THE
MORISCOS
OF
SPAIN

THE

MORISCOS

OF

SPAIN:

THEIR CONVERSION AND EXPULSION.

BY

HENRY CHARLES LEA, LL.D.

GREENWOOD PRESS, PUBLISHERS
NEW YORK 1968

Reprint Edition, 1968

LIBRARY OF CONGRESS Catalogue Card Number: 68-19286

PRINTED IN THE UNITED STATES OF AMERICA

PREFACE.

THE material on which this volume is based was collected for a chapter in a general history of the Spanish Inquisition which I hope in due time to prepare. On reviewing it the subject has seemed to me to possess interest and importance deserving fuller treatment than it could receive as a mere episode in a larger narrative, for it not only embodies a tragedy commanding the deepest sympathy, but it epitomizes nearly all the errors and tendencies which combined to cast down Spain, in little more than a century, from its splendor under Charles V. to its humiliation under Carlos II.

The labors of modern Spanish scholars have made public a mass of documentary evidence which throws much light on the inner history of the movements leading up to the final catastrophe, but this has been mostly drawn from state papers and unconsciously minimizes the part taken by intolerance and embodied in the Inquisition. To some extent I have therefore been able to supplement their researches and to make more prominent what was perhaps the most efficient agency in rendering impossible the amalgamation of the races essential to the peace and prosperity of the land. I have also been able to present in some detail the repeated efforts made to give religious instruction to the so-called converts, and the causes of their failure.

In the collection of inedited material my thanks are largely due to Señor Don Claudio Perez y Gredilla, the accomplished chief of the Archivo General of Simancas, and to Señor Don Ramon Santa Maria, formerly in charge of the Archivo Central of Alcalá de Henares.

PHILADELPHIA, JANUARY, 1901.

CONTENTS.

CHAPTER I.

THE MUDÉJARES.

CHAPTER II.

XIMENES.

CHAPTER III.

THE GERMANÍA.

CHAPTER IV.

CONVERSION BY EDICT.

CHAPTER V.

THE INQUISITION.

CHAPTER VI.

CONVERSION BY PERSUASION.

CHAPTER VII.

CONDITION OF THE MORISCOS.

CHAPTER VIII.

THE REBELLION OF GRANADA.

CHAPTER IX.

DANGERS FROM ABROAD.

CHAPTER X.

EXPULSION.

CHAPTER XI.

RESULTS.

THE MORISCOS.

CHAPTER I.

THE MUDÉJARES.

It has been the fashion to regard the war of the Reconquest, through which Spain was gradually won back from the Moslems, as a war of religion. During its progress at times it suited the purpose of the Christian princes so to represent it, when they solicited the aid of crusaders and proclaimed themselves as champions of the Cross. It was so regarded in Rome, where service against the Spanish Saracens was frequently considered as the equivalent of service in Palestine and the knights of the Temple and of the Hospital were allowed to expend their military ardor on their infidel neighbors. In fact, however, the medieval history of Spain shows that in the long struggle there was little antagonism either of race or religion. At the Moorish conquest the populations willingly submitted to the invaders, who were no harsher masters than the Goths had been, and the conquerors made no attempt to interfere with the religion of their new subjects who maintained their faith and their ecclesiastical organization until the irruption of fresh hordes of fanatic barbarians, known as Almoravides and Almohades, in the eleventh and twelfth centuries, caused their gradual disappearance. Similarly as territory was won by the Christians the peaceable population was left undisturbed; prisoners taken in war without conditions were enslaved, but the conquests were mostly the result of formal surrenders in which the inhabitants were guaranteed the possession of their property and the enjoyment of their religion and laws. They came to be known by the name of Mudéjares —the corruption of Mudegelin, an opprobrious term bestowed upon them by the Moors, derived from the word Degel which we are told was equivalent to Antichrist.[1] Enslaved prisoners could acquire liberty by various acts of public service, but baptism did not enfranchise them unless the owner were a Moor or a Jew. No forcible conversion was allowed, but only persuasion, and the convert had all the rights of the Old Christians save eligibility to holy orders; he was never to be insulted but was to be held in honor.[2]

The toleration which thus became the national policy was strengthened by the habitual alliances with Moorish neighbors of Christian princes involved in mutual civil

[1] Luis del Marmol Carbajal, Rebelion y Castigo de los Moriscos de Granada, p. 158 (Biblioteca de Autores Españoles, Tom. XXI.). Ample evidence of the nullity of the religious factor in the war of the reconquest will be found in Dozy, *Recherches sur l'Histoire et la Littérature de l'Espagne* (Leipzig, 1881), and in Francisco Fernandez y Gonzales, *Estado de los Mudéjares de Castilla* (Madrid, 1866). The ballads of the *Romancero* afford abundant proof of the absence of popular religious acerbity, even down to the capture of Granada.

[2] Las Siete Partidas P. I. Tit. v. ley 23; P. IV. Tit. xxi. ley 8; Tit. xxiii. ley 3; P. VII. Tit. xxv. ll. 2, 3.

It is evident that the Moorish slaves were often men of trained intelligence, highly trusted by their masters for another law (IV. xxi. 7) provides that the latter are bound by any contracts made by slaves whom they have placed in control of a shop or ship or any description of trade. The Spanish disinclination to labor and the monopoly of industry by Moors and Jews is readily intelligible from medieval conditions.

war. There never was the slightest hesitation in invoking the aid of the infidel, whether to foment or suppress a rebellion. When, in 1270, Alfonso X. excited disaffection by releasing Portugal from its vassalage to Leon, his brother, the Infante Philip, took advantage of the situation and organized a conspiracy with a number of the more powerful *ricosomes*. Their first thought was to solicit assistance from Abu Jusuf, King of Morocco, who willingly promised it; the Castilian prelates lent their influence to the movement; the conspirators established themselves in Granada as their head-quarters and there was prospect of desolating war with the Moors of both Africa and Spain when Queen Violante intervened and the rebellious nobles were bought off with concessions. Twelve years later, when Sancho el Bravo revolted against his father Alfonso with the support of all the nobles except the Master of Calatrava and of all the cities except Seville, Alfonso thus abandoned sent his crown to Abu Jusuf as security for a loan. The Moor at once furnished him with 60,000 doblas and came himself with large forces; Sancho made alliance with Granada, and the ensuing war, with Christians and Moors on both sides, raged until the death of Alfonso.[1] Instances such as this on a large scale could be multiplied, but a trivial occurrence will perhaps better illustrate the Christian spirit of the time. In 1299 certain knights of the military-religious Order of Santiago seized some castles of the Order on the Moorish border, filled them with Saracen troops and threatened to give them over to the enemy unless the

[1] Crónica de Don Alfonso X., cap. xix.-lviii., lxxvi.—Barrantes, Illustraciones de la Casa de Niebla, Lib. I. cap. vi., ix. (Memorial Histórico Español, IX. 72-9, 92-8).

Master and Chapter would grant them in perpetuity certain properties of the Order. Their terms were accepted; the lands were made over with solemn legal assurances that they would never be reclaimed, in spite of which complaint was made to Pope Boniface VIII., who promptly ordered the Archbishop of Toledo to compel restitution under ecclesiastical censures.[1]

The Church, in fact, had long regarded with disfavor the careless indifference which led Alfonso VI. to style himself *imperador de los dos cultos*[2]—which was satisfied to allow subject Moors to enjoy their religion in peace. When, in 1212, Alfonso IX., at the head of a crusade, won the great victory of Las Navas de Tolosa and advanced to Ubeda, where 70,000 Moors had taken refuge, they offered to become Mudéjares and to pay him a ransom of a million doblas. He accepted the terms but the clerical chiefs of the crusade, Rodrigo of Toledo and Arnaud of Narbonne, forced him to withdraw his assent, with the result that, after some further negotiation, the Moors were all massacred except such as were reserved as slaves.[3] In a similar spirit Innocent IV., in 1248, ordered Jayme I. of Aragon to permit no Moors, save as slaves, to reside in the Balearic Isles which he had conquered in 1229.[4] It is not likely that he paid any attention to this command, for when, in 1238, he added Valencia to his dominions he allowed the Moors to remain as Mudéjares. In 1266 Clement IV. returned to the charge in a brief urging upon him the expulsion of all

[1] Digard, Registres de Boniface VIII. No. 3334.

[2] Fernandez y Gonzales, Mudéjares de Castilla, p. 39.

[3] Mondéjar, Memorias de Alonso VIII., Cap. cv., cviii.—Roderici Toletani de Rebus Hispanicis Lib. VIII. cap. xii.

[4] Villanueva, Viage Literario, XXI. 131.

Saracens from the kingdoms of the crown of Aragon. The pope told him that his reputation would suffer greatly if in view of temporal profit he should longer permit such opprobrium of God, such infection of Christendom as is caused by the horrible cohabitation of Moors and Christians, while by expelling them he would fulfil his vow to God, close the mouths of his detractors and show his zeal for the faith. It was probably in return for a tithe of the ecclesiastical revenues that Jayme had pledged himself to the pope to expel the Moors, but he was too worldly wise to do so and as late as 1275 he invited additional Moorish settlers by the promise of a year's exemption from taxation. In 1276, however, on his death-bed, in consequence partly of a dangerous Moorish revolt and partly of the awakened fears shown by his taking the Cistercian habit, he enjoined his son Pedro to fulfil the promise and in a codicil to his will he emphatically repeated the injunction, but Pedro, like his father, was too sagacious to obey.[1]

In fact, obedience to the commands of the Church involved consequences to the welfare of the State which no ruler could contemplate without dismay. Except for military purposes the Mudéjares formed the most valuable portion of the population, and even in war their services were relied upon, for we find Pedro, when gathering his forces to resist the invasion of Philippe le Hardi, in 1283, summoning his faithful Moors of Valencia to

[1] Ripoll Bullarii Ord. FF. Prædicator. I 479.—Danvila y Collado, La Expulsion de los Moriscos, p. 24.—Swift, James the First of Aragon, pp. 140, 253, 290.—King Jayme is said to have made a vow, when about to undertake the conquest of Valencia, not to permit any Moors to remain in the land.

swell his ranks and in 1385, when levies were made in Murcia for the war with Portugal each *aljama*, or Moorish organization, had its allotted quota.[1] It was on their industry moreover that the prosperity of the land reposed. None of the resources of the State were more relied upon than the revenues which they furnished and assignments on these were in request as the safest security for appanages and dowers and for the income of prelates and religious corporations.[2] They were virtually indispensable to the nobles on whose lands they were settled, for they were most skilful in agriculture and unwearied in labor. They carried these characteristics into every department of industry, science and art. As physicians they ranked with the Jews, and when, in 1345, the Prior of the Order of Santiago built the church of Nuestra Señora de Uclés, we are told that he assembled "Moorish masters" and good Christian stone masons who erected the structure.[3] They were equally skilled in marine architecture and the Catalan power in the Mediterranean was largely due to their labors. The wonderful system of irrigation by which they converted Valencia into the garden of Europe still exists, with its elaborate and equitable allotments of the waters. They introduced the culture of sugar, silk, cotton, rice and many other valuable products and not a spot of available ground was left untilled by their indefatigable industry. The Mahometan law which prescribed labor as a religious duty was fully obeyed and every member of a family contributed his

[1] Fernandez y Gonzalez, pp. 221, 286.—Coleccion de Documentos de la Corona de Aragon, VI. 157, 196.

[2] Ibid. VIII. 53.—Memorial Histórico Español, I. 239, 263; III. 439.

[3] Fernandez y Gonzalez, pp. 382, 386.

share of work to the common support. In all the mechanic arts they were unexcelled. The potteries of Malaga, the cloths of Murcia, the silks of Almería and Granada, the leather hangings of Córdova, the weapons of Toledo were renowned everywhere and furnished the materials for profitable foreign commerce, which was stimulated by the universal reputation of their merchants for probity and strict fidelity to their engagements, so that it passed into a proverb that the word of a Granadan and the faith of a Castilian would make an Old Christian, or, as Hernando de Talavera, the saintly Archbishop of Granada used to say "They ought to adopt our faith and we ought to adopt their morals." They were temperate and frugal; they married early, the girls at eleven and the boys at twelve, without fear of the future, for a bed and ten libras or ducats were considered sufficient dowry. There were no beggars among them, for they took affectionate care of their own poor and orphans; they settled all quarrels between themselves and held it to be unlawful to prosecute each other before a Christian tribunal.[1] In short, they constituted the most desirable population that any land could possess, and we shall have occasion to note hereafter the curious perversity with which these good qualities were converted into accusations against them by their Christian persecutors.

It is easy for us now to see what might have been the prosperity of Spain had a population thus gifted been gradually interfused with their vigorous conquerors, to

[1] Janer, Condicion social de los Moriscos, pp. 47-50, 161.—Fonseca, Giusto Scacciamento de' Moreschi, pp. 87, 89 (Roma, 1611).—Pedraza, Historia eclesiastica de Granada, fol. 187 (Granada, 1638).

whose religion they would have been won over in time through friendly intercourse. To the conscientious medieval churchman, however, any friendship with the infidel was the denial of Christ; the infidel was not to be forcibly converted, but it was a duty to lay upon him such burdens that he would himself seek relief in conversion. Accordingly the toleration and conciliation, which were the basis of the Spanish policy, were vigorously opposed in Rome, where the effort was to keep the races as far apart as possible, through the somewhat humiliating fear that Christianity would lose more than it could gain in the intercourse between them. Even the freedom of ordinary commercial dealings, permitted by the Spanish laws, was discouraged and in 1250 the Order of Santiago felt it necessary to represent to Innocent IV. that it held numerous Moorish vassals, wherefore it asked for licence to buy and sell with them, which he granted accordingly.[1] Another device to keep the races separate, on which the Church persistently insisted, was prescribed by the Lateran council of 1216—that all Jews and Saracens should wear a distinctive garment or badge. This was not only humiliating but dangerous, as it exposed the wearer to insult and maltreatment, especially in the case of travellers, such as muleteers and merchants, on the notoriously insecure highways. A long struggle ensued between the Church and the Spanish monarchs over the enforcement of this canon. At length in Aragon an attempt in that direction was made, in 1300, by an ordinance requiring the Mudéjares to have the hair cut in a peculiar fashion, and in Castile, at the request of the córtes of Toro in 1371, Henry II. ordered all Jews and Moors to wear a

[1] Fernandez y Gonzalez, pp. 294, 321, 367.

badge, but the injunction had to be frequently repeated and received scant obedience, and when enforced we are told that it led to innumerable murders on the high roads.[1]

The Church was succeeding in gradually awakening the spirit of intolerance, but its progress was slow. The council of Vienne in 1312 complained that Saracens dwelling in Christian lands were permitted to have priests who, from the minarets of the mosques, invoked Mahomet and sounded his praises, and further, that the people were allowed to gather around the grave of one whom they adored as a saint; these practices the council declared to be insufferable; it ordered the princes to suppress them, with the alternative of winning salvation or of enduring a punishment which would render them a terrible example.[2] This was directed especially at Spain, but the princes were unmoved, and in 1329 the council of Tarragona complained of their disobedience and ordered them to enforce the canon within two months, under pain of excommunication and interdict.[3] Nothing came of this and a century later, in 1429, the council of Tortosa supplicated the King of Aragon and all prelates and nobles, by the bowels of divine mercy, to observe the canon and all other conciliar decrees for the exaltation of the faith and the humiliation of Jews and Moors and to see to their observance by their subjects if they wish to

[1] Concil. Lateran. IV. ann. 1216, cap. lxviii. (Cap. 15, Extra, v. vi.).—Raynald. Annal. ann. 1217, n 84.—Amador de los Rios, Historia de los Judíos de España, I. 361–2, 364, 554; II. 116, 329, 565.—Partidas, P. VII. Tit. xxiv. ley 11.—Fernandez y Gonzalez, p. 369.—Ayala, Crónica de Enrique II. año VI. cap. vii.

See also Robert, *Les Signes d'Infamie au Moyen Age* (Paris, 1891).

[2] Cap. 1, Clementin. Lib. v. Tit. ii.

[3] Concil. Tarraconens. ann. 1329 (Aguirre, Concil. Hispan. VI. 370).

escape the vengeance of God and of the Holy See.[1] This was equally ineffectual and it was reserved for Ferdinand and Isabella, about 1482, to enforce the canon of Vienne with a strictness which brought a remonstrance from Constantinople.[2]

The council of Vienne had likewise enacted a canon directed against the privileges accorded to the Jews in Spain. Evidently the Spanish bishops who attended the council must have been deeply impressed with the spirit which they found among their fellow prelates and they doubtless were given to understand the indignation with which Spanish tolerance was regarded elsewhere. The Spanish church hitherto had been singularly independent; it was now brought into more direct relations with the rest of Christendom and it cast off the tolerant spirit which had thus far distinguished it, but its efforts were chiefly directed against the Jews, although it strove impartially to create popular antagonism against both Moors and Jews and to put an end to the pernicious habit of these infidels frequenting divine service in Christian churches and of Christians participating in their weddings and merry-makings.[3] Already, moreover, the final policy of expulsion was suggested, in 1337, by Arnaldo, Archbishop of Tarragona, in a letter to Benedict XII. imploring the pope to order the King of Aragon to adopt it. The material objections to it, he said, had been disproved by the Abbot of Poblet, who had recently expelled the Mudéjares from the possessions of the abbey without impairing its revenues, and the resistance of the nobles

[1] Concil. Dertusan. ann. 1429, cap. xx. (Ibid. V. 340).

[2] Raynald. Annal. ann. 1483, n. 45.

[3] Concil. Vallisolet. ann. 1322, cap. xxii.; Concil. Tarraconens. ann. 1329 (Aguirre, V. 250, 371).

might be overcome by empowering them to seize and sell the persons and property of the Moors, as public enemies and infidels, while the money thus obtained would be serviceable for the defence of the kingdom[1]—an inhuman proposition which we shall see officially approved by the Church in the seventeenth and eighteenth centuries.

This constant ecclesiastical pressure began in time to produce its effect on the ruling classes and the fatal policy was adopted of separating as far as possible the races and reducing to a minimum the necessary intercourse between them. In the córtes of 1385 and 1387 laws were adopted, and in the council of Palencia in 1388 canons were decreed, punishing with heavy penalties all unnecessary conversation between them and requiring Jew and Moor to kneel when the sacrament was carried through the streets and to observe all Christian feasts by abstaining from working publicly. Moreover their employment as officials and tax-collectors was forbidden, as it had frequently been before, and the old custom in the towns of separate quarters—Morerías and Juderías—for them was insisted on and rendered more absolute.[2] In the restrictive legislation of 1412 this matter occupies the first place; Morerías and Juderías were ordered to be established everywhere, surrounded by a wall having only one gate; any one who within eight days after notice should not have settled

[1] Aguirre, V. 286-7.

[2] Córtes de los Antiguos Reinos de Leon y de Castilla, II. 322, 325, 363, 365, 369 (Madrid, 1863).—Amador de los Rios, II. 331.—Ordenanzas Reales, VIII. iii. 6.—Concil. Palentin. ann. 1388, cap. v., vi. (Aguirre, V. 300).

It is worthy of note that in the proceedings of the córtes there is vastly more antagonism manifested towards Jews than towards Moors, arising from their greater activity as money lenders and usurers and their employment as farmers of the revenue and tax-collectors.

therein forfeited all his property, with personal punishment at the king's pleasure, while severe penalties were provided for Christian women entering the forbidden precincts. It was easier to enact than to enforce such laws and in 1480 Ferdinand and Isabella state that this had been neglected, wherefore they renewed it, allowing two years for the establishment of these Ghettos after which any Jew or Moor dwelling outside of them was subjected to the prescribed penalties and no Christian woman should be found within them.[1] Under Ferdinand and Isabella laws were no longer neglected and these were enforced with their accustomed vigor.

In all this legislation Jews and Moors were included together, but clerical abhorrence was more particularly directed against the former, with the consequence that popular antipathy followed in the same direction, especially as the Jews made themselves largely disliked by their practice of usury and their efficiency as tax-gatherers. That it was difficult to arouse antagonism towards the Mudéjares would seem to be shown when Ferran Martinez, the Archdeacon of Ecija, succeeded in starting the dreadful massacres of 1391. The Jews were the objects of his inflammatory harangues, and for three months, from June to September, in one city of Castile and Aragon after another, the populace rose on the Juderías, with slaughter and rapine, only sparing those who sought safety in baptism. The Morerías escaped, though in some places we are told the people only refrained from attacking them through fear of reprisals on the Christians in

[1] Ordenamiento de Valladolid, i., xi. (Fortalicium Fidei, fol. 176). —Fernandez y Gonzalez, pp. 400, 402.—Ordenanzas Reales, VIII. iii., 10, 19.

Barbary. That the Mudéjares, in fact, felt themselves exposed to imminent danger in the savage fanaticism of the time would appear from the statement that some ten thousand of them were added to the innumerable multitude of converts from Judaism made by San Vicente Ferrer who was the apostle of militant Christianity throughout this terrible uprising.[1]

Although the Mudéjares thus escaped pillage and massacre, the event exercised a sinister influence on their ultimate fortunes. The immense number of forcibly converted Jews created a new class in Spanish society known as Marranos, conversos or New Christians, the solidity of whose faith was not unreasonably regarded as doubtful. Released from all disabilities, their superior business aptitude speedily raised many of them and their descendants to commanding positions in Church and State, intensifying the dislike and envy with which they had previously been regarded. Antagonism which had before been almost purely religious became racial, while religious antagonism became heightened and Spain, which through the earlier middle ages had been the most tolerant land in Christendom, became, as the fifteenth century advanced, the most fanatically intolerant. It was impossible for the conversos wholly to abandon the multifarious rites and customs of rabbinical Judaism in which they had been trained for so many generations; these were regarded as indubitable evidence of apostasy in those who by baptism had become subject to the Church; fiery preachers, like Alonso de Espina, were not lacking to point out the dangers to which Spanish

[1] I have treated in some detail on the massacres of 1391 in the American Historical Review, Vol. I. p. 209.

Christianity was exposed of becoming Judaized by intercourse with these apostates, and finally Ferdinand and Isabella yielded to the apparent necessity of a radical cure by the establishment of the Inquisition in 1480. The unbaptized Jews were not subject to the Inquisition, so long as they abstained from proselytism or sacrilege, but this did not protect them from the ferocious zeal of the people, which seemed to be constantly increasing in intensity, unsatisfied by legislation which oppressed them with so many disabilities. In all this, jealousy of the superior energy of the non-Christian races had its share, for in spite of these disabilities the results of their intelligent industry were a constant source of dread and provocation. In 1453 a decree of the town of Haro forbids Christians to sell their estates to Jews and Moors, giving as a reason that if this were not stopped the Christians would have no ground left to cultivate as the Moors had already obtained possession of all the best of the irrigated lands.[1] It was doubtless this jealousy which prompted the demand made on Henry IV. by the revolted nobles, in 1460, that he should expel from the land all Jews and Moors who contaminated religion and corrupted morals.[2] Whatever might have been lacking to stimulate this antagonism was supplied by the Holy See, when Eugenius IV. in 1442 and Nicholas V. in 1447 issued terrible bulls of proscription against the Jews, embodying in the canon law all the most abhorrent features of Spanish legislation,[3] and Sixtus IV. in a *motu proprio*

[1] Boletín de la Real Academía de la Historia, XXVI. 468–72.

[2] Colmenares, Historia de Segovia, cap. XXXI. § ix.

[3] Raynald. Annal. ann. 1442, n. 15.—Wadding. Annal. Ord. Minorum, ann. 1447, n. 10.

of May 31, 1484, expressed his displeasure at learning that in Spain, and especially in Andalusia, these bulls were not observed, wherefore he ordered all officials, secular and ecclesiastical, to enforce strictly the canonical decrees concerning the proscribed races.[1] Still the popular feeling seems to have been mostly directed against the Jews and Jewish conversos and we hear of no action against the Mudéjares in the bloody risings against the former in Toledo in 1449 and 1467, in Valladolid in 1470 and in Córdova and other towns of Andalusia in 1473.[2] It is true that Alfonso de Borja, Archbishop of Valencia (1429-1455), afterward Pope Calixtus III., urged upon Juan II. of Aragon the expulsion of the Mudéjares of Valencia, in which he was supported by Cardinal Juan de Torquemada, uncle of the celebrated inquisitor-general, and they made such impression on the mind of the king that he appointed a term for their departure, but he thought better of it and abandoned the measure.[3] But the greater favor shown to the Moors is observable when, in 1480, Isabella ordered the expulsion from Andalusia, where the Jewish population was most numerous, of all Jews that would not embrace Christianity and when in 1486 Ferdinand did the same in Aragon, although both of these measures were probably but financial expedients to sell exemptions and suspensions, for no positive action was taken.[4] Possibly in this allowance must be made

[1] Padre Fidel Fita (Boletín, XV. 443).

[2] Crónica de Juan II. año XLII. cap. ii., v.—Crónica de Álvaro de Luna, Tit. LXXXIII.—Valera, Memorial de diversas Hazañas, cap. xxxviii., lxxxiii.-iv.—Castillo, Crónica de Enrique IV. cap. xc., xci., cxlvi., clx.—Memorial Historico Español, VIII. 507–8.

[3] Bleda, Crónica de los Moros, p. 877 (Valencia, 1618).

[4] Pulgar, Crónica de los Reyes Católicos, II. lxxvii.—Archivo Gen-

for the fact that the Mudéjares were protected against such measures by the old capitulations to which they could appeal as guaranteeing the right of domicile and the privilege of their religion, while the Jews had neither rights nor privileges and their domicile was but a matter of sufferance. So it was in the crowning catastrophe when, in 1492, the final conquest of Granada from the Moors was signalized by the decree of expulsion of the Jews, conceived and executed in a spirit of the most arbitrary injustice, and Spain was deprived of some hundreds of thousands of its most intelligent and thrifty population.[1]

Human inconsistency has rarely been more conspicuous than in the contrast between this radical measure for purifying the faith of Spain and the politic course adopted by Ferdinand and Isabella in their gradual winning of the kingdom of Granada during the nine years' war between 1482 and 1492. The traditional course was observed of subjecting to the utmost rigor of war places taken by assault or obliged to surrender at discretion, while the sovereigns were always ready to grant the most liberal terms of capitulation. This is set forth, in 1487, in an

eral de la Corona de Aragon, Reg. 3684, fol. 96.—Padre Fidel Fita (Boletín, XV. 323–5, 327, 328, 330; XXIII. 431).

[1] The computations of the Jews expelled in 1492 range from 800,000 down. Isidore Loeb (Revue des Études Juives, 1887, p. 182), after an exhaustive examination of all the sources, Christian and Jewish, reduces the number to

Expelled	165,000
Baptized to escape expulsion	50,000
Died	20,000
	235,000

application to Sixtus IV. concerning the tithe which the Moors were accustomed to pay to their native kings, from which it would seem that the clergy laid claim to it in the conquered lands as though it were ecclesiastical. Ferdinand and Isabella represent that they cannot induce the Moors to submit if they oppress them more than their rulers have done; that the capitulations always provide that they shall pay no more taxes than they had been accustomed to and that if the crown cannot enjoy these tithes there will be no revenues to defray the cost of garrisoning the captured towns. This had been settled, they say, in the case of Aragon and Valencia and they ask Sixtus to apply the same rule to Granada. To this the pope assented and forbade all ecclesiastics from advancing any claim on the Moorish tithes.[1] So when, in 1489, the Sultan complained to the pope of the progressive conquest of Granada, saying that there were many Christians in his dominions whom he protected in their faith and that if the war were not stopped he would be obliged to make reprisals on them, the sovereigns replied that they were only recovering their own and that the Moors in their territories enjoyed full liberty of person and religion.[2]

This was not the result of a tolerant spirit for when the opportunity offered nothing could be more ferocious than their fanaticism. When they captured Malaga in August, 1487, after a desperate resistance of three months, all renegade Christians found there were tortured to death with sharp-pointed reeds, all conversos were burnt, and the inhabitants were held to ransom as

[1] Fernandez y Gonzalez, p. 412.

[2] Pulgar, Crónica, III. cxii.

slaves. Abraham Senior, the Jewish financier of Queen Isabella, paid 20,000 doblas to redeem four hundred and fifty Jews; as for the Moors, a royal decree of September 4th assented to an agreement by which they were to pay, as a ransom for themselves and their personal effects, thirty doblas a head, irrespective of age or condition of servitude, for the fulfilment of which they gave hostages; such as desired to go to Barbary were to be transported at the royal expense, the rest might go anywhere, except within the kingdom of Granada, and were guaranteed safety and freedom.[1]

As the war drew toward the end, however, capitulations were granted even more liberal than those of old. That which secured the submission of Purchena and the important valley of the Almanzora with the Sierra de Filabres, December 7, 1489, receives all the inhabitants, with their officials and alfaquíes or priests, under the royal safeguard; it permits all the Mudéjares who had come to their assistance to return freely home with their effects and free of accountability for whatever property they may have seized; it gives free transport to Barbary to certain parties and their friends, with permission to sell their lands or collect the rents while absent; it permits all others to go to Barbary whenever they choose; it appoints Moors as magistrates who are to decide all suits between the inhabitants and Christians; it pays 12,000 reales as ransom for a hundred and twenty captives held by the Moors; it promises not to force renegades to return to Christianity; it engages to exact no taxation greater than had been paid to the Kings of

[1] Zurita, Hist. de Aragon, Lib. LXX. cap. lxxi.—Amador de los Rios, III. 298-99.—Fernandez y Gonzalez, p. 415.

Granada; it allows them to live in their law and faith and to be judged according to the *zunna* or Moorish code; it declares their houses inviolable against forcible entry or the free quartering of soldiers; it guarantees them possession of their horses and arms and that they shall never be required to wear badges and finally that the land shall never be alienated from the crown. All this was pledged in the most solemn manner on the royal faith and word.[1] Subsequently, on February 11, 1490, a capitulation was drawn up for the city of Almería which was to serve for all subsequent surrenders. This was even more liberal, containing in addition to the above provisions others which assured the new Mudéjares of relief from unjust burdens laid upon them by the native kings; that children born of Christian women should choose for themselves at the age of twelve which religion to embrace; that no Jew or convert should ever hold jurisdiction over them; that no Christian should ever enter their aljamas; that any fugitive Moorish slave coming to Baza or Guadix should be free; that their rights in slaves kept in Barbary should not be disturbed, and it even included the Jews, who were placed on the same level as the Mudéjares if they were natives of Granada, while if they were renegades from Christianity they should have a year in which to return to the faith or to go to Africa.[2]

This careful detail would seem to assure to the conquered Moors all the rights and privileges which they had enjoyed under native rule, but when the final sur-

[1] Fernandez y Gonzalez, p. 416.—Coleccion de Documentos inéditos para la Historía de España, VIII. 403.

[2] Fernandez y Gonzalez, p. 419.—Coleccion, XI. 475.—Pulgar, Crónica, III. cxxv.

render was made of the city of Granada, involving the abdication of Boabdil and the establishment of Christian domination over the whole land, still greater concessions were granted. This was a solemn agreement, bearing date November 25, 1491, and ratified three days later, the surrender and delivery of the city to be made within forty days thereafter. Ferdinand and Isabella, for themselves, for their son the Infante Juan, and for all their successors, received the Moors of all places that should come into the agreement as vassals and natural subjects, to be under the royal protection, to possess all their lands in perpetuity, to be preserved from all oppression, and to be honored and respected as vassals and subjects. They were not to be disturbed in their habits and customs; those who desired to go to Barbary had full permission to sell their property or to leave it in the hands of agents, while for three years they were to be transported at the cost of the crown and subsequently at their own expense. They were never to be required to wear badges, and Jews were to have no authority over them or to be made collectors of the revenues. They were not to be deprived of their mosques, entrance to which was forbidden to Christians. Questions between themselves were to be decided under the zunna or Moorish law by their own magistrates, while suits with Christians were to be heard by a mixed tribunal consisting of the Christian alcalde and Moorish cadi. Moorish slaves of Christian masters, flying to Granada, were not to be reclaimed. Tributes were not to be exacted greater than those paid to the native kings. Those who had fled to Barbary had three years in which to return and enjoy the privileges thus granted. They had free permission to trade with

Barbary and with all places in Castile and Andalusia without heavier imposts than those paid by Christians. Renegades were not to be maltreated by act or word and Christian women married to Moors were allowed to choose their own faith, while no constraint was to be applied to Moors to induce conversion—indeed, any female Moor who through love for a Christian desired to change her religion was not to be received until she had been examined in the presence of Christians and Moors, and if she had taken anything with her it was to be restored and she was to be punished. All Christian captives were to be delivered without ransom and similarly all Moorish ones in Castile and Andalusia were to be set free. All the revenues of mosques and schools and charitable foundations were to be maintained and paid as usual into the hands of the alfaquíes, and the governors and magistrates appointed by the new sovereigns were to treat the Moors kindly and lovingly and anyone acting wrongfully was to be visited with due punishment. Even these careful and elaborate provisions did not wholly satisfy the Moors and on November 29th Ferdinand and Isabella made a solemn declaration in which they swore by God that all Moors should have full liberty to work on their lands or to go where they desired through the kingdoms in search of advantage and to maintain their religious observances and mosques as heretofore, while those who preferred could sell their property and go to Barbary.[1]

The elaborate nature of these compacts shows how carefully the Moors guarded their religious freedom and how

[1] Fernandez y Gonzalez, p. 421.—Coleccion de Documentos, VIII. 411.—Marmol Carvajal, Rebelion y Castigo, pp. 146–50.

willingly the Catholic sovereigns subordinated religious to political interests. Had these agreements been preserved inviolate the future of Spain would have been wholly different; kindly intercourse would have amalgamated the races; in time Mahometanism would have died out, and, supreme in the arts of war and peace, the prosperity and power of the Spanish kingdoms would have been enduring. This, however, was too foreign to the spirit of the age to come to pass. Fanaticism and greed led to persecution and oppression, while Castilian pride inflicted humiliation even more galling. The estrangement of the races grew ever greater, the gulf between them more impassable, until the position became intolerable, leading to a remedy which crippled the prosperity of Spain.

At first there seems to have been an intention to carry out these compacts in good faith. When Ferdinand and Isabella left Granada their instructions were to administer them in a kindly spirit and bring about the pacification and unity of the races. Iñigo Lopez de Mendoza, Count of Tendilla (subsequently Marquis of Mondéjar), was appointed captain-general and sought to follow out this policy.[1] Arrangements were promptly made for transporting to Barbary all Moors who desired to go, and many of them did so, including most of the nobles. A letter, in 1492, to the sovereigns says that the Abencerrages went almost in a body and that in the Alpujarras there were few left save laborers and officials. The continuance of this emigration shows that the Moors were not altogether confident of the good faith of their new masters, and a letter of Ferdinand in 1498 indicates that

[1] Janer, Condicion Social, p. 19.

it was still going on and that he was desirous of stimulating it.[1] If, however, he thus regarded his new subjects as undesirable he seems to have wished to increase the population of Mudéjares—of those who through generations of intercourse with Christians had accommodated themselves to the situation and were in every way undoubtedly useful to the community. When Manoel of Portugal decreed the expulsion of the Moors from his dominions, Ferdinand and Isabella issued letters, April 20, 1497, permitting them to enter Spain with all their property, either to reside or to pass through and go whither they pleased with their effects except gold and silver and other articles of which the export was prohibited. They were taken under the royal protection and all persons were warned not to molest them in any way.[2]

The contrast between this invitation and the final action of Philip III. measures the unwise statesmanship which within a century converted friendly subjects into domestic enemies. The process, indeed, was already commencing through infractions of the capitulation of Granada. Boabdil, with wise distrust, had wanted it to receive papal confirmation but was obliged to abandon the demand, and its disregard commenced with the appointment as alguazil of

[1] Coleccion de Documentos, XI. 569; XIV. 496.—Janer, p. 127.

[2] Archivo General de Simancas, Patronato Real, Inquisicion, Legajo único, fol. 4. See Appendix No. I.

When, in 1497, at the instance of the Castilian sovereigns, Manoel expelled from Portugal all Jews and Moors who refused baptism, he deprived the former of their children under fourteen years of age, causing despair which moved even the Christians to compassion. He spared to the Moors this cruelty through a dread of reprisals on his subjects by the Mahometan powers.—Damião de Goes, Chronica do Rei Dom Manoel, P. I. cap. xviii., xx.

Don Pedro Venegas, a converso, who, on his first walk through the streets, converted the mosque At-Tanavin into the church known as San Juan de los Reyes. Although the royal secretary, Hernando de Zafra, to whom was intrusted the interpretation of the compact, gave satisfaction by defeating an attempt to divert the revenues of schools and hospitals and to introduce Castilian law, still there was open disregard of the capitulation in the imposition of a tithe and a half in addition to the tithe formerly paid to the native kings. This was rendered more oppressive by farming the revenues to Moorish *almojarifes* or tax speculators whose familiarity with the wealth of their compatriots and whose covetousness rendered the collection excessively burdensome. The treasury even made a speculation out of the transportation to Africa of those who expatriated themselves.[1]

Thus one after another the guarantees given at the surrender were shown to be but a slender protection against the exigencies of the conqueror. There could be little reliance on his good faith as far as temporal interests were concerned, but thus far he had practically respected his pledges concerning religion. It remained to be seen how long he could resist the pressure to establish unity of faith.

[1] Fernandez y Gonzalez, pp. 216–18.

CHAPTER II.

XIMENES.

Hardly had Ferdinand and Isabella obtained possession of their new conquests when there were zealous prelates and frailes at the court who urged upon them that in gratitude to God they should give their new subjects the alternative of baptism or exile. By some process of reasoning they proved that this would be no violation of the capitulations and it was easy to show how the Moors would gain salvation and the land would be assured enduring peace. The sovereigns, however, rejected these counsels, not that they were not just and holy, but that their new vassals were as yet unquiet and had not wholly laid down their arms, so that such vigorous measures would infallibly provoke another war. Besides, we are told, as they had other conquests in view they did not desire to do anything unworthy of their plighted troth and as the work of conversion had commenced auspiciously they had hopes that it could be completed in good faith.[1]

In fact, there appeared at first a flattering prospect that the Moors might be won over to Christianity. Hernando de Talavera, a Jeronimite fraile, was confessor to Isabella, who had made him Bishop of Avila. He had accompanied her to the siege of Granada, and on its sur-

[1] Marmol Carvajal, p. 153.

render, impressed by the field open for missionary labor, he had asked permission to resign his see in order to devote himself to the holy work. Granada in Roman and Gothic times had been the seat of a bishopric, the memory of which had been preserved in the fifteenth century by a series of titular bishops. Isabella had the felicitous idea of reviving it in the shape of an archbishopric and bestowing it on Talavera. He consented, but, desiring to avoid all appearance of cupidity, insisted that the revenues assigned to it should be moderate, and they were fixed at 2,000,000 maravedís—considerably less than those of Avila.[1] It would have been impossible to make a happier selection. Talavera was a true apostle, whose zeal was tempered with charity and loving kindness. He speedily gained the hearts of his flock, devoting his labor and his revenue to the relief of suffering and the practical exemplification of the gospel precepts. The true Christianity which he so faithfully represented won the affectionate veneration of the Moslem and rendered abundantly successful the work of conversion which was the object of his life. Many came spontaneously to ask for baptism; the alfaquíes themselves listened willingly to him as he expounded Christian doctrine; he had houses in which he preached and taught to all who sought instruction and he not only caused his missionaries to learn Arabic but he himself in his old age acquired it sufficiently for his purposes and composed an elementary grammar and

[1] Ibid. p. 152.—Avila was one of the poorer Spanish sees, with an income of about 8000 ducats. The revenue assigned to Granada was a little over 5000, but by 1510 it had increased to 10,000.—L. Marinæi Siculi de Rebus Hispan. Lib. IV.—Pedraza, Hist. ecles. de Granada, fol. 173.

vocabulary. The traditional hardness of the Moorish heart softened in the warmth of Christian love which he poured forth and the rapidly increasing number of converts gave promise that a proselytism so conducted would solve the most serious question which confronted Spanish statesmanship.[1] As the century drew to its close there seemed indeed an encouraging tendency to general conversion. We hear of the Moors of Caspe, an important town in Aragon, turning Christians in 1499; in the district of Teruel and Albarracin, which subsequently was noted as the most defiantly obstinate of the Moorish regions, in 1493 a mosque was converted into the church of the Trinity and in 1502 the whole population became Christian, at least for the time.[2] To stimulate the process, Ferdinand and Isabella by a pragmatica of October 31, 1499, ordered that all Moorish slaves, who since the surrender had been baptized, should be set free, the owners being compensated from the royal treasury; any son of a Moor who was baptized should be entitled to receive his portion from his father and should subsequently inherit the share in the paternal estate which would otherwise enure to the crown.[3]

At the same time there were ominous symptoms of a resort to less persuasive methods of propagandism. Already, in 1498, a letter of Ferdinand, January 28th, to the inquisitor-general, shows that in Valencia the Inquisition was arrogating to itself jurisdiction over the Moors and

[1] Marmol Carvajal, p. 152.—Pedraza, Hist. ecles. de Granada, fol. 174, 186–7.

[2] Archivo de Simancas, Inquisicion, Libro 1.—Muñoz, Diario Turolense, año 1502 (Boletín, 1895, p. 10).

[3] Llorente, Añales de la Inquisicion, I. 254.

was endeavoring to suppress the use of Moorish costume, although the rule was absolute that it had no cognizance over any one who had not by baptism become subject to the Church, unless, indeed, he were guilty of sacrilege or of seeking to convert others from Christianity. It was therefore a flagrant abuse of authority when the tribunal of Valencia undertook to prevent the wearing of Moorish garments and sent officials to Serra to arrest some women for disobedience. They were not recognized by the people and were maltreated while the women were conveyed away, whereupon the tribunal adopted the arbitrary measure of seizing all the inhabitants of Serra who chanced to come to Valencia, so that the place was threatened with depopulation—an excess of zeal which the king reprimanded, ordering greater moderation to be observed in future. The ringleaders in the resistance to the officials, after three years' incarceration, were condemned to confiscation and banishment, leading to considerable correspondence in 1500, in which Ferdinand showed a commendable desire to mitigate the harshness of the inquisitors. He manifested the same disposition towards the Moorish aljama of Fraga, which was concerned in the confiscation of a certain Galcerán de Abella, and also towards the Moors of Saragossa who became involved with the Inquisition there by reason of harboring a female slave who had escaped from Borja.[1]

It was still further ominous for Granada when, in 1499, it was subjected to the Inquisition and was incorporated in the district of the tribunal of Córdova.[2] To make matters worse, on September 7th, the infamous Diego

[1] Archivo de Simancas, Inquisicion, Libro 1.

[2] Zurita, Historia del Rey Hernando, Lib. III. cap. 44.

Rodriguez Lucero was appointed inquisitor of Córdova and we learn from an *ayuda de costa* or gratuity granted to him, July 27, 1500, to reimburse him for the expenses of a journey to Granada, Malaga and other places, that he had been busy in organizing his subordinates throughout the newly acquired territory.[1] He speedily acquired the unbounded confidence of Ferdinand by unscrupulous activity which was fruitful in confiscations, and his career was a tissue of atrocious fraud and cruelty which in 1506 led to a rising in Córdova and eventually to his deposition. We have no records as to his proceedings in Granada against the Moors, baptized or unbaptized, but his persecution of the Archbishop Talavera and his family, on the most absurd and extravagant charges of being engaged in a plot to convert Spain to Judaism by the arts of witchcraft, shows how little mercy was to be expected by those of lesser degree who might provoke his cupidity or enmity.[2]

Meanwhile Talavera, unconscious of the trouble which was to embitter his closing years, was earnestly pursuing his apostolate with constantly increasing success. Unfortunately Ferdinand and Isabella, who were in Granada from July until the middle of November, 1499, were not content with the progress of the work and desiring to expedite it they summoned to Talavera's assistance the Archbishop of Toledo, Francisco Ximenes de Cisneros, who was busy at Alcalá laying the foundations for his university. Much as Spain owes to this extraordinary man, his services were far overbalanced by the irrep-

[1] Archivo de Simancas, loc. cit.

[2] I have considered the career of Lucero in some detail in a paper in the American Historical Review, Vol. II. p. 611.

arable mischief which he wrought in a work for which he was peculiarly unfitted. Of his disinterestedness there could be no question as well as of his zeal for religion as he understood it, but he was peremptory, inflexible and unforgiving, and even his admiring biographer admits that his temper was so imperious that he deemed force to be the only way of ensuring obedience and that in his atrabilious moods it was dangerous to approach him so that he sometimes acted through fury rather than prudence, as was seen in the conversion of the Granadan Moors and the attempt to conquer Africa.[1]

Such was the colleague allotted to the saintly Talavera, whose milder nature readily yielded to the stronger individuality. For awhile they worked successfully together and when the sovereigns left Granada for Seville it was with the injunction to proceed with gentleness and not provoke a revolt. Ximenes threw himself into the work with his customary ardor. He borrowed considerable sums which he lavished on the principal Moors whom he desired to win over, giving them silken vestments and crimson caps, of which we are told they were inordinately proud. In conjunction with Talavera he held conferences with the alfaquíes and morabitos—the priests and teachers—explaining to them the Christian doctrines, and leading many of them to instruct their flocks in the true faith with such effect that applications for baptism became numerous and in a single day, December 18, 1499,

[1] Gomecii de Rebus Gestis a Francisco Ximenio Lib. IV. fol. 95, Lib. V. fol. 128, Lib. VII. fol. 218. How much his zeal overran his discretion as a statesman is visible in his attempt, in 1506, to unite Ferdinand, Henry VII. and Manoel of Portugal in a crusade.—Wadding. Annal. ann. 1506, n. 73.

three thousand were baptized by the simple expedient of sprinkling them in a body, and the mosque of the Albaycin was consecrated as the church of San Salvador.[1]

All this was legitimate enough, but Ximenes showed his temper when, alarmed by the progress of Christianization some of the stricter Moslems endeavored to check it by dissuasion. He promptly had them imprisoned in chains and treated with great harshness. The most prominent among them was a Zegri, proud of his royal descent and distinguished by eminent personal gifts. Him Ximenes confided to one of his priests named Pedro Leon with instructions to break his spirit, which was duly accomplished by starvation until the Zegri begged to be taken before the Christian alfaquí. In squalor and chained hand and foot he was brought into the presence of Ximenes, when he asked to be relieved of his fetters in order that he might speak freely. When this was done he explained that the previous night Allah had appeared to him and commanded him to embrace the Christian faith, which he was ready to do. Pleased with his conquest, Ximenes had him washed, clothed in silk and baptized, when he took the name of Gonzalo Fernandez Zegri, in honor of Gonzalo of Córdova, not as yet the Great Captain, with whom he had fought during the siege of Granada, and Ximenes further gratified him with a pension of fifty thousand maravedís.

[1] It is apparent from these events that already the separation had been enforced between the Moors and the incoming Christians, the former being confined to a small Morería, of about 500 houses, in the city, known as the Antequeruela and to a larger one of some 5000 houses occupying the Albaycin, a quarter of the town on higher ground, of rocky and uneven surface. The Moorish population of the city at the time was estimated at 40,000.

Having once given way to his imperious temper it would seem that Ximenes could no longer control it. Impatient of the slow process of persuasion he imagined that he could end the matter at a blow and he refused to listen to those who urged moderation and gentleness. He summoned the alfaquíes to surrender all their religious books; five thousand were brought to him, many splendidly adorned with gold and silver and priceless illuminations. There were numerous applicants for these specimens of Moorish art, but Ximenes refused them all and the whole were publicly burnt, save a few on medicine which he reserved for the library at Alcalá. All this foreshadowed still more forcible proceedings. The Moors were becoming more and more disquieted at the increasing disregard of their guarantees and it needed but a spark to cause an explosion.

Ximenes was not long in furnishing the necessary provocation. It will be recalled that among the provisions of the capitulation was one which protected all renegades from persecution. There appears to have been many of these, who, with their children were known as *elches*. To a rigid churchman it was insupportable that one who had once, by baptism, been subjected to ecclesiastical jurisdiction, or his children who ought to have been baptized, should be exempted from it. Such cases came clearly within the cognizance of the Inquisition, which was not to be defrauded by any human compact, and Ximenes procured from Inquisitor-general Deza delegation of power to deal with them. He made use of this to arrest those who were proof against persuasion until it happened that one of his servants named Sacedo, with Bellasco de Barrionuevo, a royal alguazil, arrested in the

Albaycin a young daughter of an elche. As they were dragging her through the plaza of Bib-el-Bonut — the principal one in the Albaycin—she cried out that she was to be forcibly baptized in contravention of the capitulations; a crowd collected and commenced to insult the alguazil, who was hated by reason of his activity in making arrests; he answered disdainfully, passions were heated and in the tumult he was killed with a paving-stone while Sacedo would have shared his fate had not a Moorish woman rescued him and hidden him under a bed until midnight. The trouble spread, the Moors flew to arms, skirmished with the Christians and, regarding Ximenes as the violator of the compact, they besieged him in his house. He had a guard of two hundred men who defended him until morning, when Tendilla came down from the Alhambra with troops and raised the siege. For ten days the two archbishops and Tendilla parleyed with the Moors, pointing out the penalties they would suffer if they did not submit before forces should come from Andalusia, to which they replied that they had not risen against the sovereigns but in defence of the royal faith, that it was the officials who had caused disturbance by violating the capitulations and that everything would be pacified if these were observed. At length Talavera boldly went to the plaza Bib-el-Bonut with a chaplain and a few unarmed servants; the sight of his calm and benevolent features wrought a revulsion and the Moors kissed the hem of his gown as they had been wont to do. Tendilla followed with his halberdiers, but tossed into the crowd his crimson cap and rode bareheaded as a sign of peace; it was picked up, kissed and returned to him. Thus an armistice established itself; Tendilla and Talavera urged the Moors to lay down their arms and promised them pardon, as it should be understood that they had not revolted but only sought to maintain the capitulations, which should be strictly observed for the future. To show his confidence Tendilla brought his wife and boys and placed them in a house next to the principal mosque and the city became quiet. The cadi Cidi Ceibona promised to surrender to justice those who had slain the alguazil, which was accordingly done; the corregidor hanged four and let the rest go for the sake of peace; the Moors laid down their arms and returned to work.

To drive a population such as this to rebellion and despair required exceptional perversity and wrongheadedness, but these were not lacking. Tendilla and Talavera had counted without Ximenes, but the latter soon made himself felt. During the interval rumors had reached Seville that Granada had revolted because Ximenes had attempted to Christianize it at a stroke, and Ferdinand, who had never forgiven Isabella for promoting her confessor Ximenes in 1495 to the primatial see of Toledo, which he wanted for his son Alfonso of Saragossa, now took the opportunity to reproach her bitterly with the result, and she wrote to Ximenes blaming him severely. The court anxiously awaited tidings. On the third day of the outbreak Ximenes had dispatched letters by a slave who had the reputation of making twenty leagues a day, but at the first tavern on the road he got drunk and took five days for the journey in place of two. On receiving Isabella's reproof Ximenes sent his faithful retainer Francisco Ruiz and promised to follow as soon as the disturbances should cease. Ruiz removed the unfavorable impression and when Ximenes came and gave his version of events he was held worthy of great honor for bringing so difficult a matter to so fortunate an ending. He pointed out that, as the Moors by rebellion had forfeited their lives and property, any pardon should be conditional on their embracing Christianity or leaving the land. The sovereigns listened and yielded to his reasoning; Tendilla's promises were ignored; the opportunity of annulling the capitulations was not to be lost, the Moors were to be taught how vain was any reliance on Christian faith and although the issuing of the edict was postponed for eight months, an impassable gulf was opened between the races which all subsequent action only made wider and deeper.

Ximenes returned to Granada, where the inhabitants of the Albaycin were offered the alternative of conversion or punishment, and their readiness for baptism was stimulated by a royal judge or *pesquisidor*, sent for the purpose, who executed some of the most active insurgents and imprisoned others. With the assistance of Talavera Ximenes undertook the task of teaching the unwilling converts, but when they asked for instruction in their own language and Talavera had the offices and portions of the gospels printed in Arabic, Ximenes stoutly opposed it, saying that it was casting pearls to swine, for it was the nature of the vulgar to despise what they could understand and to reverence that which was occult and mysterious. If he could enforce outward conformity he evidently cared little for intelligent faith; he was by nature an inquisitor and not a missionary. We are not surprised therefore to learn that Talavera was obliged to baptize them without instruction or catechization, for the multitude was so great and the time was so short that there was no opportunity for such preliminaries. Nor need we wonder that such profanation of the sacrament left the neophytes as much Moslem in heart as before, with undying hatred, to be transmitted to their children, towards the religion to which they had been forced outwardly to profess conformity and towards the oppressors who had shown disregard so cynical of their solemn engagements. Nor was that hatred likely to diminish as the Inquisition, which had thus obtained jurisdiction over them, harried them ceaselessly for a century with its spies, its confiscations, and its autos de fe. They had made one vain effort to avert their fate by sending to the Soldan of Egypt to represent that they were to be converted by force and asked him to threaten reprisals on the Christians within his dominions. The soldan accordingly dispatched envoys to Ferdinand and Isabella, who explained the matter to their satisfaction and responded by sending that elegant scholar, Peter Martyr of Anghiera, on a return mission, fortified with certificates from the alcaides of Barbary that all Moors desiring to emigrate had been landed there in safety, for the sovereigns had duly accompanied the exiles with officials who saw to their delivery and took testimony as to their treatment. Peter Martyr performed his mission successfully and nothing further was heard from Egypt. The number of Christians thus brought into the fold, including those of the Vega, was estimated at from 50,000 to 70,000.[1]

[1] In all this I have principally followed Marmol Carvajal whose account is the fullest and most in detail (Rebelion y Castigo, pp. 153–6). Other relations are those of Gomez (De Rebus Gestis a Fr. Ximenio, Lib. II. fol. 30–33); Robles, Vida de Cisneros, pp. 100, 108 (s. l. 1604);

To stimulate the process Ferdinand, who had returned to Granada, issued, February 26, 1500, a general pardon to all conversos for crimes committed prior to baptism, remitting the royal rights over persons and property accruing by reason of such crimes.[1] He made no secret of his displeasure at the unlawful means employed to

Zurita, Historia del Rey Hernando, Lib. III. cap. 44; Galindez de Carvajal (Coleccion de Documentos, XVIII. 296); Bernaldez, Historia de los Reyes Católicos, p. 145; Mariana, Historia de España, Tom. IX. p. 20 (Ed. 1796); Pedraza, Hist. ecles. de Granada, fol. 193, 196.

Peter Martyr probably only repeats the stories promulgated at the court when he writes, March 1, 1500, that the Moors of the Albaycin rose in rebellion, overcame the city guard and slew its captain. Then they summoned aid from the country, where the Moors rose and for some days killed all the Christians whom they met. Those of the lower part of the city were in serious peril, but Tendilla garrisoned the wall which separated the city from the Albaycin and Talavera, who was universally beloved, threw himself among the rebels and won over the leaders partly by hope, partly by fear, so that they begged for pardon.—Pet. Mart. Angler. Epist. 212. See also Epistt. 215, 221.

Some of the earlier writers do not hesitate to criticise the inconsiderate zeal of Ximenes, although exercised in so pious a cause. This excites the ire of Fray Bleda who exclaims that such is always the reward of those who seek the conversion of this apostate race, no matter how holy is their ardor and how conformable to the rules of the Church, for it was perfectly lawful to compel the elches to conversion with torture and fire, for their parents were baptized renegades and the children consequently belonged to the Church.—Bleda, Cronica de los Moros, p. 626 (Valencia, 1618).

This, at all events, is honest. Not so much can be said of Hefele's justification of the great Cardinal, which is a model of the *suppressio veri* and *suggestio falsi*.—Der Cardinal Ximenes und die kirchlichen Zustände Spaniens in 15 Jahrhundert, pp. 52 sqq. (Tübingen, 1851).

[1] Archivo de Simancas, Patronato Real, Inquisicion, Leg. único, fol. 26. See Appendix No. II.

It is worthy of remark that this is issued in the sole name of Ferdinand, without Isabella's participation, although Granada was annexed to the crown of Castile.

procure the conversion, more especially as the affair interfered with his designs on Naples, which required all his forces. The danger at home however demanded his immediate attention, for although many of the Moors of Granada had emigrated, others had taken refuge in the mountain fastnesses of the intricate range known as the Alpujarras and had incited the hardy mountaineers to revolt. In the hope of checking this movement Ferdinand wrote to the leading Moors, January 27th, assuring them that all reports that they were to be forcibly converted were false and pledging the royal faith that not a single one should be compelled to baptism.[1] They knew too well how little Christian faith was worth, however, and were deaf to his blandishments. He had not trusted to it himself and with all speed he raised an army as large as if the conquest was to be repeated, with which he advanced on March 1st and soon crushed resistance, the rebels consenting to baptism, and to pay a fine of 50,000 ducats; but in so rugged a land, when a rising was suppressed in one place it would break out in another, and Ferdinand was occupied until the end of the year in superintending this military mission work, which was supplemented by preachers and friars sent through the mountains to instruct the neophytes—a duty not without danger for although they had guards of soldiers some of them were martyrized. The means adopted to spread the faith of Christ were not the most gentle. At Andarax the principal mosque, in which the women and children had taken refuge, was blown up with gunpowder. At the capture of Belfique all the men were put to the sword

[1] Clemencin, Elogia de la Reina Isabel, p. 291-3 (Madrid, 1821).

and the women were enslaved, while at Nijar and Guejar the whole population was enslaved, except children under eleven, who, however, were delivered to good Christians to be brought up in the faith—energetic proceedings which, we are told, led to the baptism of ten thousand Moors of Seron, Tijola and other places.[1]

The risings appeared to be suppressed and, January 14, 1501, the army was disbanded, but the example made at Belfique and Guejar produced an opposite effect on the numerous population of the district of Ronda and the Sierra Bermeja, who feared that they would be subjected to enforced conversion and who were irritated by raids and ravages made upon them by Christians—a standing grievance which frequently nullified the best intentioned efforts of pacification. They rose and committed reprisals and it was necessary to summon the levies of all Andalusia. Ferdinand issued a proclamation that all who would not be converted must leave the kingdom within ten days, and care was enjoined that converts should be well treated and that emigrants should be protected from harm. The rebels of the Sierra Bermeja, however, refused to surrender and on February 23d the army left Ronda under Alonso de Aguilar, elder brother of Gonzalo de Córdova and one of the most distinguished captains of Spain. The Moors had fortified themselves in an almost inaccessible position at Calalui; on March 16th, the undisciplined troops, eager for pillage, straggled to the attack without orders; they were beaten back, and were followed by the Moors till Aguilar advanced and drove them back, when the soldiers again fell to plundering. On seeing this the Moors

[1] Zurita—Galindez de Carvajal—Marmol Carvajal—Bernaldez, *ubi sup.*

returned to the attack, when the pillagers fled leaving Aguilar with a handful of men at nightfall to be surrounded and slain after a desperate resistance. The catastrophe made an immense sensation throughout Spain. Ferdinand hastened from Granada with all the chivalry of his court, intending to push the war vigorously, but on recognizing the cowardice of his army and the impregnable fastnesses of the mountains he saw the impossibility of accomplishing anything by force of arms, while Isabella, with feminine vehemence, declared that the Moors must all be driven out in a single day. While thus the Christians paused irresolute and uncertain, the Moors opened negotiations, asking to be allowed to expatriate themselves. Ferdinand admitted that it would be a greater service to God and to himself that they should remain Moors in Africa rather than be such Christians as they were in Spain, but he made a shrewd bargain that all might go who could pay ten doblas for the passage, while the rest, who constituted the majority, should stay and be baptized. Guards were furnished to accompany to the port of Estrepona those who desired to embark; on these terms, by the middle of April, the insurgents of the Sierra de Ronda surrendered; those of the Sierra Bermeja and other places waited to learn whether the first emigrants were safely landed in Barbary and on being assured of this they too came in. The conversos of the lowlands who had taken to the sierras were allowed to return home, surrendering their arms, and forfeiting their property, while their persons were to be at the mercy of the king, their lives being spared. Thus this dangerous rebellion, caused by the intemperate zeal of Ximenes, was finally quelled. Large numbers of the Moors crossed the sea, both under the agreement and surreptitiously, but they left multitudes behind to brood over their wrongs and to detest the faith which they had been compelled to profess.[1] As though moreover to preserve a nucleus of irritation and disaffection in the land the sternest edicts were issued prohibiting the emigration of all new converts; those attempting it were to be seized and delivered to the Inquisition, and all shipmasters receiving such passengers suffered excommunication and confiscation.[2] Baptism had incorporated them in the Church and they should not escape from its jurisdiction.

To stimulate conversion in the Alpujarras, Ferdinand had issued a royal cédula, July 30, 1500, promising that all conversos should be relieved of the special taxes imposed on Moors, both as regards persons and property and should thereafter be subject to the tithes and alcavala (a tax on sales) like other Christians. They were in all respects to be equal before the laws with Christians and their suits were to be equitably dispatched by the ordinary judges.[3] It was sound policy thus to assimilate them with the Christian population but there was too lively a recognition of the wrongs inflicted to render possible the performance of these promises, for the converts could never be regarded without suspicion. September 1, 1501, an edict forbade them to bear or possess arms, publicly or secretly, under penalty for a first offence of confiscation

[1] Zurita—Marmol Carvajal, *ubi sup.*—Bleda, Crónica, pp. 633–9.

[2] Edicts to this effect were issued Nov. 8, 1499, Jan. 15, 1502 and Sep. 15, 1519.—MSS. of Royal Library of Copenhagen, 218*b*, p. 306.

[3] Clemencin, *op. cit.* p. 603. The children of those who were slain or captured at Lanjaron and Andarax were further promised the property, real and personal, of their slain or captive parents as a reward for conversion.

and two months of prison, and of death for a second—an edict which was repeated in 1511 and again in 1515.[1] In an age of violence, when the power of self-protection was essential to every man, disarmament was one of the most cruel and humiliating of inflictions, but, as we shall see, this was but the first of a long series of such measures, for wrong could only maintain itself by injustice.

To Isabella is generally assigned the credit of the next step toward securing unity of faith under her Castilian crown. To be sure, not much confidence could be reposed in the sincerity of those who were converted in such arbitrary fashion, but it was argued that baptism gave them at least a chance of salvation and if they did not avail themselves of it the responsibility was theirs; moreover, if the parents were not even passably good Christians, the next generation, reared under the kindly influence of the Church, would surely be better; the kingdom of God would be advanced by the destruction of that of Mahomet and the earthly kingdom would have its peace secured by community of faith. Such arguments could be powerfully urged by the religious advisers who surrounded Isabella and it is not likely that Ximenes, who enjoyed her fullest confidence, would hesitate to complete the work which he had so auspiciously commenced in Granada. Strong, indeed, must have been the influences which could blind her to the infamy of her course. The enforced conversion of Granada had been, so to speak, accidental in its inception and a war measure in its development among those who were still restless and turbulent, chafing under

[1] Nueva Recopilación, Lib. VIII. Tit. ii. ley 8.

a new domination; moreover free choice was offered to the mountaineers between conversion and expatriation and all who rejected baptism were allowed to depart provided they could defray the expenses. In the older Castilian kingdoms, however, the Mudéjares were peaceful and contented subjects, contributing to the prosperity of the State under compacts centuries old which secured them in the enjoyment of their religion and laws. Deliberately to violate those compacts, to compel a change of religion with scarce a colorable pretext of alternative, was so gross an infraction of all divine and human law that even the dialectics of scholastic theology might well seem incapable of framing a justification, while the conversion of loyal and contented subjects into restless and plotting conspirators, causing sleepless anxiety to generations of statesmen, would appear to be an act of simple insanity.

Yet Isabella, in her misguided zeal, was capable of the wrong and the folly. A preliminary pragmatica of July 20, 1501, forbidding all Moors to enter the kingdom of Granada, in order to preserve the new converts from the infection of intercourse with the unconverted, shows the line of reasoning which had been adopted to work upon her conscience. It was impossible of enforcement, for the business of transportation was in the hands of the Mudéjares and the needs of Granada for supplies of wheat from its neighbors were imperative, to say nothing of the multifarious necessities of commerce. A more radical measure was requisite and, after due deliberation, on February 12, 1502, was issued the pragmatica which had such far-reaching results, beyond the possible conceptions of the short-sighted bigotry which dictated it. If Moors could not be kept out of Granada there should be no

Moors—all should be Christians under the crown of Castile, save slaves who could not be meddled with and they should be known by the perpetual wearing of fetters. Allusion was made to the scandal of allowing infidels to remain elsewhere when Granada had been purified, to the gratitude due to God which could be rightly shown by expelling his enemies, and to the necessity of protecting the neophytes from contamination by the infidel, wherefore all Moors were ordered to quit the kingdoms of Castile and Leon by the end of April—that is, all males over the age of fourteen and females over twelve, the children being retained apparently to separate them from their parents and rear them as Christians. The exiles were allowed to carry with them their property, except gold and silver and other prohibited articles. The sentence of expatriation however was purely illusory, for it was coupled with conditions rendering it impossible. They were to sail only from ports of Biscay, under pain of death and confiscation; they were not to be transported to Navarre or to the kingdoms of the crown of Aragon, and as there was war with the Turks and the Moors of Africa they were not to seek refuge with either but were told that they could go to the Soldan of Egypt or to any other land they chose. They were never to return nor were Moors ever to be admitted to the Castilian kingdoms, even temporarily, under pain of death and confiscation without trial or sentence and anyone harboring them after April was threatened with confiscation.[1] A comparison of this measure with the cordial invitation to

[1] Nueva Recop. Lib. VIII. Tit. ii. ley 4. Cf. Fernandez y Gonzalez, p. 219.

the Moors of Portugal, in 1497, demonstrates how profound was the change effected in Isabella's policy by the arbitrary methods of Ximenes in Granada.

Evidently criticism on the enforced conversion of Granada and doubts expressed whether baptism under such circumstances was valid, had made an impression and the new edict cunningly offered no alternative. That expulsion could be escaped by conversion was left to be inferred, so that the conversion could be assumed to be voluntary and spontaneous. The hypocrisy of this is evident when we learn on good authority that in reality the alternative of exile was not granted but that when the term expired those who wanted to go were not permitted to depart but all were obliged to submit to baptism.[1] Some show of preaching and instruction was made during the narrow interval allowed, sufficient presumably to satisfy the royal conscience,[2] and, as the end of the term approached, the unhappy Mudéjares professed the faith of Christ in droves. A letter of April 24th, from Avila to the sovereigns announced that the two thousand souls of the aljama there will all convert themselves and none will go away.[3] Isabella did not deceive herself as to the sincerity of her new converts, for when they manifested a purpose to leave their homes for regions where they would

[1] En el dicho mes de enero mandaron los Reyes salir de sus reinos de Castilla y Leon todos los moros que vivian y moraban en ellos por los meses de marzo, abril y mayo, y aunque los mandaron salir, despues de llegado el plazo no lo consentieron sino que se tornasen cristianos.—Galindez de Carvajal (Coleccion de Documentos, XVIII. 303–4). Zurita however (Hist. del Rey Hernando, Lib. IV. cap. 54) while quoting Carvajal, says that those who refused baptism were driven out, but he admits that the conversion was involuntary.

[2] Zurita, *loc. cit.*

[3] Coleccion de Documentos, XXXVI. 447.

be under less careful surveillance she promptly checked the movement by issuing orders, September 17th, forbidding them for two years to sell their property or to leave Castile for Aragon, Valencia or Portugal except by land, and then they must furnish security to return as soon as their business was accomplished.[1]

So signal a service rendered to God might reasonably expect reward. It was disappointing therefore that Heaven afflicted the land with visitations, for the harvests were deficient from 1503 to 1506 and this was followed in 1507 with a pestilence which fell with peculiar severity on the clergy. Bernaldez tells us that in Alcalá de Guadayra out of thirteen mass-priests twelve died; in Utrera four died and all the sacristans and the remainder were sick but recovered. In his own parish, out of 500 souls he buried 160. It was the same throughout Andalusia and Castile and was the worst pestilence since that of the year 575 when half the population of Spain perished. This was succeeded in 1508 by a plague of locusts, which flew in clouds obscuring the sun, four or five leagues in length and two or three in width, devouring all vegetation except the vines.[2]

Isabella died November 26, 1504, after which, except during the short interlude of the reign of Philip and

[1] Llorente, Añales, I. 279. The prohibition of travel by sea was evidently to prevent emigration to Africa which was doubtless adopted by many. Fray Bleda assures us (Crónica, pp. 639-41) that if Torquemada had been alive the expulsion would have been carried out as was that of the Jews, for he had not the indiscreet zeal which led others to induce the sovereign to attempt the conversion of the Moors by compulsion without the preliminary catechism and disposition required by human and divine law.

[2] Bernaldez, Historia de los Reyes Católicos, II. 291-99, 311-14.

Juana in 1506, Ferdinand remained master of Castile as well as of Aragon. While sufficiently zealous for the faith he did not allow bigotry wholly to supersede policy and he recognized that contented subjects were more desirable than discontented ones. His general attitude towards the new converts was therefore that of restraining rather than of inciting persecution. The baptism of the Castilian Mudéjares—to be known henceforth as Moriscos—had placed them under the jurisdiction of the Inquisition; it was notorious that their conversion was only external, that at heart they retained their ancestral faith and that they maintained its observances in so far as they could in secret, and thus they were liable when detected to prosecution and punishment. The extant records of the Castilian Inquisition of the period are scanty and positive conclusions from them cannot safely be drawn, but in so far as I have been able to examine the evidence it would appear that the Holy Office was still concentrating its attention on the Jewish New Christians and at first gave little heed to the Moriscos.

In 1507 Deza was forced to resign the position of inquisitor-general and Ximenes succeeded to the coveted office. One of his earliest acts in this capacity was to issue to all the churches in Spain public letters specifying how the New Christians and their children should deport themselves in religious matters, how they should regularly attend divine service and how they were to be instructed in the rudiments of the faith; also, what they should avoid, such as Judaic and Mahometan ceremonies, sorcery, magic, incantations and other superstitions introduced by demons.[1] What warrant Ximenes found in his office for

[1] Gomecii de Rebus Gestis, Lib. III. fol. 77.

issuing such instructions to the churches it might not be easy to discover, but it is not likely that any zealous defender of ecclesiastical or episcopal jurisdiction had the hardihood to raise the question and the necessity of such an order, five years after the edict of expulsion, shows how negligent the Church had been of its duty toward its neophytes. It had been more active as to its material interests, for, when the royal fisc seized the revenues of the mosques which had been closed, it interposed, claiming that the property had been given, however mistakenly, for the service of God and therefore could not be converted to secular uses.[1]

Thus already began the complaints which we shall find continue to the last, that the Church ignored its responsibility and did nothing to win over and instruct those whom the Inquisition was persecuting for their ignorance. The orders of Ximenes received scant observance for we find Ferdinand writing to him, March 20, 1510, announcing that he was sending letters to all the prelates of his realm pointing out the neglect of Catholic rites by the New Christians of Moorish and Jewish extraction; the bishops must compel their presence at mass and provide for their instruction and all parish priests must give to this their special attention.[2] Simultaneously with this Ferdinand made application to Julius II. for a brief empowering the inquisitors to treat apostate neophytes with a leniency not authorized by the canon law. As this was the first of a series of measures constantly occurring in the dealings with recalcitrant Moriscos, it may be as well to premise that inquisitors had faculties of proclaiming

[1] Pet. Mart. Angler. Epist. 286.

[2] Danvila y Collado, Expulsión de los Moriscos, p. 74 (Madrid, 1889).

what was known as an Edict of Grace, prescribing a term, usually of thirty days, during which all heretics could come forward, confess fully as to themselves and others, and escape confiscation and the stake, in lieu of which they were subjected to penance, pecuniary and spiritual, at the discretion of the inquisitor; they abjured their errors publicly and were publicly reconciled to the Church. Reconciliation of itself was a grievous penalty, for a subsequent lapse into error was regarded as relapse, for which, according to the canons, the irrevocable punishment was relaxation to the secular arm, that is, death by fire. Moreover it inflicted serious disabilities, not only on the culprit but on his descendants for two generations by the male line and for one by the female—inability to hold office of honor or profit, and to obtain ecclesiastical preferment, besides which, under the Spanish law, he was forbidden to bear arms, to ride on horseback and to wear silk or jewels or gold and silver ornaments and to follow certain occupations, such as those of physicians, surgeons, druggists, etc. The Church, it will be seen, was not merciful to its erring children, even when repentant, and the term of grace was but indifferently attractive.

As the Inquisition had no power to mitigate these provisions of the canon law and as Ferdinand was desirous to adopt milder measures which could only be authorized by the Holy See, he applied to Julius representing that since 1492 there had been converted in Spain numerous persons of Jewish and Moorish race who in consequence of deficient instruction in the faith had not observed their obligations and had committed heretical crimes. In view of their numbers and of their recent conversion it would be inhuman to proceed against them with the full rigor of the law, wherefore he had ordered them to be instructed in the faith. To give them fuller opportunity for this, and that they might more willingly confess their sins and perform penance, he asked that faculties should be granted to the inquisitors to receive to reconciliation those who should come within thirty days, confess their sins and accept penance salutary to their souls, without inflicting confiscation and the other pains and penances which the law enjoins and without requiring public abjuration, for otherwise if they should again fall into the same errors there would be no possibility of saving them.[1]

It may safely be assumed that Ferdinand's request was granted, but its only importance lies in its statement of the existing condition and in its indication of his policy, for these Edicts of Grace labored under a limitation which rendered them for the most part inoperative, except as an exhibition of apparent clemency and as affording an opportunity of objurgating the apostates for hardness of heart. In theory the penitent was received because he had experienced real conversion; as a Catholic Christian he must detest heresy and heretics; the confession of his own offences was imperfect and fictitious unless he included all of which he was cognizant in others. Imperfect and fictitious confession was one of the gravest crimes in the code of the Inquisition, it rendered nugatory all absolution gained by it and exposed the culprit to the danger of relaxation. Thus any one coming forward under an Edict of Grace was obliged to denounce all his accomplices in heresy—that is, all his family and friends

[1] Archivo de Simancas, Inquisicion, Libro 3, fol. 72.

—and to furnish such evidence as would lead to their arrest and trial and torture. The records of the Inquisition, unhappily, supply evidence only too abundant of the way in which parents incriminated children and children parents under the stress of prolonged incarceration, skilful examination and perhaps the torture-chamber, but to expect those in freedom to come forward spontaneously and betray their nearest and dearest presupposed too vile an estimate of human nature to be often realized.[1] It could only occur when a whole community took united action.

Whether the combined efforts of Ferdinand and Ximenes aroused the Church to a sense of its duties and responsibilities we have slender means of knowing, but it may safely be assumed that they did not and that the Moriscos remained as firmly Moslem as ever, while the inquisitors were not as neglectful as the prelates and when the Jewish conversos became scarcer those of Moorish extraction kept the field of operation supplied. Thus we happen

[1] The utility of confession in discovering accomplices is exemplified by the case of Francisco Zafar y Ribera, a Valencian Morisco who, in 1605, was miraculously converted and made a pilgrimage to Monserrat where he confessed to a priest who sent him to the inquisitors of Barcelona for absolution from the censures incurred by heresy. They required him to reveal the names of all whom he knew to be Moslems and on finding them to be Valencians they sent him thither, where he denounced no less than four thousand persons by their names. He had been a travelling tailor and had a large acquaintance among the Aljamas.—Bleda, Crónica, p. 929.

Guadalajara y Xavierr tells us (Expulsión de los Moriscos, fol. 159), as one of the evil characteristics of the Moriscos, that when obliged by necessity they would freely confess as to themselves but refused to reveal the crimes of their neighbors, wherefore they were burnt as *negativos* and excommunicated apostates.

to hear of the active prosecution, in 1517, by the tribunal of Calahorra, of the Moriscos of Aguilar de Rio Alhama, Cervera de Rio Alhama, Erze and Inestrillas, resulting in thirty-eight convictions. As there was no church in Aguilar where the neophytes could be taught, and as one had been commenced, King Charles generously made over half of the confiscations to assist in its construction and endowment. The next year on learning that persecuted Moriscos had commenced to remove to Granada in the hope of passing to Africa or remaining concealed, he graciously waived his right to the confiscations in favor of those who should come in under a term of grace to be designated.[1] In a similar spirit, in 1518, on hearing that the inquisitors of Cuenca were arresting and prosecuting the Moriscos, Cardinal Adrian, the inquisitor-general, ordered an Edict of Grace with a term of two years while Charles renounced the confiscations, and this was renewed in 1520. A similar measure, in 1518, with the term of one year, checked the operations of the inquisitors of Cartagena who were persecuting the Moriscos of the Val de Ricote in Murcia; in October, 1519, this was extended for another year; then, December 24, 1521, Cardinal Adrian writes to the inquisitors that the Moriscos have appealed to him for a further extension, alleging that in consequence of the disturbances they have been prevented from coming forward and confessing as to themselves and others; he therefore grants a further term of six months from January 1, 1522, during which time those who confess are not to suffer confiscation, but are to be treated mercifully as regards penance and are not to be con-

[1] Archivo de Simancas, Inquisicion, Lib. 4, fol. 7; Lib. 5, fol. 11; Lib. 9, fol. 13.

demned to perpetual prison and wearing the sanbenito, the latter being removed as soon as they have abjured their errors in the public auto de fe.[1]

All this shows that the inquisitors were proceeding with more zeal than discretion and that their superiors were disposed to listen to the appeals of the sufferers, recognizing the supreme absurdity of expecting sincere adherence to a faith imposed by force and known only as the source of persecution and spoliation. Still, there were the canons, the machinery for their enforcement and the obligation of vindicating the faith on the apostates who were legally members of the Catholic Church. A situation had been created from which there was no escape and every attempt to find an exit only aggravated the difficulties until despair of a reasonable remedy brought about the final catastrophe. Meanwhile thus far the disposition was to temporize and postpone energetic proceedings. This doubtless explains the action of Cardinal Adrian, August 5, 1521, in issuing general orders that no arrests should be made except on testimony directly conclusive of heresy and even then the evidence must first be submitted to the decision of the Suprema, or supreme council of the Inquisition.[2] As usual the inquisitors interpreted

[1] Archivo de Simancas, Inquisicion, Libro 4, fol. 97; Lib. 9, fol. 2, 29; Lib. 940, fol. 69, 131, 185.

The sanbenito, a sort of yellow tunic with a red oblique band, to be constantly worn in public, was one of the penalties attaching to reconciliation and was a very severe infliction as it was an indelible mark of disgrace. It was heightened by the fact that a counterpart, with an inscription of the name and date and offence, was hung up in the parish church in perpetual evidence of the crime and its punishment.

[2] Ibid. Libro 939, fol. 89. It should be borne in mind that mere arrest by the Inquisition was in itself a very serious punishment. All

these instructions to suit themselves, and Adrian's successor as inquisitor-general, Archbishop Manrique, was more explicit in a *carta acordada*, or general order of April 28, 1524. This recites the conversion of the Moriscos by Ferdinand and Isabella, who promised them graces and liberties, in pursuance of which Cardinal Adrian issued many provisions in their favor, ordering inquisitors not to prosecute them for trifling causes, and if any were so arrested they were to be discharged and their property be returned to them. Notwithstanding this inquisitors arrest them on trivial charges and on the evidence of single witnesses. As they are ignorant persons who cannot easily prove their innocence and have never been instructed in the faith, these arrests have greatly scandalized them and they have petitioned that they may not be worse treated, wherefore the Suprema instructs all inquisitors not to arrest any of them without evidence of their having committed some offence directly conclusive of heresy; if there is doubt on this point the testimony is first to be submitted to the Suprema. All persons held for matters not plainly heretical are to have speedy justice tempered with such clemency as conscience may permit.[1]

It is not to be imagined that these well-intentioned instructions were effective in removing the abuses of which the Moriscos complained. The inviolable secrecy

the property of the prisoner was at once seized and sequestrated and he was imprisoned *incommunicado* until his trial was ended, which usually occupied from one to three years, during which his family were in total ignorance of his fate and he could know nothing about them. The expenses of his maintenance in prison were paid out of his sequestrated estate which was apt to be consumed in the process.

[1] Danvila y Collado, Expulsión de los Moriscos, p. 89.

which shrouded all the actions of the tribunals relieved the inquisitors of responsibility and their use of the power with which they were clothed depended almost wholly on individual temperament. Whether their power was well or ill employed they at least secured outward conformity. The Moriscos of Castile were gradually assimilating themselves to their Christian neighbors; they had long since abandoned their national language and dress and they now were assiduous in attendance at mass and vespers, the confessional and the sacrament of the altar; they took part in interments and processions and were commonly regarded as Christians, whatever might be the secrets of their hearts.[1]

When, in 1512, Ferdinand conquered Navarre he annexed it to the crown of Castile, where the royal power was more absolute than in Aragon. This brought the Mudéjares there under the operation of the edict of 1502, giving them the alternative of emigration or of baptism. It cost them comparatively little to transfer themselves to the French portion of the dissevered kingdom and it would seem that, as a rule, they preferred this to baptism and subjection to the Inquisition, which Ferdinand had lost no time in introducing in his new dominions. As early as 1516 we are told that from this cause there were two hundred uninhabited houses in the town of Tudela, and thenceforth we hear nothing of Moriscos in Navarre.[2]

[1] Bleda, Crónica, p. 905.

[2] Yanguas y Miranda, Diccionario de Antigüedades del Reino de Navarra, II. 434 (Pamplona, 1840).

Yanguas (p. 428) prints the very liberal charter accorded to the Moors of Tudela by Alonso el Batallador when he obtained possession of the city in 1114. It shows the same policy as that followed in the

The properties thus abandoned were confiscated, for in 1519 a letter of the Suprema required the titles of all lands of the expelled Moors to be submitted to the inquisitors there.[1]

But a new act of the tragedy was now about to open which requires a review of some antecedent events.

rest of Spain during the Reconquest. When the crown passed to the House of Capet, Louis Hutin confirmed all the fueros and franchises of the Mudéjares in 1307, and in 1368 Charles le Mauvais granted to those of Tudela a remission of half their taxes for three years as a reward for their assistance in his wars, especially in fortification and engineering.—Ibid. p. 433.

[1] Archivo de Simancas, Inquisicion, Libro 72, P. I. fol. 173.

CHAPTER III.

THE GERMANÍA.

THUS far we have been dealing with the kingdoms of the crown of Castile, of which the policy with regard to the Moors was determined during the joint reign of Ferdinand and Isabella. Outside of these lay the kingdoms of the crown of Aragon—Aragon, Valencia and the principality of Catalonia—which were ruled by Ferdinand alone. They had preserved much more of their ancient liberties than had their sister states; they were jealous of their *fueros* or laws and privileges and their córtes still were bodies with which their princes had to reckon, for their petitions of grievances had precedence over the votes of supplies long after the córtes of Castile were forced to invert the order of procedure. The ruling classes set a high value on their Moorish vassals who cultivated the land and paid heavy imposts, while loans to their aljamas were a favorite investment for prelates and ecclesiastical foundations. It had passed into a proverb that "Mientras mas Moros mas ganancia"—"the more Moors the more profit." Strong influences were therefore at work to preserve the *status in quo;* any disturbance threatened loss, and if the Moors, on receiving baptism, should reach equality before the law with Old Christians, their lords dreaded a notable diminution of revenue. To the last this interested conservatism was the object of ceaseless objurgation by the zealots who labored at first for forcible conversion and subsequently for expulsion.

This conservatism did not fail to manifest itself as soon as the alarm was given by the occurrences in Granada and Castile—indeed, it was somewhat premature for, as early as 1495, the córtes of Tortosa obtained from Ferdinand a fuero that he would never expel or consent to the expulsion of the Moors of Catalonia. After the edict of 1502 in Castile it was currently reported that Ferdinand would follow the example, leading the córtes of Barcelona in 1503 to exact from him a pledge to the same effect, and in 1510 at the córtes of Monzon he repeated this with the addition that he would make no attempt to convert them by force nor throw any impediment on their free intercourse with Christians to all of which he solemnly swore an oath the repetition of which was exacted of Charles V. on his accession in 1518.[1]

Ferdinand, in fact, had already interposed in his imperative fashion to check the indiscreet zeal of the inquisitors who were abusing their power to compel conversions

[1] Danvila y Collado, La Expulsión, pp. 75, 76.—Fernandez y Gonzalez, p. 441.—Bleda, Crónica, p. 641.—The Latin version of this fuero, as given by Bleda (Defensio Fidei, p. 156) is—"Facimus forum sive legem novam ut Mauri vicini stantes et habitantes in villis Regiis et aliis civitatibus, villis et locis ac ruribus ecclesiasticorum, hominum divitum, nobilium, equitum, civium et aliarum quarumlibet personarum, non expellantur aut ejiciantur neque exterminentur a Regno Valentiæ neque a civitatibus aut villis Regiis illius, neque cogantur fieri Christiani; cum velimus sitque nostra voluntas ut neque per nos neque per successores nostros fiat ullum obstaculum prædictis Mauris dicti Regni in commerciis, in negotiis et contractibus inter Christianos et cum Christianis, sed potius ut libere possint haec agere in posterum sicut hactenus consueverunt."

indirectly. On the complaint of the Duke and Duchess of Cardona, the Count of Ribagorza and other magnates, he wrote in 1508 to the inquisitors, reproving them sharply for overstepping the law, with much scandal to the Moors and damage to their lords. No one, he says, should be converted or baptized by force, for God is served only when conversion is heartfelt, nor should any one be imprisoned for simply telling others not to turn Christian. In future no Moor is to be baptized unless he applies for it; any who are in prison for counselling others against conversion are to be released at once and the papers are to be sent to the Inquisitor-general of Aragon, Juan de Enguera, Bishop of Vich, for instructions, nor shall any one be arrested in future without his orders. As it is further said that some have fled in fear of forcible conversion or imprisonment, steps must be taken to bring them home with full assurance against future violence.[1] Similarly, in 1510, when some Moors in Aragon had been converted, and had consequently been abandoned by their wives and children, Ferdinand ordered the inquisitors to permit the latter to return but not to exert pressure on them or baptize them forcibly. This indicates that a slow process of conversion was going on, and the same is seen in the case of a Catalan alfaquí named Jacob Tellez, who had sought baptism and had brought over several aljamas; Ferdinand, to aid him in his missionary work, issued to him a licence to travel everywhere and to have entrance into all aljamas where the Moors were required to assemble and to listen to him.[2] Incidents such as these

[1] Archivo de Simancas, Inquisicion, Libro 926, fol. 76. (See Appendix No. III.)

[2] Ibid. Libro 3, fol. 132, 245.

might encourage the hope that in time Christianity would win its way by gentleness and persuasion. The neophytes were not always firm in the faith but the policy adopted in Aragon as in Castile was not to handle them too roughly. We have seen how, in 1502, the Moors of Teruel and Albarracin had sought baptism in a body; such wholesale conversions were apt to furnish backsliders, and when the Inquisition took action against them Charles V., in 1519, interposed; he understood, he said, that many of the children of the conversos who had relapsed were desirous of returning to the faith but were deterred by fear of punishment, wherefore he granted them a term of grace of a year during which they could come in and confess without undergoing confiscation, and similar concessions were made in Tortosa and other cities.[1]

Valencia, which had the most crowded Moorish population, was also the scene of considerable proselyting and of vigorous inquisitorial activity. The little town of Manices (partido of Moncada) must have been converted almost in mass, for we chance to have a sentence passed in bulk, by the inquisitors of Valencia, April 8, 1519, in the church there, on 232 Moriscos, then present, who had come in under an Edict of Grace, confessing and abjuring their errors, and who were received to reconciliation. Apparently there was no confiscation and the penances inflicted were purely spiritual, but they were

[1] Archivo de Simancas, Inquisicion, Libro 14, fol. 80; Libro 940, fol. 69, 131, 185.

At the same time the Moors were not allowed to establish new mosques and the Inquisition was active in preventing it. In 1514 the Suprema ordered Inquisitor Calvo of Valencia to tear down the one recently erected so that not a trace of it should be left and in 1519 it thanked the inquisitors for ordering the destruction of one recently built at Ayora.—Ibid. Libro 72, P. I. fol. 1, 64.

subjected to the severe customary disabilities and there is ghastly evidence of the cruel work that had been going on in the fact that in the list of these penitents no less than thirty-two are described as the wives or daughters of men who had been burnt.[1] However conformable

[1] Archivo Histórico Nacional, Inq. de Valencia, Legajo 98.

From the materials at my disposal it is impossible to compile absolutely accurate statistics as to the activity of the Valencian Inquisition at this time, but it can be approximated, premising that as yet there were a certain number of Judaizing conversos mingled with the Moriscos. There is a list (*ubi sup.*) of all the cases of heresy tried by that tribunal from 1461 to 1592. Starting with 1512, after two or three previous years of comparative inactivity, we find the numbers to be as follows:

1512, 32 cases.	1516, 41 cases.	1520, 36 cases.
1513, 41 "	1517, 25 "	1521, 31 "
1514, 63 "	1518, 21 "	1522, 40 "
1515, 34 "	1519, 22 "	1523, 37 "

Danvila y Collado (Expulsión, p. 87) is evidently in error when he says that unpublished records show that between 1515 and 1522 the Valencian Inquisition burnt 250 persons, scourged 155 and tried 1090. The whole number of trials for heresy in those years was 250. I cannot ascertain positively the number of burnings, but it was comparatively small. I have a record of them from 1486 to 1593, but it is imperfect, ending with the letter N.—for these indexes to the registers are always arranged alphabetically, under the Christian names. From other extensive lists I find that this portion of the alphabet comprises just four-fifths of the whole, so that if we add 25 per cent. to the following we shall have a substantially correct statement of the number of burnings—those in effigy being persons who were dead or fugitives.

	In person.	In effigy.		In person.	In effigy.
1512	1	8	1518	none	
1513	12	1	1519	none	
1514	52	8	1520	27	—
1515	none		1521	8	3
1516	none		1522	6	—
1517	4	6	1523	8	—

(Archivo Histórico Nacional, Valencia, Legajo 300).

The aggregate of these is 154, or, with the addition of 25 per cent., 192. For the years specified by Danvila the numbers would be 54 and

this may have been to the ideas of the period it necessarily acted as a powerful deterrent to the wished for conversion of the infidels, who, so long as they remained unbaptized were not subject to prosecution and who might well hesitate to render themselves liable to imprisonment, trial and confiscation for abstaining from pork and wine or for staining their nails with henna.

While thus the efforts to preserve the purity of the faith were preventing its propagation, the whole face of affairs was suddenly changed by the revolt known as the Germanía or Brotherhood, which broke out in 1520. This was a rising of the commons against the cruelty and oppression of the nobles, orderly at first, when it received the approbation of Cardinal Adrian, regent of the kingdom in the absence of Charles V. Excesses on both sides led to open civil war, in which the Moors were faithful to their lords. They formed a considerable portion of the forces with which the Duke of Segorbe won the victories of Oropesa and Almenara, early in July, 1521, and they constituted a third of the infantry under the Viceroy Mendoza in the disastrous rout of Gandía, July 25th. This revived the race hatred which had been slowly dying out and led the chiefs of the Germanía to conceive the idea of baptizing them by force, not as a measure of religious zeal but as an act of hostility to the

68—a quite sufficient evidence of the pitiless character of the persecution.

With regard to the total number of cases of all kinds it must be borne in mind that the greater portion of the business of the Inquisition consisted in the suppression of blasphemy, sorcery and the utterance of careless words, classed as "proposiciones," for all of which scourging was a frequent punishment. None of these cases would be included in the above lists which are exclusively of trials for heresy.

nobles, thus emancipating them, giving them the status of Christians, and depriving their lords of the support arising from their numbers and fidelity. The first indication of this, in the city of Valencia, was on July 4, 1521, when a Franciscan appeared at the gate of his convent, brandishing a crucifix and shouting "Long live the faith of Christ and war to the Saracens!" A crowd assembled with which he marched out of the city, but the Marquis of Zenete, deputy governor, who had the confidence of both parties, persuaded him to wait till the next day and then dispersed the band.[1] The movement however had actively commenced earlier elsewhere, for Urgellés, the chief in command of the Germanía, mortally wounded at the siege of Játiva, which surrendered July 14th, was already busily engaged in forcing baptism on the Moors in the places under his control.[2] He was succeeded by Vicente Peris, who, on July 25th, won the decisive victory of Gandía, placing all the neighboring territory at the mercy of the Agermanados, wandering bands of whom at once scattered over the country, pillaging and forcing the Moors to submit to baptism. Peris himself laid siege to the castle of Polop, in which many Christians and some eight hundred Moors had taken refuge. After a cannonade of four days the castle surrendered, paying a ransom and conceding the baptism of the Moors, who were promised safety of life and property. They were placed in the barbican of the castle, when there came a report that the Moors of Chirles were advancing to rescue

[1] Danvila y Collado, La Germanía de Valencia, pp. 146, 471.

[2] Informacio super Conversione Sarracenorum.—This is the report of a commission deputed in 1524 to ascertain whether the Moors were voluntarily or coercively baptized. I possess the original document.

them: the cry of "Kill them!" arose, they were massacred to a man and abundant spoils were obtained from the dead.[1] In September Peris returned to the city of Valencia, in order to interrupt negotiations which were on foot for a settlement; while there he held a council in which was declared a war of extermination, of which one article ordered the baptism of all Moors, so that they might pay no greater imposts than those of Old Christians.[2]

This was superfluous, save as an indication of policy, for by this time the work of conversion was wellnigh accomplished in all places which the Agermanados could reach. Although the extreme measures of Polop were not employed, there was no pretence of persuasion and there was no hesitation at murder as a means of intimidation. At Játiva the killing of two, the burning of the gate of the Morería and the threat to sack it sufficed. From there Urgellés sent word to Albayda that they must all within three days turn Christians or depart or he would kill them; the magistrates told them that they could not protect them; they sent envoys to Urgellés who replied that the banner of the Germanía would not return to Valencia until all the Moors were baptized, whereupon they submitted, especially as a force of three thousand Agermanados from Orihuela came there with threats of pillage and after the rout of Gandía sent them word that they would kill them. There were many refugees from the surrounding country in Albayda and all were taken in groups of from twenty to fifty to the church for baptism, giving every sign of unwillingness. At Consentaina, when, on July 29th, the news came of

[1] Danvila y Collado, Germanía, p. 155. [2] Ibid. p. 163.

the rout of Gandía, it was followed by a troop of men from Alcoy, who marched through the town to the Morería, and soon after came the bands from Orihuela and commenced to sack it; a Moor on the tower of the mosque killed one with a cross-bow, whereupon the Christians slew ten or fifteen of them and the rest rushed weeping and crying "Christianos!" to the church to be baptized, or sought shelter in the houses of their Christian friends, or escaped to the Sierra de Bernia. At Oliva, the soldiers of Orihuela drove the Moors in droves to the church for baptism, striking and robbing them, while the latter were crying "Sancta Maria, have mercy, the hour has come!" Subsequently a good fraile of el Pi armed with a crucifix brought in a little band of twenty or thirty to save their lives; dead Moors were lying on the road-sides, the Morería of Olevagra was set on fire and two sick Moors were burnt in their homes. At Gandía, on the very day of the rout, the Agermanados celebrated their victory by killing some Moors and dragging the rest to the church, shouting "Death to the Moors!" and "Dogs be baptized!" They ordered the priests to get to work and the process lasted for several days as bands were brought in from the vicinage, and a witness stated that he saw a hundred and fifty dead Moors between the tower gate and San Antonio. At Valldigna the men of Alcira came with two frailes carrying crucifixes and proclaiming that all Moors must turn Christians or die; they pillaged the monastery and castle where property had been stored for safety, killed some of the Moors who had sought refuge in the mountain of Toro, and gave the rest two hours in which to choose between baptism and death—a term which was subsequently extended to eight or ten days. Such were the scenes which were enacted in all places controlled by the Agermanados and the only redeeming feature of the cruel business is the frequent evidence through it all of friendly relations between Christian and Moor, of refuge and protection willingly given to the terrified victims, showing how the antagonism of race had been dying out and its extinction might have been hopefully anticipated but for this new infliction of wrong.[1]

There was also an attempt to convert the mosques into churches. In a few places they were consecrated; in others a paper picture of Christ or the Virgin was hung up, or was placed on the door. Occasionally divine service was performed, which the new converts attended with more or less regularity, but their adhesion to the faith imposed on them was brief. In some cases it lasted but for three weeks, in others for a few months; as soon as they felt that danger was over they reverted to their Moslem rites and worshipped in their mosques as before. For the most part they were encouraged to this by their lords, who assured them that the enforced baptism which they had received was invalid and that they were free to return to their old religion. There was also a certain Micer Torrent, a jurist of Játiva, who seems to have followed closely after the proselyting bands, assuring the conversos that they were not truly baptized. We hear of him at Alcira, Alberich and Valldigna, at the latter of which places he uttered threats as to what King Charles would do and assured them that the king had ordered that those who had received baptism with-

[1] MS. Informacio.

out chrism were not Christians, while those on whom chrism had been used could nullify it with the use of lye and water—a doctrine which relieved the fears of many.[1] Others made matters safe by escaping to Africa and it was estimated that no less than five thousand houses were thus left vacant, which would infer an emigration of some 25,000 souls.[2]

The Germanía was suppressed in 1522, its last strongholds, Alcira and Játiva holding out until December. With the restoration of order the Inquisition began to take steps to garner the new harvest which the violence of the Agermanados had procured for it. Inquisitor Churruca had no conscientious doubts as to the validity of the sacraments which brought under his jurisdiction so large an accession of notorious apostates, but in order to prosecute it was necessary to prove in each individual case that the party had undergone the ceremony. The haste and confusion had been great and the multitudes greater; in the majority of places the officiating priests had been unable to make out lists or registers of the converts and identification was difficult. Where such lists had been kept he demanded their surrender, evidently for the purpose of compiling records which would prove serviceable to the tribunal in its future operations and toward the close of 1523 we find him busy in examining witnesses who could furnish him with the names of those

[1] Ibid.—Danvila (Germanía, p. 379) prints evidence to the effect that at Alberich Micer Torrent offered to enable the baptized to live as Moors for half a ducat a piece; also that he would communicate a papal brief, for a ducat per family, whereby they could turn Moors on washing the body and forehead with lye and ashes.

[2] Danvila, p. 184.

whom they had seen baptized.[1] At the same time he was prosecuting those on whom he could lay his hands. In October, 1523, the fragment of a trial of Haçan, son of En Catola, otherwise Jeronimo, shows that the case turned on the proof of his being among the Moors who were baptized at Játiva. In November testimony is being taken against Haxus, a Moorish girl, whose father and mother must also have been on trial for they testified that they and all their eight children had turned Christians and had then lived as Moors. Haxus said that she had never gone to mass, for fifteen days she had lived neither as Christian nor Moor and then had returned to Moorish ways in which she intended to persevere, but on December 18th she weakened and begged for mercy. There was no disposition to be harsh with such cases and under instruction from the Suprema she was simply penanced by being required to go for two months to the church of San Juan, to give some alms and to learn the Catholic prayers.[2] A reference in the sentence, moreover, to absolution being temporary until an expected brief of the pope is received shows that the perplexities of the situation were recognized and that application had been made to the Holy See for a remedy. It would further appear that Cardinal Adrian adopted the policy of a wise toleration which, after his elevation to the papacy, the advocates of the Moriscos argued amounted to a dispensation for their apostasy.[3]

[1] MS. Informacio.—Danvila, Germanía, p. 473.

[2] Archivo Histórico Nacional, Inquisicion de Valencia, Legajo 299, fol. 400.—Danvila, p. 474.

[3] Loazes, Tractatus super nova paganorum Regni Valentiæ Conversione, col. 12 (Valentiæ, 1525).—"Et quod summi pontificis dispen-

The situation, in fact, was quite sufficiently complex. In Granada and the Castilian kingdoms, enforced conversion had been universal. Every Moor had, constructively at least, become a Morisco or convert and could be legally held to the consequences, but in Valencia conversion had been partial and tumultuous, records were lacking and no one knew what part of the population was Moorish and what part was technically Christian, nor even whether, in any given case, the sacrament so hurriedly and irregularly administered had been rightfully performed. The simplest solution which offered itself seemed to be to complete the work so auspiciously commenced and to convert the whole Moorish population, and for this purpose missionaries were sent to try the art of persuasion, while the opposition of the nobles was averted by conceding that their rights over their Moorish vassals should not be impaired by conversion and that converts should not be allowed to change their domicile.[1] The most prominent of these missionaries was the well-known humanist, Fray Antonio de Guevara, subsequently Bishop of Guadix and then of Mondoñedo, who, in a letter of May 22, 1524, says that by command of the emperor

satio intervenerit patet ; nam summus pontifex Adrianus, dum in istis Aragoniæ partibus resideret et plenam notitiam dicti baptismi sic violenter recepti et qualiter pagani postea cessante violentia ad primævos ritus redierunt haberet, visus fuerit eos tollerando et aliter non providendo super eorum tollerantiam cum eisdem dispensare."

Adrian, after his election to the papacy, January 9, 1522, remained in Spain until August 4th, without resigning his office as inquisitor-general.

[1] Danvila, Germanía, p. 489.

The nobles derived from the Moors double the imposts and revenues that they could from Christians.—Sandoval, Historia de Carlos V., Lib. XIII. § xxviii.

he had labored for three years in Valencia, during which he had done nothing but dispute in the aljamas, preach in the Morerías and baptize in the houses, besides suffering many insults. He reveals one of the secrets which go far to explain the ill-success of the Spaniards in their efforts to win the Moors to Christianity, for he tells the friend to whom he is writing that, after great labor and the opposition of the whole Morisma of Oliva, he had converted and baptized the honored Cidi Abducarim after which his friend had called Cidi a dog of a Moor and an infidel. When he reproved his friend the latter made matters worse by saying that in his country it was an old custom to call all new converts Moors or Marranos —a term of infinite contempt. Guevara points out to him the evils resulting from this and the depth of insult which it conveys, as it infers perjury, treachery and apostasy.[1]

Not only thus was there uncertainty as to the baptism of individuals but the question was raised as to the validity of the sacrament as administered under the terrorism of the Agermanados. In Granada the Moors had been rebels and their conversion was a condition agreed to on pacification. In Castile there had been the simple edict of expulsion with a tacit understanding that it would not be enforced on those who asked for baptism. In Valencia however the sovereign was under a solemn oath that no compulsion should be employed; the Agermanados had themselves been rebels and as soon as their

[1] Ant. de Guevara, Epistolas familiares, pp. 639–42 (Madrid, 1595). Charles V. in the Edict of Granada, 1526, forbade the mutual calling each other dogs under penalty for a Morisco of ten days' imprisonment and for a Christian of six days, with double for a second offence. —Nueva Recop. Lib. VIII. Tit. ii. ley 13.

power was withdrawn the Moors had universally treated the baptism as invalid and had returned to the rites of their fathers, while the Inquisition had assumed its validity and had prosecuted such apostates as it could reach. A discussion inevitably arose both as to the validity of enforced baptism, the degree of coercion exerted in the present case and the sufficiency of the rite so hastily and irregularly performed.

It was a principle of the Church, handed down from primitive times, that the faith is not to be spread by force or violence. It was also a dogma that the sacrament of baptism impresses an indelible *character;* that the neophyte belongs irrevocably to the Church. Even before Christianity had so lost its early purity as to render compulsory conversion possible, St. Augustin, in his controversy with the Donatists over the question of the integrity of the sacraments in unworthy hands, had asserted that the belief and intention of him who is baptized has much to do with his salvation but has nothing to do with the validity of the sacrament.[1] A further step was taken when the Spanish Goths undertook to persecute their Jews into Christianity; they formulated the policy which became current in the Church—that the Jews ought not to be coerced to baptism but that when baptized in whatever fashion they were to be forced to remain in the Church lest the name of the Lord be blasphemed and their adopted faith be rendered contemptible—a hideous principle which was duly carried through the canons and served as a justification for vitiating in practice the essential genius of Christianity and as an excuse for unnum-

[1] S. Augustini de Baptismo, Lib. III. cap. xiv.

bered horrors.[1] In the repeated papal instructions to the early inquisitors to treat as heretics all Jews and Saracens who had been converted and relapsed, there is no exception in favor of those whose conversion had been coerced, and Boniface VIII., while pretending to exempt those whose coercion had been absolute, took care to define that the fear of death is not such coercion, a decision which was embodied in the canon law.[2] When the schoolmen came to reduce these incongruities to a system they discovered that there were two kinds of coercion, conditional or interpretative and absolute, and that coerced volition is still volition, while their definition of conditional coercion was so elastic that there was nothing left for absolute save that if a man were tied hand and foot and was baptized in that condition while uttering protests, the baptism would be invalid.[3] The sacrament thus

[1] Concil. Toletan. IV. ann. 633, cap. 57.—Ivonis Decret. P. I. cap. 276.—Gratiani Decret. P. I. Dist. xlv. cap. 5.

[2] Gregor. PP. X. Bull. *Turbato corde,* ann. 1273; Nicholai PP. IV. Bull. *Turbato corde*, ann. 1288; Gregorii PP. XI. Bull. *Admodum,* ann. 1372 (Bullar. Roman. I. 155, 159, 263).—Cap. 13 in Sexto, Lib. v. Tit. ii.

[3] Hostiensis Aureæ Summæ Lib. III. de Baptismo § 11; Lib. v. de Judæis § 5.—S. Th. Aquin. Summæ P. III. Q. lxviii. Art. 8 ad 4; Q. lxix. Art. 9 ad 1.—S. Bonaventura in IV. Sentt. Dist. IV. P. i. Art. 2, Q. 1.—S. Antonini Summæ P. II. Tit. xii. cap. 2, § 1.—Summa Sylvestrina s. v. *Baptismus* IV. § 10.—Loazes, Tractatus, col. 14. Albertus Magnus, however, admits that a protest uttered at the time of baptism invalidates it (In IV. Sentt. Dist. VI. Art. 10). Duns Scotus agrees with this and adds that internal opposition prevents the reception of the sacrament although the Church assumes consent and coerces the convert to the observance of the faith (In IV. Sentt. Dist. IV. Q. 4, 5). Towards the end of the fifteenth century Angiolo da Chivasso admits that the question is doubtful and that some doctors deny validity under coercion (Summa Angelica s. v. *Baptismus* VI. §§ 6, 12).

became a fetish, reverence for which overcame all consideration for its real significance. Yet to the last there were learned doctors who maintained that the coerced baptism of the Moriscos was a sacrilege and invalid and so was the continued baptism of the children against the wish of the parents; nor do the defenders of the work seem to realize the true import of the miracles which they triumphantly allege—that when the Moors of Aragon were forcibly converted, in 1526, an image of the Holy Sepulchre in the Carmelite Convent of Saragossa wept for twenty-four hours and the images of Our Lady of Tobet and some associated angels sweated profusely for thirty-six hours, so that a vase of this precious liquor was collected and preserved, of which, in 1590, Philip II. devoutly begged a portion. When the Moriscos were expelled in 1610 this marvellous fluid suddenly evaporated, even that belonging to the king.[1]

There could, in fact, be no question as to the law and practice of the Church, but to silence all discussion as to its applicability to the present case some pretence of consultation and investigation must be made. Charles V. had already resolved on his policy and had applied to Clement VII. to be released from his oath not to impose Christianity on the Moors, but the Valencian nobles were becoming restive under the prosecuting zeal of Inquisitor

[1] Bleda, Crónica, pp. 941, 1050.—Lanuza, Historias de Aragon, II. 426.—Fonseca, Giusto Scacciamento, pp. 38, 269–96.—Guadalajara y Xavierr, Expulsión de los Moriscos, fol. 78.

In 1579 San Luis Bertran, at the request of the Duke of Najera, then Viceroy of Valencia, drew up a paper on the situation in which he says that the original baptism was ill-done and he wished it had not been done, but being done it stands and the custom of the Church must be enforced.—Bledæ Defensio Fidei, p. 457.

Churruca and there must be at least a show of deliberation, if only to gain time. Charles therefore ordered the Governor of Valencia to consult with the inquisitors and other learned theologians and jurists, who should decide upon the matter, but this was manifestly a body of too little weight for the comprehensive measures in view. The new Inquisitor-general, Cardinal Manrique, Archbishop of Seville, therefore addressed to the emperor, January 23, 1524, a letter suggesting that he should hold this junta, adding to it some members of the royal councils, so that the whole subject of the Moors and Moriscos of the kingdom could be considered; while if necessary some theologians and jurists of Valencia might participate, in view of the opposition of the nobles and gentry who dreaded the loss to arise from the Christianization of their vassals. The tone of the letter indicates that the matter was prejudged in advance and that any investigation into the degree of coercion employed was only to save appearances.[1] Charles, on February 11th, ordered the junta to be held at the court, but, as though to show that its deliberations were superfluous, on the same day he wrote to Queen Germaine, the vice-queen of Valencia, ordering the inquisitors and vicar-general to take due action with the apostate Moriscos.[2] Then, on February 20th, Manrique issued a commission to Churruca and his assessor Andrés Palacio to make a complete investigation of all that had occurred in the conversion of the baptized Moors, what they had since done and what reasons they alleged for not living as Christians, together with whatever else was

[1] Archivo de Simancas, Inquisicion, Libro 4, fol. 97. (See Appendix No. IV.)

[2] Danvila, Expulsión, p. 88.

necessary to throw light on the affair. There was evidently no haste desired, for the next document is dated September 14th and consists of a series of interrogations on which the examination was to be conducted; these necessarily limited the scope of the enquiry and were somewhat perfunctory in character, although special stress was laid on the necessity of thorough investigation into the use of force to bring about the conversion.[1] As Churruca and Palacio were already committed by their action as inquisitors the indecency of entrusting such an investigation to them is apparent, and this was increased when, October 10th, the provisor of Valencia, Antonio de Luna, empowered Churruca to act in his place, but it was somewhat relieved by the addition of two other commissioners, Martín Sanchez and Marco Juan de Bas.[2]

It was not until November 4th that the commission got to work at Alcira, although during October Churruca and Palacio were examining witnesses on their own account. The commission labored until November 24th moving from place to place in the narrow territory between Alcira and Denia and examined 128 witnesses. The animus of the inquisitors was evident and though the prescribed formula of interrogation avoided the question of the regularity with which the sacrament was administered a large portion of the evidence was devoted to this. The priests who officiated seem to have been carefully summoned as witnesses and they expatiated at length on the care with which they had put the preliminary questions as to the desires of the converts and on the completeness with which the rites had been performed, pass-

[1] See Appendix No. V. [2] MS. Infor macio.

ing discreetly over the absence of all enquiry as to the converts' knowledge of the doctrines which they were presumed to be eagerly embracing. In only one instance moreover is there an allusion to an interpreter, which, as the Moors for the most part understood only Arabic, would seem to have been a necessity. It was amply in evidence however that in the crowds which filled the churches there could rarely be any individualization of the ceremony, that holy water was scattered over them at random with an aspergillum or from a crock, and that when holy water was not to be had spring water was freely employed. Of course the use of chrism was impossible.[1] As baptism can, in cases of necessity, be the simplest of ceremonies and be performed even by a woman, such deficiencies did not invalidate it, but there is significance in the care with which the commission elicited from the clerical witnesses all possible testimony in favor of its due performance.

This report was supplemented by a learned argument in due scholastic form by Fernando Loazes, fiscal of the Valencia tribunal. It is dated April 22, 1525, and therefore, unless previously circulated in MS., cannot have had any influence on the result, but it is interesting as showing that there was no pretence that the baptism of the Moors was other than coerced by violence and terror.[2] The violence used, he admits, was a crime and the criminals should be punished, but the effect was good

[1] MS. Informacio.

[2] "Cum enim ita et taliter notorium sit quod nullatenus celari potest, dicti regni Valentiæ populares . . . terroribus et maximis minis et pœnis dictos paganos ad baptismi suscipiendum sacramentum induxisse."—Loazes, Tractatus, col. 1.

and should be preserved; it is the way, he piously adds, that God works to educe good out of evil. The Moors have been saved from perdition and from slavery to the demon and as this is a public benefit the baptisms must be held good, the converts must be compelled to adhere to the Catholic faith and those who uphold them in apostasy are to be prosecuted by the Inquisition as fautors and defenders of heresy. It is noteworthy that he wastes no time in defending the regularity of the baptismal rites, showing that that was assumed as a matter of course, and there is an ominous assertion that if the converts are allowed to relapse it will create doubt in the minds of the faithful as to the efficacy of baptism, while all the doctors agree that when there is danger of infecting the faith the prince can compel uniformity or can expel the unbelievers from the kingdom.[1]

The report of the commission, limited and imperfect as it was, was duly laid before a junta of all the leading statesmen, lay and ecclesiastic, for the assembly consisted of a reunion of the councils of Castile, of Aragon, of the Inquisition, of Military Orders and of the Indies, together with eminent theologians, and was presided over

[1] Ibid. col. 17, 45, 60–61, 62.

Loazes was a man of culture; in his dedication to Inquisitor-general Manrique he displays his learning by references to Homer and Virgil, Hesiod and Terence, Suetonius, Aulus Gellius and Valerius Maximus. He tells us that he was born in Orihuela, sprung from the knightly race of Loazes of Galicia and that he studied in Padua. He became inquisitor of Barcelona, where he distinguished himself by his arrogant and inflexible insistance on the prerogatives of the Holy Office and was involved in bitter quarrels with his colleague, Juan Dominguez Molon. In 1542 he was made bishop of Elna and he successively obtained the sees of Lerida in 1544 and Tortosa in 1553; in 1560 he became archbishop of Tarragona and in 1567 of Valencia.

by Cardinal Manrique. It met in the Franciscan convent of Madrid and sat for twenty-two days; the matter was elaborately argued; some of the theologians, with Jayme Benet, the most distinguished canonist of Spain, at their head, denied the validity of the baptisms, but no decision in that sense was possible and it was agreed that, as the Moors had made no resistance or complaint, they should keep the faith which they had accepted, whether they wished it or not. On March 23, 1525, the emperor was present in the junta; Cardinal Manrique announced the result to him, when he confirmed it and ordered the necessary measures to be taken for its enforcement. Accordingly, on April 4th, he issued a cédula reciting the care with which the question had been examined and the unanimous conclusion reached, wherefore he declared the baptized Moors to be Christians, that their children must be baptized and that churches in which mass had been celebrated must not be used as mosques.[1]

The weighty decision was taken and the fate of the Spanish Moors was sealed, for all subsequent events were the natural consequence of the policy on which Charles had resolved and of which this was the first step. No time was lost in sending as inquisitorial commissioners Gaspar de Avalos Bishop of Guadix, Fray Antonio de Guevara, the Dominican Fray Juan de Salamanca and Doctor Escanier royal judge of Catalonia, with a retinue of counsellors and familiars, constituting a most formidable tribunal. They reached Valencia May 10th and on Sunday the 14th the bishop preached, explained his commission and ordered the publication of Charles's

[1] Sandoval, Historia de Carlos V., Lib. XIII. § xxviii.—Sayas, Añales de Aragon, cap. cxxvii.—Danvila, Expulsión, pp. 90-1.

cédula and of an edict granting thirty days in which apostates could return with security for life and property, after which they should forfeit both.[1] It was easy to issue proclamations but not so easy to identify those who had undergone baptism and were living with their unconverted brethren. To this task the commissioners therefore addressed themselves, travelling through the land, investigating and making out lists and administering confirmation to all whom they could identify.[2] This of course was preliminary to prosecuting those who had returned to Moorish rites, but they were too numerous to be subjected to the full hardship of the ordinary inquisitorial procedure. To moderate this required papal authority which was invoked; a brief of Clement VII. to Cardinal Manrique, June 16, 1525, recites that Charles had applied to him for a remedy; the multitude of the delinquents calls for gentleness and clemency wherefore they are to be prosecuted with a benignant asperity, and those who return to the light of truth, publicly abjure their errors and swear never to relapse may be absolved without incurring the customary disabilities and infamy.[3]

In spite of this effort to mitigate the rigor of the canons against heresy and apostasy, this laborious and doubtless unsatisfactory investigation had a double result. On the one hand it served to confirm Charles and his advisers in the conviction that the only way to be sure of the baptism of a Moor was to baptize them all; on the

[1] Sandoval, *ubi sup.*—Sayas, *ubi sup.*—Bleda, Crónica, p. 647.

[2] Fonseca, Giusto Scacciamento, p. 11.—Bleda, Crónica, p. 647; Defensio Fidei, p. 123.

[3] Archivo de Simancas, Inquisicion, Libro 926, fol. 47.—Bulario de la Orden de Santiago, Libro II. fol. 58 (Archivo Histórico Nacional).

other it naturally created great alarm and excitement in the Moorish population, especially among the ten or fifteen thousand who had passed under the hands of the Agermanados. They had the sympathy moreover of the ruling classes. Charles was moved to indignation on hearing that the magistrates of Valencia had asked the commission to act with caution and not to ill-treat the alfaquíes because the prosperity of the kingdom depended on the preservation of the Moors, and when the baptized ones took refuge in the Sierra de Bernia the nobles not only would not reduce them but favored them, hoping that the trouble would lead the emperor to suspend action. Charles was inflexible, however; he reproved the recalcitrant nobles, praised those who showed a disposition to assist, and ordered them all to go to their estates and urge their vassals to become Christians, promising them favor and good treatment. At length preparations were made to attack the refugees of Bernia, who had held out from April until August; they agreed to surrender on promise of immunity, and were taken to Murla, where they received absolution and were kindly treated.[1]

The Bishop of Guadix fell sick and left the field; the other commissioners grew tired of the work and were on the point of returning to Castile when despatches were received from Charles saying that as God had granted him the victory of Pavia he could show his gratitude in no better way than by compelling all the infidels of his realms to be baptized; they were therefore ordered to remain and undertake this new conversion, in conjunction

[1] Sandoval, *ubi sup.*—Danvila, pp 92–3.—Sayas, *ubi sup.*

with a new colleague, Fray Calcena. Although Charles had long been preparing for this, there may be partial truth in the story that he was stirred to immediate action by the gibes of his captive, Francis I., who landed at Valencia June 30, 1525, and was taken to the castle of Benisano, where he was scandalized on seeing from a window Moors at work in the fields on a feast day.[1] It was doubtless as a persuasive to conversion that in October and November severe restrictions were placed on all unbaptized Moors. They were required to wear on the cap a half-moon of purple cloth, they were forbidden to leave their domiciles under pain of being enslaved by the first comer, they were forbidden to sell anything, they were deprived of their arms and the practice of their religious rites, they were required to rest on feast days and to uncover and prostrate themselves on meeting the sacrament.[2]

The Germanía had builded better than it knew. It had given an impulse which blind fanaticism had eagerly developed until the movement was spreading far beyond the narrow boundaries of Valencia, and the wild work of the lawless bands of Agermanados was to be adopted and systematized and perfected by the supreme powers in State and Church.

[1] Bledæ Defensio Fidei, p. 124.

[2] Danvila, p. 92.—Sayas, *ubi sup.*—Bledæ Defensio Fidei, p. 123.

CHAPTER IV.

CONVERSION BY EDICT.

EVEN before the question of the validity of the Valencian baptisms had been settled, Charles V. had resolved that he would have uniformity of faith in his Spanish dominions. Whatever tolerant tendencies he might have had in the earlier years of his reign had disappeared in the fierce struggle with the Lutheran revolt. By the edict of Worms, May 26, 1521 he had put Luther and his followers under the ban of the Empire; under his orders the magistrates of the Low Countries were burning reformers; he had learned to regard dissidence of belief as rebellion against both the temporal and the spiritual power and as both a statesman and a sincere Catholic it was his duty to suppress it. His demands for religious unity in Germany were fatally weakened if it could be said that in Spain, where his authority was almost absolute, he permitted hundreds of thousands of his subjects openly to worship Allah and his prophet.

His grand-dame Isabella had enforced outward conformity in the kingdoms of Castile, but for those of Aragon there was the obstacle of the solemn oath taken by Ferdinand for himself and his successors, an oath which Charles himself had repeated when he was recognized and had received the allegiance of his Aragonese subjects. It was a binding compact between them but fortunately for him the Vice-gerent of God had assumed the power of releasing men from their oaths, of abrogating compacts and of setting aside all human laws. To Clement VII. therefore Charles applied in the latter part of 1523, or beginning of 1524, for relief from the obligations which worked such disservice to God, and it is to the credit of Clement that he refused at first, declaring that the request was scandalous.[1] His resistance however gave way before the earnest pressure of the Duke of Sesa, Charles's ambassador, and on May 12, 1524, the fateful brief was issued.

It recites the papal grief at learning that in Valencia, Catalonia and Aragon Charles has many subjects who are Moors and with whom the faithful cannot hold intercourse without danger; they even live with the temporal lords who make no effort for their conversion, all of which is a scandal to the faith and a dishonor to the emperor, besides which they serve as spies for those of Africa to whom they reveal the designs of the Christians. It therefore exhorts Charles to order the inquisitors to preach the word of God to them and if they persist in their obstinacy the inquisitors shall designate a term and warn them that on its expiration they shall be exiled under pain of perpetual slavery, which shall be rigorously executed. The tithes of their temporal possessions, which they have never hitherto paid, shall accrue to their lords in recompense for the damage caused to them by the expulsion, under condition that the lords shall provide the churches with what is necessary for divine service, while the revenues of the mosques shall be converted into

[1] Llorente, Añales, II. 287.

benefices. The portentous document concludes with a formal release to Charles from the oath sworn to the córtes not to expel the Moors; it absolves him from all censures and penalties of perjury thence arising and grants him whatever dispensation is necessary for the execution of the premises. Moreover it confers on the inquisitors ample faculties to suppress all opposition with censures and other remedies, invoking if necessary the aid of the secular arm, notwithstanding all apostolical constitutions and the privileges and statutes of the land.[1]

If Clement had hesitated at first in thus authorizing this breach of faith he had gotten bravely over his scruples; there is no word in the brief signifying that it had been asked of him; he took the responsibility of the initiative and Spanish writers were justified in assigning to him the credit of having suggested the action and induced Charles to adopt it. The whole matter was treated as belonging exclusively to ecclesiastical jurisdiction and its execution was committed wholly to the Inquisition as the most appropriate and efficient instrument.

For eighteen months Charles held the papal brief without publishing it, but it untied his hands. Apparently

[1] Archivo de Simancas, Libro 927, fol. 285.—Bledæ Defensio Fidei, pp. 463–66.—Sayas, Añales, cap. cx.

March 20th Charles had instructed the Duke of Sesa to ask Clement not to entertain any appeals from the Moriscos but to refer them all to the inquisitor-general (Llorente, Añales, II. 293). It is not likely that the pope gave any written assurance to this effect, as the question of appeals from the Inquisition was a burning one and was at this moment the subject of a specially vigorous controversy. It is worth noting however that while the documents up to the close of the century show frequent endeavors by Judaizing heretics to escape by recourse to Rome I do not remember to have met with a single instance of the kind on the part of a Morisco.

he waited until the weighty question of the validity of the baptisms was settled and then the disturbances in Valencia counselled further delay before taking decisive action. On being satisfied as to this early in September, 1525, he addressed, on the 13th, letters to the nobles informing them of his irrevocable determination not to allow a Moor or other infidel to remain in his dominions except as a slave; he recognized that expulsion would affect their revenues and leave their lands depopulated, wherefore he earnestly desired to avoid it and consequently urged them to go to their estates and co-operate with the inquisitorial commissioners in procuring the conversion and instruction of their vassals. A brief letter of the same date to the Moors informs them of the determination to which he has been inspired by Almighty God that His law shall prevail throughout the land, and of his desire for their salvation and release from error, wherefore he exhorts and commands them to submit to baptism; if they do so, they shall have the liberties of Christians and good treatment; if they refuse he will provide for it by other means. This was followed the next day by an edict for proclamation everywhere; it was addressed to the Moors telling them of his resolve that no one of another faith should remain except in slavery; as he desires their salvation and protection from all ill-treatment he gives them this notice before executing his intention; he guarantees them all the privileges of Christians and, under a penalty of 5000 florins and the royal wrath, every one is ordered not to impede the conversion and to respect all converts. A letter of the same date to Queen Germaine is worth noting as the first of a long series which reveals the absurdity of the attempt to deprive the Moors of their religion without providing a substitute. He is told, he says, that in many of the villages of the new converts there are no priests to instruct them or to celebrate mass, and he orders her to see that the converts are instructed and ministered to, but in lands subject to the royal jurisdiction care must be taken to reserve to the crown the patronage of the new churches.[1] It remained thus to the end; there were always eager hands stretched out to seize the revenues of the mosques and the tithes, but few to train the new converts in the faith which they were compelled to profess.

Guevara and his colleagues, armed with full power as inquisitors, set to work, announcing to the Moors the unchangeable will of the Emperor, with a term of grace of eight days, after which they would proceed to execute his decrees. The frightened aljamas met and deputed twelve alfaquíes to supplicate Charles for clemency and the revocation of the edict. Queen Germaine gave them a safe-conduct and they were solemnly received at court, whither, it is said, they carried 50,000 ducats wherewith to influence persons of importance. For the moment they could accomplish nothing although subsequently they obtained, nominally at least, some mitigation of rigor.[2]

At length Charles concluded that the time had come to show his hand. On November 3d he enclosed the papal brief in a letter addressed to the inquisitor-general and all inquisitors and ordered them to put it into execution as speedily as possible. Under the same date he ad-

[1] Danvila, pp. 94-8.—Fernandez y Gonzalez, p. 443.—Sayas, Añales, cap. cxxvii.

[2] Sayas, *loc. cit.*—Danvila, pp. 97-8.

dressed the authorities, secular and ecclesiastical, of Valencia (and presumably of the other kingdoms) informing them of the brief and that it derogated all the fueros, privileges and constitutions of the kingdom to which he had sworn. He stated that he had instructed the Inquisition to execute the papal command, and he ordered the local authorities, under pain of 10,000 florins, to enforce whatever the inquisitors might decree.[1] Having thus paved the way, on November 25th he issued a general edict of expulsion. All the Moors of Valencia were to be out of Spain by December 31, 1525, and those of Aragon and Catalonia by January 31, 1526. Following Isabella's example, there was no exemption promised for conversion but the difficulties thrown in the way of the exiles showed, as in 1502, the real object in view. The Valencians were ordered to register and obtain passports at Sieteaguas, on the frontier of Cuenca, and thence take their weary way through Requena, Utiel, Madrid, Valladolid, Benavente and Villafranca to Coruña where they were to embark for strange lands under pain of slavery and confiscation. The nobles were warned not to retain or harbor Moors under penalty of 5000 ducats for each one and other penalties. At the same time was published a papal brief ordering, under pain of major excommunication, all Christians to aid in enforcing the imperial decrees and that the Moors must listen without replying to the teaching of the Gospel. Another edict commanding that all Moors should be baptized by December 8th or be prepared to leave the kingdom showed by implication that exile might be averted by baptism.

[1] Archivo de Simancas, Libro 927, fol. 285.

Then the Inquisition gave notice that it was prepared for action; tremendous censures were published against those who failed to denounce transgressors, together with a penalty of a thousand florins on all who, when called upon, should fail to aid it against those who obstinately resisted the sweetness of the gospel and the benignant plans of the emperor. Some of these obstinate ones, in fact, in Aragon and Catalonia, managed to make their way to France and thence to Barbary.[1]

In Aragon, even before the issue of the edict, the anticipation of what was to come had caused a lively agitation among the Moors. They ceased to labor in their fields and shops causing the greatest anxiety to the Christian population. The *Diputados*, or standing committee of the córtes, were summoned to save the prosperity of the land; they called into counsel prominent representatives of the interests concerned and resolved to send envoys to remonstrate with Charles. One of their number, the Count of Ribagorza, a great noble of royal blood, chanced to be at the court, and to him they sent a detailed instruction for immediate action. This appealed to the solemn oath taken by Ferdinand and repeated by Charles; it represented that the whole industry and prosperity of the land rested upon the Moors, whose labors raised the harvests and produced the manufactures, while on their *censales* depended the income of churches and convents, of benefices and the gentry, of

[1] Sayas, Añales, cap. cxxvii.—Llorente, Añales, II. 296.—Danvila p. 99

The *Diario Turolense* says that the Moors of Aragon were ordered to depart by the port of Coruña and those of Valencia by the way of Fuentarabia.—Boletín de la R. Acad. de Historia, XXVII. 56.

widows and orphans.[1] They were practically the slaves of the gentry and nobles, to whom they were obedient and peaceable, and they had never been known to pervert a Christian or cause scandal to the faith; they lived at a distance from the coast, so that they could hold no communication with Barbary and by the law they were enslaved if they attempted to leave the kingdom. Their expulsion would mean ruin, while if converted they would be enfranchised and enabled to go abroad, weakening Spain and strengthening its enemies. As they had ceased to sow their lands, immediate action by the king relieving their fears was necessary to avert a famine. The influence of Ribagorza procured a brief delay in the issue of the edict, but Charles was inflexible, and his practical reply was a proclamation, published in Saragossa, December 22d, forbidding any Moor from leaving Aragon and ordering absentees to return within a month, prohibiting any communication between those of the nobles and those living on *realengos* or lands under royal jurisdiction, ordering that no one should purchase property of them, closing their mosques and depriving them of their public shambles.[2]

This naturally increased the agitation and risings oc-

[1] The *censo* or *censal* was a debt or obligation, bearing interest usually at the rate of five or six per cent., and charged upon an individual or community or land—in the latter case like the modern ground-rent. It formed at the period almost the only investment available for capital and was particularly a favorite with the ecclesiastical foundations. The Moors were large borrowers and their recognized mercantile integrity rendered their censos peculiarly desirable. We shall see hereafter the frightful confusion arising from this at the final expulsion.

[2] Sayas, Añales, cap. cxxx.—Dormer, Añales de Aragon, Lib. II. cap. 1.

curred. The Moors of Almonacir, indeed, had not waited for these developments but in October had closed their gates against some preachers sent for their conversion and they held out until January when the town was taken by assault, the leaders were executed and the rest submitted to baptism. After the publication of the edict other places rose; they fortified themselves in the Castillo de Maria, near Saragossa, placing their hopes in succor from Africa and in the promised resurrection of the Moor Alfatimi on his green horse, but as these expectations died away they seem to have recognized their hopeless position and to have submitted. No little trouble, however, was caused by Christians who seized and enslaved many Moors on the pretext that they were preparing to take to the mountains, causing great scandal and angering the lords who were seeking to keep their populations of vassals intact. Restlessness continued and the repugnance to baptism was hard to overcome; hopes were entertained when an alfaquí of Quarto, said to be more than a hundred years old and of great authority among them, was converted, but only a few followed his example. The date of expulsion was postponed until March 15th and as it approached there were risings in the lands of the lords of Luna and the Count of Aranda, but the insurgents were suppressed and disarmed, and finally the Moorish population as a whole submitted to baptism.[1]

The problem was a still more troublesome one in Valencia, where the Moors were more numerous, were nearer the coast and in more constant communication with Barbary, and where the great nobles had more at stake in

[1] Sandoval, Lib. XIII. § xxviii.—Dormer, Lib. II. cap. 1.

protecting their vassals. When the alfaquíes returned from their fruitless mission to the court the great bulk of the Moors submitted and outwardly accepted baptism. Antonio de Guevara, who was foremost in the work, boasts that in Valencia he baptized 27,000 families of Moors, but the Moriscos subsequently related that this wholesale administration of the sacrament was accomplished by corralling them in pens and scattering water over them, when some would endeavor to hide themselves and others would shout "no water has touched me." They submitted to it, they said, because their alfaquíes assured them that deceit was permissible and that they need not believe the religion which they were compelled to profess.[1] Many also eluded it by hiding themselves but the first open resistance was at Benaguacil, in which the Moors of the neighboring villages took refuge and closed the gates, whereupon Don Luis Ferrer, lieutenant of the governor, ravaged their lands with a hundred troopers. This failed to overcome their obstinacy, when the great standard of Valencia was raised and the governor, Don Valencio Cabanillas, marched with two thousand men and proclaimed war with fire and sword—*guerra á fuego y á sangre*—the pitiless and unsparing warfare which so often meets us in the history of these deplorable conflicts. Even with the aid of artillery and reinforcements, swelling the army to 5000 men, it took the besiegers five weeks to force a capitulation, March

[1] Guevara, Epistolas familiares, p. 543.—Archivo de Simancas, Inquisicion de Valencia, Legajo 205, fol. 3.

Bleda (Defensio Fidei, p. 125) says that Guevara's boast is an exaggeration, for in 1573 there were but 19,801 families of Moriscos in Valencia, and in 1602 they had increased only to about 30,000.

27th, with promise of quarter, letters of pardon having been sent by Charles through Guevara who entered with the governor. The Moors, except some who escaped to the Sierra de Espadan, were duly baptized and the penalty of slavery and confiscation was commuted to a fine of 12,000 ducats, except in the case of some Aragonese Moors who had come to the assistance of the besieged.[1] A further significant incident was that of the lord of Cortea who was residing at Requena. Moved by pious zeal he started for Cortea with seventeen valiant hidalgos to baptize his Moors, but they were beforehand with him, for they ambushed him at night and slew the whole party.[2]

More serious was the rebellion which had its stronghold in the Sierra de Espadan, consisting mainly of the vassals of Alonso de Aragon, Duke of Segorbe. Of all the great nobles he had been the most recalcitrant to the measures of the emperor, which had probably strengthened the spirit of resistance in that district, where his estates were enormous. The refugees were joined by others, even from as far as Aragon, who came with their families and property. They organized for a desperate resistance, electing as king a Moor named Carban who took the name of Selim Almanzo, they built huts and entrenched themselves in the fastnesses of the mountains, from which they made forays upon the adjoining valleys, laying in stores of provisions and we are told that they had the sympathy of the people, who willingly suffered privation for the benefit of those who were defending the cause of Mahomet. Queen Germaine raised a force of

[1] Dormer, *loc. cit.* [2] Sandoval, *loc. cit.*—Diario Turolense, *loc. cit.*

3000 men and sent them to the Duke of Segorbe, but he was repulsed with considerable loss and his army, discouraged and accusing him of being half-hearted in the business, melted away until he had only a thousand men left. With these he garrisoned Onda, but could not prevent the Moorish forays, in one of which the village of Chilches was captured and some consecrated hosts were carried off. Immediate use of this was made to inflame the people; all the altars in the province were draped with mourning, only the wickets in the church-doors were opened, all services were performed without display and the procession of Corpus Christi (May 31st) was postponed. Enthusiasm was thus aroused; the great standard of Valencia was unfurled and a second army was raised which set forth July 11th. As it neared Onda it was met by the Moors in vigorous sallies, in which booty to the amount of more than 30,000 ducats was obtained, which explains the large accessions of volunteers who came to join the troops. After reaching Onda, July 19th, there was desperate fighting in which the Moors were gradually driven back to the sierra from the lowlands which they had occupied, an important advantage as it checked the tendency to rise which was spreading and only awaiting a prospect of favorable success. The duke summoned the Moors to surrender within three days under pain of slavery for all prisoners, but they rejected his proposals and as he deemed his forces insufficient for an assault on the mountain he called for reinforcements. Many came from Aragon and Catalonia, while the papal legate Salviati, happening to pass through Valencia, issued a plenary indulgence *a culpa et a poena* to all who should serve, thus converting the campaign into a crusade. It made little difference that he had no power to do this; the offer was tempting to sinners and brought large accessions to the army. There was another difficulty to be overcome, for Charles was as usual impecunious and furnished no money for the payment of the troops, but the clergy and the nobles and the city of Valencia were appealed to and raised sufficient funds to keep the men in the field. All this time the Moors were defending themselves obstinately and even making sallies into the lowlands; the duke sought to obtain reinforcements from Aragon and finally appealed to the emperor who recalled from Barcelona a detachment of 3000 German veterans about to embark for Italy and placed them under the duke's orders. This swelled his force to 7000 men, besides, as we are told, great numbers of adventurers—a feature common enough in these campaigns—partly men attracted by honor, but mostly those whose object was plunder and speculators who came in the hope of bargains in slaves or other miscellaneous articles which the soldiers might wish to dispose of on the spot. The war was now nearing its end; on September 18th the troops carried a ridge and on the 19th a general assault was made from four sides; the Moors defended themselves as best they could with slings and bows, killing seventy-two of the assailants, of whom thirty-three were Germans. The Spaniards, we are told, only slew the old men and the women, reserving the rest for slaves; the Germans, in revenge for their thirty-three comrades massacred all, in number about 5000. Great booty was obtained; what was sold on the spot fetched more than 200,000 ducats, while the adventurers and the Aragonese, Catalans and Germans carried off much more. The Moors who escaped took refuge in the fastnesses of the Muela de Cortes, but they were soon hard-pressed and surrendered at discretion, when three of their leaders were strangled, the rest were deprived of their arms, their books were burnt and they were compelled to submit to the Gospel. There were other rebels who found refuge in the Sierra de Bernia and in Guadaleste and Confridas, but they mostly succeeded in escaping to Africa. Thus was Valencia Christianized and pacified; the Moriscos, as we may now call them, were disarmed, the pulpits used by their alfaquíes were torn down, their Korans were burnt and orders were given to instruct them completely in the faith—orders, as we shall see, perpetually repeated and never executed.[1]

The whole Morisco population was now at the mercy of the Inquisition. Considering the circumstances of the conversion, the ignorance of the neophytes and their notorious attachment to their ancestral faith every consideration both of policy and charity dictated a tolerant spirit until they could be instructed and won over, and the Suprema recognized this by ordering that they should be treated with great moderation.[2] As usual, however, the tribunal of Valencia was a law unto itself and its records show that, with the exception of the years 1525 and 1527, when it stayed its hands and had no trials or burnings for heresy, it continued its operations with rather more activity than before.[3] In fact, it seemed impossible for the Moris-

[1] Sandoval, Lib. XIII. § xxix.—Dormer, Lib. II. cap. viii., ix.—Bleda, Crónica, p. 649.—The córtes of 1528 granted amnesty to the insurgents.—Danvila, Expulsión, p. 101.

[2] Archivo de Simancas, Inquisicion, Libro 939, fol. 108.

[3] The trials for heresy in 1524 were 40, in 1526, 47, in 1528, 42, in 1529, 44, in 1530, 20.—Archivo Hist. Nacional, Inqu de Valencia, Legajo 98.

The burnings in person, adding as before 25 per cent. for the imper-

cos to be treated with fairness. The twelve alfaquíes whom we have seen sent to the court in 1525, with 50,000 ducats to avert the edict of expulsion had succeeded in obtaining important concessions in a *concordia* of January 6, 1526, in which it was agreed, with the assent of Cardinal Manrique, that on submitting to baptism, as they could not at once divest themselves of their customs and habits, they should not, for forty years, be subject to prosecution by the Inquisition, a grace of that kind having been granted to Granada at the time of its conversion. This however was kept secret until 1528, when it was sent to the bayle general of Valencia, who published it May 21st in accordance with orders from Charles, but was reproved for so doing by Cardinal Manrique. That year the córtes of the three states of Aragon met at Monzon and petitioned Charles to prevent the Inquisition from proceeding against the new converts until they should be instructed in the faith, to which he replied that he had already granted to Valencia the exemption formerly allowed to Granada and he now extended it to Aragon. The Inquisition, however, was already an *imperium in imperio*, which held itself above all human laws, and when the Aragonese nobles in 1529 presented a series of remonstrances about the treatment of the new converts to the emperor and another nearly identical to Cardinal Manrique the latter replied evasively June 2d, that it was not their injury but their salvation that was desired and that he hopes God may lay his hand on them, so that all may eventuate well. Charles had laid his hands on them by a decree of December 5, 1528 in which he ordered all the Moors of

fection of the record, may be stated as 16 in 1524, 19 in 1526, 29 in 1528, 30 in 1529 and 1 in 1530.—Ibid. Legajo 300.

Aragon and Catalonia to have themselves baptized within four years.[1]

In fact the Inquisition construed the concordia to suit itself and in a few months after its promulgation the Suprema declared that it did not condone the use of Moorish rites and ceremonies and that those who performed them or relapsed from the faith were to be considered as apostates and to be duly prosecuted, to all of which the emperor acceded.[2] We have just seen that the activity of the Inquisition of Valencia continued through 1529 and was slightly diminished in 1530. In Aragon it mitigated its severity somewhat, for early in the latter year it reported to the Suprema that a number of Moriscos had been reconciled in the preceding auto de fe, for whom confiscation and perpetual prison were commuted to fines and in some cases to scourging; that the fines had been applied to a cleric who should instruct the penitents and teach their children to read, but that the receiver of confiscations had refused to disburse the money.[3] In Valencia it signalized the year

[1] Danvila, Expulsión, pp. 102, 105, 108.—Dormer, Lib. II. cap. 1.—Llorente, Añales, II. 341.—Archivo de Simancas, Inq^{n}, Libro 76, fol. 183.

Danvila states (*loc. cit.*) that at the close of 1529 Charles ordered the expulsion of all the Moriscos of Valencia, probably moved by the discovery of a plot, the leader of which was executed. If such expulsion was ordered it must have been promptly countermanded, as there seems to be no other trace of it.

[2] Danvila, *loc. cit.*

[3] Arch. de Simancas, *ubi sup.* fol. 312.

The Suprema replied, May 7, 1530, that the receiver was responsible for the collection of the fines, but, to remove suspicion that they are for the benefit of the Inquisition, it would be well to appoint proper persons in the Morisco villages to collect the fines and with them pay the salaries of instructors.

1531 with 58 trials for heresy and about 45 burnings in person.[1] This was perhaps the moderation and benignity on which Cardinal Manrique dwelt in reply about this time to an indignant complaint of the córtes of the three kingdoms that the Moors had not been taught and had no churches provided for them and yet were prosecuted for heresy.[2] On the other hand Clement VII. grew impatient at the slow progress of the work and issued a brief, June 11, 1533, to Manrique, which Charles by a decree of January 13, 1534, ordered him to execute. In this he asserted that the Moors of Valencia, Aragon and Catalonia held relations with those of Africa, they converted many Christians to their faith and introduced many superstitions among the simple people, to the great danger of the Christian religion; he had exhorted the emperor as to all this in his brief of May 12, 1524, and repeatedly since then, and he now orders Manrique at once to depute persons of learning to instruct the Moors and that if they do not embrace Christianity within a term to be fixed, he must expel them from the kingdom or reduce them all to slavery without mercy.[3]

[1] Arch. Hist. Nacional, Inq^{n} de Valencia, Legajos 98, 300. The figures for the next few years are—

	Trials.	Burnings.		Trials.	Burnings.
1532	1	none	1537	69	1
1533	61	10	1538	112	14
1534	25	none	1539	79	5
1535	2	none	1540	53	5
1536	39	15			

[2] Archivo de Simancas, Patronato Real, Legajo único, fol. 38. (See Appendix No. VI.)

[3] Guadalajara y Xavierr, fol. 48.—Dormer, Lib. II. cap. lxx.—Danvila, p. 116.

Thus stimulated the Inquisition increased its activity. The figures on the preceding page show what it was doing in Valencia, although this may perhaps be partly explained by orders to the tribunal to punish with the utmost rigor those detected in fasting for the success of Barbarossa in his resistance to the Tunis expedition of Charles V.[1] In a list of the heretics relaxed or reconciled in Majorca, the first appearance of Moriscos is in 1535, when five were burnt in person and four in effigy.[2] They did not always submit without resistance. In 1538, when Gaspar de Alfrex, a fugitive, was being conveyed from Saragossa to the Inquisition of Valencia, the party was set upon near Nules, two of the officials were killed and the rescued and rescuers escaped to Africa.[3]

With 1540 the operations of the Valencia Inquisition came to a temporary stop and in the three years, 1541, 1542, 1543, there was not a single prosecution for heresy.[4] The nobles had complained earnestly of the disquiet caused among their vassals by its operations and the córtes petitioned that thirty or forty years might be given for their instruction, during which they should be exempt from prosecution. The emperor assembled a junta of prelates and clerics who counselled various plans of moderation and conciliation among which he selected that of granting a term of grace for former offences during which they could be confessed sacramentally to confessors and that a period should be named for their instruction during which the Inquisition should not prosecute them.

[1] Archivo de Simancas, Inquisicion, Libro 78, fol. 34, 152.

[2] Ibid. Libro 595. After this, however, they occur but sparingly.

[3] Danvila, p. 124.

[4] Archivo Hist. Nacional, Inqn de Valencia, Legajo 98.

This period was liberally fixed at twenty-six years, with the warning that it would be shortened or extended according as they should abuse or use it. The result was not satisfactory; they commenced to live openly as Moors, circumcising their boys, fasting the Ramadan, working on feast-days, abstaining from mass and saying that as they had thirty years in which to live as they pleased they would take full advantage of it.[1] This well-meant effort to employ persuasion came to a speedy end. The Inquisition resumed operations with renewed vigor and in 1544 it had 79 cases, in 1545, 37 and in 1546, 49.[2]

In 1547 there was a reversion to a milder policy. In the endeavor to frame and conduct an organization for the instruction of the Moriscos, of which more hereafter, two "apostolic commissioners," Fray Antonio de Calcena, afterwards Bishop of Tortosa, and Antonio Ramirez de Haro, afterwards Bishop of Segovia, had been sent to Valencia. They had the faculties of inquisitors and bore that title, to give them greater authority, but they were instructed not to act as such or to interfere with the operations of the tribunal.[3] In 1540, Haro's commission was renewed under the same conditions. Then a brief was obtained from Paul III., August 2, 1546, which completely superseded the Inquisition, as it granted faculties to appoint confessors empowered to hear confessions of the Moriscos and absolve them *in utroque foro*—both sacramentally and judicially—even if they had been

[1] Danvila, p. 130.

[2] Arch. Hist. Nac., Inq^n de Valencia, Leg. 98.

[3] Archivo de Simancas, Inquisicion, Libro 4, fol. 110; Lib. 77, fol. 353; Lib. 78, fol. 275.

tried and condemned by the Inquisition, and to prescribe for them either public or private abjuration on their professing contrition and swearing in future to abstain from heresy. They and their descendants were relieved from all disabilities and from confiscation and Old Christians could consort and trade with them freely.[1] This was a most liberal measure, although St. Tomás de Vilanova, Archbishop of Valencia, says that it was ineffective because it required the penitent to abjure *de vehementi*—for vehement suspicion of heresy—which none of them would do, wherefore he suggested that more extensive faculties should be obtained to absolve and pardon without observing legal forms, considering that these people were converted as it were by force, that they never have been instructed and that their intercourse with the Algerine Moors renders them averse to Christianity.[2]

It made little difference what were the powers conferred on the Bishop of Segovia, as the only effect of his commission was to render the Inquisition powerless and supersede also the episcopal jurisdiction. He left Valencia early in 1547 and never returned. April 12th the archbishop wrote to Prince Philip that since he had gone the Moriscos become daily bolder in performing their Moorish ceremonies as there is no one to restrain or punish them. The bishop had left no one to represent him and some one should speedily be sent with powers subdelegated by him. A promise was made that a person should shortly be sent, but the customary habit of procrastination pre-

[1] Bulario de la Orden de Santiago, Libro III. fol. 33 (Archivo Histórico Nacional).

[2] Coleccion de Docum. inéd. T. V. p. 104. Abjuration *de vehementi*—for vehement suspicion of heresy—irrevocably entailed burning in case of relapse.

vailed. On November 10th the archbishop wrote again representing the complete liberty enjoyed by the conversos with no one to look after them, but no attention was paid to him, and, in 1551 and 1552, we find him still calling for some one empowered to keep the Moriscos in order; if no one can be sent they should be subjected to the Inquisition as formerly, or a papal faculty should be obtained enabling the episcopal ordinary to punish them moderately. Even when, in 1551, the Bishop of Segovia appointed the Inquisitor Gregorio de Miranda as commissioner for the Moriscos he granted him no inquisitorial power and the Moriscos of Valencia remained free from persecution for ten years longer.[1] This explains why the records of the Inquisition show only twelve cases in 1547, fifteen in 1548, four in 1549 and then an entire cessation of trials up to and including 1562, except two in 1558 and fifteen in 1560.[2] In 1561 the Inquisitor-general Valdés was empowered by Paul IV. to enable the Archbishop of Valencia and his Ordinary to reconcile secretly relapsed New Christians; in those cases which could be judicially proved, the confessions were to be made before a notary and delivered to the Inquisition, while in those which could not be proved the penances were to be purely spiritual.[3] This indicates that

[1] Coleccion de Docum. inéd. T. V. pp. 100, 101, 107, 108, 122.

[2] Archivo Hist. Nacional, Inqn de Valencia, Legajo 98. The cases in 1547, 1548 and 1549 may be unfinished business of previous years or heretics other than Moriscos, and the latter supposition may explain those of 1558 and 1560. So far as heresy was concerned however the business of the Valencia tribunal was almost exclusively with Moriscos.

[3] Archivo de Simancas, Libro 4, fol. 262. (See Appendix No. VII.)

The futility of these apparent concessions arose from the insistence upon confessions being taken down by notaries and becoming matters of record not only against the penitent himself but against all his accomplices.

attention at last was being given to the anomalous condition existing. In 1562, accordingly, the Inquisition of Valencia commenced to act in Teruel, where the town of Xea had the reputation of being an asylum of malefactors; it was exclusively Morisco and no Christian was allowed to reside there.[1] Finally all restrictions were removed and, in 1563, the Inquisition was vigorously at work with sixty-two cases. It held two autos de fe in that year in which appeared nine culprits from Xea.[2]

In 1564, after the customary discussion by a junta, Philip II. essayed a tolerably comprehensive plan of conciliation in which the Inquisition was instructed to use its powers with the utmost moderation, except in the case of alfaquíes, dogmatizers (those who taught and preached heresy), midwives (who were asserted to shield infants from baptism and to circumcise the males) and those who profane the sacraments, all of whom were to be prosecuted with the utmost rigor. The instructions issued in pursuance of this by the Suprema to the Inquisition of Valencia, while not directly contravening it, allowed a latitude of which the tribunal could avail itself to frustrate the project of conciliation, and its activity during the following years would seem to show that it felt itself under no restrictions.[3]

[1] Danvila, p. 164. Teruel and Albarracin, although a province of Aragon were under the jurisdiction of the Inquisition of Valencia.

[2] Archivo Hist. Nacional, Inq^{n} de Valencia, Leg. 98.—Danvila, p. 167.

[3] Archivo Hist. Nacional, Inq^{n} de Valencia, Leg. 2, MS. 16, fol. 187; Leg. 98. The number of cases in Valencia were—

1564	38	1566	41	1568	68
1565	66	1567	54	1569	none

That the instructions with regard to the alfaquíes were observed would appear from the fact that in 1568 there were nine of them penanced.—Danvila, p. 178.

During this period the Inquisition by no means neglected the converted Mudéjares of Castile. I have the records of a number of trials between 1540 and 1550 of Moriscos of Daimiel, a town within the district of the Inquisition of Toledo, which represent what was going on with more or less frequency throughout the land. The Moors of Daimiel had been baptized in 1502 under the edict of Isabella—Mayor Garcia testified, in 1550, that she was 55 or 56 years old and that she was baptized in the general conversion of the Moors of Daimiel when she was 7 or 8 years old.[1] Apparently they had been overlooked by the Inquisition until Juan Yañes, Inquisitor of Toledo and subsequently Bishop of Calahorra, came there in his visitation of 1538 and Catalina, wife of Pedro de Baños spontaneously testified that some thirteen years before she had lived with the Moriscos for about twelve years and saw that they did not eat pork or drink wine on the plea that these things did not agree with them. Long immunity had rendered them somewhat careless as to Catholic observances; Yañes says that, prior to his visitation of 1538, they never went to mass, but they had learned enough of the externals of religion to maintain an outward appearance of orthodoxy —indeed it was believed among them that a decree of the emperor and inquisitor-general had exempted them from the jurisdiction of the Inquisition, and that this exemption had been purchased by a general assessment laid upon those of Daimiel or of the province of Calatrava. Possibly some knavish official may have speculated upon them, for Mari Gomez, when on trial, said that formerly

[1] Proceso de Mayor Garcia, fol. iv. (MS. *penes me*).

there had been a penalty imposed on those who avoided pork and wine, but that this had ceased to be collected and they had all given up consuming those articles.[1] Yañes returned to Daimiel, in 1543, and gathered further abundant testimony and the trials dragged on for a considerable period. The number of the accused was large, for a single *clamosa*, or denunciation by the fiscal, includes the names of ten defendants, although in general practice a separate clamosa is required for each one, and the number of prisoners must have exceeded the capacity of the *carceles secretas* for, in 1541, we happen to hear of nine women confined in one cell and further that the great hall of the Inquisition was being used as a prison.[2] Vigorous as were these raids they did not root out apostasy in Daimiel, for in 1597 we find the Inquisition of Toledo busy with sundry delinquents from there.[3]

A series of reports, nearly complete, of the Inquisition of Toledo to the Suprema, from 1575 to 1610, affords us an insight into the relations of the Holy Office with the Moriscos, its influence on their daily lives and its inevitable result of perpetuating and intensifying their hatred of the religion of which it was the exponent. We find in it 190 cases of Moriscos as against 174 of Judaizers and 47 of Protestants, showing that, in so far as heresy was concerned, the Moriscos afforded the largest amount of business for the tribunal. In these thirty-five years there were only eleven Moriscos relaxed—the euphemistic synonym for burning—being those who either persistently

[1] Proceso de Mari Naranja, fol. 2; Proceso de Mari Gomez, fol. viii., ix. (MS. *penes me*).

[2] Proceso de Maria Paredes, fol. i., xxiii. (MS. *penes me*).

[3] MSS. of Library of University of Halle, Yc. 20, Tom. I.

affirmed their faith or persistently denied the accusation in the face of what was considered sufficient evidence, for this was regarded by the Inquisition as a proof of impenitent guilt. For the most part the tribunal succeeded in obtaining confession with show of repentance entitling the accused to reconciliation or some milder infliction. But perhaps the most instructive feature of the record is the number of trivial cases which reveal how jealously the Moriscos were watched by their Christian neighbors, eager to denounce them on the slightest suspicion, and how easy it was to provoke them in an altercation to some careless word which would justify seizing them and throwing them in gaol until the Inquisition could be notified to send and fetch them. The Morisco thus lived in a perpetual atmosphere of anxiety, never knowing at what moment he might be put on trial for his life. In 1575 Garci Rodriguez is tried on an accusation of saying that in the war of Granada a certain captain had been saved by a soldier and not by invoking God and the Virgin, and he escapes with abjuration *de levi* in a penitential habit. Diego Herrez, when a man called Mahomet a knave, had the imprudence to say "What is Mahomet to you?" and was sentenced to abjure *de levi*, to receive a hundred lashes and four months' instruction from his parish priest. In 1579 Gabriel de Carmona, a youth of 17, travelling with four other Moriscos, was accused by three chance road companions of singing the *Zambra antigua*—a song customary at Moorish weddings. The secular officials of Orgaz promptly threw all five in gaol and handed them over to the Inquisition which duly tried them. Gabriel denied the charge and that he even knew the zambra and when the witnesses came to ratify their testimony it appeared that none of them knew Arabic, or what the zambra was, or what Gabriel had been singing. They were all acquitted but there could be no compensation for their suffering and the interference with their affairs. Isabel, a Morisca girl aged 20, was accused by her mistress and daughter and another witness, of having in a quarrel sent all Christians to the devil and spoken of her having a different law from theirs. On trial she admitted certain imprudent utterances when her mistress called her a bitch and a hound, but she disabled their testimony by proving enmity and when the inquisitors differed as to the sentence the Suprema ordered the case dismissed. In 1584 Alonso de la Guarda was accused by his wife of denying the virginity of the Virgin and she arranged with the commissioner of the Inquisition that he and three other witnesses should be concealed while she led her husband on to talk; unluckily for the plot he answered her questions in Arabic so that they did not understand what he said, but he was arrested, sent to Toledo and tried. In his defence he proved that his wife was too intimate with one of the witnesses; she and the latter were examined, but the truth could not be ascertained, the evidence was not considered sufficient to justify torture and the case was dismissed. Less fortunate was Alonso de Soria who, becoming irritated in a discussion on being told that the Moriscos never confessed fully, exclaimed that confession was nothing—the real confession was in heaven. Fearing that he would be denounced for this he went voluntarily to the Inquisition and denounced himself. The witnesses summoned confirmed his story, but the inquisitors were not satisfied and tortured him to see whether they could find out something more, but without success, so he was let off with abjuration *de levi*, hearing mass as a penitent and a fine of ten ducats. Juan Gomez, an Algerine Moor, was a voluntary convert who on the road-side was bitten by some dogs. He beat them off, when their master came and abused him, beat him, and denounced him for saying that the Moorish law was better than the Christian and that he would live and die in it. On his trial he defended himself by asserting that he was a good Christian but his Spanish was imperfect and that in his passion he had meant to say that the Moors observed their law better than the Christians for they welcomed converts and treated them well. The inquisitors humanely took his recent conversion into consideration and agreed to regard his imprisonment during trial as sufficient punishment, so he escaped with a reprimand and two months' seclusion in a convent for instruction. The very triviality of these cases is their chief importance as they show how the Moriscos lived on a lava-crust which might at any moment give way and how ready a means the Inquisition furnished for enmity to satisfy a grudge in safety, protected by its suppression of the names of witnesses. A simple trial for heresy was in itself, as we have seen, no slight infliction and besides there was the ready resort to torture which, in the jurisprudence of the period, was the universal solvent of judicial doubts. In the 190 cases contained in the record before us, it was employed in 55—in four of them twice—and in a considerable portion of those which were suspended or discontinued the accused had been tortured without extracting a confession.[1]

But these trivial accusations were by no means all that the Moriscos had to dread. At any moment the treachery or trial of one might involve a whole community. In

[1] MSS. of Library of University of Halle, Yc. 20, Tom. I.

1606, a girl of nineteen named Maria Paez, daughter of Diego Paez Limpati, brought desolation on the Moriscos of Almagro by accusing her parents, sisters, uncles, cousins, kindred and friends. Incriminations of course spread. The girl's father was burnt as an impenitent because he would not confess; her mother, who confessed, was reconciled and condemned to imprisonment for life and in all twenty-five Moriscos of Almagro suffered, of whom four were relaxed to the secular arm. As confiscation accompanied the sentence in every case the Inquisition probably gathered a fairly abundant harvest.[1] The Moorish com-

[1] A summary of the sentences passed on Moriscos in the MS. cited above shows—

Died during trial	5
Acquittals	14
Cases dismissed	5
Cases suspended	30
Abjuration *de levi*	24
Abjuration *de vehementi*	15
Instruction ordered	32
Reprimand in audience chamber	8
Spiritual penance	6
Reconciliation with confiscation	78
Reconciliation without confiscation	5
Fines (the highest 100 ducats)	5
Exile	2
Wearing sanbenito	5
Sanbenito and prison for a term	27
Sanbenito and prison perpetual (usually discharged after three years)	32
Sanbenito and prison perpetual, irremissible	3
Scourging (mostly 100 lashes, but sometimes 200)	15
Galleys (for terms of from 3 to 10 years)	14
Relaxed to secular arm for burning	11

In the Seville auto de fe of September 24, 1559, there were three Moriscos burned and eight reconciled with sanbenito and prison; of these six were also scourged, including three women.—Archivo de Simancas, Hacienda, Legajo 25, fol. 2.

munities were constantly subject to devastation of this kind. In 1585, at an auto de fe in Cuenca, there were twenty-one of them—one relaxed, seventeen reconciled and three required to abjure *de vehementi*—of whom thirteen were from the village of Soquellamos and seven from Villaescusa de Haro.[1] In 1589 the Inquisition of Valencia penanced eighty-three Moriscos of Mislata and in 1590 it added seventeen more.[2]

Such were the conditions of existence of the Moriscos of Castile—of the old Mudéjares who for generations had been loyal and faithful subjects and industrious citizens contributing to the prosperity of the land. Such was the gentleness with which Fonseca says the Inquisition sought to induce them to obedience without frightening them and such were the benignant methods which a recent writer assures us were employed by the Inquisition to win them over.[3] The learned Juan Bautista Perez, Bishop of Segorbe, knew better when, in 1595, in enumerating fifteen impediments to their conversion he included their fear of the Inquisition and its punishments which make them hate religion[4]—that is, the religion of their persecutors. If it were not so tragic there would be food for grim mirth in the rhetorical amplification with which the clerical writers of the period dilate on the devilish and inexpugnable obstinacy with which the Moriscos clung to their false faith and resisted the kindly efforts made for their salvation.

[1] Archivo de Simancas, Inquisicion, Leg. 1157, fol. 155.

[2] Archivo Hist. Nacional, Inqn de Valencia, Leg. 98.

[3] Fonseca, Giusto Scacciamento, p. 346.—Menendez y Pelayo, Heterodoxos españoles II. 628.—"La Inquisicion apuraba todos los medios benignos y conciliatorios."

[4] Archivo de Simancas, Inqn de Valencia, Leg. 205, fol. 3.

CHAPTER V.

THE INQUISITION.

In order properly to understand the influence exerted by the Inquisition a brief summary of its processes and methods is necessary. The impenetrable secrecy which shrouded all its operations invested it with a terror possessed by no other tribunal. When a prisoner was arrested he disappeared from human view as though the earth had opened to swallow him; his trial might last two, three, or four years, during which his family knew not whether he were dead or alive, until in some public auto de fe he reappeared and sentence was read, condemning him to relaxation, or the galleys, or perpetual imprisonment, or perhaps discharging him with some trivial penalty. Geronimo Moraga, a Morisco, when on trial in Saragossa in 1577, explained how he met certain persons in December, 1576, while on his way to the city to be present at an auto de fe announced for that time, in order to see whether his father and brother, who had been arrested some time previously, would appear in it.[1] It was the only way in which he could learn their fate and put an end to agonizing suspense. The prisoner at his first audience was sworn not to reveal anything that should occur while he was in prison, and after the auto de fe, if he was not burnt, a similar but more solemn oath was

[1] Archivo de Simancas, Inq^{n} de Valencia, Leg. 205, fol. 4.

administered to him before he was discharged to undergo his penance. All officials and witnesses were likewise bound to inviolable secrecy. The tribunal was thus shielded from all criticism and released from all responsibility save to the Suprema. No one could call in question its justice and no one could complain of its acts for every mouth was sealed. Human nature is not fitted to wield wholly irresponsible power over the lives and fortunes of men, and such a system, while it gave free rein to the evil-disposed, could not but affect injuriously even the well-intentioned judge.

A corollary to this system of secrecy was the careful suppression of the names and identity of the witnesses, who thus were likewise released from all personal responsibility, save in the exceedingly rare cases of prosecution for perjury. Their evidence was taken in secret by the inquisitor, there was no cross-examination or endeavor to test its accuracy, and when, at a subsequent stage of the trial, it was "published" or read to the accused, it was in a garbled form, drawn up so as to prevent, as far as possible, any identification of the witnesses by him. All this, of course, threw almost insuperable difficulties in the way of the defence, nor were they much diminished by the simulacrum of allowing him counsel. He was offered a choice between two or three advocates who formed part of the official staff of the tribunal, and with the one selected he was permitted to communicate only in presence of the inquisitors. In the majority of cases the main duty of the advocate consisted in urging his client to confess and throw himself on the mercy of the court, and in case a serious defence was undertaken he was forbidden to communicate with the friends and kindred of the accused, for this would be a violation of the indispensable secrecy. Defence was possible in but two ways, *tachas* and *abonos*. The former consisted in guessing the names of the adverse witnesses and if possible disabling them for enmity, the latter in adducing testimony of good character. Even this modicum of defence was seriously limited by the rule that New Christians, while freely admitted as witnesses for the prosecution, were not allowed to testify in favor of the accused. It is true that, in 1526 and 1529, the inquisitors were instructed that in cases of Moriscos who could call no other witnesses they might use their discretion in admitting them.[1]

The whole theory of the inquisitorial process was the assumption that the accused would not have been arrested if he were not guilty, and the effort throughout the trial was to make him confess, with the powerful agency in reserve of torture to compel him to do so. Simple confession, moreover, was insufficient to merit the doubtful mercy of reconciliation combined with confiscation and other penalties; to be efficacious it must be the result of conversion and repentance, implying the denunciation of all accomplices in the crime of heresy, including the nearest and dearest; the wife could scarce have been guilty without the husband's participation; the child could scarce have gone astray without the guidance of the parents, and thus, when one member of a family fell into the hands of the Inquisition, the rest as a rule speedily followed and the whole household recognized each other in the resultant auto de fe. Denial of guilt and persistent assertion of orthodoxy were of no service as against the

[1] MSS. of Royal Library of Copenhagen, 318*b*. p. 306.

evidence of two witnesses; it merely demonstrated that the accused was impenitent—a *negativo*—and as such he was relaxed to the secular arm for burning.

How scanty were the chances of escape, when the presumption was always against the accused, is seen in the case of Francisco Doquin Frare and his wife Maria Gilo tried, in 1575, by the Inquisition of Valencia. There was but one witness against them—a man who had been convicted and burnt. The accused chanced to identify him and proved that he was a personal enemy of Frare. Notwithstanding this, when the case came to be voted on there was *discordia*, or disagreement. One of the inquisitors and the episcopal Ordinary voted to make them appear in an auto de fe, to fine them and send them to the prison of penitents for instruction; the other inquisitor and the *consultores* voted for torture in order to further enlightenment. This prevailed and was executed on the husband, though the wife was mercifully spared because she was suckling a child—the final result being fine and imprisonment for an unproved offence.[1]

Still more illustrative of inquisitorial methods and of the hatred of Christianity, which they naturally provoked, is the case of Mari Gomez, one of the Moriscos of Daimiel. May 1, 1540, she was arrested on evidence which had been accumulating since 1538. After commencing with protestations of orthodoxy, the interrogatories of her well-trained judges in successive audiences drove her to one admission after another. In June she managed to convey to her daughter, María Cassilla, an injunction to confess, the result of which was that, on September 1st, the daughter

[1] Archivo Hist. Nacional, Inq^{n} de Valencia, Legajo 396.

made a confession in which her mother was represented as a confirmed and persistent Moor. When this and some other new testimony was read to Mari Gomez she could not be induced to admit it all, she vacillated and revoked some of her admissions—a most serious offence in the inquisitorial system, which brought on her a sentence of torture, April 4, 1541. On June 8th, after a long and strenuous effort to make her confess, she was taken to the torture chamber and stripped, which extracted a confession with the explanation that she had not made it earlier in hopes of saving her daughter. She was made to tell all she knew about others and the torture was suspended. After duly ratifying her confession, June 9th, on the 12th she was sentenced to reconciliation, confiscation and perpetual imprisonment with the sanbenito. After nearly three years, on the testimony of the alcaide of the prison that she was *buen penitente*, on May 31, 1544, her prison was changed to Daimiel, where she was never to leave her house without the sanbenito, she was to hear mass on all Sundays and feast-days and to confess and commune on the three great feasts of Christmas, Easter and Pentecost—a fairly effective way of rendering odious the observances of religion. A few days later, on June 4th, she presented a pitiful petition representing that her husband is in the penitential prison; he is in great necessity and requires her services, wherefore she begs that she may be allowed to remain in Toledo, where she will reside near the prison and succor him; furthermore she prays that she may be allowed to take with her the bedding from her confiscated property, on which she has been sleeping, and retain it till her penance is completed. Then, on November 18, 1545, she presented an order which she had procured from the Suprema, reciting that she has been a good penitent and ordering the inquisitors to commute her prison and sanbenito into spiritual penances of fasts, prayers and pilgrimages, conditioned on her not leaving the kingdoms of Castile and Leon. The sanbenito was at once removed and she was discharged, the penances enjoined being Friday fasting for a year, recitation of five Paternosters and Ave Marias on all Sundays and feast-days and visiting the hermitage nearest to Daimiel. Her troubles, however, were by no means over. In 1550 she was included, as a simulated confessor and relapsed impenitent, in a batch of Daimiel women to be tried again—Mari Lopez la Brava, Mayor la Roya, Juana Diaz, Mari Hernandez, Mari Herrera and Isabel del Niño—and on July 14th she was thrown into the secret prison. Her confession was held to have been fictitious and imperfect because she had omitted in it to mention certain matters, as for instance a fact contained in the evidence of a prisoner, in 1541, that, nine or ten years before, a kid had been killed in her house after the fashion of the Moors, by cutting its throat; also she had not mentioned all the persons who had changed linen and rested on Thursday nights and Fridays and she had not confessed to irregular attendance at mass. Then she was a relapsed impenitent because since her penance she had proposed to marry a son to a girl within the prohibited degrees without obtaining a dispensation and she had twice spoken of Allah. In the course of her trial she attempted defence by both *tachas* and *abonos*, but on January 22, 1551, it was voted that the evidence required to be purged, wherefore she should be tortured as much as she could bear. She endeavored to escape this by alleging a rupture, but the midwife called in to examine her reported that this was not the case, although her belly was swelled. On March 5th she was tortured with great severity—sixteen turns of the sharp cords around legs and arms, then the *escalera*—a sort of inclined frame in which the head was lower than the feet—and finally a cord twisted around the head while two jars of water (about half a gallon) were made to trickle down the throat by means of a rag thrust down. She shrieked and screamed, appealed to God and begged to be killed, but persistently declared that she had nothing to confess and when her tormentors were satisfied the torture was suspended. On March 9th she was voted to be punished arbitrarily, with reclusion in her house and spiritual penances if she were poor and had nothing, but on investigation it was found that she possessed some property and that on her return to Daimiel after her first imprisonment she had succeeded in recovering 9000 maravedís from the receiver of confiscations, so she was fined twenty ducats for the expenses of the Inquisition and was sentenced to keep her house in Daimiel as a prison for four months, never leaving it except to attend mass and sermons and from Easter to Pentecost of that year she was to fast on Fridays and recite four Paters and Aves.[1] Now all this was the ordinary everyday routine of the Inquisition and there is small cause for surprise if the Moriscos were confirmed more and more in their abhorrence of a faith propagated after this fashion.

The faith, however, was, to some extent, rather a pretext and the Inquisition recognized that if its operations incited to discontent and rebellion, its severity was

[1] Proceso de Mari Gomez (MS. *penes me*).

an important factor in keeping the Moriscos in subjection. A letter to Philip II. from the inquisitors of Saragossa, June 6, 1585, enclosing a relation of an auto de fe held that day, in which there were five culprits burnt and 63 reconciled, who were nearly all Moriscos, dwells on the service rendered in repressing their insolence; they have been deprived of their leaders, they now seem quiet and obedient and no longer manifest their customary impudence and effrontery.[1] The inquisitors also call special attention to their usefulness in another direction, for they take care to point out that they have sent twenty-nine Moriscos to serve in the galleys, besides three left over from the auto de fe of the previous September. Galley slaves were always in demand and although such brutal punishment was usually reserved for specially blasphemous cases of heresy, the Suprema issued orders, May 8, 1573, to send the new converts to the galleys even when they confessed readily and well, a command which it repeated in 1591.[2]

There doubtless is some truth in the assertion that the terror of the Inquisition was less for the Moriscos than for Spaniards, since the former when punished were naturally regarded by their fellows as martyrs and were consequently held in high esteem. It was for them an honor to appear on the scaffold of an auto de fe and thus the infamy which was one of the severest inflictions accompanying the penances of the Holy Office was ineffective, especially in Morisco communities, where we are told that such martyrs

[1] Biblioteca Nacional, Seccion de MSS. PV. 3, No. 20.

[2] Archivo Hist. Nacional, Inqn de Valencia, Leg. 5, No. 1, fol. 285, 329. The *buen confitente* was always regarded as entitled to mitigation of punishment.

were frequently rewarded with rich brides. There is a story of a woman who, when the sanbenito was put on her, asked for another for her child, as the weather was cold. Another story illustrates this and also the care with which all expenses were thrown upon the culprits. A number of Moriscos of Gestalgar were scourged in an auto de fe, after which the executioner went there to collect his fees from his patients; one from whom he demanded payment refused on the ground that he had not been flogged, and on investigation it was found that he had been inadvertently omitted, whereupon the lashes were duly administered, to his great satisfaction.[1]

Pecuniary penances and confiscation, however, were of another character and were acutely felt, not only by the Moriscos themselves but by their lords, who naturally objected to the impoverishment of their vassals, as they desired to extort all that patient industry could earn, over and above a bare existence. When, after the fall of the Roman Empire, heresy first became the subject of systematic persecution in the twelfth and thirteenth centuries, confiscation was one of the penalties decreed for it under the canon law and princes who did not enforce this vigorously were threatened with the censures of the Church.[2] The monarch who profited by the spoliation of his subjects could therefore, strictly speaking, not forego it without papal authorization, leading at times to some curious and intricate questions. Although in Spain, as elsewhere, the confiscations enured to the royal fisc and in the earlier times of Ferdinand and Isabella they had

[1] Bledæ Defensio Fidei, p. 98; Crónica, p. 883.—Fonseca, p. 85.

[2] Cap. 10 Extra, V. vii.—Innoc. P.P. IV. Bull. *Cum fratres* (Bullar. Roman. I. 90).

been a source of large income, as they diminished in amount they had practically been diverted to the Inquisition, which was always pleading poverty, and little attention was paid to the degrading spectacle of judges pronouncing sentences in which they were personally interested as a source from which their salaries were to be paid. Fines, or pecuniary penances as they were euphemistically termed, occupied virtually the same position. In the early days of the Spanish Inquisition they were its perquisite; then the crown claimed and took them, but finally the Inquisition recovered them by the device of imposing them for its extraordinary expenses.

In the kingdoms of Castile there was no question as to the applicability of all this to the Moriscos, but in those of Aragon it was different. This was especially the case in Valencia, where the Moriscos were most numerous and the interest of the nobles and gentry in them was greatest. The earliest *fuero*, granted by Jayme I. after the conquest, provided that in case of condemnation to death for heresy, treason or other crime, the allodial lands and personal property of the offender should be confiscated to the king, but feudal lands or those held under a censo or rent-charge, or other service, should revert to the lord. When the new Inquisition was established, it paid no attention to this and, in 1488, the ecclesiastics and nobles in the córtes of Orihuela complained to Ferdinand and demanded its observance to which he assented. This proved nugatory, for the Inquisition continued to confiscate and, in the córtes of 1510, the nobles repeated the complaint and asked that he should compound for the lands illegally obtained and that purchasers should be compelled to pay all rent-charges and fines for transfer, to all of which he gave his assent. This was as ineffectual as the previous promises and, in 1533, the complaint was repeated in the córtes of Monzon ; it was the lords and the churches that suffered by the confiscation imposed on their vassals; only corporal punishments should be inflicted, not pecuniary ones, and some compromise should be reached as to past infractions of the fuero to be determined by a commission. To this the reply was equivocal ; there was no confiscation and, please God, with the efforts now on foot for the instruction of the new converts, there will be no necessity for it in future, but, if there should be, provision will be made to protect the lords, and meanwhile a commission can decide what is just as to the past.[1]

The next year, at Saragossa, Charles issued a solemn pragmatica for Aragon in which, after consultation with the inquisitor-general and Suprema, he promulgated as a law to be inviolably observed that, if any of the new converts should commit apostasy requiring confiscation, the property should be made over to the legal Catholic heirs, or in default of such be distributed in accordance with the intestate laws of Aragon, and perpetual silence was imposed on the royal fisc which was declared to have no claim, and all this without prejudice to the lords of the culprits. This he swore to publicly with his hand on the gospel and ordered its enforcement by his son Philip and all royal officials.[2]

[1] Coleccion de Doc. inéd. XVIII. 106–13.—Archivo de Simancas, Patronato Real, Legajo único, fol. 37.

[2] Archivo de Simancas, Inq^{n}, Libro 939, fol. 9.

A brief of Paul III., under date of 1536, asks Charles to adopt exactly this policy and habilitates the descendants of offenders to hold such property. There may be a mistake in the date, and it may have given the impulse to Charles. In any event it was practically a papal

As the crown no longer had any interest in the confiscations, Charles could waive his rights without sacrifice, but the Inquisition was not disposed to abandon its claims. The córtes of the three kingdoms, in 1537, presented formal complaints that it seized lands that were held in fief and on ground-rents and even such as had been bought in good faith from Moriscos and had been improved by the new owners. The Inquisition denied these charges, but the córtes instanced lands of which the *dominium directum* belonged to the chapter of Valencia and other churches, and they asked the emperor to issue positive commands to the inquisitors to obey the laws, which he promised to do.[1] The Suprema however replied in a consulta in which it argued that confiscation was the most efficient penalty for the repression of heresy; the heretic could escape burning by confession and reconciliation and if there were no confiscation heresy would be unpunished.[2] With imperturbable obstinacy therefore the Inquisition maintained its position and the córtes of Monzon, in 1542, reiterated the complaint that the inquisitors wholly disregarded the law; its officials refused to do justice and the secular courts were afraid to interfere. It was asked that, in cases of condemnation for heresy, the *dominium utile* of the convict should revert to the

confirmation of the policy.—Biblioteca Nacional, Seccion de MSS. Dd. 145, fol. 352.

[1] Archivo de Simancas, Patronato Real, Inqⁿ, Legajo único, fol. 37, 38 (See Appendix No. VI.).—Coleccion de Doc. inéd. XVIII. 114.—One of the worst features of confiscation was that it was held to operate as soon as an act of heresy was performed; ownership then at once enured to the fisc and any subsequent sale by the apparent owner was void and the buyer was stripped of it.

[2] Archivo de Simancas, Inquisicion, Libro 78, fol. 192.

dominium directum of the lord and that the royal officials should be compelled to act and put the lord in possession under pain of 1000 florins, to all of which Charles gave his assent.[1] Then Paul III. intervened, in his brief of August 2, 1546, which virtually superseded the Inquisition, and decreed that for ten years and subsequently during the pleasure of the Holy See, there should be no confiscation of the property of Moriscos nor any pecuniary penalties imposed.[2]

No attention seems to have been paid to this papal utterance. In 1547 the córtes of Valencia renewed the complaint that the Inquisition disregarded the law which in confiscation reunited the *dominium utile* with the *directum*. In order that it might be enforced they therefore asked that the inquisitor-general should sign the fuero and send instructions to his subordinates to obey it. It was thus recognized that the emperor's signature was insufficient; that the Holy Office was an independent body in the state, bound by no law save of its own making. Prince Philip admitted this when he gave his assent to the article—*Plau a sa Alteza*—adding that he would order the inquisitor-general and the apostolic commissioner entrusted with the affairs of the Moriscos to be treated with and when the matter was concluded the necessary letters would be issued. There was no intention of concluding the matter, for the córtes of 1552 complained that the agreement with the inquisitor-general had not yet been reached, and those of 1564 reviewed the whole question. They said that in 1533 Charles V.

[1] Coleccion de Doc. inéd. XVIII. 116.

[2] Bulario de la Orden de Santiago, Lib. III. fol. 33.

had granted that in cases of confiscation for heresy the property should go not to the fisc but to the kindred and that in 1537 he had repeated this and promised its confirmation by the inquisitor-general and pope; this confirmation had never come and they asked that it be obtained as well as that of the law consolidating the *dominium utile* with the *directum*.[1] To this the reply of Philip II. was that he would ask the consent of the inquisitor-general. How safe he was in making this promise is seen in the instructions issued this same year by the Suprema to the inquisitors of Valencia in which they are specifically told to confiscate the property of the Moriscos no matter what the people may say about having a privilege against confiscation.[2] Its obstinacy is intelligible when we see how frequently it drew upon that tribunal for the salaries of its members and officials.[3]

Meanwhile in Aragon the pragmatica of 1534, which had received the assent of the Inquisition, was dexterously evaded. The córtes of 1547 complained to the inquisitor-general that, as the inquisitors could no longer confiscate property, they had adopted a system of pecuniary penances that was worse than confiscation, for fines were imposed greater than the wealth of the penitents who were obliged to sell all their property and in addition to impoverish their kinsfolk—to which the contemptuous reply was that

[1] Coleccion de Doc. inéd. XVIII. 119-24.—Bledæ Defensio Fidei, pp. 333-6.

[2] Archivo Hist. Nacional, Inq^{n} de Valencia, Legajo 2, MS. 16, fol. 187.

[3] Archivo de Simancas, Inquisicion, Libro 940, fol. 34-60.

if any one was aggrieved he could apply for relief to the inquisitors or to the Suprema.[1]

At length, in Valencia, a satisfactory concordia or agreement was reached. Already, in 1537, a compromise had been proposed by the córtes of Valencia of a payment to the Inquisition of 400 ducats per annum if the inquisitors should be restrained from levying fines on Moriscos in the guise of pecuniary penance, but the Suprema rejected it as inadequate and as a disservice to God.[2] In 1571, however, there was more disposition to listen to such suggestions. The rebellion of the Moriscos of Granada had just been suppressed after a prolonged effort which had exhausted the resources of Spain in men and money and had depopulated that flourishing kingdom. It was a warning not to push oppression too far and consideration was given to the complaints of the syndics of the Valencia aljamas at the court. Cosme Aben-Amir, a noble Morisco, himself under prosecution by the Inquisition, was residing at the court in possession of considerable influence and aided their efforts, which resulted in a royal cédula of October 12, 1571. This recited the moderation with which the apostasy of the Moriscos had hitherto been treated, but now, in order that in future there may be no excuse and that they may be punished with all merited rigor, the Inquisitor-general Espinosa has condescended to grant to the Moriscos of Valencia the articles presented by them. These articles provided that, in consideration of a payment of 50,000 sueldos (equivalent to 2500 ducats) per annum to the

[1] Archivo de Simancas, Inquisicion, Libro 922, fol. 15.
[2] Ibid. Libro 78, fol. 168.

Inquisition, the property of the conversos and their descendants entering into the arrangement shall not be subject to confiscation for heresy, including dogmatizers, alfaquíes, circumcisers, relapsed and prisoners under trial but not sentenced, and no sequestration was to be made on arrest. Pecuniary penances moreover were limited to ten ducats, but the aljamas of the culprits were liable for them. Any aljama could decline to come into the arrangement, and in such case its members were liable to confiscation which should be computed as part of the 50,000 sueldos, but any one could come in at any time on agreeing to pay its share, and even individuals of outside aljamas were to be received on paying the proper assessment on their property. A grace of 500 or 600 ducats moreover was allowed in consideration of confiscations decreed but not covered in. To confirm this agreement papal briefs and privileges from the king and inquisitor-general were to be procured at the cost of the Moriscos and if they desired it to be included as a fuero in the next córtes the king promised to assent to it. So large a portion of the aljamas accepted this commutation that thereafter it is always spoken of as in force throughout Valencia, but a document of 1585 shows that there were still some which held aloof.[1] This arrangement was mutually satisfactory from a financial point of view. The Holy Office was assured of an annual revenue of which it was in need, while the Moriscos felt that they were paying for insurance against the impoverishment of their families and the miseries of sequestration which was the invariable accom-

[1] Danvila, pp. 183–88.—Archivo Hist. Nacional, Inqn de Valençia, Cartas del Consejo, Leg. 5, No. 1, fol. 107.

paniment of arrest on charges however flimsy. The nobles and churches moreover were secured against the alienation of their lands and the disabling of their vassals from paying the customary tribute.

It was difficult however to compel the inquisitors to observe any limitations on their power to oppress. In 1595 the aljamas made complaint of infractions of the concordia.[1] The power to impose fines of ten ducats also was a direct source of revenue which was naturally exploited. In the auto de fe of January 7, 1607 there were twenty fines of ten ducats on Moriscos of whom only eight were reconciled. To this the Suprema took exception saying that when there was not reconciliation the fine was uncalled for, unless there was some special offence deserving it. In the same auto, moreover, there was a fine of twenty ducats, one of thirty and one of fifty. The judges evidently took care that there should be funds to pay their salaries.[2]

The comparative leniency of the concordia was displeasing to some of the more rigid churchmen. In 1595 Bishop Perez of Segorbe drew up by command an elaborate report of the situation in which he advocated its revocation, as under it he says that the Moriscos deemed themselves at liberty to live as they pleased and confiscation would be a restraint on their offences.[3] That same year, however, the juntas of Madrid and Valencia, which had charge of the Morisco question, agreed that there was less apostasy in places where confiscation was not permitted under the

[1] Archivo Hist. Nacional, Inq^{n} de Valencia, Leg. 5, No. 2, fol. 14, 15.

[2] Ibid. Leg. 2, MS. 10, fol. 79.

[3] Archivo de Simancas, Inq^{n} de Valencia, Leg. 205, fol. 3.

concordia and Philip II. resolved that it should be continued during the period agreed upon for instruction.[1]

The statistics of the Inquisition of Valencia subsequent to the concordia would indicate that that measure had no definite influence on its activity, although the numbers fluctuate from year to year in a manner not easy to explain.[2] Towards the close of the century and during the opening years of the seventeenth its vigor seems to increase; at an auto de fe held September 5, 1604, there were twenty-eight abjurations *de levi*, forty-nine *de vehementi*, eight reconciliations and two relaxations—all Moriscos except a Frenchman penanced for blasphemy.[3] In that of January 7, 1607, there were thirty-three Moriscos, of whom one was relaxed for relapse, besides six whose cases were suspended, and in their trials torture had been employed fifteen times.[4] That there were not more was not for lack of material, for we are told that in the town of Carlet there were two hundred and forty

[1] Danvila, p. 228.

[2] From 1570 to 1592 the number of cases of heresy in the Inquisition of Valencia are (Arch. Hist. Nac. Inqn de Valencia, Leg. 98):

1570, 16 cases	1576, 16 cases	1582, none	1588, 21 cases
1571, 55 "	1577, 13 "	1583, 8 cases	1589, 94 "
1572, 32 "	1578, 15 "	1584, 29 "	1590, 49 "
1573, 34 "	1579, 24 "	1585, none	1591, 290 "
1574, 16 "	1580, 37 "	1586, 64 cases	1592, 117 "
1575, 20 "	1581, 22 "	1587, 35 "	

In 1591 the number of the reconciled was so great that Archbishop Ribera asked that on Sundays and feast-days they should not be allowed to come to the cathedral, as the crowd disturbed the services.—Arch. Hist. Nac. Inqn de Valencia, Leg. 5, No. 2, fol. 314.

[3] Danvila, p. 263.

[4] Archivo Hist. Nac. Inqn de Valencia, Leg. 2, MS. 10.

Morisco households in which the fast of Ramadan was kept.[1]

In fact the bungling and misguided efforts at conversion had been so complete a failure that one can only wonder that the whole Morisco population did not pass through the hands of the inquisitors. Evidence sufficient to warrant arrest and trial was easily obtainable, for it was impossible to eradicate ancestral customs, while any of these, even when not strictly connected with religion, was held to justify suspicion of heresy, which in itself was a crime requiring purgation and penance. In the case of Bartolomé Sanchez, who appeared in the Toledo auto de fe of 1597, cleanliness was regarded as a suspicious circumstance—doubtless from the Moorish habit of bathing—and though he overcame the torture he was finally brought to confess and was punished with three years in the galleys, perpetual prison and confiscation. Miguel Cañete, a gardener, for washing himself in the fields while at work, was tried in 1606; there was nothing else against him but he was tortured without success and his case was suspended. The same year María Roayne, with her daughter Mari Lopez, was tried because when her son was to be married she took to the bride's house some sweetmeats and cakes to be thrown in the mattresses according to an old Moorish custom, but as nothing else could be proved against them the cases were suspended. Putting clean linen on a corpse for burial was a highly suspicious practice which warranted prosecution, though if nothing else could be proved or

[1] Ibid. Legajo 99.

obtained in confession it does not seem to be always regarded as punishable; still, in 1591, Isabel Ruiz for so treating her husband's body appeared in the auto de fe, abjured *de levi* and was fined in 10,000 maravedís.[1] Abstinence from pork and wine was of course a highly suspicious circumstance, which frequently appears in the trials; nothing else seems to be recorded against Juan de Mediana, who appeared in a Saragossa auto de fe in 1585 and was sentenced to two hundred lashes.[2] Refusal to eat of animals that had died a natural death was also a very compromising practice. In the Daimiel trials of 1540-50 this was evidently a novel idea to the tribunal which inquired curiously into it, apparently regarding it as a remarkable custom. In the accusation of Mari Naranja one of the articles is that when one of their cattle died they gave it to the herdsman or threw it to the dogs, and in that of Mari Serrana it is charged that when one of her goats died she sold it to an Old Christian for what he would give. Apparently Old Christians had no such scruples. Staining the nails with henna also figures prominently in charges against women although Mari Gomez la Sazeda pleaded that it was not specially a Moorish custom, for Christian women frequently stained their nails and hair.[3] If it was denied that these customs were relig-

[1] MS. of Library of University of Halle, Yc. 20, Tom. I.—Biblioteca Nacional, Seccion de MSS. D, 111, fol. 127.

[2] Biblioteca Nacional, Seccion de MSS. PV. 3, No. 20.

[3] MSS. *penes me*. The Edict of Granada, in 1526, forbade the use of henna, but it was suspended and when, about 1530, Antonio de Guevara, then Bishop of Guadix, endeavored to prevent its use by the Morisco women, they complained to the chancillery of Granada and the Captain-general Mondéjar, who intervened and told him it had nothing to do with the faith (Marmol Carvajal, Rebelion y Castigo, p. 164).

ious observances there was always the resource of torture to ascertain the intention, or skilful pressure and the despairing weariness of prolonged incarceration might lead to the admission of formal rites—the fasting of the Ramadan, the Guadoc, or bath accompanied with a ritual, or the Taor, another kind of bath prior to reciting the Zala, which was certain prayers uttered with the face to the East at sunrise, noon, sunset and night. The possession of books or papers in Arabic was almost conclusive proof. A general rule is enunciated that in such case, if the party denies intention, he is to be sent to the auto de fe with or without scourging as the circumstances may indicate.[1] That this was the practice is shown by the case of Nofre Blanch and his wife Angela Carroz, who appeared in the Saragossa auto of 1607. It appeared that officials, making a levy and execution in their house, found under the bed a book and some papers in Arabic, for which they were promptly imprisoned and tried. Each declared that the articles had belonged to an uncle of the husband and that they were ignorant of the contents. Both were tortured without confessing and were sentenced to abjure *de vehementi,* to 100 lashes apiece and a year's imprisonment, with the addition of a ten ducat fine on the woman.[2] So in the case of Isabel Zacim; in searching her house (apparently for arms) the officials found a Koran in Arabic in a chest. She denied all knowledge of it and there was no other evidence against her. As she was ninety years old she was spared torture and scourging but appeared in a Valencia auto de fe of

[1] Miguel Calvo (Archivo de Alcalá, Hacienda, Leg. 544^2, Libro 4).
[2] Archivo Hist. Nac., Inqn de Valencia, Leg. 2, MS. 10, fol. 48–9.

1604, abjured *de vehementi*, was exposed to a *vergüenza publica*—parading through the streets on an ass with an inscription setting forth her name and offence—imprisonment till she should be instructed in the faith, and the inevitable ten ducat fine.[1] In fact, the presumption was always in favor of guilt, when a Morisco was concerned, and inquisitorial methods were well adapted to convert that presumption into certainty. Unfortunately the Spanish statesmen could not see that the inevitable result was aversion and not conversion.

The time-honored principle that baptism was necessary to subject any one to the jurisdiction of the Inquisition came to be violated in the eagerness of the Holy Office to extend its functions. Bishop Simancas represents the older doctrine when he says that it has no cognizance in the case of an unbaptized dogmatizer who performs circumcision on a Christian boy or seeks to make converts; they must be left to the secular courts and there are laws enough to punish such offences. Not long afterwards, however, Rojas controverts this and asserts that in Valencia the inquisitors can proceed against unbaptized Jews and Moors who dogmatize among Christians, and this became the established rule. It was even extended to those who might defend or conceal heretics in general.[2]

Fautorship—the favoring or defending of heretics by Christians—had been from the first establishment of the Inquisition a crime subject to its jurisdiction and severely

[1] Ibid. MS. 7, fol. 3.

[2] Simancæ Enchiridion, Tit. XVII. n. 2.—Rojas de Hæreticis, P. I. n. 552-3.—Elucidationes Sancti Officii, § 48 (Archivo de Alcalá, Hacienda, Leg. 544², Libro 4).

punished. It was capable of very extended definition and the struggle with the Moriscos gave to the Inquisition the opportunity of striking salutary terror in a class which did not often fall into its hands. It was not only fautors like butchers who slaughtered in Moorish fashion or permitted others to do so, alguaziles who for bribes overlooked Morisco apostates, or midwives who consented to perform their ceremonies, all of whom were to be punished with appearance in an auto de fe, scourging, deprivation of functions and banishment from Morisco communities.[1] The feudal lords had antagonized the Inquisition in their repeated endeavors to secure for their own benefit the confiscations of their vassals ; they deprecated the interference which inquisitorial raids were apt to cause with the industry of those from whom their revenues were derived and perhaps sometimes they manifested this with too little discretion. Rojas has no hesitation in blaming the bishops and nobles who permitted their vassals openly to practice Moorish rites to the opprobrium of the Christian name, and, in 1567, Gaspar Cocolla, who seemed intimately acquainted with the Morisco population, told the Inquisition that the best way to convert them was to begin by converting their lords. On being asked who were the lords, he answered the Duke of Segorbe, the Admiral and other barons ; he knew nothing about them personally but the Moriscos had told him their lords desired them to remain Moors. Possibly some may have gone even further, for in an instruction of the Suprema to the tribunal of Valencia, in 1565, it is ordered to prosecute the lords and Old Christians who give aid and

[1] Miguel Calvo (Archivo de Alcalá, *loc. cit.*).

favor or use coercion to compel the conversos to live as Moors.[1]

The earliest instance I have met of such action is against an ecclesiastic, Padre Juan Oliver, archdeacon of Albarracin, in 1538, as a fautor of the sect of Mahomet.[2] In 1542 the Inquisition had a more distinguished victim in the person of Don Rodrigo de Beaumont, of the family of the constables of Navarre and akin to the Dukes of Alva and Segorbe, who was prosecuted as a great protector of the Moriscos, even of those who were in correspondence with Algiers. The most celebrated case however was that of Don Sancho de Córdova, Admiral of Aragon, who was condemned to abjuration *de levi*, to a fine of 2000 ducats and to reclusion at the pleasure of the Supréma. This proved perpetual, for at the age of 73 he was confined in a convent at Cuenca; falling sick he was transferred to one in Valencia where he lay till released by death. In an auto de fe of 1571 there appeared the Grand Master of the Order of Montesa and two nobles, Don Luis Pallas and Don Francisco Castellví, and in 1578 evidence was taken against two brothers, Francisco and Ramon Carroz, lords of Ciral and Tega, for keeping the Moriscos excited by telling them that they had been forcibly baptized, that they were not subject to the Inquisition and that they should appeal to the pope.[3] Such proceedings could not fail to strike terror throughout all ranks of the nobility, for public penance inflicted by the Inquisition not only brought incurable disgrace on all the kindred of the culprit but destroyed for his

[1] Rojas de Hæreticis, P. I. n. 12-13.—Danvila, pp. 172, 174-5.

[2] Archivo Hist. Nacional, Inq^{n} de Valencia, Leg. 390.

[3] Danvila, p. 126, 129, 181, 183, 194.

descendants the *limpieza*, or purity of blood, which was a condition precedent to admission to the great Military Orders and to much valuable preferment. This rule was only becoming established at this period, but it was rapidly spreading, and, in time, inability to prove *limpieza* was one of the sorest misfortunes that could befall any man.

It was not often that the Moriscos mustered courage openly to resist the Inquisition, but when this occurred the tribunal visited the offence with exemplary severity. The Morisco town of Xea, near Teruel, was notorious for the turbulence of the population, and when, in 1589, the Inquisitor Pedro Pacheco was making a visitation of the district even his vicinity did not prevent their continuing openly the practice of their religion. From Teruel he issued a warrant for the arrest in Xea of Lope de la Paridera, which was executed by the alguazil Miguel de Alegria. The people rose in arms to the number, it is said, of a thousand, attacked the house in which Lope was confined and set him free. In the melée the alguazil was struck on the head with a stone, thrown by Luis Garan, who was seized and tried. He did not deny throwing the stone but asserted that he did not know Alegria to be an official of the Inquisition. For this he was sentenced to abjure *de vehementi*, to receive 200 lashes, to serve six years in the galleys and to be perpetually banished from Xea. This was not the first occurrence of the kind at Xea for only a few years before another prisoner had been similarly rescued.[1]

[1] Archivo Hist. Nacional, Inq^{n} de Valencia, Legajo 383. In the accounts for this visitation there is an item of sixty reales paid to the

Thus the Inquisition fully performed its part in stimulating the aversion of the Moriscos to Christianity and in rendering impossible the amalgamation of the races on which depended the peace and prosperity of Spain.

medico and the barbero for curing Alegria and of ninety to him for confinement to his bed for many days.—Ibid.

CHAPTER VI.

CONVERSION BY PERSUASION.

It is not to be supposed that Spanish statesmen relied wholly on persecution to win the unwilling converts to the faith. It is true that in the earlier wholesale baptism under Isabella, in 1502, no traces have been left of any organized attempt to instruct the Mudéjares, save the perfunctory orders of Ximenes and Ferdinand (pp. 47, 48), but when the events of the Germanía led to the edict of 1525 it was recognized that a grave responsibility was incurred and that if the instruction which should precede baptism was impossible, the sacrament should at least be followed by earnest and systematic efforts to render the neophytes Christians in fact as well as in name. These efforts were constant and prolonged and, if they were futile, the cause is largely attributable to the incurable vices of Spanish administration, the greed and corruption which rendered the Moriscos a subject of speculation and the impossibility of following a consistent course of kindly persuasion and toleration when the fierce fanaticism of the age insisted upon regarding all aberrations as crimes for which God demanded instant punishment.

Clement VII., in his brief of May 12, 1524, had merely alluded to preaching by the inquisitors as a preliminary to giving the Moors the choice between conversion and exile. It is true, as we have seen, that, after the Germanía, missionaries had been sent to do what they could by disputation and persuasion (p. 69) but if they effected anything it has not been recorded, and Charles preceded his edict of 1525 with commands that priests should be provided and instruction be given in the dogmas of the faith (p. 85). Guevara, for a time, was transferred from Valencia to Granada where the situation was similar, as described, in 1526, by the shrewd Venetian envoy Navagero—the Moors were Christianized partly by force, but they are so little instructed in the faith and there is so little care about teaching them, priestly gains being the chief object, that they either are as much Moors as ever or have no religion of any kind.[1]

Those of Valencia seem to have been abandoned to the Inquisition as a missionary agent until the concordia of 1528 suspended it for a time and involved the necessity of milder methods of propagating the faith. Frailes were accordingly selected and commissioned to preach to them. The only one of these whose name has reached us was the Observantine Bartolomé de los Angeles, who had the recommendation of familiarity with Arabic, but unfortunately his evil character unfitted him for the work. A letter of the Suprema, September 27, 1529, to the inquisitors of Valencia, expresses astonishment at the report of his ill doings and orders them at once to send proper persons to the places which he had visited in order to remove the impression created by his scandals, but, with the customary regard for the reputation of the Church and churchmen, he is not to be named and no charges are to be brought against him.[2]

[1] Gachard, Voyages des Souverains des Bays-Bas, I. 208.
[2] Archivo de Simancas, Inquisicion, Libro 76, fol. 235.

This was of evil augury and portended the troubles which never ceased to exist in the dealings with the Moriscos. It soon became evident however that to Christianize a large population, living for the most part in exclusive communities scattered over the land, would require a complete organization of new parish churches with schools and all the appliances for instruction and the administration of the sacraments. The bishops of Valencia had done nothing; it was necessary to take the matter out of their hands and place it under one head, who should be superior to all episcopal authority in the dioceses. Papal delegation was essential for this and application was made to Clement VII., who responded with a brief of December 9, 1532, addressed to Inquisitor-general Manrique, in which he accepted for himself the responsibility of Charles's edict of 1525 and its happy result of the general baptism. Subsequently however, he said, in consequence of the neglect and absence of their priests the converts had returned to their vomit, and worse consequences were to be feared unless due provision was made, wherefore he granted to Manrique full power, during his lifetime, to provide persons to teach the converts, to erect and unite churches and chapels, to appoint and dismiss priests, to regulate tithes, in short to organize and govern the whole necessary ecclesiastical establishment, independently of the local bishops. Power was further given to decide all suits that might arise on the part of archbishops, bishops, chapters, abbeys, priests and secular lords, compelling obedience by censures and the secular arm and by depriving recalcitrants of their benefices, with perpetual disability for preferment, and in fine to do whatever was necessary to effect the object. It was a grant of enormous power, including that of crushing resistance expected from the existing hierarchy. There must have been remonstrances, for in about a month, January 11, 1533, the brief was followed by another, limiting to a twelvemonth the faculties for effecting the proposed organization. It doubtless was renewed after opposition had been subdued, for, November 26, 1540, Paul III. issued a brief to Inquisitor-general Tabera in which that of 1532 is recited, adding that the emperor had represented that, although Manrique had accomplished much yet much remained to be done, and doubts had arisen whether his successor as inquisitor-general enjoyed the same powers, wherefore Paul subrogates Tabera and confers on him the same faculties.[1]

The main trouble now, as it continued to be to the end, was money, for all classes who saw a chance of gain, in the confusion caused by the forcible conversion, grasped at what share of the spoils they could. Clement VII., in the brief of 1524, had ordered all mosques to be consecrated as churches; the Moors had paid tithes only on a few things; they were now to pay on all, not to the Church but to their lords, to recompense the latter for the expected loss of tribute arising from their becoming Christians, for they were promised that in all things they were to be treated as Christians. In return, their lords were to provide the churches with what was requisite for divine service and the revenues of the mosques were to

[1] Bulario de la Orden de Santiago, Libro II. fol. 94, 96, 145.

The supineness of the Valencia hierarchy was attributed to the Archbishop of Valencia, Everard de la Marche, one of the Flemings promoted by Charles in his younger days. He was non-resident and occupied the see from 1520 to 1538.

be converted into benefices. There was delay in carrying this out, which interfered with the conversion, for the lords held back until assured of what they should get, but, April 28, 1526, Charles procured from the Legate Salviati a bull on the subject, which we are told gave rise to innumerable suits, some of them carried up to the Roman Rota, as the measure was attacked for invalidity. It provided that the Moriscos should pay tithes like Christians, but to the king or their other lords in lieu of the old tribute; the funds of the mosques were to be used for the churches, and what tithes the Moors had paid to their mosques were still to be continued; if the funds thus were more than what was necessary to support the churches, the surplus was to be paid to the lords, to whom was assured the patronage of these churches and of all new ones erected, and all were to be free from any impost to the episcopal Ordinaries.[1] The lords, secular and ecclesiastical, thus sold their consent to the conversion of their vassals at a good price, to the impoverishment of the new establishment. The churches thus founded came to be known as rectories, of which we shall hear much hereafter.

Such was the foundation on which Manrique had to build. There had been 213 mosques converted into churches in the archbishopric of Valencia, 14 in Tortosa, 10 in Segorbe and 14 in Orihuela, but the object kept in view had been the revenues and not the instruction of the Moriscos.[2] Acting under the papal faculties, Manrique, January 14, 1534 despatched to Valencia Fray Alonso de Calcena and Don Antonio Ramirez de Haro, after-

[1] Sayas, Añales, cap. 110.—Dormer, Añales, Lib. II. cap. 2.

[2] Danvila, p. 116.—Bledæ Defensio Fidei, p. 190.

wards Bishop of Segovia, as his subdelegates armed with full powers and also with the title of inquisitors. Their instructions were that after consultation with the viceroy, the Duke of Calabria, husband of Queen Germaine, they were to complete the ecclesiastical arrangements for the Moriscos. If the rectors, who apparently were not expected to reside but merely to enjoy the revenues, have income sufficient to provide chaplains and sacristans they must do so; where they cannot, these must be furnished by the prelates who receive the tithes and first-fruits. If the nobles endow benefices they are to be patrons with power of presentation; where they do not, the preferment is to be given to persons belonging to the place or the nearest vicinity, taking care that the appointees are fitted for the work and that moderate salaries be assigned to them by the commissioners in conjunction with the Ordinaries. Careful selection must be made of sacristans who will administer justice, keep the churches clean and instruct the children in the faith, while, for the adults, preachers must be provided and means found for their support. A college must be founded for the education of children, who in turn will instruct their parents, and the means for this must be discussed. Arrangements must be made with the Ordinaries for the administration of the sacraments gratuitously, or very cheaply, so that the Moriscos may not be repelled from them, and confession is not to be obligatory except at Easter, Annunciation, Ascension of the Virgin and All Saints. Marriage fees must be reduced; if the Ordinaries will not consent to this the matter is to be referred back to Manrique.[1]

[1] Archivo de Simancas, Inq^{n}, Libro 77, fol. 227. (See Appendix No. VIII.)

While much of this was intelligently adapted to the situation one cannot but reflect that eight years had passed since the enforced baptism of the Moriscos, that all this elementary work had still to be done, and that the most prominent feature of the difficulties to be encountered is revealed to be the money question. The Moriscos were wellnigh supporting the whole kingdom with the products of their toil, yet all their earnings, beyond a bare subsistence, were so greedily clutched by noble and prelate that it was impossible to find means for the religious training that was essential to the safety of the state. When the final expulsion took place we are told that it reduced the revenues of the archbishop from 70,000 ducats to 50,000 showing how large was the income contributed by the Moriscos, yet all that could be drawn from the archiepiscopal and other ecclesiastical revenues by papal authority, for the support of a hundred and ninety new rectories founded by the commissioners was 2000 ducats per annum, to endow with 30 crowns a year those which were not supported by the first-fruits, and when St. Tomás de Vilanova assumed the archbishopric, in 1544, it was burdened with this pension, then designated as suggested by the commissioners for the foundation of the college, and a further pension of 3000 ducats for his predecessor Jorje de Austria who had accepted the benefice of Liége. At the same time St. Tomás urged Charles to place zealous and exemplary rectors in the Morisco villages with ample salaries to enable them to distribute alms, but it does not seem to have occurred to him that this was part of his duty and that of the Church.[1] No change was made and

[1] Cabrera, Relaciones, p. 464 (Madrid, 1857).—Fonseca, p. 21.—Coleccion de Doc. inéd. T. V. p. 81. In 1588 Philip ordered the Arch-

in 1559 a formal report to Philip II. stated that men could not be found to serve as rectors for the beggarly pittance of thirty ducats a year.[1]

It seemed impossible to eradicate the idea that persuasion must be supplemented or superseded by force. In 1535 we hear that in the Val de Alfandecheln the commissioners appointed an alguazil to drive the Moriscos to church on Sundays and feast-days and to punish those who did not go. His arbitrary proceedings displeased the Duke of Gandía who complained to the viceroy that so evil a man should have been selected. The viceroy sent for the alguazil who, on the road to Valencia, was murdered by Gandía's servants, whereupon the inquisitors applied to the Suprema for instructions and were ordered to prosecute the murderers vigorously and to inquire why the viceroy dared to summon an official of the Inquisition. How little had been accomplished by thus attempting to enforce this outward conformity is seen in the report of the inquisitors that the new converts live as Moors, circumcise their sons and fast so that Allah may grant victory to Barbarossa against Charles V. before Tunis.[2] The Córtes of 1537 might well embody in their complaints against the Inquisition that the Moriscos had not been instructed in the faith nor properly provided with churches and yet they were prosecuted for heresy, to which the Suprema loftily replied that they had been treated with all moderation and benignity; as for the

bishop of Valencia and Bishop of Segorbe to establish a seminary for Moriscos to be supported by 1000 ducats a year levied on the *tabla* or bourse of Valencia.—Danvila, p. 217.

[1] Danvila, p. 159.

[2] Archivo de Simancas, Inquisicion, Libro 77, fol. 353.

rest, provision would be made with the emperor's assent.[1] How slender was the provision may be gathered from a letter of the empress-queen, September 30, 1536, to the commissioner Haro stating that in the town of Oxea, with a population of four hundred households, mostly Moriscos, there was but one priest, who was manifestly insufficient for their instruction and guidance, wherefore he was ordered to establish two more there.[2] There must have been a considerable revenue derived from a place of that size and some one was doubtless enjoying it.

There appears to have been some episcopal co-operation when we are told that the Archbishop Jorje de Austria on leaving his see for Flanders, in 1539, issued new constitutions for the conversion of the Moriscos and renewed the commission of Benito de Santo Maria to preach to them.[3] The commissions granted by Manrique to Calcena and Haro were held to expire with his death in 1538 and the work was suspended until his successor Tabera was reinvested with the papal faculties. As soon as this occurred Haro, now Bishop of Ciudad Rodrigo, was again commissioned and sent to Valencia with full power to prosecute the work.[4] He remained until 1545 when he withdrew in obedience to a summons to attend the council of Trent (he was then Bishop of Segovia) from which, however he succeeded in getting himself excused, when Prince Philip asked the Archbishop Tomás de Vilanova to take charge of the matter. The latter assented, although as he truly said, the work was so important and

[1] Archivo de Simancas, Patronato Real, Inquisicion, Leg. único, fol. 38.

[2] Ibid. Inquisicion, Libro 926, fol. 79.

[3] Danvila, p. 126.

[4] Archivo de Simancas, Inquisicion, Libro 78, fol. 275.

so difficult that it ought to have the exclusive care of the person entrusted with it and he could not do justice to it in connection with the business of his see.[1]

The promised successor to Haro, as we have seen, was never appointed and matters were allowed to drift along in neglect. In 1547 the Archbishop furnished a detailed report of the situation. The Moriscos were daily becoming bolder in publicly performing their rites. The college consisted of a house with a large garden, in which there were thirty children under instruction, but a site should be chosen and a new building erected. There had been 147 new rectories established, each with a donation of 30 libras (or ducats), defrayed partly by appropriating two-thirds of the 2000 ducats taken from the archbishopric and partly from the first-fruits and the assessments on the provostships, dignities of the cathedral and other benefices, but this leaves a deficiency of 106 ll. 13 sols, 11 dineros for the rectories, which will have to be taken from the college as there is no other source from which to get it. Rectors have been appointed and vacancies are filled by the Ordinary. Printed instructions have been furnished for the rectors and catechisms for the converts. In many places alguaziles have been appointed to enforce the regulations and compel the converts to attend mass and live like Christians. Preachers have been sent to instruct, to baptize and to administer the sacraments but they have not remained long. A collector of the revenues of the former mosques has been appointed and instructed as to disbursements; also a collector of the 2000 ducats and other dotations, although

[1] Coleccion de Doc. inéd. T. V. pp. 92, 93.

he has not been able to perform his functions completely, owing to the resistance of the contributors.

Then the good archbishop proceeds with suggestions, which show a deplorable state of things. What is most necessary is a rigid inspection and supervision, to see whether the converts are trained and taught, to know whether the rectors reside and do their duty and live decently, what revenues they have from the former mosques and how they spend them. For lack of this inspection the rectors neglect their duties, they do not reside in the rectories, and some of them live dissolutely. The revenues of the former mosques are largely embezzled; they should be ascertained and accounted for and steps be taken to apply them to the Morisco churches, and a strict accounting should also be demanded from the receivers and collectors of the 2000 ducats. As some ecclesiastics have refused to pay their assessments for the support of the rectories, the king should provide for compelling payment. Measures should be adopted for the instruction of the converts, so that they may no longer be able to plead ignorance, and meanwhile they should be coerced into at least external observance, while action should be taken against the lords who favor them and impede the rectors and alguaziles from compelling them to attend mass.[1] Twenty years had elapsed since the Moors were forcibly baptized, yet practically nothing had been done to convert them. Spoliation, embezzlement, malversation of every kind had been rife; a few hundred benefices had been created, which neglect rendered virtually sinecures, and the revenues of which in not a few cases were squan-

[1] Coleccion de Doc. inéd. T. V. pp. 102–7.

dered in riotous living; the Inquisition had been afforded a new source of victims, after having nearly exhausted the old one of Judaic conversos, but the ostensible object for which the great crime of 1525 had been committed had not been advanced a step. Under the maladministration which had become chronic in Spanish affairs, persecution and persuasion only made Christianity more abhorrent to the New Christians. So it remained to the end and Spanish statesmen might well begin to look forward anxiously and ask what was to be the outcome.

The efforts to supplement the missionary efforts of the rectors and alguaziles by sending learned and eloquent friars throughout the land were equally unsuccessful. In 1543 Charles resolved on an earnest attempt. He announced to the Moriscos that he had procured from the pope a suspension of the Inquisition and was sending among them preachers to whom they must listen with reverence and incline their hearts to win salvation for if they hardened themselves the penalties provided by human and divine law would be enforced.[1] One of these preachers was the Dominican Juan Micon who shone in miracles. His commission empowered him to preach anywhere; all officials were ordered to aid him under pain of 1000 florins, he was authorized to summon the Moriscos to listen to him and to impose penalties on the disobedient.[2] Another was the Observantine Bartolomé de los Angeles, who had been tried in 1529 and dismissed in disgrace on account of the scandals he caused. He was again furnished with the most ample credentials and powers and a list of 128 towns was furnished which he

[1] Janer, p. 235.

[2] Fonseca, p. 20.

was to visit. At first Bishop Haro congratulated him on his success, although the priests were not helping him—though in many places there were none of the latter in consequence of the danger to which they were exposed. As early as 1544, however, charges were brought against him of associating with the Moriscos and using his mission as a source of gain. Still he was kept at the work until 1548, but his conduct seems to have become insufferable; he was formally tried, deprived of his functions and confined in a convent.[1]

The prolonged employment of so unworthy a missionary as Fray Bartolomé is probably explicable by his familiarity with Arabic, for, incredible as it may seem, the preachers as a rule were expected to convert populations of whose tongue they were ignorant. In the agricultural villages, where the bulk of the Moriscos resided, knowledge of Castilian or Lemosin was a comparatively rare accomplishment and one possessed by very few women or children. When, in 1564, Philip II. awoke to the necessity of action and ordered a spasmodic effort to reform abuses and instruct the Moriscos, the visitors who were sent to inspect the rectories were to carry with them money for liberal almsgiving and preachers who knew Arabic, and Archbishop Martin de Ayala sought to aid by printing the catechism in Arabic—the first time this device had been thought of since Hernando de Talavera earned the rebuke of Ximenes by such a profanation.[2] On the other hand, St. Luis Bertran, when called upon, in 1579, for suggestions by the Viceroy Duke of Najera,

[1] Janer, pp. 228-41.—Danvila, p. 130.

[2] Danvila, p. 169.—Archivo de Simancas, Inq^{n} de Valencia, Leg. 205, fol. 3.

urged the importance of forcing the Moriscos to learn the vernacular so that they might understand the preachers—the girls should not be allowed to marry till they comprehended the catechism and on feast-days in church there should be a fine imposed for each time that Arabic was spoken.[1] In 1695 Bishop Perez of Segorbe, in response to a demand for a report on the situation, included among his suggestions the employment of priests familiar with the language and he met the opposition to this by citing the examples of Talavera and Ayala.[2] There appears about this time to have been considerable discussion of a project to establish a chair of Arabic in the University of Valencia. Those who advocated it urged that the Council of Vienne, in 1312, ordered Arabic to be taught in Rome, Bologna, Paris, Oxford and Salamanca; that St. Ramon de Peñafort had obtained from the Dominican General permission that friars should be instructed in it and that schools were opened in Murcia and Tunis with the aid of the kings of Castile and Aragon; that the preachers thus trained had converted more than ten thousand Moors and that Gregory XIII. had established in Rome a press for printing in Hebrew, Greek, Latin and Arabic which the popes maintained at great expense. They further pointed out that, as the Moors believed the Koran to be the word of God, those who were unacquainted with it had no chance of winning them over, for they believed that if it were studied its truth would be recognized; they also had many books in Arabic controverting Christianity and these could only be met by those who were familiar with the tongue and the dogmas of the Moors. All this seems

[1] Ximenez, Vida de Ribera, pp. 365-7.

[2] Archivo de Simancas, *loc. cit.*

too plain to admit of refutation, but on the other hand it was argued that it would take too long; besides there was Fray Juan de Puegentos with his disciples and many others who preached to them in Arabic without success, and further that in Aragon the Moriscos had nearly forgotten their ancestral tongue while those of Castile had wholly abandoned it and they were as impenetrably heretic as those of Valencia. These arguments were successful, Philip decided against the professorship, and ordered that Morisco children should be taught the vernacular.[1] There is a world of significance in the scorn with which Fray Bleda tells us that, in the junta of 1604, there were people who even urged that it would be serviceable if the preachers would learn Arabic.[2]

Another method, which seems based on common sense, was to bring about a fusion of the races by mingling them together. The Morerías, or separate quarters in the towns, divided by a wall under the legislation of Ferdinand and Isabella, still existed and the Moriscos thus dwelt apart from the Christians. If this could be broken up not only would they be exposed to Christian influences but it would be much easier to keep them under supervision and punish them for backsliding. The earliest suggestion that I have met with as to this occurs in 1515, when the Inquisitor Enzinas, during a visit to Ágreda, ordered that thirty or forty of the baptized Moriscos should live in the town and as many Old Christians be transferred to the Mota or Morería. The municipal authorities appealed to Ferdinand, representing that to accomplish this the gate of the Mota would have to be

[1] Fonseca, pp. 346–60.—Danvila, p. 230.
[2] Bleda, Crónica, p. 883.

left open and another gate be opened so as to make a street connecting the quarters. This Ferdinand refused to sanction and suggested that those to be moved, both New and Old Christians, should be persons who have no houses of their own.[1] During the baptismal process in Valencia the Inquisition took a different view and, when the aljama of Albarracin was converted, the inquisitors arbitrarily issued an edict forbidding all Moors to enter the city, in order to prevent all intercourse between the unconverted and the neophytes. This worked great hardship on the citizens as it deprived them of the supplies which the Moors were accustomed to bring, and as the city was a place of transit it prevented Moors from passing through, wherefore Charles, March 4, 1526, asked the inquisitors to relax their edict in so far as to allow travelling Moors to pass two days and nights inside the city wall, but not to enter that of the Morería.[2] In 1528 the córtes of Castile saw the unwisdom of keeping the races apart and petitioned that the Moors should be obliged to live among Christians to facilitate their conversion.[3]

On the other hand, in this same year, 1528, the concordia between the Inquisition and the Moriscos of Valencia provided that the independent organizations of the latter in the royal cities, such as Valencia, Játiva, Castellon de la Plana, etc., should be preserved,[4] but in 1529

[1] Archivo de Simancas, Inquisicion, Libro 3, fol. 427 ; Libro 927, fol. 276.

[2] Ibid. Libro 927, fol. 284.

[3] Colmeiro, Córtes de los antiguos Reinos de Leon y de Castilla, II. 155.

[4] Danvila, p. 105.

Charles changed his policy; he wrote to all the corregidores and Manrique to all the inquisitors, ordering them to consult together and also with representatives of the Moriscos as to the best means of removing the latter from their *barrios* or Morerías, in order to facilitate their conversion without inflicting too great inconvenience and loss on them, and the result of these deliberations was to be submitted to the Suprema.[1]

Like so much else in this unhappy business of perpetual consultations and non-action little or nothing came of this. It is true that Inquisitor-general Valdés, in a letter to Charles V. November 5, 1549, says that the experiment had been tried in various places with happy results,[2] but the almost insuperable difficulties attending it are seen in the attempt made in Valladolid, where, in 1541, it had been proposed to tear down the wall of separation and throw open the *barrio* of the Moriscos. This involved the destruction of certain houses, the value of which was appraised at 3000 ducats and, in 1542, the city agreed to defray one-third, another third was to be obtained by assessing benefits on property that would be improved, while the Inquisition promised to furnish the other third out of fines to be imposed on Moriscos coming in under an Edict of Grace. The matter then rested until 1549, when the work of demolition commenced, but the house owners resisted; in the squabble two officials of the Inquisition were arrested by the alcaldes de corte (the court at that time was residing in Valladolid) and for this insult the tribunal vainly clamored for satisfaction. The work was suspended indefinitely and when, October 8, 1549, Valdés calmly

[1] Archivo de Simancas, *loc. cit.* fol. 277.

[2] Ibid. Libro 13, fol. 306.

ordered that Old and New Christians should occupy alternate houses, the Suprema replied to him November 18th with a report of the whole affair. It also wrote to the emperor, then in Germany, November 7th and December 23d. The position was simply that the Inquisition was asked to advance the whole 3000 ducats and take its chances of collecting the 2000. The Suprema declined; it had not money enough to pay its salaries and if it should borrow the amount the prospects of recovery were too vague to justify the risk; besides it demanded as a condition precedent satisfaction for the arrest of its officials.[1] How the matter terminated we have no means of knowing, but it is fairly safe to assume that the Moriscos were left undisturbed in their barrio until the final expulsion. In 1572 Philip II. recurred to the idea and ordered the Moriscos to live among Old Christians in order that they could be watched and denounced to the Inquisition, but no attention seems to have been paid to the commands,[2] and I have met with no trace of further efforts in this direction.

In his letter of October 8, 1849, to the Inquisitors of Valladolid, Valdés made a valuable suggestion in the same line by ordering them to encourage intermarriage in every way; the dower which a Morisca bride may bring to an Old Christian should never be subject to confiscation, and it should be the same with the property possessed by a Morisco at the time of his marriage with a Christian.[3] Unfortunately fanaticism could not endure such liberality; in 1603 Archbishop Ribera boasted that he never granted licences for such marriages as the Christian spouse was apt to be perverted, and Bleda devotes a whole section to

[1] Ibid. Libro 4, fol. 183; Libro 79, fol. 43, 51. [2] Fonseca, p. 71.

[3] Archivo de Simancas, Inquisicion, Libro 4, fol. 183.

proving that they ought to be prohibited.[1] Valdés further ordered that instructors should be appointed, to teach the Moriscos and their children, whose salaries should be paid in such wise as the inquisitors should determine. The question of payment was solved by the thrifty bishops of Valencia who sent *doctrineros*, or catechizers through their sees at wages of two reales per diem, to be paid by the Moriscos in addition to all their other burdens of tithes and oblations.[2]

We have seen the fluctuating policy adopted with regard to confiscations and the occasional suspension of the Inquisition. This had the vice inherent in all uncertain lines of action, for temporary leniency only increased exasperation when severity was resumed. Yet it was explicable by the hope persistently entertained that the perpetual efforts at so-called instruction would prove successful in spite of the fact, which should have been self-evident, that the whole machinery, however honestly devised, was in the hands of those whose only object was to make what they could out of the oppressed race. The Spanish statesmen had a duty to perform of tremendous import and complexity and they earnestly sought to discharge it according to their imperfect lights, but their efforts were neutralized by the greedy and self-seeking hands to which the most delicate and responsible functions were of necessity confided. The extent of self-deception of which they were the victims is seen in the repeated efforts to gather in a harvest of true converts as the fruit

[1] Guadalajara y Xavierr, fol. 90.—Bledæ Defensio Fidei, pp. 359–63.

[2] Archivo de Simancas, Inquisicion de Valencia, Leg. 205, fol. 3.

of the work which they supposed to be going on. To do this it was necessary to remit the penalties which the Church imposed on its erring children who sought to return to its bosom, as we have seen tentatively essayed in the brief of Clement VII., June 16, 1525 (p. 17). A more regular method was through the Edicts of Grace, which specified a term during which the heretic and apostate could come forward, confess and be reconciled under lightened conditions. The Inquisition had power at all times to publish such edicts in the ordinary form, but something more was desirable in this case and a remarkable series of papal briefs was procured which manifest an earnest desire on the part of the government to win over the Moriscos, although the rulers were too blind to see that what they regarded as leniency was sufficiently deterrent to neutralize the attraction.

The first of these briefs, granted by Clement VII., July 7, 1527, recited that the converts, through the absence of their bishops, the negligence of their priests and the lack of instruction, had relapsed into their errors; that Charles, desirous to show mercy, had decided that apostates could, within a term to be named, confess secretly to persons deputed by Manrique and be absolved *in utroque foro*, without public penance and without confiscation, wherefore Clement confirms this and, for abundant caution, empowers priests appointed by Manrique and his successors to absolve *in utroque foro* even for crimes reserved to the Holy See, to impose salutary penance and to restore them to baptismal innocence.[1]

[1] Bulario de la Orden de Santiago, Libro II. fol. 67 (Archivo Hist. Nacional).

It was soon found, however, that something more than even this was required. The New Christians were apt to regard absolution, whether thus obtained or through formal reconciliation or abjuration *de vehementi* in the Inquisition, as merely a licence to resume their old ways, thus committing the crime of relapse which was unpardonable under the canon law. For the relapsed the Church had no mercy; they might save their souls by craving readmission to her bosom and she did not deny them the sacraments, but their bodies were irrevocably committed to the flames.[1] The Inquisition had rightfully no power to remit this penalty and a specially delegated papal faculty was requisite to prevent the number of victims consigned to the stake from outweighing all the fair promises of benignity and moderation. The earliest delegation of this kind that I have met with occurs in a brief of Clement VII. December 2, 1530, empowering Manrique, as long as he is inquisitor-general, to appoint confessors with power to absolve penitents, even if they have relapsed repeatedly, with secret absolution and penance and to release them and their descendants from all penalties, disabilities and confiscations, the reason alleged for this mercy being the lack of priests in the Morisco districts to instruct the converts in the faith.[2] If, on Manrique's death, this power was conferred on his successor Tavera,

[1] Cap. 4, 8, in Sexto, v. 2.

[2] Archivo de Simancas, Inquisicion, Libro 926, fol. 57.—Bulario de la Orden de Santiago, Libro II. fol. 79.—It was not until 1535 that Manrique transmitted this to the inquisitors of Valencia, with orders to execute it (Ibid. fol. 80) but it does not seem to have exercised much influence on the number of burnings (p. 98).

the brief would seem not to have been preserved, and then followed the suspension, in 1546, of the operations of the Inquisition. At length, in 1556, Paul IV. conferred the same powers on Inquisitor-general Valdés which Pius IV. repeated in 1561,[1] and we have seen (p. 102) that Valdés promptly delegated them to the Archbishop of Valencia and his ordinary. Then, in 1565, the briefs take a somewhat different shape. One of August 25th from Pius IV. to Valdés recites that the latter had represented that dread of inquisitorial penalties led many to escape to Africa wherefore the pope authorizes him to publish a term of grace for a year, during which those who come forward and confess may be absolved, even if they have repeatedly relapsed, and moreover if those now absolved shall hereafter relapse

1 Archivo de Simancas, Inquisicion, Libro 926, fol. 49, 53.—Bulario de la Orden de Santiago, Libro III. fol. 51, 85.—Archivo de Alcalá, Hacienda, Legajo 1049.

In 1556, when an active effort was made in Aragon to win over the Moriscos and the inquisitors were ordered to visit the whole kingdom and proclaim an edict of grace, Valdés claims that under the brief he has all the powers of his predecessor Manrique. He points out however that this only extends to relapsed converts and not to their descendants. Application for this will be made to Rome and until it comes such cases must be suspended.—Archivo de Simancas, Inquisicion, Libro 4, fol. 220-1. The briefs of 1556 and 1561 include descendants.

There was the odor of lucre about this. An assessment was made on the Moriscos who took advantage of the grace and in three months 8000 sueldos had been collected. The term was for six months, and on its expiration an extension of three months was granted for the benefit of those who should obligate themselves to pay the assessment imposed on them of the sum offered by the new converts for the maintenance of the Holy Office.—Ibid. fol. 222.

they can be reconciled without punishment, even pecuniary, or relaxation, or, if it be thought best, fines can be imposed for the ornamentation of their churches or for the Christian poor. Pius IV. died, December 9th, and his successor, Pius V., August 25, 1567, renewed the provision with the condition that the edict be published within six months, that it should give a term of not less than three years during which penitents could come in and that there should be no pecuniary penalties. Valdés, however, was now incapacitated by old age; Espinosa was appointed as his deputy with the reversion of the office, and to him Pius repeated the brief, September 6th.[1]

Possibly questions may have arisen as to the interpretation of these faculties for the next brief, issued August 6, 1574, to Inquisitor-general Quiroga, is more explicit. It recites that Quiroga had represented that there were Moriscos punished and reconciled by the Inquisition who yet, as rustics and imperfectly instructed, had relapsed and now ask for penance which cannot be granted without special licence, wherefore the pope authorizes him to empower the inquisitors to absolve them with secret or public abjuration and penance, and without confiscation or disabilities for themselves or their descendants. This was exceedingly liberal, as it imposed no limitation of time and might apply to prisoners on trial, but when it was repeated by Sixtus V., January 25, 1588, to Quiroga it required him to publish a term of grace during which

[1] Archivo de Simancas, Inquisicion, Libro 926, fol. 63, 67.—Bulario de la Orden de Santiago, Libro III. fol. 88, 109.—Archivo de Alcalá, Hacienda, Legajo 1049.

it should operate and excluded all who were under arrest.[1] When Clement VIII., May 31, 1593 renewed the grant to Quiroga he limited its duration to three years and extended its operation to prisoners on trial and after condemnation to relaxation or the galleys or exile or imprisonment, all of which could be commuted to public or private penance, not pecuniary; confiscations could be restored to them and all disabilities for themselves and their descendants be removed. This was the most comprehensive grant made as yet and before its expiration Philip II., in 1595, applied for its extension, which was doubtless granted.[2]

I have recited these briefs thus in detail because they are the most impressive evidence of a desire on the part of the government to mitigate the most odious feature of the canon law against heresy and to avoid driving the Moriscos to desperation. In themselves they made little difference in the situation. The edicts of grace, with which they were mostly connected, brought few or no penitents to come forward and denounce themselves and their kindred by confessions which were reduced to writing and remained of record against all concerned. Nevertheless it is a fact that during the latter half of the century the number of burnings fell off, while that of the trials, as we have seen, fluctuated with a tendency to increase.[3]

[1] Archivo de Simancas, Inquisicion, Libro 926, fol. 59.—Bulario de la Orden de Santiago, Libro IV. fol. 24, 103.

[2] Bulario de la Orden de Santiago, Libro IV. fol. 112.—Danvila, p. 228.

[3] The number of burnings in Valencia as shown by the record (Archivo Hist. Nacional, Inq^{n} de Valencia, Legajo 300) is as follows. It

Forty years had elapsed since the portentous brief of Clement VII. ordered the enforced baptism of the Moriscos when, in 1564, the córtes of Monzon called the attention of Philip II. to the failure of all the plans for instructing the converts, who were punished for their ignorance. The work had still to be done and the córtes petitioned that 3000 ducats more should be appropriated from episcopal revenues for the endowment of rectories and churches which should be supervised watchfully by the episcopal Ordinaries and that the whole matter should be exclusively under the control of the bishops and archbishop. Philip promised to consult the inquisitor-general and in December a junta met under the presidency of Valdés, the conclusions of which were embodied in a royal cédula. The business of instruction was confided to the bishops in their respective dioceses, who should appoint proper persons for that purpose and send commissioners to see to its performance. These were to treat the Moriscos with the utmost kindness, to punish those who insulted them, to reward the good according to their

will be borne in mind that this register is incomplete and that an addition of about 25 per cent. should be allowed for.

1544	3	1557	none	1570	none	1583	5
1545	3	1558	none	1571	1	1584	2
1546	none	1559	none	1572	5	1585	none
1547	none	1560	none	1573	3	1586	5
1548	none	1561	none	1574	7	1587	none
1549	none	1562	none	1575	3	1588	none
1550	none	1563	6	1576	3	1589	none
1551	none	1564	5	1577	5	1590	4
1552	none	1565	none	1578	4	1591	none
1553	1	1566	3	1579	1	1592	10
1554	15	1567	4	1580	none	1593	5
1555	none	1568	2	1581	2		
1556	none	1569	none	1582	none		

deserts and the leading ones were to be made familiars of the Inquisition. The use of Arabic was forbidden and schools were to be established for teaching the vernacular; alguaziles and officials were to be appointed under the protection of the Inquisition; the nobles who permitted their vassals to practise Moorish rites were to be punished. How little had yet been accomplished is seen in the clause ordering the mosques to be converted into churches and the books, trumpets and instruments to be removed. The baths in Valencia were to be placed in charge of Old Christians and no bathing was to be permitted on feast-days.[1]

The most striking feature in all this is its recognition that nothing had yet been done and that the work had to be commenced anew under different auspices. The conciliatory spirit manifested was admirable and might have proved effective, even at that late day, if the perpetual irritation of the Inquisition could have been suppressed and if the execution of the plan could have been confided to honest, zealous and capable hands. The spirit in which the bishops undertook the duties entrusted to them is seen in a provincial council assembled by Archbishop Ayala on his return from the junta. This body busied itself, not with plans for instructing the Moriscos and furnishing the necessary funds, but with imposing heavy fines on those who did not have their children baptized immediately at birth and in the best clothes they could furnish, on alfaquíes who visited the sick and on secular officials who did not denounce any Moorish observances—even the Zambras and Leilas, or songs and

[1] Danvila, pp. 167-71.—Bledæ Defensio Fidei, p. 192.

performances customary in wedding festivities. The pious hope is expressed that by compelling them to attend church on Ash Wednesday, Maundy Thursday, Good Friday and All Saints they may be attracted to Christian worship, and their salvation is cared for by ordering them when dying to instruct their heirs to give something for the benefit of their souls, in default of which the heirs must at least have three masses sung for them.[1]

The conciliatory policy confided to narrow-minded and greedy churchmen such as these was not likely to win over the Moriscos or to make much progress in their instruction. We hear nothing of the 3000 ducats which the córtes of Monzon had considered essential for the dotation of rectories, and in 1570 the Suprema, in sending de Soto Salazar as visitor to Valencia, instructed him to find out why nothing had as yet been done to carry out the plans of the junta of 1564.[2] In 1567 Ayala had been succeeded by Loazes, who issued some new instructions framed in conjunction with the other bishops of the kingdom, but in a year the see was again vacant and was filled by Juan de Ribera, Patriarch of Antioch, who held it for forty-three years and was an efficient agent in the final catastrophe—a service tardily recognized by his beatification in 1796. We are told that he addressed himself earnestly to the work; heedless of comfort, and of safety, he personally visited every part of his extensive and rugged see, many portions of which had never seen a prelate; he disputed with the alfaquíes and made himself familiar with the necessities of the situation. In a long memorial

[1] Aguirre Concil. Hispan. V. 415, 419, 432.

[2] Archivo de Simancas, Inquisicion, Libro 13, fol. 371

addressed to Philip he deplored the deficiency of churches and rectors owing to the inadequate salaries paid, which was the chief cause of the long ill-success in the conversion. He had built churches and increased salaries; he had promised the Moriscos a suspension of the Inquisition, and if, after all this preparation, nothing is done they will be more obstinate than ever. Spiritual remedies must be accompanied with temporal pressure, and this he asked the king to apply and also to order the Bishops of Orihuela, Tortosa and Segorbe to co-operate, for thus far they had done nothing.[1] That Ribera's well-meant efforts should have proved useless is perhaps explained by the account given by a well-informed contemporary, who tells us that he held a meeting with the bishops of Orihuela and Tortosa (the see of Segorbe was vacant from 1575 to 1578) who resolved that the stipends of the rectors were insufficient, as there were no offerings at the altar, wherefore many abandoned their positions and it was necessary to take whomsoever could be got, who were mostly ignorant and of indifferent character. It was therefore resolved to increase the number of churches and raise the salary to a hundred crowns, which was duly confirmed by the pope. The king contributed three thousand ducats a year, besides the pension levied on the archbishopric, but so many difficulties sprang up that the salaries were not raised and the revenue accumulated

[1] Ximenez, Vida de Juan de Ribera, pp. 61–2, 347–52.

The winning character of Ribera's missionary work is illustrated by a prophecy attributed to one of his preachers, the Bishop of Sidonia, in a sermon on April 14, 1578, the natal day of Philip III.—"Since you will not eradicate from your hardened hearts this infernal and cursed sect of Mahomet, know that to-day is born the prince who will drive you from Spain."—Guadalajara y Xavierr, fol. 60.

greatly, so that eventually 60,000 ducats were taken to increase the income of the college for Moriscos in Valencia and 40,000 for a new seminary for women and children.[1] As usual, the money question dominated and the mission-work came to naught.

If the oblations at the altar were lacking the priests had another mode of increasing their stipends which was the source of great discontent. The council of Toledo in 1582 instructs all priests to make lists of their Morisco parishioners over five years of age; on every Sunday and feast-day he is to call this roll and fine all absentees, dividing the result between himself, the sacristan and the fabric of the Church.[2] In 1584 the Venetian envoy Gradenigo says that they prefer to pay rather than attend church, which may have been the case with the well-to-do, but Leonardo Donato attributes the rebellion of Granada largely to this and the other vexations inflicted on them by their priests, not from religious zeal but from greed.[3]

Still the endless ineffectual work went on. In 1586 Philip resolved on another effort to convert the converts and as usual he called a junta to devise the means. This and a successor met and deliberated and recommended that resolutions adopted in 1573 should be put into execution. There was a bustle of consultation with the bishops and viceroy of Valencia, public prayers were

[1] Fonseca, p. 28.

[2] Concil. Toletan. ann. 1582, Decr. 48 (Aguirre, VI. 14).

[3] Relazioni Venete, Serie I. Tom. V. p. 392; Tom. VI. p. 408.—Archbishop Ayala endeavored to suppress the observance of the Ramadan and other Moorish fasts by ordering the secular officials to watch for it and fine all delinquents two crowns.—Fonseca, p. 54.

ordered for the success of the attempt and, in a final consulta of January 30, 1588, Philip was advised that rectors should be provided for all the Morisco villages, that endowments for them should be had from the episcopal and capitular revenues and from the tithes of the villages, that the business of instruction should be pushed and in order that this might have a better chance, that a papal brief for an edict of grace be procured.[1] We have seen that Sixtus V. and Clement VIII. made no difficulty in granting the amplest faculties of pardon, but when it came to action the customary paralysis benumbed the effort and nothing was accomplished.

In 1595, Philip convened another junta to continue the consideration of the eternal question as to the instruction of the Moriscos. It was doubtless for the enlightenment of this body that reports were called for from the Valencian bishops, of which that of the learned Juan Bautista Perez, Bishop of Segorbe, reviews the whole question thoroughly and says the more he thinks of it the more difficulties it presents, for all efforts thus far have been fruitless. He enumerates fifteen impediments to the conversion of the Moriscos—their ignorance, deceit and fanatic obstinacy, their living apart and by themselves, their ignorance of the vernacular, the tradition of the violent baptism of their forefathers, their fear of the Inquisition and its punishments which make them hate religion,

[1] Danvila, pp. 214-16.—Fonseca, p. 32.

Bishop Perez of Segorbe explains that Ribera sought to raise the salaries of the rectors to 100 crowns by a pension on his table and the tithes of the canonries and of the lords, but though this was confirmed by the pope at the request of the king, it never took effect, owing to the appeals interjected.—Archivo de Simancas, Inq^{n} de Valencia, Leg. 205, fol. 3.

the fact that when some really wish to be converted and confess the priest cannot absolve them, as heresy is reserved to the inquisitors to whom nothing will induce them to go, the favor shown to them by the nobles for the heavy imposts they pay, and lastly, if the truth must be told, there are not enough rectors who can reside and instruct them, for they only go on Sundays and feast-days. The salary ought to be 100 ducats and a house, and power should be obtained from the pope to effect this summarily and without appeal from the parties affected. The poverty of the rectories arises from the tithes having been given to the lords and to canons and other dignitaries of the churches. Then some monasteries, which had acquired the revenues of many of them, obtained in 1567 from Pius V. a *motu proprio* fixing at fifty crowns a year the *portio congrua* which they were obliged to leave to the rectories;[1] and in this they included all uncertain emoluments. Only ignorant priests would accept this beggarly stipend and these could not reside; some of them brought suits against the canons and others, but ecclesiastical suits are interminable. The bishops cannot compel them to residence, knowing that they cannot live on the stipend. The Moriscos never summon them, even when dying, although there is a penalty for dying without a priest, for they always prove by witnesses that the death was sudden. There are many wise men, he adds, who hold that the failure to instruct the Moriscos is only a question of money. The colleges founded in Valencia and Tortosa have had no result; only three or four per-

[1] This is the bull *Ad exequendum*, Nov. 25, 1567 (Bullar. Roman. II. 259). It names from 50 to 100 crowns a year as the *portio congrua*, and the monasteries naturally took the benefit of the minimum.

sons of consideration have issued from that of Valencia and they have preferred to live in the city on their benefices rather than to preach among their people; the rest return home to labor and presumably are as much Moors as before.[1]

Such was the condition of the Morisco question after seventy years of striving, in which the designs, more or less sagacious, of the rulers had been wrecked by the supineness, the greed and the corruption of those whose duty it was to save the hundreds of thousands of souls confided to their charge, to say nothing of the overwhelming political interests involved. Bishop Perez may be taken as an unexceptionable witness, for he was not only a remarkably intelligent prelate—as shown by his exposure of the forgeries of the *plomos del Sacro Monte*—but he was by no means inclined to favor the Moriscos and did not hesitate to recommend greater severity on the part of the Inquisition and to suggest expulsion if all other means failed.

Politically the question was becoming year by year more pressing as the alternative of real conversion or of expulsion presented itself ever more strongly to Spanish statesmen as inevitable. During the whole of 1595 and a great part of 1596 a junta sat, engaged in interminable debates and submitting conflicting opinions to the king, according to the fashion in which Philip carried on his

[1] Archivo de Simancas, Inqn de Valencia, Leg. 205, fol. 3.

A similar report was presented by Bishop Esteban of Orihuela. He recommends a reduction of the exactions of the lords, greater activity by the prelates and priests, the establishment of schools, greater restrictions and disabilities on the Moriscos and then, if within a given term they were not converted, they should all be reduced to slavery and be scattered throughout Spain.—Danvila, p. 229.

government. On December 20th petitions were discussed, presented by the aljamas, complaining that they were not instructed owing to the negligence of the prelates and rectors and asking that proper persons be sent, the existing ones being simple ignorant clerics, mostly foreigners and Frenchmen. This was promptly followed, December 24th, by a royal decree ordering Archbishop Ribera to fill the rectories at once with the best appointees he could find and that the Bishops of Segorbe, Tortosa and Orihuela should immediately erect and endow the rectories in their dioceses so that the work of instruction might commence promptly and preachers be sent through all the bishoprics—provisions the importance of which consists in the evidence they give of how little rational work had been done in christianizing the Moriscos since the edict of 1525.[1]

Interminable debates followed as to whether the matter should be entrusted to one supreme commissioner or whether each bishopric should have its own, and what should be their functions and powers; also as to the sources from which the dotations of the rectories and the pay of the preachers should be drawn, together with numerous other details. Everybody had a different opinion and the king, in place of deciding, asked to be advised about the respective opinions—a perfectly finished example of the most elaborate methods which human wit has devised of how not to do it.[2] The wearied old mon-

[1] Danvila, pp. 230-1.

[2] This perpetual discussion and irresolution was not the least of the causes contributing to the decay of the Spanish monarchy. Introduced by Philip II., it continued to the last of the Hapsburgs; the diminishing resources of the nation were frittered away for lack of vigorous action at critical moments by a government combining the

arch was breaking down; he died, September 13, 1598, busy to the last with plans to pay for the rectories out of the balance of the funds which had been accumulating for twenty years and with endeavoring to persuade Clement VIII. to reconsider his refusal of a brief which should exempt the Moriscos from the obligation to denounce their accomplices, for without this there could be no hope of voluntary conversions.[1] As we have seen, no priest could absolve for heresy and admit to reconciliation, while to the inquisitor a confession was fictitious and invalid which did not contain full information about all the heretics known to the convert. The rules of the Church demanded this, however impassable was the obstacle which it erected in the path of the returning sinner. It is true that, at the request of the king, Clement had granted, February 28, 1597, an edict of grace covering relapse, and had conceded that confession could be made to the episcopal Ordinaries, but he had insisted that the confession must include full denunciation of the apostasy of others.[2]

peculiar and seemingly irreconcilable vices of autocracy and bureaucracy. It is well described by a contemporary—"Con semejante lentitud se desatendió siempre en todo el gobierno de Phelipe segundo á las mayores urgencias, empleando el tiempo que debiera lograrse en prevenir los peligros para evitarles con providencia en consultas prolixas y en informes inutiles, no creyendo nunca á quien los prevenia, aumentando los gastos despues la morosidad de sus resoluciones."—Historia de la Casa de Mondéjar (Morel-Fatio, L'Espagne au XVIe et au XVIIe Siècle, p. 69).

These perpetual delays were the despair of the foreign diplomats at the Spanish court. See the despatch of the Nuncio Sega, March 1, 1578, in Hinojosa, *Los Despachos de la Diplomacia Pontificia*, I. 243 (Madrid, 1896).

[1] Danvila, p. 232.

[2] Bulario de la Orden de Santiago, Libro IV. fol. 128.—Archivo de Simancas, Inquisicion, Libro 926, fol. 71. (See Appendix No. IX.)

The Junta, which by this time was a virtually perpetual body, though with varying membership, and in full control of the Morisco question, continued to report to Rome that the trouble arose from the avarice of the bishops and the evil example of the priests, and that the Moriscos sinned because there was no one to instruct them.[1] Archbishop Ribera, in 1602, argued on the other hand that it was because they were determined not to learn, in support of which he adduced the evidence of the inquisitors who would keep them in prison for two or three years, teaching them on every feast-day, yet they would be discharged without knowing a word of Christian doctrine, and he tells us that the aljamas publicly reprehended their syndics at the court for asking for a term of delay in which they could be instructed.[2]

Still, whatever were his convictions, Ribera had not refused his co-operation in another vigorously futile attempt to instruct and convert, with which Philip III. inaugurated his reign. A new edict of grace had been applied for from Clement, and in preparation for it, in 1599, Ribera held in Valencia a provincial council, at which assisted the royal confessor, Gaspar de Córdova, and the Licentiate Sebastian de Covarrubias, for the purpose of organizing instruction, which was to commence forthwith. Rectors and preachers were to be appointed and money provided to pay for them, the catechism was to be printed, the inquisitors were to name commissioners and the barons were to found schools with teachers where all children between 7 and 12 were to be taught; Ribera was to borrow 60,000 ducats for the college of Valencia

[1] Bleda, Crónica, p. 882.

[2] Ximenez, Vida de Ribera, p. 386.

and the viceroys and their wives were to take charge of a hermandad or confraternity to place the daughters of Moriscos in convents and houses of Old Christians.[1] All the work which had been so fruitlessly attempted so many times was commenced anew as if nothing had yet been tried.

The eagerly expected papal brief was duly received, addressed as usual to the inquisitor-general and the subdelegation of his powers was necessarily made to the Valencian inquisitors. August 6, 1599, Philip III. forwarded to them these powers in a letter in which he congratulated himself that the labors and expenditure of his father and his own have at last borne fruit in instructing the converts; the great difficulties were overcome and nothing more was needed but the publication of the edict and the appointment of commissioners in each of the dioceses. The edict was only a repetition of those which we have seen so repeatedly issued with such nullity of result. It granted only the term of one year, it excepted those who were under arrest, it gave power to absolve for relapse, and though it exempted from all punishment those who voluntarily came forward and confessed, it required the confession to include all those of whose errors the penitent was cognizant. It was duly published August 22d in the cathedral of Valencia, and on April 28, 1600, in view of the approaching expiration of the term, Inquisitor-general Guevara extended it to February 28, 1601. Philip awaited the result and on

[1] Danvila, p. 241. For Ribera's instructions to the priests and preachers, see Ximenez, pp. 352–64. He is emphatic in ordering them to make it clear to the Moriscos that they cannot evade denouncing their accomplices to the Inquisition (p. 360).

July 24th and 27th he wrote to the inquisitors of Valencia for a report and an opinion as to the advisability of applying to the pope for an extension of the term. August 22d the inquisitors replied. During the eighteen months of the edict, they said, only thirteen persons had presented themselves to take advantage of it and these had made such fallacious confessions and had so protected their accomplices that they deserved condemnation rather than absolution; some of them had already been denounced to the Inquisition, so that they evidently came from fear rather than from conversion. On the general mass the effect had been that they regarded it as giving licence to sin with liberty and scandal, fasting the Ramadan without pretence of concealment. The experience of this tribunal had long been, and was now more than ever, that few or none of those reconciled told the truth or were converted in heart. Their lords and their priests and all who have converse with them say that they are and always will be Moors if God does not enlighten them with special mercy; they do not desire instruction; if they go to mass, it is only to escape the penalty of absence and when there they behave carelessly and contemptuously and turn away their eyes at the elevation of the host. Therefore there is no result to be expected from the royal mercy, and if the Inquisition does not convert them it at least forces them to act with less publicity and thus diminishes the evil which they do to Christians.[1] If the Edict of Grace had been a failure

[1] Archivo Hist. Nacional, Inqn de Valencia, Legajo 5, fol. 185, 186, 220, 295, 297–99. (See Appendix No. X.)—Bledæ Defensio Fidei, p. 468.

It was customarily said that but one person came forward to claim

this was not for lack of inquisitorial industry on those who hesitated to avail themselves of it, for a record of the tribunal of Valencia from January, 1598, to December, 1602, shows that out of a total of 392 cases, 194 were of Moriscos.[1]

This hopeless view of the situation taken by the inquisitors was confirmed by the reports of the bishops, who expatiated at length on the earnest zeal of their labors and their liberal expenditure in the endeavor to render the edict of grace effective. All concurred in stating that nothing had been accomplished and Ribera towards the end of 1601 and beginning of 1602 addressed to Philip two vigorous memorials to prove that the evil was irremediable without the most decisive measures.[2]

the benefit of the edict (Danvila, p. 242) which was epigrammatic but not exact.

[1] Ibid. Legajo 99.—From June 30, 1602, to September 5, 1604, there were but 30 cases in all, of which 17 were of Moriscos.—Ibid. Legajo 2, MS. 7.

In comparison with all this active work in Valencia it is worthy of remark that, in 1597, Inquisitor Heredia of Barcelona made a visitation of the province of Tarragona and parts of the sees of Barcelona, Vich and Urgel. His report of his labors includes eighty-eight cases, among which there is but a single one of a Morisco and with him it was for going to Algiers in a Moorish vessel.—Archivo de Simancas, Inquisicion, Visitas de Barcelona, Leg. 15, fol. 4.

[2] Fonseca, pp. 35-9.—Ximenez, Vida de Ribera, pp. 367, 376.

Bleda says (Defensio Fidei, pp. 96-7) that the bishops of Orihuela and Segorbe were at first deceived by the professed readiness for conversion of the Moriscos and their letters greatly encouraged Philip, but they subsequently learned the truth. The Bishop of Segorbe, he tells us, was particularly won by the zeal of a convert named Miguel Xavari and proposed to admit him to communion on Corpus Christi day, which falls on the Thursday after Trinity Sunday, but his chapter persuaded him to defer it. The next day (Friday) one of his officials chanced to visit the convert's house and found six or eight *ollas* cooking enough

Doubtless it was so by this time. For seventy years everything had been done to render Christianity odious and its ministers hated or despised. The most solemn promises had been violated in the name of religion and under its cloak for generations the Moriscos had known only persecution and oppression. It is one of the mysteries of human intelligence that men, learned, acute, and trained in philosophy and statecraft could be so blinded by their conviction of laboring in the cause of God that they persistently threw the blame on the Moriscos for perversity, obstinacy and hardness of heart. Ribera had a glimmering of this when, in his instructions to the preachers whom he sent out, he told them that the task was difficult but not impossible, for they had to deal with people who hated them for the difference of race, for the perpetual discord between Moors and Christians, and for the lack of charity with which they were treated, so that it is a proverb among them that they are regarded as slaves; besides, they are hardened in the heresy which they have inherited from their forefathers. But Ribera cannot resist adding an allusion to the Devil who seeks to render it impossible for them to learn Christianity, and it does not occur to him to couple the Inquisition with Satan as an efficient agent.[1]

In spite of this discouragement, Philip made a new effort along the old lines. In 1604 the córtes of Valencia demanded that the fifty-five rectories still lacking of

meat for the whole aljama; he summoned the people and on ransacking the house some eight or ten volumes of the Koran were discovered in a locked chest. Miguel was the alfaquí of the place; he escaped and went to Mecca.

[1] Ximenez, Vida de Ribera, pp. 356-7.

the 129 decreed in 1572 should be endowed. Philip sent Canon Francisco de Quesada as a special agent to Rome where he obtained from Paul V. a brief, March 6, 1606, revoking three letters of Clement VIII. and confirming one of Gregory XIII. in favor of 190 rectories in the archbishopric, of twenty in Segorbe, of twenty in Tortosa and of eleven in Orihuela. The chapters were required by the pope, against their previous refusal, to grant pensions on the tithes, and rectors were to be sent to all the Moorish villages. Ribera, we are told, had always paid his quota; the Bishop of Tortosa now agreed to furnish 400 ducats a year for the support of the new rectories and the Bishop of Segorbe promised to do his share but questions arose which prevented a settlement. The money difficulty, which had from the beginning been the impediment to the carrying out of all plans, seemed at last to be reaching a solution. To render these exertions effective Philip instructed Quesada to procure a brief ordering the Valencian bishops to meet in consultation. It was dated May 11, 1606, and required Ribera to assemble his colleagues and discuss the best means of conversion and report their conclusions to him, and it especially urged the importance of providing endowments for the churches and seminaries, a matter which was represented as the chief object of the conference in the letters addressed to the several bishops. It was not however until April 6, 1608, that Philip forwarded these briefs to the bishops, who did not assemble until October, when they spent four months in deliberations, the result of which they duly forwarded to the king, being principally that a new edict of grace should be procured during which instruction should be carried on, and the Inquisition be suspended, the money question being prudently evaded.[1] It mattered little what their conclusions were. The anxieties of the rulers of Spain were growing too acute to permit much longer delay, and, as the all-powerful Duke of Lerma said, instruction was useless but it must be kept up in order to blind the Moriscos to the preparations for sterner measures which were in progress.[2]

To appreciate those anxieties it is necessary for us to take a glance at the secular aspects of the Morisco question and the position which the New Christians occupied amid the surrounding populations.

[1] Danvila, pp. 263–4, 270–1. —Fonseca, pp. 39–50. —Bleda, Crónica, p. 975.

[2] Danvila, p. 283.

CHAPTER VII.

THE CONDITION OF THE MORISCOS.

It was not only in matters of religion that the Moriscos had legitimate cause of discontent. In their relations with their Christian neighbors they were the objects of oppression and injustice, which created an enduring sense of wrong, rendering their fidelity suspect and leading to harsh measures of repression which increased their disaffection. The blundering policy of Spain moved in a vicious circle, ever aggravating the difficulties of the situation until the statesmanship of the age could find no outlet from it save self-destructive violence.

In the older time, as we have seen, there had been no necessary antagonism between the races, even when the Mudéjares were allowed peaceably to follow their ancestral faith, but with the development of Christian fanaticism there came a change which led the Spaniard to treat the Morisco with the galling contempt which Bishop Guevara deprecated and which inevitably was repaid with hatred. So little respect had been shown by the rulers to plighted faith, where the Moriscos were concerned, that this contempt not unnaturally led the people to regard them as entitled to no protection from the law and as subject to arbitrary abuse and oppression. The relations between the races are illustrated by a trouble which arose in Aragon in 1585. Pedro Perez, a native of Sandinies in the Valle de Terra—

one of the most remote and rugged in the Pyrenees—in the winter of 1584–5 drove his cattle to pasture in the valley of the Tagus, not far south of Saragossa. In some quarrel he was slain by the Moriscos of Codo, whereupon his nephew, Antonio Marton, an infanzon or gentleman of Sallent, resolved to avenge him, in spite of the dissuasion of his friends, among whom was Lanuza the narrator of the event. He and his comrades believed that the killing of Moriscos was a most acceptable service to God and that if they perished in the attempt their souls would be a grateful offering to the Creator. Marton, with four companions, stationed himself before sunrise at the gate of Codo and when the Moriscos came forth to their daily labor they were set upon, five or six being killed while the rest fled back to the town and barred themselves in, and the Montañeses returned home in triumph. Some days later Marton came back with a force of twenty-five men; they concealed themselves in a valley and attacked the Moriscos who came to work in the fields, but found them armed and watchful; a skirmish ensued in which some fifteen Moriscos and one Christian were killed and Marton had five wounds. The Montañeses continued to despatch all the Moriscos they could find; the latter formed an organization, known as the "Conjuracion" or "Moros de la venganza," and murdered Christians wherever they could—on one occasion, between la Almunía and la Muela they slew fifteen, including two frailes who were peaceably travelling from Calatayud to Saragossa. The whole kingdom was disturbed, homicides were frequent and the high-roads were full of dangers. This went on for several years till, in 1588, the Montañeses assembled in force and descended upon Codo, which they utterly destroyed; then turning upon Pina, where there was a mixed population, the houses of the Old Christians were spared, but those of the Moriscos were levelled; they massacred without sparing age or sex and it was reckoned that the slaughter amounted to seven hundred souls. There was talk of making an end with all the Moriscos of Aragon, but the catastrophe of Codo and Pina at length aroused the authorities. Forces were raised and garrisons placed in Benasque, Balbastro and other places and the crusading zeal of the Montañeses was curbed. The next thing was to break up the Morisco "Conjuracion," which had its headquarters in Pleytas, a town near Saragossa. Alonso Celso, the deputy-governor of Aragon, on the night of January 30, 1589, quietly surrounded Pleytas and ordered the gates opened in the name of the king. The Moriscos refused and rang their bells for assistance, as agreed upon in the Conjuracion, but Celso forced the gates, losing a few men wounded, and by threats of fire and sword compelled surrender. He tore down some houses of the most guilty and carried off twenty-nine men, together with three who had come in response to the call for aid. The twenty-nine were garrotted and the three were discharged at the instance of the Justicia of Aragon, whose vassals they were, while two leaders who had escaped were subsequently captured and executed. Perhaps the most characteristic feature of the affair was that the Montañeses felt remorse for what they had done and voluntarily came to Saragossa and surrendered themselves. Marton was put to death and his comrades were pardoned on condition of serving in the army of Italy, but the factions which had been formed long continued to disturb the peace of the kingdom.[1]

That, under such circumstances, the Moriscos made reprisals when they safely could may well be believed, though we may reasonably reject the stories told by the ecclesiastical writers to excite abhorrence—that they were taught by their alfaquíes to slay Christians whenever they could without risk, that they became pastry-cooks in order to poison their customers and physicians in order to despatch their patients. Bleda relates that, during the four years in which he was in the baronies of the Duke of Infantado teaching the Moriscos, a friend of his among them, named Juan Vleyme, seemed one day much disturbed because the aljama had ordered him to rent the ferry-boat. On being asked what was the rent he said he did not care whether he made or lost money but he disliked the duty imposed on the ferry-man, which was to kill all the Christians who employed him when he could do so without being discovered; that a spade was kept in the boat with which the passenger was knocked on the head from behind and then buried in the sand. Not content with assassination, it was said that the Moriscos used to drink the blood of their victims and Bleda even goes so far as to assert that these murders sensibly

[1] Lanuza, Historias Ecclesiasticas y Seculares de Aragon, II. 90–97, 139–45.

It should be borne in mind that the right of private warfare seems still to have been one of the recognized privileges of Aragon. At this time there was a ferocious struggle going on for years between Hernando, Duke of Villahermosa and Count of Ribagorza, and his vassals of Ribagorza, who were endeavoring to throw off their subjection to him and there was no interference by the viceroy.—Ibid.

diminished the population of Spain, already reduced by emigration and foreign wars. This martyrdom did not lack its Santo Niño—a Santa Niña Catalina de Oliva, martyrized November 26, 1600, with bestial cruelty.[1]

There is probably more reliance to be placed in the account we have of Hornachos, a town in the province of Badajos, inhabited almost exclusively by Moriscos. They had bought from Philip II., for 30,000 ducats, the privilege of bearing arms; they had a regular organization and treasury and a mint for counterfeit money employing thirteen operatives; they robbed and murdered strangers passing through the town as well as all who informed against them or aided the Inquisition and by judicious bribery of the officials of the court they protected the assassins when detected. At length the hidalgo Juan de Chaves Xaramillo denounced them to the king as confederating with the disaffected throughout the kingdom in preparation for a rising and in October, 1608, the licentiate Gregorio Lopez Madera, alcalde of the court, was sent there to investigate and punish. Alcaldes of the court sent on these errands were noted for the stern and speedy justice which they administered, and Madera justified this reputation. He made an inquest and found eighty-three dead bodies in the fields; he hanged ten of the council of Hornachos and its executioner; he sent a hundred and seventy to the galleys, scourged a large number, and left the place peaceful for the brief period which remained before it was depopulated by the expulsion.[2]

[1] Bleda, Crónica, pp. 861–66; Defensio Fidei, p. 512.

[2] Bleda, Crónica, p. 921.—Guadalajara y Xavierr, fol. 122–3.—Cabrera, Relaciones, p. 355.

In Castile, the chief complaint was as to those who had been deported

It was not, however, so much lawlessness with which the Moriscos had to contend as with the laws and customs which deprived them of nearly all rights and reduced them to a condition akin to serfdom, in flagrant disregard of faith pledged to them. Enforced conversion had added to their burdens and had brought no compensatory privileges—they were Christians as regarded duties and responsibilities and subjection to the Inquisition, but remained Moors as respected liabilities and inequality before the law. When enforced conversion was decreed, in 1525, we have seen (p. 85) that Charles V. solemnly promised them all the liberties of Christians, and in pursuance of this the syndics of the aljamas represented that in order to enjoy their religion they had been subjected to many servitudes and imposts by their lords which as Christians they could not pay, as they would not be allowed to work on Sundays and feast-days, wherefore they asked to be taxed only as Christians. In the concordia of 1528 the answer to this was that they should be treated as Christians and to avoid injury to parties investigation would be made to prevent injustice. It was ominous however that, in this same year 1528, the córtes of Valencia declared that the lords of Morisco vassals retained all their rights over the converts and forbade them to change their domiciles.[1] The nobles made good

from Granada after the rebellion. An official report of a commission appointed by the royal council states that, between 1577 and 1581, more than two hundred persons had been found murdered in the vicinity of populous cities such as Toledo, Alcalá, Seville, etc., and it was proved that all this was the work of seven or eight bands. They had only commenced in 1577, by which time they had become acquainted with the country.—Janer, p. 272.

[1] Dormer, Lib. II. cap. 1.—Danvila, pp. 101, 105.

If there had been felt need of justification for the perpetual breaches

their claims, although they had been allowed the tithes and first-fruits as a compensation, and the Moriscos were powerless to resist. Charles seems to have felt himself equally impotent and had recourse to the pope in hopes that faculties granted to the Inquisition might enable that dreaded tribunal to enforce what he dared not attempt. Clement VII. responded, July 15, 1531, in a brief which is perhaps the most remarkable of all that the Inquisition has ever received. It was addressed to Inquisitor-general Manrique and recited that when the Saracens were converted the barons and knights who held the converts as vassals, to recompense them for the loss inflicted on them by the conversion, were by apostolic authority empowered to exact from them the tithes and first-fruits, but the nobles not only collect these but also extort the personal services and açofras[1] and other demands which were rendered prior to conversion, whence it arises that the converts, unable to endure these burdens, allege them as a reason for resorting to their old customs, eating flesh and disregarding the Christian feasts and ceremonies. As Charles had asked him for a remedy and as he had no knowledge of the matter he commissioned Manrique

of faith pledged to the Moriscos it could have been found in the allegation that they were all constructively heretics and apostates and it was a recognized principle that faith was not to be kept with heretics if there were any valid reason for its violation. As Bishop Simancas says "cum hæreticis nullum commercium nec pax ulla catholicis esse debet; quamobrem fides illis data, etiam juramento firmata, contra publicum bonum, contra salutem animarum, contra jura divina et humana, nulla modo servanda est."—De Catholicis Institutionibus, Tit. XLVI. n. 53 (Romæ, 1575).

[1] The *zofres* or *zofras* were imposts or excise paid by the Mudéjares in addition to the division of crops. It remained a grievance to the last Ribera alludes to it twice (Ximenez, Vida de Ribera, pp. 362, 444).

to diligently inform himself and if he found the conversos unduly oppressed he was to order by papal authority the nobles to exact no more from their Morisco vassals than from the Old Christians on their lands and not to molest them under pain of excommunication and other penalties at his discretion. In case of disobedience he was to hear complaints and render justice, for which full powers were granted to him, and he was to enforce his decisions by censures, invoking if necessary the secular arm.[1] Under this, when, in January, 1534, Manrique sent Calcena and Haro to Valencia as commissioners to organize the Morisco churches, in his instructions he informed them that the king ordered the concordia to be enforced and that in all things the New Christians were to be treated like the Old and they were secretly to investigate and report whether this was the case.[2] The rôle of protector in lieu of persecutor was a new one for the Inquisition; there is no trace of its functions in this line and it doubtless held that Moriscos should prove themselves Christians before they were entitled to its aid. What prosecutions it undertook against their lords were for favoring their vassals, which meant endeavoring to prevent their being interfered with and disquieted for their apostasy. As little could they look for assistance from the córtes, where no measures were ever adopted for their relief; the only effort was to increase their burdens and, in case of prosecution, to profit by the confiscations.[3]

The lords, in fact, had been accustomed to get from their Moorish vassals double the imposts which they could

[1] Bulario de la Orden de Santiago, Libro I. de copias, fol. 118.
[2] Archivo de Simancas, Inquisicion, Libro 77, fol. 227.
[3] Danvila, p. 141.

exact from Christians and the declaration of the córtes of 1528 showed their determination to adhere to this. The share of the produce of the land which they obtained varied from a third to a half; in addition to this they secured the tithes and first-fruits and in time the Church put in its claim also to these and made it good. Besides these were the *zofras* and servitudes and forced loans and benevolences. There were fines for non-attendance at mass and licences for abstaining from wine and pork. They were terrorized by officials of the Inquisition into cultivating their lands gratuitously. In short they were defenceless and every one, cleric and layman, pillaged them systematically. Even their pitiless ecclesiastical enemies are almost moved to compassion in describing their miserable condition. Fray Bleda speaks of the ceaseless exactions with which they were ground to earth, and tells us that these were continually increasing, so that the wretches could not endure them and were always plotting rebellion. Ribera finds fault with them for growing rich in spite of giving their lords a third of the crops together with the "ordinary services" and many arbitrary gifts and loans. Padre Fonseca says that they paid the tithes and first-fruits to the church, but only in consequence of the great pressure and diligence employed by the rectors, and he adds that it often happened that when the harvest came to be divided—one-half or one-third to the lord according to the custom of the place, so much for the tithe and first-fruits and so much for the balance of old indebtedness, which they always had, the husbandman would return home with little or nothing of his crop. There was no compassion felt for this, he says, for it was generally deemed advisable to keep them impoverished and in subjection.[1] They were virtually *taillables et corvéables à merci* and their oppression was only tempered by the ever-present apprehension of rebellion and, in the maritime districts, by the facilities of escape to Africa.

As far as possible moreover in Valencia and Granada they were reduced to the condition of predial serfs. A pragmatica of Charles V., in 1541, recites that they only changed their residence for the purpose of escaping to Barbary and if no one would receive them they could not do this. They were therefore forbidden, under pain of death and confiscation, from changing either domicile or lord and any one accepting them as vassals without special royal licence was fined five hundred florins or stripes in default of it. The same penalty, with the addition of exile, was denounced for sheltering Granadan and Castilian Moriscos, who moreover were threatened with death and confiscation if they entered Valencia. This ferocious legislation was repeated, in 1545, with the inclusion of those of Aragon in the prohibition of entering Valencia, and similar edicts were issued in 1563 and 1586.[2]

As the muleteers and carriers were nearly all Moriscos these regulations exposed them to the most vexatious interference. In 1576, one of them named Miguel Fernandez, of Granada, complained to the king that, in his business of transporting goods to Córdova, Seville and other places, he was continually stopped and his freight seized,

[1] Sandoval, Libro XII. § xxviii.—Archivo de Simancas, Inquisicion, Libro 922, fol. 15.—Concil. Tarraconens ann. 1591, Lib. III. Tit. xviii. cap. 2 (Aguirre, VI. 292).—Bleda, Crónica, p. 1030; Defensio Fidei, pp. 47, 51.—Ximenez, Vida de Ribera, pp. 362, 378.—Fonseca, p. 65.

[2] Danvila, pp. 128, 133, 211.—Boletín de la Real Acad. de la Hist. Abril, 1887, p. 288.

although he carried a passport, and it is easy to conceive of the extortions thus practised by local officials, but the only result of his petition was the issue of a royal order reminding the authorities of the regulation forbidding Granadan Moriscos to absent themselves for a single night from their abodes without a special licence for a limited time after furnishing due security, the strict observance of which was enjoined. It may be added that this occupation of muleteering was regarded with a jealous eye; the muleteer was the carrier of news as well as of merchandise and the Moriscos were suspected of organizing in this way the treasonable conspiracies of which we hear so much and see so little.[1]

They were not even allowed the poor privilege of expatriation, especially to Barbary. We have seen (p. 41) with what stern penalties Ferdinand and Isabella forbade the emigration of their Granadan converts and this policy continued. Intercourse of every kind with Africa was subject to rigid limitations and seems to have been *mixti fori*—under jurisdiction both of the Inquisition and the secular authorities. In 1548 we find the Suprema permitting communication with Barbary for the redemption of captives, while, in 1553, a royal pragmatica says that as emigration is increasing from all the coast districts it repeats the prohibition to go to Barbary without a licence from the Bayle general, the fees for which amounted to 100 sueldos, or five ducats.[2] In 1558 the Suprema, in a letter of September 9th to Paul

[1] Janer, p. 247.—Ximenez, Vida de Ribera, p. 378.—Guadalajara y Xavierr, fol. 74.

[2] Archivo de Simancas, Inqn de Canarias, Expedtes de Visitas, Lib. III. fol. 15.—Danvila, pp. 142, 259.

IV., says that the Inquisition has been much occupied in checking this movement.[1] How effectually it sought to accomplish this is seen in the great Seville auto de fe of September 24, 1559, where two Morisco apostates were burnt and among their crimes was enumerated that one had carried Moriscos to Barbary and the other had taken his wife and children there.[2] It was not only to Barbary, however, that the Inquisition sought to prevent the escape of those whom it persecuted. In 1561 the Spanish ambassador at Venice repeated previous advices that many Moriscos of Valencia and Aragon were passing to the Levant; there were at that time more than thirty, some with their wives and children, awaiting passage and more were coming daily. They were expecting others from Granada, urged by a merchant known in Constantinople as Abraham and in Granada as Her-

[1] Archivo de Simancas, Inquisicion, Libro 4, fol. 232.

[2] A case illustrating the jealousy between the competing jurisdictions of the anomalous Spanish government occurred in 1562. Moriscos of Granada, endeavoring to escape to Barbary, were put to death by the captain-general, but if the Inquisition chanced to have anything against them it was first to try them and, after it was done with them, return them to him for execution. A certain Luis Alboacen, on his way to Africa, was taken at Almuñecar, condemned to death by Tendilla and delivered to the Inquisition which sentenced him to relaxation as a *negativo*. Tendilla claimed him, but the tribunal refused to surrender him and appealed to the Suprema. Philip II. decided in its favor, because it was better for the people to see him burnt for heresy, and ordered this course to be followed in future.—Bulario de la Orden de Santiago, Libro III. fol. 97.—Archivo de Simancas, Inquisicion, Libro 926, fol. 249.

In 1593, however, the Suprema seems disposed to call upon the secular arm when it asks why the royal officials do not punish Moriscos who after reconciliation pay a visit to Algiers.—Archivo Hist. Nacional, Inq^{n} de Valencia, Leg. 5 No. 2, fol. 372.

nando de Talavera. May 19, 1561, the Suprema forwarded this to the inquisitors of Saragossa and Valencia with orders to be vigilant and to put a stop to such evil business.[1] It was doubtless under this impulsion that the tribunal of Saragossa published edicts prohibiting Moriscos from leaving Aragon and Christians from guiding them over the Pyrenees, and in the auto de fe of June 6, 1585, it had the satisfaction of punishing four culprits—two who had served as guides and two who were seeking to emigrate—with scourging and the galleys for three men and scourging with imprisonment and sanbenito for a woman.[2] In time, however, when expulsion was drawing near this vigilance was relaxed; the Junta proposed, June 24, 1608, to instruct the viceroy of Catalonia to watch the Moriscos who were going to France, to arrest those who were rich and influential in order to learn their intentions, but to allow the rest to pass, for the fewer there were of them the better, as it was proposed to carry them all to Barbary.[3]

One of the sorest disabilities inflicted on the Moriscos was the deprivation of arms, for it was not only a humiliation but it left them defenceless at a time when violence was constant and to an Old Christian the blood of the despised race was little more than that of a dog. We have seen (p. 41) that in the pacification of Granada, in 1501, the population was disarmed and the possession of weapons was forbidden under the severest penalties. The Moriscos were skilful armorers and, like

[1] Archivo de Simancas, Libro 4, fol. 263.

[2] Biblioteca Nacional, Seccion de MSS. PV. 3 No. 20.

[3] Danvila, p. 269.

most other handicrafts, this was largely in their hands. Under these circumstances the continued enforcement of such a law was difficult, and the repetition of the edict, in 1511 and again in 1515, shows how it was eluded or disregarded. The royal cédula, however, in 1511, in consequence of the inconvenience to which they were exposed by the strict construction of the law, permits the use of round-pointed knives, but forbids sharp-pointed ones. Licences to bear arms were issued, however, under greater or less authority and were doubtless lucrative to those who assumed to grant them. The attention of Charles V. was called to this and, in his Edict of Granada, in 1526, he ordered that all such licences should be presented to the corregidores, after which he would determine what action to take respecting them, and at the same time he prohibited the nobles from issuing them to their vassals—regulations which in 1528 he extended to all the kingdoms.[1] These licences became recognized and abused; those who had them were said to procure more arms than they needed, which they sold to the *monfíes* or outlaws of the sierras, to remedy which they were ordered, in 1552, to present them to the captain-general together with their arms and have them sealed under pain of five years of galleys —an order which was repeated in 1563 and which in both cases was slackly obeyed.[2]

In Valencia, as a prudent preliminary to baptism, the Moors were all disarmed in November, 1525. In the negotiations for the concordia of 1528 they asked for the

[1] Nueva Recop. Lib. VIII. Tit. ii. ley 13.—Coleccion de Doc. inéd. XXXVI. 569.

[2] Janer, p. 52.—Marmól Carvajal, p. 159.—Danvila, p. 172.

return of their arms, which they had hitherto used loyally in the king's service and would continue to do so to the death. To this the answer was that they should be treated as Old Christians.[1] Like all the other pledges, this was made only to be broken. Among the restrictions of the pragmatica of 1541 was the prohibition to carry arms, whether offensive or defensive. With the customary laxity of administration this was not enforced and, in 1545, fresh orders were sent to disarm them. That it was regarded as a work of no little danger is shown by a letter of the viceroy, the Duke of Calabria, to Prince Philip, February 3, 1545. He had consulted with the archbishop and others, sworn to secrecy, who all agreed that the measure was necessary, leaving them only a knife apiece and reducing them to the condition of those of Granada. It is thought best to notify the great lords secretly in advance, such as the Dukes of Segorbe and Gandía and the Count of Oliva, while the viceroy promised to start it in the baronies of Alberich and Alcocer, which were under his charge and were the largest Morerías in the kingdom, and when he and the other three set the example the other lords will not venture to hold back, though they fear their Moriscos will be so outraged that they will flee to Barbary. The sierras of Bernia and Espadan must be seized and there must be sufficient troops within call if necessary. It was better to make the lords do it and not the royal officials as ordered, but the latter should be present so that the Moriscos might understand that the measure was general.[2]

[1] Bleda, Crónica, p. 648.—Dormer, Libro II. cap. 1.—Danvila, pp. 92, 104.

[2] Danvila, p. 127.—Coleccion de Doc. inéd. V. 88.—Janer, p. 242.

These consultations led to no action—possibly the lords were afraid to act—and, in 1547, Archbishop Tomás de Vilanova suggested that, for the security of the preachers sent out to convert the Moriscos, it would be well to disarm them, at least of missile weapons, such as arquebusses and cross-bows. Still nothing was done and, in 1552, St. Tomás wrote in much trepidation to Prince Philip about a Turkish fleet reported to have been seen off Majorca; he begged for 2000 troops to be sent at once to prevent a rising, and if not needed for this they could be used to disarm the Moriscos, which ought to have been done long before.[1] As usual, procrastination ruled and, in 1561, the inquisitor Gregorio de Miranda, in response to a command for his advice, specified disarmament as the indispensable preliminary measure. It should be done in winter, when the corsairs dare not approach the shore, and should be commenced by the great nobles under threat that if they do not do it the king will.[2] Finally, in 1563, the measure was executed. Preparations were secretly made for carrying it out simultaneously everywhere by the barons, who were subjected to a fine of 2000 florins for non-compliance. The royal pragmatica of January 19, 1563, forbade all conversos and their descendants from possessing or carrying arms under pain of forfeiture of the arms, perpetual galleys, confiscation of houses in which they might be found and arbitrary penalties including death. Inventories were to be made of all arms seized with their value, which was to be repaid to the owners, and only four hours were allowed for the surrender. This was accompanied with

[1] Coleccion de Doc. inéd. V. 102, 123. [2] Danvila, p. 163.

a proclamation of the captain-general taking all Moriscos under the royal safeguard; as some persons maltreated and insulted them, those who should call them dogs or the like were to be fined 25 ducats or imprisoned for thirty days; those who should strike or wound them or damage their property should, if honorable persons, be exiled from Spain for two years, if plebeians should be sent to the galleys for the same term. The disarmament was fairly thorough. The inventories show that, in a total of 16,377 Morisco houses, there were seized 14,930 swords, 3454 cross-bows and a long list of other arms, offensive and defensive, proving that the Moriscos had industriously provided themselves with weapons.[1]

In Aragon the matter of disarmament was placed in the hands of the Inquisition which, November 4, 1559, issued a decree forbidding all Moriscos from bearing arms, but the nobles appealed from this to the Suprema and had influence enough to procure an indefinite postponement of its execution, the reason alleged being that without arms no one would be able to maintain his rights in the irrigating canals.[2] In 1590 the matter was taken up again, on a proposition to surrender their weapons in consideration of a general pardon. After consulting with the king, the Suprema instructed the inquisitors of Saragossa to discuss the matter with the archbishop, the Viceroy Almenara and the Count of Sástago. It is illustrative of the methods of the period that when they asked the archbishop to fix a day and hour for the meet-

[1] Danvila (Boletín de la R. Acad. de la Hist., Abril, 1877, pp. 276-306).

[2] Guadalajara y Xavierr, fol. 62.—Archivo de Simancas, Inquisicion, Libro 13, fol. 372.—Relazioni Venete, Serie I. Tom. VI. p. 407.

ing and he replied requesting them to name the time, but in a manner to show that he expected the junta to be held in the archiepiscopal palace, to which the inquisitors were to go like the nobles, their dignity was so touched that they reported to the Suprema, May 22, 1590, and asked for instructions. The Suprema pondered over the matter until January 18, 1591, and then ordered that the junta should be held in the Aljafería, where the Inquisition was established, giving notice to the archbishop, and, if he did not choose to come, they were to consult the others without him.[1] Then further delay occurred, owing to the revolt growing out of the affair of Antonio Perez, and it was not until after the pacification and the córtes of Tarazona that the matter was taken up again. March 20, 1593, Philip ordered the disarmament and sent Pedro Pacheco, a member of the Suprema, and Don Ladron de Guevara to Saragossa to consult with the inquisitors as to details. They determined to issue edicts in the name of the Inquisition and the inquisitors shut themselves up in the morning with their secretaries and labored until six o'clock the next morning preparing edicts for more than 130 places. On Palm Sunday, April 4th, these were published throughout the kingdom, ordering all arms to be surrendered within thirty days and none thereafter to be owned by New Christians under pain of a hundred lashes and a hundred ducats. Accompanying this was an edict of Inquisitor-general Quiroga pardoning all errors and apostasy that should be confessed. Two inquisitors were sent throughout the kingdom to see to the disarmament and to reconcile those who should take advantage

[1] Archivo de Simancas, Inquisicion, Libro 940, fol. 296.

of the Edict of Grace. No resistance was made; besides weapons buried or secretly sold, there were collected 7076 swords, 1356 pikes, lances and halberds, 489 cross-bows, 3783 arquebusses and other weapons in large numbers. The edict permitted the retention of knives, and these were gradually increased in size till they became formidable weapons. After two or three officials of the Inquisition had been killed with them, when attempting to make arrests, a royal edict of 1603 limited the length to the third of an ell and required them to be pointless.[1]

In Catalonia, to the last, there was no distinction in the matter of arms between Old and New Christians, which led to some apprehension at the time of expulsion, but it was groundless, for no use was made of them.[2]

In addition to the deprivation of self-defence the limitations which the strict construction of these edicts imposed on the daily labors of the husbandman or artificer was a perpetual irritation and serious disability. In the sugar-culture, for instance, the heavy *machete* was almost essential for cutting the cane, but it came within the proscription and in a thousand ways the labor of the Morisco was crippled for the lack of implements which the official might regard as dangerous weapons. In 1576 a Morisco muleteer of Granada, named Miguel Rodriguez, petitioned the king to be allowed to carry a pointless dagger such as was permitted in Granada and was necessary to his busi-

[1] Guadalajara y Xavierr, fol. 64.—Lanuza, Historias de Aragon, II. 417.

In 1593 we find an *ayuda de costa* of 40 ducats granted to Juan del Olmo, notary of the Inquisition of Valencia, for his labors in the disarming of the Moriscos of Xea, Albarracin and Teruel.—Arch. Hist. Nacional, Inq^{n} de Valencia, Legajo 5, No. 1, fol. 403.

[2] Bleda, Crónica, p. 1049.

ness. The reply to this was a royal order recapitulating a provision of the pragmatica of Granada forbidding any Morisco of that kingdom from carrying any weapon, offensive or defensive, save a pointless knife, under penalty, for a first offence, of confiscation, for a second of six years of galleys and for a third of galleys for life, all of which was ordered to be strictly enforced.[1]

The imputation of broken faith can scarce be cast on the disabilities as to holding office or benefices, which in the latter part of the sixteenth century weighed upon the Moriscos, but nevertheless it was deeply felt by the rich and educated among them, many of whom were Christians in heart as well as in externals. It was a matter not prominent at the time of the enforced baptisms and promises of equality with Old Christians, but was a later outgrowth of the increasing development of fanatic intolerance, attributable in part to the passions aroused by the Reformation. Space is lacking to treat here the portentous subject of *limpieza*, or purity of blood, which in time filled the land of Spain with envy, hatred and all uncharitableness. It must suffice to say that, towards the middle of the sixteenth century, the doors were closed on all descendants of Jews and Moors, or of heretics publicly penanced by the Inquisition, for admission to many of the colleges and universities, to benefices in many cathedral churches, to most of the religious and all the military Orders, to positions in the Inquisition and even in some places to municipal offices. The exact extent to which this prevailed it would be impossible now to define, for each body was a law unto itself in this respect.

[1] Janer, p. 251.

Thus in Granada, we are told, the cathedral and collegiate churches did not require limpieza, while in Bilboa it was a condition for municipal office.[1] In the great universities, such as Salamanca and Alcalá, the condition of limpieza must have been confined to the faculties and officials, for it would have been impossible to require the crowds of students to go through the tedious and expensive process of presenting proofs of limpieza, but in the college of the Dominican house of Santa Maria of Toledo it was enforced on all students of arts and theology.[2] In a land where a career in ecclesiastical or secular office was

[1] Escobar de Puritate et Nobilitate probanda, P. I. Q. xiii. § 3 No. 71.—Ordenanzas de la Noble Villa de Bilbao, Tit. I. cap. ii. (Bilbao, 1682).

The Basque Provinces seem to have been particularly antagonistic to Moors and Jews. As early as 1482 Guipuscoa had a statute forbidding conversos to reside or to marry there (Pulgar, Letra xxxi. p. 61). In 1511 Biscay procured a royal pragmatica expelling all conversos and Moors and their descendants. In 1561 it petitioned the Council of Castile for the enforcement of this, but the council decided that it had never been enforced and that its enforcement was inexpedient, so the procurators were told to depart and they would be summoned when the subject was to be considered. Not content with this rebuff they made another application in 1565, with the same result.—Autos y Acuerdos del Consejo, fol. 5, 8 (Madrid, 1649).—Autos Acordados, Lib. VIII. Tit. ii. Auto 1.—Novis. Recop. Lib. XII. Tit. i. ley. 4.

[2] Ripoll, Bullar. Ord. FF. Prædic. IV. 163.—In the letter, June 19, 1547, of Archbishop Siliceo of Toledo and his chapter to the Royal Council, arguing in favor of the statute of limpieza which they had adopted, they say it is in force in all the Spanish colleges and even in that of Bologna, founded by Albornoz, none but Old Christians were received as collegians, chaplains or familiars and from these colleges were drawn, for the most part, the members of councils and chancelleries and other judicial officers, and all other members of councils and chancelleries, are Old Christians, except through ignorance.—Burriel, Vidas de los Arzobispos de Toledo, Vol. II. fol. 2, 3 (Biblioteca Nacional, Seccion de MSS. Ff. 194).

the ambition of almost every one who had even a smattering of education, the barrier thus erected was a severe infliction on the more intelligent and influential Moriscos and could scarcely fail to excite disaffection and discontent. Navarrete, indeed, thinks that the necessity for the expulsion could have been avoided but for this—that they could have been Christianized if they had been admitted to a share of the honors of public life and had not been driven to desperation and hatred of religion by the indelible mark of infamy which was imposed on them.[1]

Yet in the earlier period of this development there seems rather to have been a desire to shield the Moriscos from its blighting influence. The office of familiar of the Inquisition, although unsalaried, was one eagerly sought, both on account of a certain amount of social distinction which it conferred and of the exemption which it carried from the jurisdiction of the secular courts. The first application of *limpieza* to familiars occurs in an order by the Suprema, October 10, 1546, that none shall be admitted who is not an Old Christian, but when, in 1547, the córtes of Monzon complained that many Moriscos were appointed, the reply of the Suprema was that the Inquisition regards as capable of holding office all who are baptized and live as Christians, except heretics and apostates and their fautors. It was not long before there was a change as to this, for, in a letter of 1552 to the inquisitors of Valencia, Inquisitor-general Valdés orders that they appoint as familiars none who are descended from Jews or Moors, and a royal cédula of March 10, 1553, prescribes as a universal rule that

[1] Navarrete, Conservacion de Monarquias, pp. 51-3 (Ed. 1626).

familiars shall be Old Christians. Yet in 1565, when Philip II. was essaying conciliation, he ordered that leading and influential Moriscos shall be appointed. It was not long after this, however, in 1568, that we find the inquisitors of Barcelona reproved for inobservance of the rule and ordered to see that in future all familiars shall be *limpios*.[1] Even more marked was the consideration shown with respect to clerical careers. When, in 1566, Archbishop Ayala introduced the rule of *limpieza* in the Valencian church, he prohibited any descendant of Jews or heretics to the fourth generation direct, or the second degree collateral, from obtaining any ecclesiastical dignity or preferment.[2] In this the omission of Moriscos is significant. Paul IV. had forbidden admission to holy orders to the descendants of Jews to the fourth generation and, in 1573, Gregory XIII. extended this to Moors, but in 1564, at the córtes of Monzon, it was decreed that those trained in the Morisco college of Valencia should be allowed to hold benefices and the cure of souls among their people,[3] and we are told that they graduated some good priests and preachers and doctors of theology.[4] As time wore on, however, and as hatred and contempt were intensified, the exclusion became general; able and

[1] Archivo de Simancas, Inquisicion, Libro 4, fol. 208, 215; Libro 922, fol. 15; Libro 926, fol. 33; Visitas de Barcelona, Legajo 15, fol. 20.—Danvila, p. 169.

[2] Aguirre, Concil. Hispan., V. 495.

[3] Bledæ Defensio Fidei, p. 372.

[4] Fonseca, p. 377. Fonseca however tells us (p. 67) that Archbishop Ribera suspended from their functions all Morisco priests, though among them there were doctors and vicars of good life and reputation, who had been educated in the seminaries, owing to a probable doubt as to whether they had been baptized.

ambitious men, who might have done the state service and have been useful in winning over their fellows, were rendered hopeless and were reduced to expend their vigor in spreading disaffection and stimulating the spirit of revolt.

If the relations of the Moriscos to the state and to society were thus deplorable, those which they bore to the Church, even apart from persecution, were little better. It was only under the fiction that they were Christians that they were allowed to exist in the land of their ancestors; it was the duty of the Church to make them conform to its observances, externally at least, and they were therefore subjected to perpetual espionage and the enforced performance of practices at which they revolted. They were exposed to the extortions, legal and illegal, of alguaziles, appointed by the bishops, but with the privileges of familiars, whose duty it was to keep close watch over them and collect the fines for working on feast-days, absence from mass, or doing other things prohibited in the printed instructions issued for their guidance. In 1595 Bishop Perez of Segorbe describes these gentry as paid by a half or a third of their collections, and as this amounted to a bare pittance the position was only accepted by the very poor, who were bribed to conceal the offences committed and were afraid to do their duty, threatened as they were by the lords and also by the Moriscos in remote districts.[4]

To one practice the Moriscos were particularly attached —the treatment of their dead, arraying them in clean

[1] Archivo de Simancas, Inq^{n} de Valencia, Leg. 205, fol. 3.

grave-clothes and burying them in virgin earth. We have seen (p. 129) how the former gave rise to prosecutions by the Inquisition. As for the latter, in the concordia of 1528, the syndics of the aljamas asked that, where they lived together with Old Christians, they could have their own cemeteries, to which the answer was that cemeteries could be established near the churches changed from mosques, but Old Christians were not to be debarred from burial there if they wished.[1] This partially satisfied them and it continued until 1591, when it was ordered that they should be buried inside of the churches, which was so abhorrent to them that they vainly offered more than thirty thousand ducats if king or pope would allow them to be interred elsewhere, even though in dunghills.[2]

The baptism of their children was the source of perpetual irritation. It was the duty of the Church to see that none escaped, for only thus could they have a chance of salvation and only thus could it claim jurisdiction over them. The most rigid regulations were consequently prescribed to ensure that the sacrament was duly administered. No Morisca woman was allowed to act as midwife. In every Morisco village there was a Christian midwife, carefully selected and instructed. She kept watch on all pregnant women and was fined in a hundred reales for every case she missed. After putting the infant to the mother's breast, her first duty was to notify the priest or alguazil and then she never left the bedside save to attend to indispensable duties about the house. The baptism

[1] Danvila, p. 103.

[2] Bledæ Defensio Fidei, p. 71 ; Crónica, p. 950.

took place on the same day or the next, and careful registers were kept so that all could be identified. It is the universal statement, and doubtless true, that on returning home the father scraped and washed the spots touched with the chrism, thinking thereby to efface the sacrament.[1]

Marriage was another subject in which the Church was brought into conflict with the customs and convictions of the Moriscos. Even before matrimony had been erected into a sacrament, the Church had assumed to control it and had defined the degrees of kinship within which it was permissible. After at one time extending this to the shadowy relationship expressed by the seventh degree, it had been satisfied with the sufficiently distant one of the fourth and, by the invention of so-called

[1] Bleda, Crónica, pp. 951-2. Bleda here controverts an absurd statement of Fonseca that to elude baptism they would present one child repeatedly. Thus in Buñol, he says, there were twenty births within eight days; of these one child was selected who was baptized twenty times. Children were even lent for this purpose from one village to another. Along the river Mijares it was the custom that the one first born in a space of two months served for all the rest during that time (Fonseca, p. 67). The foundation of this was a statement sent to Archbishop Ribera from Oran, purporting to come from Miguel Ferrer, a refugee Moor of Ayodar. Ribera was so impressed by it that he suspended, as we have seen, all Morisco priests as being doubtfully baptized, and in a pastoral of August 3, 1610, he ordered that all children below the age of reason, retained at the expulsion, should be conditionally baptized. Bleda also gave credit to it at first (Defensio Fidei, p. 422). His subsequent refutation of it shows how credulous were all churchmen where the Moriscos were concerned. First there were the two sexes to be considered, and no girl could be presented for a boy. Then no priest would accept an infant two weeks or two months old for one new-born. Then in the whole baronies of Ayodar and Fuentes, in the valley of the Mijares, there were not more that fifty Morisco households and there was not over a birth a month.

affinity, spiritual and otherwise, it had enlarged the prohibited area and had introduced a number of perplexing questions. At the same time it had created for the pope the power of issuing dispensations, disregarding the fact that this implied the admission that the prohibition was purely artificial and without basis in natural or moral law. This gave to the Holy See not only vast political influence, in its ability to permit or forbid dynastic marriages, but an abundant source of income in the sale of dispensations, the price for which was made to depend on the needs or ability of the purchaser.[1]

Among the Moors, marriage was permitted between first cousins, and as, for the most part, they lived in small isolated agricultural communities, intermarriage for generations had created such a complexity of kinships that probably few or none within them could be found whose unions were not incestuous and invalid under ecclesiastical definitions. The same was true of those living in cities, walled off in their Morerías, where mixed marriages with Christians could not have been common. In 1501, when those of Castile were forcibly converted, as soon as they were baptized their unions became incestuous and invalid and their children illegitimate, but what action was taken in this supremely important matter does not appear, though, as we have seen in Daimiel, in 1550, in the trial of Mari

[1] In 1301 Boniface VIII. sold, for the enormous sum of ten thousand silver marks, the legitimation of Fernando IV., of Castile, the marriage of whose father Sancho IV. was invalid for lack of a dispensation (Cronica de Don Fernando IV. cap. viii.).

For the varying legislation of the Church respecting the forbidden degrees of consanguinity, from the fourth to the seventh, see Gratian, *Decreti* P. II. Caus. xxxv. Quæst. 2-5.—For the canons on affinity see Tit. xi.-xiv. in Sexto, Lib. IV.

Gomez, one of the charges was that she had proposed to marry a son to a girl within the prohibited degrees without applying for a dispensation.[1] In Valencia, after the wholesale baptisms of 1526, one of the petitions of the syndics of the aljamas represented the hardship that would ensue by invalidating such marriages existing and contracted, wherefore the inquisitor-general was supplicated to induce the legate to dispense for such consummated marriages and for all that might be contracted for forty years to come, to which the reply was that the legate had already been consulted and was willing to do so as respected existing marriages and those agreed upon prior to the conversion, but his faculties did not extend to future ones; he had been asked to apply to the pope, but the Moriscos hereafter must conform to the canons.[2]

It was impossible for them to do so. They continued to intermarry although their unions in the eye of the Church and the law were mere concubinage. Doubtless the rectors sought to make them purchase dispensations and in their absence refused to perform the rites. We are told that they rarely sought for dispensations and would never have done so but for fear of the Inquisition; that in some places they contented themselves with informing the lord that the parties were of kin and if he made no objection the marriage would take place—a degree of carelessness on the part of the nobles for which more than one was prosecuted by the Inquisition and publicly penanced.[3] This probably explains why the córtes of Monzon, in 1564, petitioned that facilities should be given for obtaining dispensations from the

[1] Proceso de Mari Gomez (MS. *penes me*). [2] Danvila, p. 104.
[3] Fonseca, p. 72. Cf. Bleda, Crónica, p. 905.

Commissioner of the Santa Cruzada, who had the necessary faculties; also that the children sprung from such unions should be regarded as legitimate. The response to this by the bishops, at the council of Valencia in 1565, was a series of canons threatening excommunication and other severe penalties on all marrying within the prohibited degrees and on all concerned in evasions of the rule.[1]

Like everything else in this unhappy business, the matter, despite its importance, was allowed to drift along. At length, in 1587, Philip II. represented to Sixtus V. that the Moriscos were contracting marriages, both clandestine and within the prohibited degrees, which were therefore invalid and the children illegitimate, but all that he obtained was a brief, January 25, 1588, directed to Archbishop Ribera, granting to him and his bishops, for six months only, faculties to validate such marriages, legitimate the children and absolve the parents *in utroque foro*, imposing on them salutary penance, for all of which it was strictly forbidden to charge fees.[2] Under such conditions it is not likely that the episcopal officials took much pains to promulgate the brief or that the Moriscos were eager to avail themselves of it. The last that we hear of the matter is that, in 1595, Philip resolved to apply to Rome for another brief conferring faculties for dispensation.[3] Doubtless it was granted and was as little efficient as the previous ones.

Among the minor inflictions may be mentioned the restrictions placed on the Moriscos to prevent their having

[1] Danvila, p. 169.—Aguirre, Tom. V. p. 418.

[2] Bulario de la Orden de Santiago, Libro IV. fol. 101, 102 (Archivo Hist. Nacional).

[3] Danvila, pp. 228, 230.

meat killed in accordance with their customs. They were forbidden to exercise the trade of butchers or even to kill a fowl for a sick man, nor were they allowed to approach the shambles when slaughtering was going on. It was probably difficult to enforce this, especially in the remoter Morisco communities, for the law was repeated as late as 1595.[1]

A Dutch archer of Philip II., who accompanied the king in his journey to the córtes of Monzon in 1585, affords us a contemporary glimpse of the Moriscos of the time. On crossing the Aragon border he observes that the population of the lands of the nobles is almost exclusively Moorish while that of the royal towns is Old Christian. The Moors, he says, are with difficulty brought to live in the latter. The town of Muel, the seat of a flourishing industry of Hispano-Moresque lustre ware, belonged to the Marquis of Camarasa and was populous with New Christians, who had maintained their laws since they conquered the land. They would not taste pork or wine, and he saw that, on the departure of the royal train, they broke all the glassware and pottery that had been used for the obnoxious food and drink. There were about two hundred households and only three Old Christians—the priest, the notary and the inn-keeper—while all the rest would rather make a pilgrimage to Mecca than to Compostella. The church was naturally little visited, as it was closed except on Sundays and feast-days, when the New Christians were forced to hear mass.[2]

[1] Nueva Recop. Lib. VIII. Tit. ii. ley 13.—Bledæ Defensio Fidei, pp. 57, 421.—Danvila, p. 230.

[2] Henrique Cock, Relacion del Viage hecho por Felipe II. en 1585, pp. 30-1 (Madrid, 1876).

Thus in the kingdoms of Aragon the races kept apart and were no nearer amalgamation than they had been when Charles V. made his ill-starred attempt to enforce uniformity of faith. In the kingdom of Castile there was greater approximation in externals but not much more in essentials. A more general view, expressing moreover the popular prejudices against the race, is afforded by Archbishop Ribera in his second memorial. The Moriscos, he says, are of two classes. One is free from vassalage to lords, such as all those expelled from Granada, although they may have settled on feudal lands, and those who are scattered in various places of Castile such as Avila, Olmeda and many others. The other class are born vassals of lords, such as those of Aragon and Valencia. The first live among Christians and for the most part speak our language and use our dress and bear arms, but are as thoroughly Moors as those of Valencia, with greater opportunities to live as such, for, as they have not public aljamas nor live apart, they are not watched by their priests, which is no small reproach to the latter and their bishops. The latter dwell in communities, having their aljamas and a superintendent. The former bear arms and many of them being muleteers they maintain communication with the others throughout Spain. In the army they serve as spies. They are avaricious and economical and are the sponge of the wealth of Spain; there is no doubt that they possess most of the gold and silver, for though there is great scarcity of money they are rich, although they pay heavy tribute and give their lords one-third of what they produce and their lords exact from them not only the ordinary rents and services but many gifts and loans. Wherever they go they reduce the people to poverty. He had seen in Andalusia how the competition of those driven from Granada had reduced the number of Old Christians. They are hard-working and thrifty and, spending little on food or drink and clothing, they work for what would not support an Old Christian, so they are preferred by purchasers and employers; they monopolize the mechanic arts and commerce as well as working by day's labor. As they do not buy bread or meat or wine the excise for the king and for local needs, which is mostly levied on these articles, falls more heavily on the Old Christians. Thus we are peopling our country with heretics and destroying the faithful.[1]

This indictment of underselling and cheapening labor indicates one of the grievances which stimulated popular enmity. The Venetian envoy, in 1595, describes the Moriscos as constantly increasing in numbers and wealth; they never go to war but devote themselves exclusively to trade and gain.[2] Bleda, it is true, argues that if they worked or sold cheaper than Old Christians they at least raised families and spent money and thus were far less injurious than the foreigners who brought gewgaws to Spain and carried the money away, thus impoverishing the land.[3] Cervantes, on the other hand, gave utterance to the popular feeling in his *Colloquio de los perros:* the Moriscos multiply, they all marry, they never put their children into religion or the army, they pay nothing for teaching them, for all their science is to rob us. They spend little and hoard what

[1] Ximenez, Vida de Ribera, pp. 377–9.
[2] Relazioni Venete, Serie I. Tom. V. p. 451.
[3] Bleda, Crónica, p. 906.

they gain, so that they now have most of the money in Spain; it is a slow fever which kills as certainly as a raging one.[1] All this found official expression in the Castilian córtes of 1592, which represented to Philip that previous ones had asked him to remedy the evils of the Granadan Moriscos scattered through the land. These evils, they say, are daily increasing, for the longer the cure is delayed the greater are their numbers; they have obtained possession of trade, especially in provisions, which is the crucible in which money is melted, for they gather and hide it at the harvest time so that the crops must pass through their hands. With this object they become shopkeepers, caterers, bakers, butchers, inn-keepers, water-carriers etc., whereby they get and hoard all the money. They never buy land and thus become rich and powerful so that they control the secular and ecclesiastical courts which so favor them that they live openly in disregard of religion. They daily emigrate to Barbary; they marry among themselves and never ask for dispensations but celebrate their weddings with *zambras* and they bear arms publicly. The most atrocious crimes committed within these ten years are their work. In assessing the *servicio* or subsidy, they have been numbered and counted, whereby it is evident that they can cause the State some disquiet—for all of which a remedy is sought at the king's hands. The remedy was an edict ordering all the magistrates of the kingdom to enforce with rigor the severe restrictive legislation directed against them.[2]

It is evident that the causes of complaint in the king-

[1] Obras de Cervantes, p. 242 (Madrid, 1864).

[2] Janer, p. 270.—Bleda, Crónica, p. 905.—Nueva Recop. Lib. VIII. Tit. ii. ley 24.

doms of Castile were not the same as in those of Aragon, but the underlying motives were similar. It was not alone religious hatred, but the fact that the Spaniards were to a great extent consumers and the Moriscos were producers. The Spaniard sought a career in the church or the army or the service of the state; he despised those on whose labor he lived, he grudged them the earnings of toil and thrift; to them he attributed the gradual depauperization which was the result of his own false view of life and mistaken policy, and he was eager to find some excuse for stripping them of their accumulations and reducing them to a greater depth of poverty.

A curious custom in Valencia, as described by an eye-witness, illustrates the quality of the religious fervor directed against the Moriscos. When a criminal of the race was to be executed he was asked whether he desired to die as a Christian or as a Moor. In the former case he was hanged in the market-place; in the latter he was taken to a spot outside the walls, known as the Rambla, where he was stoned to death and afterwards burnt, according to the command of God for idolaters (Deut. xvii. 5). To escape this they usually professed Christianity with great zeal and then on the gallows invoked Mahomet. The populace were prepared for this and, to ensure the execution of the divine command, they stood with stones in their hands and as soon as the word Mahomet was uttered they sent a volley like a hailstorm which not only killed the culprit but broke not a few Christian heads. Next morning not a stone could be found on the ground where the previous evening they had lain by the thousand—all were carried off during the night and were treasured as the relics of a martyr.[1]

[1] Fonseca, p. 73.

Race hatred, religious hatred and the assumed antagonism of interests combined to render the situation impossible in the absence of a wise statesmanship of which the Spain of the period was incapable. Enforced conversion had rendered the condition of the Moriscos distinctly worse. In place of enjoying the promised benefits of the status of Old Christians they were subjected to all the former burdens with new ones superadded; they were exposed to the constant supervision and extortions of sacristans and alguaziles, with the ever-present terror of the Inquisition impending over them and they could only regard as a mockery the interest felt by their persecutors for the salvation of their souls and as an intolerable intermeddling the gratuitous interference with their habits and customs. That they should grow restive under incessant provocation and ready to welcome any mode of deliverance from intolerable bondage was inevitable.

CHAPTER VIII.

THE REBELLION OF GRANADA.

In Granada the experiment was pushed to the uttermost of how far the endurance of a population could be tried by oppression and wrong of every kind. In the severe repression of the rising of 1500 the more turbulent spirits had been allowed to seek refuge in Barbary and the remainder had settled down peacefully, had pursued their industries and had formed, if not a contented, at least a fairly prosperous community, constituting, as they did, a vast majority of the inhabitants. Pedraza, himself a canon of the cathedral of Granada, and almost a contemporary, gives a most favorable account of them. There were few idlers among them, they were moral, strictly honorable in their dealings, and most charitable to their poor, but the avarice of the judges and the insolence of the officials of the law rendered them disaffected through the abuses to which they were subjected and, as the ministers of the Church were no better, they lost all affection for religion. Archbishop Guerrero, in 1565, held a provincial council to reform these evils, but his chapter appealed from its provisions as an illegal invasion of their privileges and matters went on as before. The Moriscos had submitted to baptism but were heretics at heart; they went to mass to escape the fine; they worked behind doors on feast-days with more pleasure than on other days and they kept Fridays better than Sundays; they washed themselves even in December and regularly performed the accompanying *zala;* to comply with the law they had their children baptized and then washed off the chrism, performed circumcision on the boys, and gave them Moorish names. Brides went to church in borrowed Christian garments and on returning home changed them to Moorish and celebrated the nuptials with *zambras* and *leilas*. They learned the prayers in order to marry and then forgot them; they confessed during Lent in order to get the requisite certificate, but their confessions were imperfect and one year merely repeated another.[1] They at least were loyal subjects for, in 1522, they were among the first to take up arms against the Comuneros; Don Juan de Granada, brother of the last native king Abdelehi, served as general in Castile and did his full duty.[2]

In 1526 Charles, while in Granada, was appealed to, in the name of the Moriscos, by three descendants of the old Moorish kings, Fernando Venegas, Miguel de Aragon and Diego Lopez Benexara, for protection against their ill-treatment by the priests, judges, alguaziles, and other officials, whereupon he appointed a commission to investigate and report.[3] Fray Antonio de Guevara was one of the commissioners and hurried from his baptismal work in Valencia to the Alpujarras where he describes, in a letter to a friend, the New Christians as requiring so much to correct that it had better be done in secret rather than to punish them publicly; they have been so ill-taught in

[1] Pedraza, Historia eclesiastica de Granada, fol. 236-8 (Granada, 1638).

[2] Marmol Carvajal, Rebelion y Castigo, p. 164.

[3] Sandoval, xiv. 18.—Dormer, Lib. II. cap. vii.

the faith, and the magistrates have so winked at their errors that it will be enough to remedy it in the future without meddling with the past.[1] There can be no doubt as to the nature of the commissioners' reports which Charles received in Granada; they confirmed the complaints of ill-usage but stated that there were not to be found among the Moriscos more than seven true Christians. He referred the reports to a junta of important personages, under the presidency of Inquisitor-general Manrique, and the outcome was the Edict of Granada, December 7, 1526. As might be expected this did not address itself to the redress of the admitted grievances of the Moriscos but to the repression of their apostasy—not by providing them with instruction but by restrictions and threats. It granted an amnesty for past offences but as a means of salutary terrorizing it ordered the transfer to Granada of the Inquisition of Jaen.[2] A term of grace was granted for those who would come forward and confess, after which the laws against heresy would be rigorously enforced, except that for some years, fines were in practice, substituted for confiscation and time was given to allow the culprits to earn them.[3]

The Edict imposed many restrictions which were trifling but vexatious, and some that were oppressive to no small degree. It forbade the use of Arabic and the wearing of Moorish dress; tailors were not to make garments

[1] Guevara, Epistolas familiares, p. 543.

[2] Sandoval, Dormer, *ubi sup.* The papal brief authorizing this transfer was dated July 7, 1527, in the castle of Sant' Angelo where Clement was kept a prisoner by Charles's troops.—Llorente, Añales, II. 315.

[3] Archivo de Simancas, Libro 926, fol. 80 (see Appendix No. XI.).

nor silversmiths jewels after their fashion; their baths were prohibited; all births were to be watched by Christian midwives to see that no Moorish rites were performed; disarmament was to be enforced by a rigid inspection of licences; their doors were to be kept open on feast-days, Fridays, Saturdays and during weddings, to see that Moorish rites were abandoned and Christian ones observed; schools for the education of children in Castilian were to be established in Granada, Guadix and Almería; no Moorish names were to be used and they were not to keep *gacis* or unbaptized Moors either free or as slaves.[1]

[1] Dormer, Lib. I. cap. vii.—Bleda, Crónica, p. 566.—Marmol Carvajal, p. 158.—Nueva Recop. Lib. VIII. Tit. ii. leyes 13, 15, 17.

The wearing of Moorish garments had been forbidden under Ferdinand, but the prohibition was suspended until, in 1518, Charles ordered it enforced and again suspended it at the petition of the Moriscos.—(Marmol Carvajal, Bleda, *ubi sup.*) It and the abandonment of Arabic were ordered in Valencia, but in the concordia of 1528 they were suspended for ten years (Danvila, p. 102).

In 1572 Philip II. again prohibited the use of Arabic by the exiles from Granada as we shall see below. The Moorish ritual was in Arabic and seems never to have been translated. In the trials the prayers are always spoken of as being in Arabic. Francisca de Ribera, reconciled in the Toledo auto de fe of 1603, confessed that she had the intention of being a Moor and desired to learn some prayers but was unable in consequence of her ignorance of Arabic.—(MSS. of Library of Univ. of Halle, Yc. 20, Tom. I.) In the middle of the seventeenth century, after the final expulsion, a manual of religious observances for the use of the exiles in Tunis was composed in Spanish, the author of which lamented that Arabic was unknown to them and the rites of worship forgotten.—Tratados de Legislacion Musulmana, p. 7 (Madrid, 1853).

Fray Bleda, in a letter to Philip III. in 1605, treats with contempt the project of Christianizing the Moriscos by forcing them to abandon their dress and language. Their greatest alfaquíes, he says, dress like Christians and use the vernacular so as not to be identified; he would

This naturally caused great agitation among the Moriscos. They held a general assembly and raised 80,000 ducats which they offered to Charles in addition to the ordinary tribute if he would recall the edict. Money doubtless was not spared among his advisers and before he left Granada he suspended it during his pleasure and also permitted them to carry sword and dagger in the towns and a lance when in the country, but not to keep other arms in their houses. In 1530, however, during his absence in Germany, the Empress-regent revived the provision respecting dress, but on an appeal made to him he revoked her order, until he should return.[1] It was doubtless then that the matter was compromised by the imposition of a special tax or licence known as *farda*, by the payment of which the use in Granada of the Moorish language and vestments was conceded. In 1563 we happen to know that this contributed 20,000 ducats to the royal treasury.[2] The matter thus remained in abeyance for many years, and when the Archbishop Gaspar de Avalos (about 1540) endeavored to compel the Moriscos to abandon their costume, the secular authorities, with the captain-general at their head, made him abandon the attempt.[3]

rather see them distinguished by dressing in yellow or blue, like the Jews in Rome.—Crónica, p. 968. Cf. Defensionem Fidei, p. 425.

In the older time costume was not of so much moment. The Cid was buried in a Moorish garment. At the battle of Grados, in 1063, Sadada, one of the Moorish chiefs, who wore a Christian dress and spoke Romance, was enabled to penetrate the Spanish lines and mortally wound Ramiro I. of Aragon.—Dozy, Recherches, II. 232, 243.

[1] Dormer, Marmol Carvajal, Bleda, *ubi sup.*

[2] Relazioni Venete, Serie I. Tom. V. p. 37.

[3] Marmol Carvajal, p. 163.

The Inquisition was duly established, but for awhile it seems to have been inert for, in 1532, the Captain-general Mondéjar suggested to the emperor its suspension, on the ground that it had done nothing for it could find nothing against the converts, to which the Suprema replied that he was prejudiced and the matter was dropped. It is probable that this stimulated the tribunal to greater activity for, in 1537, the Moriscos petitioned that a general pardon should be granted, that fines and confiscations be abandoned and that other means of support be found for the tribunal, to which the reply was that confiscation and pecuniary penance were required by both the canon and secular law and were indispensable; as for the pardon, if they really desired to save their souls by embracing the faith, a term of grace might be conceded during which they could confess in writing before the inquisitors and be absolved.[1] The pressure on the part of the Holy Office seems to have gone on increasing for, in 1539, with the support of Mondéjar, the Moriscos again petitioned Charles for a general pardon without the necessity of confession and further that those condemned to burning or reconciliation should not have their property taken by confiscation or composition or consumed by excessive charges for support in prison during trial. This time Charles ordered a junta to consider the matter, consisting of Guevara, now Bishop of Mondoñedo with the prelates

[1] Confession before an ordinary priest was auricular and was covered by the seal. In the Inquisition all confessions were written out by the notary or secretary and remained of record against the culprit. The one was sacramental, the other judicial. This, together with the obligation to denounce accomplices, explains much of the objection to confess to the inquisitors.

of Granada and other distinguished personages, which reported unanimously against the requests ; they had had two terms of grace and if the Emperor desired to be merciful he could grant them a third, during which they could confess in writing and be absolved without confiscation or sanbenito, but that confiscation was a matter of law and could not be abolished.[1]

In 1543 a more determined effort was made. They arranged to pay six or seven thousand ducats to Christóbal Mexía, brother of the royal confessor Pedro do Soto, and twenty thousand to Mondéjar,[2] and repeated the prayer for pardon without confession or reconciliation. Inquisitor-general Tavera and the Suprema replied by referring to the report of the previous junta and offering a term of grace on the old conditions. Mondéjar replied that they would not accept this, for by written confessions they ran the risk incident to relapse and they preferred to take their chances as they were ; that papal faculties could be obtained and the king could waive confiscation whenever

[1] Archivo de Simancas, Inquisicion, Libro 926, fol. 80.

[2] By this time Mondéjar was no longer captain-general of Granada. He accompanied Charles V. to Tunis in 1535, after which he became Viceroy of Navarre until 1560, when he was made president of the council of Castile, the highest post in the kingdom. It will perhaps make the narrative clearer to explain that Iñigo Lopez de Mendoza, Count of Tendilla, the first Captain-general of Granada, became Marquis of Mondéjar, after which the eldest sons were known as Counts of Tendilla, and held the post of Alcalde of the Alhambra. Iñigo Lopez died in 1512 and was succeeded as captain-general by his son Luis Hurtado de Mendoza, the second marquis. In 1535, the latter was succeeded in the captain-generalship by his son Iñigo Lopez, known as the Count of Tendilla until 1566, when, on the death of his father, he became the third marquis.—Memorial of the Fifth Marquis of Mondéjar (Morel Fatio, L'Espagne au XVIe et XVIIe Siécle, p. 59).

he pleased. Powerful influences were brought to bear in the imperial court including the offer of a subsidy of 120,000 ducats and Charles wrote, October 27, 1543, from Avesnes to Mondéjar, warmly thanking him, and to Prince Philip and Tavera that the Moriscos could have a general pardon without preceding confession and reconciliation and that there should be no confiscation for twenty-five or thirty years. The Inquisition by this time was not always obedient to royal commands. Tavera and the Suprema replied as they had done before, and that the *servicio* of 120,000 ducats offered by the Moriscos would be little enough for a general pardon with written confessions and remission of confiscation. They could not in conscience advise suspending confiscation for twenty-five or thirty years, as it would be offering impunity for transgression besides being repugnant to the canons; it would be sufficient mercy to confiscate one-half of the property and give the other half to Catholic descendants, which would encourage the children to be good Catholics. They added that those who interceded for the Moriscos could readily induce them to accept this, but when the proposal was submitted to Mondéjar he said it would not satisfy them.[1]

Charles wrote in reply from Metz, July 6, 1544, insisting on compliance with his orders; his ambassador at Rome, Juan de Vega, had reported that he was obtaining the brief necessary for completing the arrangement. When Juan de Vega sent the brief, however, it proved to be very different from what the Moriscos had demanded.[2] Then a Mudéjar Morisco named Antonio Ser-

[1] Archivo de Simancas, Inquisicion, Libro 926, fol. 81–2.

[2] A memorial concerning Vega's negotiations in Rome shows that Charles was earnestly endeavoring to obtain the powers necessary for

rano informed Tavera that the Moriscos would moderate their demands and be content with what was just and would pay the emperor a large subsidy, if a commission was appointed to treat with them. Diego de Deza, Bishop of Canaries, then serving as judge in the chancellery of Granada, was appointed and sent for the principal Moriscos, who, after obtaining permission from the Count of Tendilla, said that they would content themselves with what was just and would pay Charles 200,000 ducats, but when Tendilla heard of the negotiation he set his friends among the Moriscos to work and broke it off, sparing neither threats nor promises. Then, in 1555, he proposed to the Moriscos that he should procure from the pope permission for them to confess to confessors of their own selection who should absolve them without solemnity or penance; that the Emperor should waive the confiscations which they had incurred and that the Inquisition should be wholly suspended for forty years. He sent emissaries throughout the kingdom to explain the advantages of this and persuade the Moriscos to offer all the money they could, so as to furnish a good subsidy and recompense those who should intercede for them with Charles and the pope. The Inquisition took the alarm and interfered with the plan by prosecuting Tendilla's emissaries, and a long correspondence ensued between

conceding the requests of the Moriscos. The cardinals to whom the affair was referred objected to the provisions for the future, regarding them as offering encouragement to sinners, and they desired to retain the penalty of burning for relapse. Many months were spent in discussion and finally a compromise was drawn up.—Ibid. fol. 86–7.

It would not, I think, be doing injustice to the Inquisition to suggest that it had a hand in creating obstacles in the curia. It had a permanent agent in Rome to attend to its business.

Tendilla, Prince Philip, Guerrero, Archbishop of Granada, and Valdés, then inquisitor-general.[1] Meanwhile, in 1549, letters passing between the Archbishop and Valdés show that an effort had been made to quiet the Moriscos by granting a term of grace in which some had come in and confessed. Another was conceded in 1553, when a commission was sent to the inquisitors, empowering them to absolve for relapse.[2]

After the abdication of Charles V. the Moriscos made another attempt by sending envoys to Philip II. in Flanders. They complained that Mondéjar and Tendilla amused them with fair words, but their demands were still greater than before, for they added to their former requests that the seal of secrecy be removed from the prisons and the names of witnesses and that when they sinned they should not be prosecuted but be taught, in return for which they offered a subsidy of 100,000 ducats and a perpetual contribution of three thousand ducats a year for the support of the Inquisition. Philip referred the petition to the Suprema to report to him on his return to Spain. Then the Moriscos asked licence to assemble for discussion and the appointment of delegates with full powers, but the Suprema in granting the permission required the meeting to be held in the presence of the archbishop, an inquisitor and the president and two judges of the chancellery, which was done and the powers

[1] Archivo de Simancas, Inquisicion, Libro 926, fol. 82–3.

I have no means of controlling these statements which are from an official report of the Suprema. Allowance should be made for the inveterate hostility between the Inquisition and the secular authorities which seems to have been peculiarly bitter in Granada.

[2] Ibid. Libro 4, fol. 174, 178, 214.

were issued. Archbishop Guerrero earnestly urged Philip not to abandon the confiscations, while the Moriscos continued, at least until the close of 1561, to besiege him with petitions to grant their request or at least such relief as had been afforded to those of Aragon and Valladolid.[1]

The document from which these details are drawn ends here, but we may safely assume that nothing came of the effort of the Moriscos to obtain complete or partial relief from the Inquisition, and it is not unjust to infer from their persistence, and from a complaint of the expense to which they had been put in their journeys to the court in Flanders and elsewhere, that there were not lacking persons in high station who buoyed them up with false hopes in return for liberal donations. These transactions, however fruitless, are not without their importance, in the absence of statistics concerning the activity of the Holy Office, as showing how great was its pressure and how keenly felt by its victims. In every way, indeed, the condition of the Moriscos had been growing worse. The Inquisition, perhaps in retaliation for their efforts to restrict it, became more rigorous than ever.[2] All the old abuses and oppressions by the priests and the petty officers of justice were flourishing rankly and a further cause of intense irritation was the progressive spoliation of their lands by judicial process; "judges of boundaries" were established and claims were put forth in the name of the king by which they were deprived without a hearing of properties purchased or inherited from their ances-

[1] Archivo de Simancas, Inquisicion, Libro 926, fol. 83–4.

[2] Mendoza, Guerra de Granada, p. 71 (Biblioteca de Autores Españoles, Tom. XXI.).

tors—they were in short "gente sin lengua y sin fabor"—friendless and defenceless.[1]

Another fresh cause of trouble was the sudden revival, about 1565, of a dormant law of 1526 which deprived the lands of the feudal nobles of the right of asylum by extending over them the royal jurisdiction, and further reducing to three days the right of asylum in churches. There were numerous Moriscos who had made terms with their enemies and had settled on lands of nobles, where they lived in peace supporting their families, their crimes having been forgotten for years. The scriveners and justices, eager for fees, now examined the records for all the old cases and the alguaziles went in pursuit until there were scarce a Morisco in the land who did not live in daily fear of arrest. To this was added the oppression of the captain-general, of the archbishop and of the Inquisition, so that many peaceable men as well as criminals took to the mountains, joining the monfíes or outlaws, and forming armed bands which committed many outrages that the ordinary justices could not prevent without soldiers. The suppression of these disorders naturally belonged to the captain-general, but there had been numerous competitions of jurisdiction between him and the judicial authorities which broke out afresh and the matter was confided to the President of the Chancellery, Alonso de Santillana, who formed squads of eight men to perform the duty, to whom extravagant pay was given and who were appointed from among the kindred and retainers of the president and alcaldes. They were useless and inexperienced, they exercised brutal licence at will and no one dared to com-

[1] Mendoza, *loc. cit.*

plain of them. This drove many more Moriscos to the mountains or to Africa, the bands of monfíes increased and the relations of the Moriscos with Barbary were strengthened.[1]

It was markedly imprudent thus to aggravate the disquiet of the kingdom for it had long been recognized that the condition of Granada was dangerously explosive. To cut off all intercourse with it Moriscos from elsewhere had been prohibited from going there on any pretext, under pain of slavery, which was a severe hardship, as the chancellery of Granada was the highest court for all the territories of New Castile, as that of Valladolid was for Old Castile, but when the córtes of Madrid, in 1551, petitioned that this prohibition should be relaxed in favor of those who had lawsuits or other pressing business, the prayer was refused—the risk of intercommunication was too great.[2] The prudence which dictated this might have also dictated an effort to soothe discontent, in place of which fresh causes of trouble were sought. In 1563 the order to present to the captain-general all licences to bear arms was revived, under a penalty of six years of galleys.[3] The good Archbishop, Pedro Guerrero, on his return from the council of Trent in 1563, paused in Rome, where he lamented to Pius IV. that his Morisco flock were Christians only in name, and was commanded to tell King Philip that he should remedy it and save their souls, a message which was re-enforced by orders to

[1] Marmol Carvajal, p. 160.—Cabrera, Felipe Segondo, pp. 393, 429 (Madrid, 1619).—Memoria de Mondéjar, pp. 14-16 (Morel-Fatio, L'Espagne au XVIe et XVIIe Siècle).—Mendoza, p. 71.—Pedraza, fol. 239.

[2] Colmeiro, Córtes de Leon y Castilla, II. 245. [3] Danvila, p. 172.

the Bishop of Rosano, papal nuncio, to labor with the king for their conversion. On reaching home Guerrero assembled his provincial council of 1565, the action of which for the protection of the Moriscos was nugatory, but that for their irritation was effective. The bishops agreed to urge the king to adopt such measures as might prevent them from longer concealing their infidelity, and Guerrero accordingly wrote, begging him to purify his kingdom of the filthy sect; it could readily be found who were Christians by prohibiting some things by which they concealed their rites. The Archbishop of Valencia, Tomás of Vilanova, also wrote, saying that he had refused the see of Granada in order not to be the pastor of so evil a flock, but he had found that it was worse in Valencia.[1]

Diego de Espinosa, Philip's evil genius, was then rising high in favor. He had just been appointed to the presidency of the council of Castile; he was shortly to be made inquisitor-general, Bishop of Sigüenza and cardinal, to die, in 1572, of mortification when the king reproached him severely with mendacity as to certain despatches from Flanders.[2] In the present case he was stubbornly impracticable and, as Cabrera says, two priests' caps wrought irreparable mischief in a matter which concerned helmets. To him, with a junta of kindred spirits, including the Duke of Alva, Philip referred Guerrero's memorial and the answer was that, assuming the Moriscos to

[1] Cabrera, Felipe Segondo, p. 393.—Pedraza, fol. 238.

[2] Cabrera, *op. cit.* p. 699. Yet at his tomb Philip declared him to have been the best minister he had ever had—"Aquí está enterrado et mejor ministro que he tenido en mis coronas."—Biblioteca Nacional, Seccion de MSS., Ii. 16.

be Christians by baptism, they must be so in fact, wherefore they must be ordered to abandon the garments, language and customs of Moors, to which end the edict of 1526 should be revived and enforced, and this they solemnly charged upon the royal conscience. On this Philip consulted privately Dr. Otadui, professor of theology in Alcalá and subsequently Bishop of Avila, who in his reply told the king that if any of the lords of the Moriscos cited the old Castilian proverb, "The more Moors the more profit" he should remember that there was an older and truer one—"The fewer enemies the better," and he could combine the two into "The more dead Moors the more profit, for there will be fewer enemies," which we are told pleased Philip greatly.[1]

In the ecclesiastical atmosphere of Philip's court there could be no doubt as to the policy to be adopted. A pragmatica was speedily framed embodying the most offensive features of the edict of 1526; Pedro de Deza, a member of the junta and of the Suprema, was appointed president of the chancellery of Granada and was sent there May 4, 1566, with orders to publish and enforce it without listening to any remonstrances.[2] Tendilla, now

[1] Cabrera, pp. 394, 466.—Pedraza, fol. 238-9.

[2] Deza's character is summed up in a letter of August 14, 1570, near the close of the rebellion, from Don John of Austria to his brother the king.—"V. M. must have heard from several sources that the methods of Deza with this people are very different from what they ought to be. The general opinion is that he was the great cause of the rebellion—so el Habaqui has told me—and the greatest obstacle to their reduction is their fear of being judged by him, of which I think there is no doubt. I entreat V. M. to consider carefully about him and give him a bishopric or some other preferment and remove him from here, which is one of the things most desirable for the service of V. M."—Coleccion de Doc. inéd. XXVIII. 126.

Marquis of Mondéjar, with his thirty years' experience as captain-general, was not consulted or notified in advance. Although he was at the court, the first intimation he had of it was an order conveyed through Espinosa to return to Granada and be present at the publication. He complained of the adoption of a measure of such importance without apprising him, he represented that the condition of Granada, destitute of troops and munitions, was not such as to justify putting a strain so severe on the loyalty of the Moriscos and he begged that either the measure be suspended or that he be furnished with forces to suppress the revolt that he foresaw. It was all in vain; Espinosa curtly told him to go to his post and mind his own business. The Council of War supported him, but the Royal Council considered the judicial power sufficient to keep in subjection a despised race who were disarmed, unorganized and without military knowledge; he was granted only three hundred soldiers to guard the coast, where he was ordered to reside during certain months of the year and to visit frequently.[1] A crazy enterprise could scarce be undertaken with a crazier lack of foresight.

May 25, 1566, Deza reached Granada with the fateful edict and at once assembled the court and took possession of his office. He had the articles printed so that they might be distributed everywhere in readiness for publication on January 1, 1567, the anniversary of the capture of the city by Ferdinand and Isabella. There was a belief held by some at the time that the object in view was to drive the Moriscos to despair so as to make an end of them and the nature of the articles almost justifies

[1] Cabrera, p. 465.—Memoria de Mondéjar (Morel-Fatio, p. 17).—Pedraza, fol. 239.—Marmol Carvajal, p. 167.

such a theory, for there is nothing in them as to instruction in religion while their whole tenor was a mere arbitrary and exasperating interference with ancestral habits. The Moriscos were ordered to learn Castilian within three years, after which no one was to speak, read or write Arabic, either publicly or privately, and all contracts in that tongue should be invalid. All books in Arabic were to be delivered to Deza within thirty days; such as he deemed innocent were to be returned to the owners for three years and no longer. No provision was made for instruction in Castilian, but Deza and Guerrero were ordered to adopt such measures as they deemed expedient. No garments were hereafter to be made in Moorish fashion; existing ones, wholly or partly of silk, could be worn for a year and no longer, those of cloth for two years, and meanwhile women were to go with faces uncovered. Betrothal and marriage ceremonies and feasts must conform to the usages of the Church and, during their celebration, as well as on Friday afternoons and feast-days, the house doors must be kept open. Zambras and leilas—festivities with song and dance—even though not contrary to religion, were forbidden on Fridays and feast-days. Moorish names and surnames were not to be employed and the staining with henna was to be abandoned. All artificial baths were to be destroyed, both public and private ones, and no one in future was to use them. No Morisco was to hold a Moorish slave, even though he had a licence to do so, and all licences to keep negro slaves were to be submitted to Deza for consideration.[1]

[1] Marmol Carvajal, p. 161–2.—Pedraza, fol. 239.

A special law, without date, preserved in the *Nueva Recopilacion* (Lib. VIII. Tit. ii. ley 21) commands the destruction of all artificial baths

All this could only seem to the Moriscos a wanton and objectless exercise of power. Forty years before they had been similarly threatened and had succeeded in buying themselves off and they doubtless expected to do so again, but now they had to deal with sterner and more impracticable bigots. Deza counselled with the archbishop as to the easiest method of enforcing the pragmatica and they called into service Canon Horozco, of the church of San Salvador, who was very friendly with the Moriscos and fluent in Arabic. By their instructions Horozco assembled the principal Moriscos, explained to them the new laws and promised them honors and offices from the king if they would induce their people to obedience, but they declared they would not dare to attempt it, for they would be stoned to death. A second attempt only found them firmer than before, although he used Deza's name and argued that, as the king was resolved to enforce the measure, they had better get what advantage they could out of it.[1]

January 1, 1567, the pragmatica was formally published with great solemnity and produced among the Moriscos an indescribable excitement as its provisions became known. As an earnest of its enforcement, all baths were forthwith destroyed, commencing with those of the king. All the aljamas sent envoys to consult the Albaycin and all were unanimous that if relief were not

in the kingdom of Granada. Any one keeping or using them, either at home or elsewhere, is for a first offence to be imprisoned for fifty days in chains, with a fine of 10,000 maravedís and two years of exile; for a second offence, double; for a third, loss of half his property and five years of galleys.

[1] Marmol Carvajal, p. 161.

to be had by entreaty resort must be had to rebellion—it were better to die fighting for independence than to live under such tyranny. Deza himself was so impressed with the threatening prospect that he wrote to the court that precautions should be taken against a rising and during the year 1567 he mitigated in some degree the harshness of the law; he did not allow any punishments under it and, as the ordinary alguaziles were rude and insulting, he substituted others with instructions to be courteous to the Moriscas whom they had to arrest for wearing veils. Meanwhile Don Juan Enriquez of Baza, a man of high rank, consented to bear a memorial to the court and to labor for a suspension of the pragmatica, but was met by letters from Deza to Espinosa and the king saying that the Moriscos had been submissive but were becoming turbulent since he had espoused their cause. Philip referred the memorial to Espinosa, as President of Castile, who replied that no suspension could be entertained; religious men had charged the king's conscience, telling him he was responsible for the souls of the apostates. Then appeal was made to the Council of State, where the Duke of Alva and Luis de Avila, Grand Commander of Alcántara, were in favor of suspension and the council suggested a compromise of enforcing only one article a year, but Espinosa and Deza had more influence than all the soldiers and statesmen in the royal councils.[1]

When the time came for abandoning silk garments, the archbishop instructed all priests to notify the Moriscos at high mass on New Year's day of 1568 and Deza ordered

[1] Cabrera, p. 465.—Pedrazá, fol. 240.—Marmol Carvajal, pp. 166, 168.

the priests to take all children between three and fifteen years of age and place them in schools where they should be taught Christian doctrine and Castilian. This increased the agitation and a deputation was sent to remonstrate with Deza, who assured them that the children were not to be taken from them, but that the king was resolved to save their souls and to enforce the new laws.[1] The Moriscos had come to the parting of the ways; there was no middle course and they had the naked alternative of submission or rebellion.

Rebellion at first sight seemed hopeless, even to despair. They had been disarmed, they had no military training, no munitions of war, no fortresses, and but little money, while against them was the great Spanish monarchy, regarded as the most powerful in the civilized world, with its navies on every sea and its armies in almost every land. But already the great Spanish monarchy was little better than a shell, hollow within, notwithstanding its imposing outward appearance. All the relations of the Venetian envoys of the period dwell upon the absence of military resources in Spain, the difficulty of raising troops and the unfamiliarity with arms of those who made such splendid soldiers when disciplined and sent abroad. In this very year 1567, Antonio Tiepolo, when commenting upon the strange neglect which left the southern coasts unguarded to be ravaged by Barbary corsairs, expresses apprehension that an invasion from Africa, supported by the Moriscos, who are only Christians in outward show, might expose the monarchy to the same dangers which it experienced of old.[2] Spain had

[1] Marmol Carvajal, p. 167.—Pedraza, fol. 241.
[2] Relazioni Venete, Serie I. T. V. p. 145.

been bled to exhaustion by Charles V. and Philip continued the process. Fray Bleda points out that during the whole course of the ensuing war, when every nerve was strained, there never were a thousand horse brought together, while Ferdinand and Isabella had twelve thousand at the siege of Málaga and as many at the conquest of Baza.[1] The financial condition was no better. Charles had left such a fearful accumulation of indebtedness that Philip, on his accession, seriously considered the expediency of repudiation, and, despite the treasures of the New World, he staggered ever under an increasing burden; his revenues were consumed in advance and when the rebellion was to be suppressed it was with difficulty that moderate sums could be provided for the most pressing exigencies.[2] That under such circumstances the supplies of arms and munitions should be deficient was a matter of course.

The intelligent Moriscos of the Albaycin could not be

[1] Bleda, Crónica, p. 755.

[2] In the correspondence of Don John of Austria during the war his demands for money are incessant. Sept. 23, 1569 he says to Philip that every one is trying to hunt for it from some one else and it is got with so much difficulty that everything suffers. Oct. 4th he hopes that money will come to pay the soldiers and buy provisions; without it nothing can be done. Feb. 19, 1570 he says that supplies of money are indispensable and about the same date he thanks Espinosa for promising to see that it is furnished for it is the one great necessity. July 6th he asks the favorite Ruy Gomez to see that the two things necessary—money and troops—are provided and Aug. 14th he tells Espinosa that what is necessary now is to have money, even if the king has to sell his patrimony; the 40,000 ducats coming are already eaten up. Aug. 29th he complains to Ruy Gomez that people at court seem to think that money is wanted only for the camp; there are over-due debts to be paid and the garrisons—and so forth.—Coleccion de Doc. inéd. XXVIII. 26, 31, 49, 56, 58, 110, 113, 124, 133, 147.

wholly ignorant of all this, however it might be disregarded by the clerical counsellors who were leading Philip to the precipice here, as they did with respect to the Low Countries. They knew that they had the natural fortresses of the sierras to fall back upon, they hoped for effective aid from Turk and Moor, whose fighting qualities were fully equal to anything that Spain could show, they argued that there were 85,000 households which paid the impost of the farda, besides 15,000 concealed by the assessors, and that these could readily furnish 100,000 fighting men, and they placed faith in three *jofores* or prophecies, handed down from the time of the conquest by Ferdinand and Isabella, from which they drew promises of success.[1] At the least, they could hope that a show of force might compel the suspension of the pragmatica. Marmol Carvajal tells us that the wealthier ones, while promising their concurrence, did not want a general rebellion but only a partial rising, by which they could attain this at the expense of the rude and ignorant mountaineers. However this may be, the agitation was stimulated and it was agreed that the rebellion should break out on Holy Thursday (April 15) 1568; this spread from one to another; the monfíes grew more audacious, marching openly with banners flying, robbing and murdering Christians; many friars and others among them notified the king of the increasing disquiet and accurate information was sent to the archbishop and to Mondéjar, who was

[1] The feelings and the hopes of the Moriscos are well depicted in a ballad by Mohammad ben Mohammad aben Daud, one of the leaders of the rising, intercepted in April, 1568, by Mondéjar and sent to the court with a translation by Alonso del Castillo. A version of it will be found in the Appendix No. XII.

then at the court, by Francisco de Torrijos, priest of Darrical, who spoke Arabic and had many friends among the Moriscos. Mondéjar hastened to Granada, where his son Tendilla was strengthening the Alhambra and arming the citizens, seeing which the leaders of the Albaycin notified the mountaineers that the plot was discovered and that it must be abandoned. With a show of indignation they went to Deza and complained of being suspected, offering to place two or three hundred of their chief men in prison as hostages. He pretended to be perfectly assured of their loyalty; as for hostages, there was no need to offer them, as he would take them whenever the king's service required; but as soon as the audience was over he sent for the alcaldes of the chancellery and told them to look up all prosecutions against Moriscos, both as principals and as securities, and arrest them gradually, so that in a short time many of those suspected were thrown in prison. He also ordered the seizure of all cross-bows and arquebusses belonging to those who held licences.[1]

It illustrates the tension of the public mind that, on the night of April 16th, an accident caused a false alarm that the Albaycin had risen. The women rushed to the churches and the Alhambra, while the men assembled in arms. The corregidores placed guards on the streets leading to the Albaycin, but this, we are told, would not have restrained the rapacity of the Christians who were eager to sack it, but for the fact that rain was falling in torrents rendering the streets almost impassable. The alarm proved groundless but as a precaution for the future the

[1] Marmol Carvajal, pp. 169, 174.—Cabrera, p. 468.

people were armed and organized.[1] About the same time a letter from the Moriscos to the King of Fez was intercepted, asking for assistance. Mondéjar forwarded this to the king, begging him either to send troops or to suspend, or at least moderate, the rigor of the pragmatica, but Philip relied on Deza's reports that the Moriscos were submissive and that no danger was to be expected; he ordered the enforcement of the pragmatica and provided no troops.[2]

Under the appearance of submission, organization and preparation were carried on industriously and a rising was determined upon for Christmas night, when the people would be in the churches and prolonged darkness would enable the mountaineers to reach the city undiscovered. Only twenty-five guards had been provided for the Albaycin, which had been taken out of Mondéjar's hands, so there was little to prevent a terrible catastrophe. December 23d risings commenced in the sierras and in a few days 182 places had revolted; the churches were desecrated, the priests and such Christians as could be seized were tortured and slain, while the women and children were kept to be sent to Barbary in exchange for arms and munitions. Eight thousand men were enrolled in the Vega to enter the Albaycin and lay waste the city with fire and sword. The plot was well planned, but at the last moment the leaders in the Albaycin thought that it had been discovered and sent word to postpone it. In spite of this Farax aben Farax, one of the most resolute of them, gathered a hundred and fifty monfíes with whom he broke open one of the gates, killed one or two of the guards and endeavored ineffectually to arouse his country-

[1] Marmol Carvajal, p. 176.

[2] Ibid. p. 179.—Memorial de Mondéjar (Morel-Fatio, p. 19).

men, although he proclaimed that the Kings of Morocco and Algiers had landed. He remained unmolested all night and departed in the morning. The corregidor had been able to assemble but twenty-three men, while Mondéjar, in the Alhambra, had but a hundred and forty foot and fifty horse—a small garrison for the fortress, which he dared not abandon, the whole affair showing how easily the Moriscos might have succeeded had they carried out their designs.[1]

The rebellion was now fairly on foot. It speedily provided itself with a king in the person of Don Hernando de Córdova y de Valor, a descendant of the Abderrahamanes, the old kings of Córdova. He was a veintecuatro, or town-councillor of Granada, and at the time a prisoner in his house for drawing a dagger in the council; he was rich but a spendthrift and angered at the imprisonment of his father for a crime, in revenge for which he had killed the accuser and some of the witnesses. He fled to the mountains and was solemnly crowned December 29th at Andarax, when he assumed the name of Aben Humeya; he endeavored to restrain the slaughter of Christians; he became unpopular and after a reign of nine months he was strangled by his Turkish and Algerine auxiliaries, who replaced him with Abdallah Abenabó. With his last breath he declared that he died a Christian; he had revolted in order to obtain revenge on those who had persecuted his father, he had glutted his vengeance and was content to die.[2]

[1] Marmol Carvajal, pp. 181–5.—Cabrera, pp. 537–40.—Memoria de Mondéjar, p. 19.

[2] Cabrera, pp. 501, 547.—Marmol Carvajal, pp. 187, 292.—Mendoza, pp. 74, 102.

The news that came pouring in from all quarters and was brought by the scouting parties which Mondéjar sent out showed that the whole land was ablaze. He had been left destitute of resources to meet the emergency which he had foreseen and he could expect no co-operation from Deza or the local authorities with whom he was in bitter discord. Deza, in fact, at once seized the opportunity to humiliate and embarrass him by writing to the Adelantado of Murcia, the Marquis of los Velez, his hereditary enemy, to raise the militia of Murcia and attack the Moriscos, which was a direct invasion of Mondéjar's territory. Los Velez, who was ambitious, arrogant and opinionated and who entertained a deadly hatred of the Moriscos, who called him "the devil with the iron head," eagerly took advantage of the invitation; he raised troops at his own expense, thrust himself into the war and mismanaged it at every turn, but he was a favorite of the king, who supported him through it all.[1]

The military system of Spain, inherited from the time when the conquests were settled by the conquerors, required the communities and towns to furnish troops when called upon. These were known as *concegiles*—raised by the town-councils; they were obliged to serve at their own cost for as long as they could subsist on the rations carried in their knapsacks, which was reckoned as a week; after this they served three months, paid by their communities, and then six months more, paid half by the latter and half by the king; when they returned home, others were sent. They were necessarily raw and undisciplined and, through long internal peace, so unused to

[1] Marmol Carvajal, pp. 207, 230.—Mendoza, p. 77.—Morel-Fatio, p. 275.

weapons that the Venetian envoy in 1570 tells us that many were afraid to discharge their arquebusses. As the pay was uncertain it was impossible to control them or make them stay by the colors, and their principal motive in serving was the prospect of booty. By a custom dating from the earliest times, the spoils were sold and the proceeds distributed, reserving one-fifth for the king, but it was found more inspiriting to give to each what he had captured and the fifth to all. But, as Mendoza remarks, this degenerates into greed; every one holds what he gets and to guard it abandons his duty; some let themselves be killed, overburdened and weakened by it, others desert and go home with it.[1] So it was throughout the war; armies disintegrated more rapidly after a victory than after a defeat; we hear of whole companies marching away and beating off those sent to detain them. The war degenerated into a pandemonium of massacre and pillage; nothing could restrain the ferocious rapacity of the troops; the armies were followed by merchant adventurers ready to buy on the spot whatever was brought in—goods or cattle or slaves—and in fact many of the so-called military movements were merely slave-hunts. There had been a question, indeed, at first, whether prisoners, who were at least nominally Christians, could be enslaved, and in Madrid there were superserviceable lawyers and theologians who denied it, but the king referred the matter to Deza and his court who promptly decided in the affirmative, whereupon the king issued a pragmatica to that effect, humanely excepting boys under 10 and girls under 11, who were to be given in charge to

[1] Mendoza, pp. 77, 96.—Relazioni Venete, Serie I. T. V. p. 163.

Christians for support and instruction in the faith, but no attention was paid to this exception.[1] As a rule the men were slaughtered and the women and children brought in droves, sometimes of two thousand or more, to the auction block. For many years thereafter the tribunals of the Inquisition throughout Spain were occupied with trials of slaves from the sierras of Granada.

Such were the conditions under which Mondéjar had to meet the crisis which burst upon Granada on the morning of December 27, 1568. He met it with resolute energy. He was eminently suited to the work in hand, for his thirty years' experience as captain-general gave him an accurate knowledge of the country and its people; he was trained to vigorous discipline, accustomed to command and impatient of contradiction; he was self-reliant, kept his own counsel and admitted few to his confidence.[2] He needed these qualities for he was without men, money, artillery, munitions and provisions. He forthwith summoned the cities of Andalusia to furnish their quotas, but they were tardy in obeying, for there had been repeated false alarms before; the contractors in Málaga were ordered to buy up all the provisions they could and to furnish powder, lead and matches; the coast defences were looked to; the municipal authorities armed and organized the citizens, and by January 2d a little army, drawn from the city and its vicinity, was on foot. His

[1] Marmol Carvajal, p. 247. There seems to have been some special royal claim on slaves. Mondéjar alludes (Memoria, p. 47) to about a thousand women, the survivors of a massacre at Jubíles, who were sent to Granada, sold at auction, and the proceeds handed to the royal officials.

[2] Mendoza, p. 84.

first experience was an earnest of much that was to come. The bridge over the deep gorge at Tablate was the key to the sierras; to secure this important point he had sent Diego de Quesada with a few hundred raw and undisciplined men; they scattered to plunder, the Moriscos set upon them and Quesada had difficulty in escaping with the remnant of his forces. The recapture of the bridge was indispensable and, on January 3d, Mondéjar set out on his campaign with 2500 foot and 250 horse, to which were added, the next day, reinforcements of 2000 more. When Tablate was reached it was found that the Moriscos had so dismantled the bridge that but one man could cross at a time and this with no little danger. They were in force on the farther side and the army paused in hesitation, till a friar rushed forward, a crucifix in one hand and a sword in the other, and boldly led the way. Two men followed him, one of whom fell from the narrow timbers and was dashed to pieces on the rocks below. Then others took heart, and, covered by the fire of the arquebusiers, enough got across to drive away the enemy; the bridge was secured and repaired.[1]

It is not necessary to follow in detail Mondéjar's short but brilliant campaign. Through heavy snows and intense cold and over almost inaccessible mountains he fought battle after battle, giving the enemy no respite and following up every advantage gained. The Moriscos speedily lost heart and sought terms of surrender. Already, by January 18th, the priest Torrijos brought to him at Jubíles seventeen of the principal alguaziles or magistrates of the sierra, who threw themselves at his feet, offered to sur-

[1] Memoria de Mondéjar, pp. 23-4.—Marmol Carvajal, p. 227.

render at discretion and begged his intercession. He received them kindly, promised them security and ordered that no harm should befall them, for the soldiers, eager for booty, were bent on prolonging the war, and murmured loudly when he gave the envoys safe-conducts and sent them back with instructions to tell their people to return to their homes. His object was to pacify the land as speedily as possible, and, while he granted letters of security to all places which submitted, he relaxed nothing in the vigor of his military operations ; he ordered that no prisoners should be taken and at the Guajaras, in revenge for a preliminary reverse, by his command there was a general massacre, without sparing age or sex. He justified this on the ground that the contrast between kindness for submission and cruelty for resistance was the surest mode of bringing peace. By the middle of February the rebellion was practically suppressed. Aben Humeya was a wanderer, hiding in caves by day and seeking shelter at night in houses which had letters of surety. Of the 182 places that had risen every one submitted at discretion, except Valor el alto which was depopulated. One of the conditions was the surrender of arms, to be deposited in designated churches, and to these he sent the priest Torrijos with twenty men to bring them in, a mission which was accomplished peacefully and seventy loads of them were taken to the Alhambra. His orders were obeyed more promptly than before the rising ; when he sent to arrest some who had not submitted and were especially guilty, they were brought in by dozens through the mountains and were executed without a finger lifted in their behalf. Pacification was complete except when bands of Christian marauders traversed the country, murdering and despoiling.[1]

Perhaps the most signal instance of submission concerns an incident too characteristic to be omitted. At the capture of Jubíles, January 18th, the non-combatants, who had taken refuge in the castle, surrendered to the number of 300 men and 2100 women. They were brought down to the town and the women were placed for safety in the church, but, as it held only about one-half, the rest bivouacked in the gardens with guards around them. During the night a soldier tried to carry off a girl; a young Morisco in female dress defended her with a dagger and wounded a soldier, others crowded in with the result that in a wild tumult all the prisoners were butchered save those in the church, who were saved only by barricading the doors. The next day three of the ringleaders of the massacre were hanged and Mondéjar distributed the surviving prisoners among their kindred to be fed and kept till he should call for them. When the district was pacified he demanded them and their husbands and fathers unresistingly delivered them up to be sold into slavery. There could, as he says, be no greater proof of obedience than bringing their wives and children from the furthest points of the Alpujarras to such a fate. It was not without pardonable pride that he boasted of having accomplished all this with insufficient forces in the space of a little over two months at a cost of fifteen thousand ducats, a large portion of which

[1] Marmol Carvajal, pp. 234-48.—Mendoza, pp. 82-4.—Memoria de Mondéjar, pp. 45-6.

was defrayed by the royal fifths of the spoils and the sale of the slaves of Jubíles.[1]

His dream of pacification however was rudely broken. Philip's system of government concentrated all power in the crown and distributed authority among subordinates independent of each other, whose mutual jealousies rendered concerted action impossible and whose jarring policies required constant reference to the king for ultimate and dilatory decision. There were too many interests and hatreds and ambitions seething around Granada for any wise and consistent line of action to be followed. When Mondéjar reported to los Velez the arrangements he was making for pacification, the latter haughtily replied that he intended to carry on the war to the bitter end. He had rightfully no authority in Mondéjar's territory, but he had been invited by Deza, who had no power to do so, and his vanity was inflated by a victory which he had won at Felix, killing seven hundred Moriscos with the loss of only a few men, a victory which emphasizes the character of the struggle between his well-armed soldiers and the poor wretches who were struggling for their rights, for we are told that the Morisco women fought desperately, endeavoring to stab the horses of the cavaliers with knives, while those who had no other weapons gathered handfuls of dust to cast in the faces of the Christians and blind them.[2]

[1] Marmol Carvajal, pp. 235, 239.—Memoria de Mondéjar, pp. 47, 53.

[2] Marmol Carvajal, pp. 236, 239.—Cabrera, pp. 560, 561.—So in Mondéjar's campaign at Pitres, on January 16th, the Moriscos attacked his camp under cover of a fog and got so near that the stones they threw by hand reached the parade ground of the camp, but when the fog lifted the arquebusiers drove them back.—Marmol Carvajal, p. 232.

There was bitter opposition to peace also among the lawless and undisciplined soldiery whose ferocious greed was not to be satiated. It was impossible to make them respect Mondéjar's letters of safety. Thus, under pretext of capturing Aben Humaya, Bernardino de Villalta obtained three companies from Tendilla with which he made a raid on Laróles, a place under safeguard, where many of the pacified Moriscos had taken refuge; he carried off a multitude of women and much other booty and when Mondéjar proposed to punish him he pleaded that he had found fighting men there and was allowed to sell the women as slaves. Even worse was what occurred at Valor el bajo, where Aben Humaya was reported to be concealed. Mondéjar sent a force there under Alvaro Flores and Antonio de Avila with orders to require his surrender and to summon those who had harbored him to appear for trial. When the troops reached the village, the chief men came out, exhibited their safeguard and asked what was required of them, for they would obey. In reply the Spaniards fell upon them, killing about two hundred—in fact all who did not escape to the mountains while the troops were pillaging and gathering in the women and children. The men organized and came down; they asked whether Mondéjar had given orders to sack the place, for if so they would submit, but as no such orders could be shown they attacked the soldiers encumbered with spoils, routed them, killed Antonio de Avila, recovered their women and gained a quantity of arms. Then they sent a deputation to Mondéjar to exculpate themselves and offered to return the arms; he was inclined to listen to them, which excited furious indignation and bitter complaints were sent to the king against him.[1]

These outrages by a licentious and brutal soldiery had a double effect. In more than one instance the Moriscos had the advantage over the marauders which encouraged them and supplied them with arms. They found moreover that Mondéjar's safeguards were not respected, that they had gained nothing by submission and that their only chance of safety lay in taking to the mountains and defending themselves, so that Aben Humaya, in place of being a fugitive in hiding, speedily gathered an army of four thousand men. Even more disastrous however was the effect upon the policy of the court. Mondéjar's enemies—Deza, the inquisitors, the municipal authorities of Granada and those whose interests lay in the prolongation of the war, or who sought the extermination of the Moriscos—had never ceased to calumniate him to Espinosa and to Philip. He held large possessions in Granada and he was represented as actuated solely by the desire to preserve their value, his successes were belittled and those of los Velez extolled. When, therefore, he reported to Philip the pacification of the land and asked for instructions whether to show clemency to the vanquished or to punish them with rigor, he was told, March 17th, that it had been determined to send Don John of Austria, the king's half-brother, to Granada to take supreme command; he was to return to the city himself, leaving a competent force in the Alpujarras, while the whole eastern portion of the kingdom was placed under los Velez.[2] This was

[1] Marmol Carvajal, pp. 250, 253.—Mendoza, p. 86.—Memoria de Mondéjar, p. 47.

[2] Mendoza, pp. 84–5, 87.—Marmol Carvajal, p. 251.—Memoria de Mondéjar, p. 48.

virtually relieving him in disgrace. He obeyed and with his absence there followed general licence. No check was placed on the disorders of the troops, stimulated by those who desired to see the peaceable Moriscos driven to rebellion, by those who had interest in increasing the troubles and by the ministers of justice who were impatient for the time of punishment. The Vega was ready to rise and whole towns and neighborhoods passed over to the rebels unable to endure the robberies and murders and outrages on women.[1]

Great preparations were made to give Don John a force which befitted his dignity and should speedily crush all resistance. The towns and cities were summoned to furnish their quotas and the Spanish ambassador at Rome, Don Luis de Requesenes, was ordered to bring the Italian galleys to Spain, to aid the home squadron in guarding the coast and intercepting succors from Africa, and also to convey the *tercio* of Naples, of about three thousand regular troops.[2] These elaborate preparations, however, were neutralized by the jealous care with which all initiative was hampered. Don John was an inexperienced youth, of about twenty-four, eager to win distinction, but modest, affable, distrustful of his own abilities, who felt himself surrounded by pitfalls and who chafed against the orders which strictly forbade him to take the field in person.[3] He brought with him as his chief counsellor his former tutor, Luis Quijada, a man of high military reputa-

[1] Mendoza, p. 89.

[2] Marmol Carvajal, p. 257.—Mendoza, p. 89.

[3] His correspondence at this time gives a most favorable impression of his character. See Coleccion de Doc. inéd. T. XXVIII. pp. 8–11, 60, 72, 86, 92.

tion, and was soon joined by Gonzalo Hernandez de Córdova, Duke of Sesa, grandson of the Great Captain, who had been viceroy of Milan and had acquitted himself well in the Lombard wars. These, with Mondéjar, Deza and Archbishop Guerrero formed his council, without whose advice he was to do nothing. Quijada was rough and obstinate and wedded to the traditions of Charles V. Sesa knew only the well-paid regular troops of Italy and Flanders. Mondéjar was trained to the limitations of the local militia, serving with little pay, but not to open war. Deza and Guerrero knew nothing. Then los Velez and Sesa, although uncle and nephew, had a standing quarrel, which bred suspicions and rendered cordial co-operation between them impossible. To crown all, nothing was to be done without referring the matter to Madrid and awaiting instructions. The results of this impracticable mode of carrying on war soon made themselves apparent.[1]

Don John arrived at Granada, April 12th, and had a magnificent reception, including a parade of ten thousand troops. The most significant feature, however, was a procession of four hundred women, whom Mondéjar had rescued from the Moriscos of the Alpujarras, and who now were marshalled by his enemies to appeal to Don John for vengeance for their murdered husbands and fathers and to tell him that they felt less grief for their losses than for seeing the murderers pardoned.[2] After awaiting the arrival of Sesa, Don John held his first council, April 22d. Mondéjar proposed three alternative lines of policy;

[1] Mendoza, p. 91.—Marmol Carvajal, p. 251.—Coleccion de Doc. inéd. XXVIII. 8.

[2] Marmol Carvajal, p. 257.—Historia de la Casa de Mondéjar (Morel. Fatio, p. 91).

Deza declared that they must begin by removing to places further inland all the Moriscos of the Albaycin, the Vega and the sierra and then placate God for the sacrileges committed, by inflicting exemplary punishment, commencing with those of Albuñuela, who under pretext of having submitted, were robbing the Christians. These conflicting opinions led to prolonged discussions during which nothing was done; the campaign went to pieces; the pacified Moriscos, reduced to despair by the withdrawal of Mondéjar, sent back their safeguards and withdrew their oaths of allegiance and with them went many places that had previously remained loyal. Military operations degenerated into sporadic raids for plunder in which the marauders more than once were cut to pieces, giving both arms and encouragement to the rebels. Granada was virtually besieged, for the Moriscos ravaged the Vega up to the gates. Los Velez had been furnished independently by Philip with an army of twelve thousand men, with which he remained virtually inactive until it dwindled away to 1000 foot and 200 horse—he claimed because the necessary provisions were not supplied, while Don John stoutly declared that he had been furnished with all that he required. The rebellion, which had hitherto been confined to the Alpujarras and Sierra Nevada, spread on the one side to the mountains of Almería and on the other to those of Málaga. The whole land was aflame and it looked as though the power of Spain was inadequate to extinguish the conflagration.[1]

[1] Marmol Carvajal, pp. 258-9, 283-6, 303.—Mendoza, pp. 91-2.—Historia de la Casa de Mondéjar, p. 90.—Coleccion de Doc. inéd. XXVIII. 13, 17, 18, 19, 22.

In all this disaster Deza at least had the satisfaction of seeing his policy carried out. June 1st an expedition was sent against Albuñuela, the pacified town which he wanted destroyed. The troops killed all the men who did not escape and brought back fifteen hundred women and children whom Don John divided among the soldiers as slaves.[1] His other favorite measure, the depopulation of the Albaycin, occupied the council to the exclusion of planning military operations. As the danger of the rebellion from without grew greater, the more pressure was there to get rid of presumable enemies within. At length Philip was induced to issue an order to transfer to Andalusia and elsewhere all the Moriscos of the city and Albaycin over ten years of age and under sixty; they were to be delivered to the *justicias* of the designated places, with lists so that they might all be accounted for, and to induce them to go peaceably they were to be told that it was for their safety and that when peace should come they would be taken care of and those who were loyal rewarded. By this time Granada was well garrisoned with troops under royal pay; they were put under arms and, on June 23d, Don John issued a proclamation that all the men of the Albaycin should assemble in their parish churches, to which they replied that they would not leave their houses alive. This had been done without the knowledge of Mondéjar, who had always opposed the proposition, but Don John sent for him and expressed his intention of putting them all to the sword. In the narrow hilly streets of the Albaycin this would have been a desperate expedient, and Mondéjar dissuaded him. The

[1] Marmol Carvajal, p. 272.

council was summoned and could suggest nothing to extricate Don John from his awkward position until Mondéjar offered to persuade the Moriscos to submit. With his guard of thirty halberdiers and his són Francisco, he proceeded to the plaza of Bib el Bonut, summoned the leaders and induced them to comply with the order. He remained till they were all in the churches, locked the doors, placed his halberdiers on guard and returned to Don John, telling him to send additional troops and provisions and to give orders that they were to be well treated and that no house should be entered. The next day they were transferred to the great Hospital Real, a gunshot from the city. Then lists were made out, they were divided up into gangs with their hands tied to ropes, like galley-slaves, and were marched off to their destinations under guard of foot and horse. The women were left for a time in their houses to sell their effects and follow to support their husbands. The number of men thus deported was 3500; that of the women considerably greater. Even the chroniclers are moved to pity in describing the misery and despair of the unfortunates thus torn suddenly from their homes, forced without warning to leave everything behind them and hurried off to the unknown. Many died on the road of grief, of weariness, of hunger, or were slain by those set to protect them, or were robbed and sold as slaves. It relieved the people of fear, we are told, but it was most distressing to see the destruction of prosperity and the vacuity left where there had been so much life and industry.[1]

[1] Historia de la Casa de Mondéjar, p. 93.—Marmol Carvajal, p. 277. —Mendoza, p. 92.

Thus matters dragged on through the summer and autumn of 1569. On September 3d Mondéjar was summoned to the court and disappears henceforth from the scene, for he took no further part in the war.[1] His absence relieved the other members of the council, but as his advice had never been followed it made no other difference. It was in the highest degree fortunate for Spain that the Mahometan powers took no advantage of the dreary struggle, contenting themselves with expressions of good-will for the rebels and granting permission to such of their subjects as desired to go to their assistance. Under this some six or eight hundred went and formed a most valuable nucleus for the Morisco armies. Arms and munitions were likewise sent across from Africa as objects of trade and it seemed impossible for the Spanish navy to prevent the free communication between the coasts.

At length, on October 19th, Philip issued two edicts. The first one characteristically ordered the removal from the Albaycin of some remnants that had been left there —old men and children, mechanics and laborers whose services were valuable, and Mudéjares who had claimed that they were not included in the earlier measure. The second edict was more serious. The forces which had been

[1] This recall was virtually in disgrace, though softened in terms by the alleged reason of desiring his advice. He remained nominally captain-general until 1572, when he was appointed viceroy of Valencia and from there he was transferred to Naples, one of the most distinguished posts under the crown. The promotion however was only apparent. The viceroyalties were held for an uncertain and usually short term of years, while the captain-generalate of Granada had been for life and heritable. Probably Philip was glad of an opportunity to break up a system which gave such power to great nobles.

raised for Don John and los Velez in the spring, had melted away without checking the progress of the rebellion and it had become a problem how to replace them. The king therefore now proclaimed a *guerra á fuego y á sangre*, for hitherto the official talk had been about punishing a rebellion. At the same time he conceded *campo franco* to the soldiers—that is, that every man should enjoy whatever plunder he could get, whether slaves, cattle or property, without paying a fifth to the commander, so as to animate the dispirited people who had been much scandalized by the complaints of the deserters from los Velez. He also increased the pay to that of service in Italy—four gold crowns a month for the arquebusier and cuirassier and three for the pikeman. Further, as the cities and nobles throughout Spain were exhausted by paying their men, and as the octroi which they had laid on provisions did not suffice, Philip, in calling upon them again to fill up their companies and increase them, offered to pay the infantry while they should pay the horse. These measures we are told produced great results, but their necessity reveals how slender were the resources of the monarchy. Efforts, not very successful, were likewise made to reform the corruption which rendered the army inefficient through padded muster rolls and indescribable fraud in the commissariat and contracts for arms and munitions, and thirty-two captains were cashiered.[1]

This was in preparation for a final effort, and to give it greater assurance of success Philip at last yielded to Don John's urgency and gave him permission to take

[1] Marmol Carvajal, pp. 292, 309.—Mendoza, p. 107.

the field in person. This in itself aided in swelling the forces, for numbers of nobles and gentlemen, eager to distinguish themselves in the presence of the king's brother, came as volunteers with their retainers. In December everything was ready for the campaign planned to recapture Galera and the valley of the Almanzora in the eastern portion of the kingdom, but before starting it was necessary to take Guéjara from which a Morisco garrison annoyed the city. A force of 9000 foot and 700 horse was collected for this enterprise, when it was delayed by a characteristic incident. The command of the city contingent belonged by custom to the Count of Tendilla, but at the last moment it was claimed by Juan Rodriguez de Villafuerte, the corregidor who was a special enemy of Mondéjar. Over this matter the council wrangled without being able to reach a decision; it had to be referred to Madrid and the answer awaited, which of course was in favor of Villafuerte. The expedition, which started December 23d, was somewhat ludicrous. Spies had reported the garrison of Guéjara at 6000 arquebusiers; a reconnoissance reduced the number to 4000; in reality there were but 120 Turks and Berbers and 430 natives, who had had ample warning and who discreetly retired in time with all the portable property. Don John returned to Granada a wiser man and he treasured up the lesson to see and think and act for himself.[1]

He finally started December 29th and by January 19, 1570, he was in front of Galera with 12,000 men. February 21st, the Duke of Sesa followed with 8000 foot

[1] Mendoza, p. 109.—Marmol Carvajal, p. 306.

and 350 horse for a campaign in the Alpujarras, leaving Deza in command at Granada as captain-general with 4000 men to guard the city.[1] Spain had strained every nerve and had raised an overwhelming force to accomplish what Mondéjar had done with a few thousand men a twelvemonth earlier. It is not necessary to follow the vicissitudes of the campaign, in which the vicious ineptitude of los Velez and the incompetence of Sesa were balanced by the rapid development of Don John, in spite of the tutelage in which he was kept and the meddlesome interference from Philip. The war was carried on with vigor, though with the same rapacity and brutality. At the storming of Galera Don John gave no quarter to the men and had four hundred women and children butchered in cold blood because their captors endeavored to secure them for themselves, while forty-five hundred others were preserved as slaves; soon afterwards, at Seron, he lost his tutor Luis Quijada with a third of his force and a thousand arquebusses and swords because his men scattered to plunder.[2] He was subject to the same difficulties as his predecessors from the worthless quality of his troops. After reducing the valley of the Almanzora, on his return to Guadix he writes, August 8th, to Philip that he will endeavor to collect forces to enter the Alpujarras in obedience to instructions, but at present he has but 1200 men. On June 7th he had called the king's attention to the manner in which certain frailes, especially in Granada and Guadix, inveighed in the pulpit against the benignity and clemency which the king had commanded to be shown to these people. It is a matter,

[1] Mendoza, p. 111.—Marmol Carvajal, p. 310.
[2] Marmol Carvajal, pp. 314, 316.

he adds, of profound regret that a point has been reached in which the soldiers who should fight are given to robbing and running away and the religious, who ought to intercede for these miserable people, the greater part of whom have sinned through ignorance, exert themselves to decry clemency and impudently interfere with matters foreign to them.[1]

The whole tragedy had been the result of clerical interference, but it is difficult to appreciate in what even the ferocious bigotry of the frailes could complain of Philip's so-called clemency, for only universal massacre would have been more cruel. Long before this the end was seen to be inevitable, the clearer-sighted Moriscos were negotiating for submission and the pitiless policy of expulsion had been commenced. As early as February 24, 1570, Philip ordered Don John to collect, with as little scandal as possible, all the peaceable Moriscos of Guadix and Baza and other places within his command, and deport them inland, allowing them to keep their women and children and to carry with them their movables. Don John replied from Seron that he could not leave there or divide his forces, to which the king assented on March 5th, saying that the royal council had determined that not a single Morisco should be left in the kingdom of Granada and that he placed the matter in Deza's hands. Deza lost no time in performing so agreeable a duty. He commenced with those of the Vega who were shut up in their churches on Palm Sunday (March 19th), from which they were transferred to the Hospital Real. They were allowed to sell their

[1] Coleccion de Doc. inéd. T. XXVIII. pp. 100, 118.

movables, to facilitate which their wheat and cattle were taken for the army to be paid for at current prices. No resistance was encountered; they were carried under guard to various places in Castile and distributed around. In April those of Guadix were shut up in their churches, but this threatened to interfere with the submission of those of the mountains who were preparing to lay down their arms. To reassure them the movement was suspended and they were told that it was merely to get them out of harm's way and that on the conclusion of peace they would be brought back with rewards from the king.[1]

This process of deportation in many places degenerated into raids of robbery and murder. The Moriscos of Ronda and the Sierra Bermeja, to the extreme west of the kingdom, had remained peaceable and had not joined in the rebellion. In April, under orders from Philip, Antonio de Luna was sent to Ronda to remove them to Andalusia and Estremadura. He was furnished with 4000 foot and 100 horse, with which he occupied the sierra before his errand was known and sent his troops out in companies to shut all the men up in the churches and carry them away. As soon as the soldiers appeared, however, the men fled to the mountains, leaving their families, and the undisciplined troops at once seized the women and children and plundered the houses and cattle, slaying all who attempted resistance, on seeing which, the men came down from the mountains and killed many of the scattered soldiers, encumbered with plunder. At Genalguacil there was a sharp skirmish in which the

[1] Marmol Carvajal, pp. 323, 336.

17

Moriscos recovered their women and children. De Luna succeeded in gathering together fifteen hundred of his men, laden with women and children and spoils, which they sold at Ronda, as though gained in open war, and then dispersed. Luna forwarded to Castile such Moriscos as he had been able to gather and then went to Philip, who was in Seville, to disculpate himself from the charges brought by the Moriscos of violating the royal safeguard. They professed readiness to lay down their arms and obey the king if their women and children and property were returned, which they said could readily be done. Luna's excuses were admitted; the blame was thrown on the disorderly troops and the result was an obstinate rebellion in the Sierra Bermeja which kept the Dukes of Medina Sidonia and Arcos busy and was not subdued until the opening months of 1571.[1]

Somewhat similar was the experience at Torrox, near Málaga, where Arévalo de Zuazo was commissioned to deport the peaceable Moriscos. He ordered his men to shut them up quietly in the church, and he placed guards around the town, but many escaped to the mountains with their families and cattle and joined the insurgents of the Sierra Bermeja. Torrox being thus depopulated, he left there Juan de Pajariego, with a small force, to gather up the portable property. The latter, understanding that the refugees had 3000 head of cattle and many women and children who could be captured, as the men were unarmed, organized a force of 120 adventurers to secure the spoils, but the Moriscos caught them in an

[1] Marmol Carvajal, pp. 342, 355, 357, 362.—Mendoza, pp. 116, 118–20.

ambuscade and the survivors were only rescued by reinforcements from Málaga and Torrox. Then the latter place was abandoned, when the refugees descended and burnt the church and the houses of the Christians.[1]

Thus the process of deportation went on everywhere with varying fortune. Formal terms of surrender had been agreed upon as early as May 19, 1570, under which it was understood that those who submitted should be removed, but in the reduced districts along the Almanzora there were disturbances, owing to the irrepressible rapacity of the soldiery. At Baza, Don Alonso de Carvajal succeeded in enticing them into the churches under the pretext of a distribution of wheat and cattle. This had been done under final instructions, October 28, 1570, from Philip to Don John, ordering the deportation of all, both the loyal and the submissive rebels. Those of the city and Vega of Granada, the valley of Lecrin and province of Málaga were to be taken to Córdova and thence to be distributed through Estremadura and Galicia; those of Guadix, Baza and the river Almanzora were to be distributed from Toledo through Old Castile as far as Leon; those of Almería and its district were to be carried in galleys as far as Seville. None were to go to Murcia or other places near Valencia, nor to Andalusia which was already encumbered with them. Families were not to be separated; they were to move in bands of 1500 men with their women and children, under escort of 200 foot and 20 horse, with a commissioner who made lists of those under his charge, provided them with food and distributed them in their destinations. Don John applied himself to the execution

[1] Marmol Carvajal, p. 344.

of these orders energetically, for he was most anxious to leave Granada and assume command of the great armada against the Turk. November 5th he writes from Guadix to Ruy Gomez that the number sent away from this district alone has been large and it has all been done with a thousand soldiers. The last party was sent off that day and was the most unfortunate affair in the world, for there was such a tempest of wind, rain and snow that the mother will lose her daughter on the road, the wife her husband and the widow her infant. It cannot be denied, he adds, that the depopulation of a kingdom is the most pitiful thing that can be imagined.[1]

Although organized resistance had ceased after the terms of surrender had been agreed upon in May, and although under it, to the lasting humiliation of Spanish pride, the Berber auxiliaries had been allowed to depart in June, still desultory fighting was kept up for a considerable time. Large numbers came down from the mountains and surrendered, but many still hesitated to trust the insecurity of the roads and the faith of the victors, as they well might, for, when a considerable body from Felix hurried with their families to Almería to surrender, they were followed by a party of soldiers who reached the town at the same time and claimed them as slaves. García de Villaroel, the commandant, accepted the surrender, but the soldiers complained to Don John and he sent a judge to decide the matter who awarded them all as slaves. King Abenabó had accepted the terms of capitulation, but it happened that a party of two hun-

[1] Marmol Carvajal, pp. 341, 364.—Coleccion de Doc. inéd. T. XXVIII. p. 156.

dred Berbers managed to land and reach the Alpujarras where they amused him with stories of large succors soon to arrive and he resolved to defend himself to the last. To meet this the sierra, in September, 1570, was attacked simultaneously from both ends with a war of ruthless devastation, destroying all harvests, killing the men and bringing in women and children by the thousand as slaves. What few prisoners were taken were executed or sent to the galleys. The caves were sought for and the inmates captured or smothered to death; nothing was left but desolation; forts were built and the troops were kept constantly on the move so that the survivors, reduced to extreme misery, fled from cave to cave.[1]

Still, so long as Abenabó remained at large, the Spaniards felt that the war was not over. He lay in hiding among caves in the most inaccessible parts of the sierra, until, in March, 1571, one of his most trusted followers, Gonzalo el Xenis, a famous monfí, guilty of many crimes, agreed to despatch him. El Xenis had wanted to escape to Barbary, but Abenabó had his vessel burnt and forbade him to approach the coast, which angered him. Through Francisco Barredo, a silversmith of Granada, he made overtures and, by Deza's order, Alonso del Castillo wrote offering to him and to all who would come in with him, bringing Abenabó's head, free pardon for person and property; they should not be slain or sent to the galleys, and as for the Inquisition, they should be let off with light penalties, and they should be allowed to select their own places of residence. Besides this Gonzalo himself should regain his wife and daughter who had been

[1] Marmol Carvajal, pp. 347, 349, 359.

enslaved, fifty captives should be given to him without ransom, he should be empowered to name six persons who might bear arms like Old Christians and should have pardon for certain murders and robberies of which he stood charged before the rebellion.[1]

Gonzalo's conference with Barredo had not escaped observation. Abenabó went at night to his cave and taxed him with it. Gonzalo showed him the letter; they quarrelled and Gonzalo and his followers despatched him, throwing his body down the rocks that the rest might see that they had no king. Nearly all took advantage of the letter of pardon and went in with him. They were marched in procession through the streets of Granada with Abenabó's body clothed and mounted on a horse as though alive. The arquebusiers fired a salute, responded to by the guns of the Alhambra, as the procession moved to the Audiencia, where it was received by the Duke of Arcos, Deza and a crowd of gentlemen. Gonzalo kissed the hands of Arcos and Deza and handed them the matchlock and scimitar of Abenabó, saying that, like a good shepherd, if he could not bring the sheep to his master he at least brought the pelt. The corpse was drawn and quartered and the head, in an iron cage over the arch of the Puerta del Rastro, for years looked out on the Alpujarras. The lately disturbed districts were industriously traversed by small companies of soldiers who were paid twenty ducats a head for all the strag-

[1] Cartulario de Alonso del Castillo, pp. 35–9, 154 (Memorial Histórico Español, T. III.).

Castillo wrote a similar letter to another Morisco leader named Andrés el Rindati, but he made use of it to escape to Barbary with a number of companions.—Ibid.

glers they could bring to Deza; he examined them and sent them to the galleys, except the more prominent among them who were torn with hot pincers and hanged.[1]

Thus ended a war, brought on by unreasoning fanaticism, which through blundering incapacity was reckoned to have cost sixty thousand Spanish lives and three million ducats and left a flourishing kingdom depopulated. That Leonardo Donato, the Venetian envoy, pronounces the depopulation a measure of great wisdom only emphasizes the wrongheadedness which rendered it the wisest alternative. He points out that if the Turk, in place of turning his arms against Venice, had sent effective succor to the rebels he would have kindled a flame almost impossible to extinguish, and had the revolt extended to Murcia, Valencia, Catalonia and Aragon, Spanish statesmen expected the Huguenots of France to pour over the Pyrenees.[2] It is characteristic that Deza, who was the malignant spirit of the whole, was left triumphant in Granada as captain-general, that through Philip's favor he rose to the cardinalate and long flourished in Rome as a wealthy prince of the Church.[3]

No time was lost in seeking to repopulate the desert

[1] Marmol Carvajal, p. 363.—Mendoza, p. 121.

[2] Relazioni Venete, Serie I. Tom. VI. p. 408.—Ximenez, Vida de Ribera, p. 375.

[3] At Philip's request he was created Cardinal priest of S. Prisca, in 1578, by Gregory XIII. He went to Rome in 1580 where in time he became Cardinal bishop of Albano and died, in 1600, full of years and honors. He built a splendid palace which after his death passed into the hands of Cardinal Borghese, subsequently Paul V.—Ciaconii Hist. Pontiff. Roman. et Cardinalium, IV. 60 (Ed. 1676). Padre Bleda (Crónica, pp. 658, 963) mentions his having an audience with Deza on his visit to Rome in 1591.

which had been created. February 24, 1571, Mondéjar was directed to return to Granada to superintend the process under an edict which gave to new settlers the houses and properties of the exiles, but he did not remain long. A subsequent edict of September 27, 1571, offered to give to immigrants vacated houses subject to a nominal ground-rent of a real per annum; the lands, in addition to the old tithes, were to pay another to the king in kind, while mulberry and olive plantations were to pay him a fifth of the produce for ten years from January, 1572, and a third thereafter. All this shows that the landed property of the exiles was held to be confiscated to the crown, in the *realengos* or districts subject to the royal jurisdiction, and that in inviting settlers the interests of the revenue were not disregarded. The process of recuperation was very slow. A series of elaborate regulations, issued August 31, 1574, seems to assume that little progress had as yet been made. Commissioners of population were provided for the several districts and the object apparently was to get persons with some capital to take up larger tracts and divide them by lot in equal holdings between actual settlers. The provisions respecting oil and grain mills, dilapidated houses, rights to water from irrigating canals, common pasturage for villages, public ovens, the rights of churches and Old Christians, and the settlement of disputes show how intricate and difficult was the task of rebuilding a civilization so ruthlessly destroyed. In the lands of the feudal nobles the property was held to revert to the lords who were ordered to distribute it in equal lots to settlers and not to exact greater imposts than had been paid by the Moriscos. It is probable that a goodly portion of the confiscated lands was frittered away in satisfying claims for damages suffered during the war, for this was the mode adopted to meet them as least burdensome to the royal treasury.[1] As for the young children who had been captured during the war, a provision issued in 1572 declared that they should not be enslaved but be distributed among Old Christians to be well brought up and to serve for their food and clothing up to the age of 20.[2] Thus slowly and painfully the effort was made to repair the havoc and desolation which could so easily have been avoided.

The fate of the exiles was hard. Leonardo Donato, tells us, as an eyewitness, that many perished through miseries and afflictions, which can readily be believed.[3] They were scattered throughout Spain to the borders of Portugal, their distribution being in charge of a temporary *Consejo de Poblaciones*. That they were not regarded as welcome guests is visible in the complaints of Córdova, in 1572, as to their harboring their enslaved countrymen, committing crimes and purchasing, for eight or ten ducats, licences to bear arms and move around in contravention of the laws.[4] After due deliberation, an elaborate edict of October 6, 1572, in twenty-three sections, prescribed the regulations under which they were permitted to exist.

[1] Historia de la Casa de Mondéjar (Morel-Fatio, p. 95).—Janer, pp. 246, 258–66.—Distribucion de los Memoriales (Morel-Fatio, p. 213). The Venetian envoy Donato, in his relation of 1573, says that Philip was deriving a revenue of 125,000 crowns from the lands of the Moriscos of Granada which had passed into his hands.—Relazioni Venete, Serie I. Tom. VI. p. 378.

[2] Nueva Recop. Lib. VIII. Tit. ii. ley 22 § 14.

[3] Relazioni Venete, Serie I. Tom. VI. p. 407.

[4] Janer, pp. 254–6.

They were to be kept under perpetual surveillance. Every individual was to be registered in his place of domicile, and lists of them were to be made out in duplicate to be preserved by the proper officials, in which lists all births and deaths were to be entered as they occurred. In each chief town a superintendent of Moriscos was appointed who was required to visit them every fortnight; in each parish a *jurado* had the same functions who, with the priest, was to visit them every week, in addition to which the justicia of the district was to visit them monthly, all this, it is said, not only to keep watch over them but to make sure that they were supported, special care being exercised to help the poor and to cure the sick, while the magistrates were ordered to see that they had work, each in his own line of industry. No one was permitted to change his residence without a special royal licence, application for which must specify all the reasons therefor, nor was any one even to pass a night away from his domicile without a licence from the justicia of the place containing a description of his person, his destination and the duration of his absence; such licences were not to be charged for and were to be freely given to all not suspected of wishing to return to Granada or to go beyond seas, but if necessary, security might be demanded. Access to Granada was sternly prohibited; any Morisco found within ten leagues of the Granada border was to suffer death, if a male over the age of 16; between that and ten and a half, and all females over nine and a half were to be enslaved, while younger children were to be given to Old Christians to be brought up until they reached the age of twenty. If found within ten leagues of Valencia, Aragon or Navarre the penalties were the same, except that death was commuted to service for life in the galleys. If found elsewhere away from their domiciles men were punished with a hundred lashes and four years of galleys, women with four years of servitude. As soon as any one was absent from his home for a day, his family, or the inmates of his house, were required under penalties to report him, when he was to be tracked by the Santa Hermandad; any one harboring him was to be punished, any one finding such a fugitive was to take him to the nearest magistrate and receive a reward of eight ducats. Where there were numbers of them they were not to live in a Morería apart but in houses scattered among Old Christians; the children, as far as possible, were to be brought up in Christian families, and the magistrates were to see that they were taught to read and write and the elements of Christian faith. Arms were rigorously prohibited, save a pointless knife, under penalty, for a first offence, of confiscation, for a second, of six years of galleys, for a third, of galleys for life. The pragmática of 1566 was declared to be fully in force, and the provisions respecting the use of Arabic were especially severe; any one speaking or writing it, even in his own house, incurred for a first offence thirty days' prison in chains, for a second, double, for a third, men a hundred lashes and four years of galleys, women and youths under seventeen, four years of servitude.[1]

If anything could obviate the dangers always apprehended from the Moriscos, such a system would effect it, but it was not calculated to merge them with the population or diminish their abhorrence of Christianity. The

[1] Nueva Recop. Lib. VIII. Tit. ii. ley 22.

impossible rigor of the clauses respecting Arabic, applied to those ignorant of any other tongue, shocked even the town-council of Córdova, which, as we have seen, was not favorably disposed to the exiles. November 28th it appointed a committee to represent to the alcalde mayor that God alone was able to render them capable of speaking a language which they did not know, especially as they were harassed by the alguaziles constantly arresting and punishing them, wherefore they asked him to suspend action till the king could be consulted and schools be organized, at the expense of the Moriscos, to instruct them, to all of which the alcalde replied that he had no choice but to obey the royal pragmática and inflict the punishment on all brought before him.[1]

Spanish legislation was apt to defeat itself by its exuberance and violence and its execution to be thwarted by the neglect or cupidity of the officials. In 1576 and 1583 it was felt necessary to repeat the prohibition of absence from domicile without a licence, and, in 1581, to reiterate the provisions as to keeping lists of Moriscos. Even the ferocious penalties for returning to Granada were powerless to prevent them from attempting it successfully, especially as no judge or alcalde was found willing to sentence them to death. The law thus was a dead letter and it was resolved to commute the punishment to the galleys. Philip proposed, in 1582, to have them all seized simultaneously; the Council of Poblaciones represented that there were not officials enough to accomplish this, to which the king replied that he wanted men for his galleys and that it must be done without

[1] Janer, p. 256.

delay; he gave minute instructions how it was to be accomplished by surprise in a single day; all the men between 17 and 55, fit for the oar, were to be sent to the galleys, the rest and the women and children to be taken to the places allotted to them; there was to be no hearing allowed and no trials.[1] He was more lenient, in 1585, on learning that three thousand of the exiles had succeeded in getting into Valencia, for he ordered the Viceroy Aytona to hang six of them as a warning and then issue a proclamation that the rest would be treated in the same way if within two months they did not return to their allotted places of residence.[2] Many of those deported claimed that they were not subject to the conditions of the law of 1572, asserting themselves to be Old Christians because their ancestors had been baptized prior to the general coerced conversion; they sometimes made good these claims before the courts, but, in 1585, Philip ordered all these matters referred to the Consejo de Poblaciones and directed that, notwithstanding favorable sentence obtained in the courts, they should be subject to the prescriptions of the law as to residence and deprivation of arms. To the same council were referred the petitions of those who asked for grants of Morisco slaves or that wandering Moriscos might be assigned to them as slaves, from which it would appear that many of them were reduced to servitude.[3] The Inquisition

[1] Janer, pp. 246, 252, 273.—Danvila, pp. 200, 202, 204.—Mr. Martin A. S. Hume (Spain, its Greatness and Decay, p. 154) computes at thirteen thousand the Moriscos who were sent to the galleys or the mines or were hanged as the result of the rebellion.

[2] Danvila, pp. 205, 206.

[3] Nueva Recop. Lib. VIII. Tit. ii. ley 23.—Distribucion de los Memoriales (Morel-Fatio, pp. 213, 214).

also found in the exiles, both free and enslaved, a field for active operations. A considerable portion of the Morisco trials for years, in the tribunals of Castile, were of those brought from Granada, and it was decided that they were liable to prosecution for Moorish rites which they had performed during the rebellion. A somewhat unusual case was that of Diego de Ortega, a youth of twenty, who, in 1581, denounced himself to the Inquisition of Toledo. He said that, as a boy in the sierra, he had practised Moorish ceremonies and that for some years after coming to Toledo he had entertained doubts as to the truth of Christianity. There was no other testimony, and he was sentenced merely to reconciliation privately in the audience chamber, to which the Suprema mercifully added "without confiscation."[1] Yet in spite of these limitations and disadvantages the indomitable industry and thrift of the strangers, thus violently scattered among a hostile population, soon created for them a prosperous career which excited the jealousy of their neighbors. Only ten years after the exile an official report says that their numbers are increasing because none go to war or into religion and they are so industrious that, after coming to Castile ten years ago without owning a handsbreadth of land, they are all well-off and many are rich, so that if it continues in the same proportion in twenty years the natives will be their servants.[2] It was evident that trampling on them was of no avail and Spain could never be satisfied short of extermination or expulsion.

[1] MSS. of Library of University of Halle, Yc. 20, Tom. I.—Archivo de Simancas, Inquisicion, Libro 939, fol. 108.

[2] Janer, p. 272.

CHAPTER IX.

DANGERS FROM ABROAD.

It is not to be supposed that the Moriscos, thus subjected to hopeless oppression, failed to seek relief from their powerful co-religionists in foreign lands. For more than five centuries the cross and the crescent had waged internecine war throughout the length and breadth of the Mediterranean basin and Turk and Algerine might be expected to sympathize with the miseries of their brethren and be eager to use them as a means of disabling the power which, in the sixteenth century, was foremost among the enemies of Islam. It was a real peril, ever present to the minds of Spanish statesmen, and the means adopted to avert it, by increasing the disabilities piled upon the Moriscos, only augmented it by stimulating disaffection, rendering more earnest the appeals for assistance and strengthening the temptation of the enemy to strike at so vital and unguarded a spot. The Mudéjares had been loyal subjects, but fanaticism, by insisting on their Christianization, had converted them into the most dangerous of internal enemies. Even as early as 1512 Peter Martyr, in describing the disturbed condition of Granada, says that if some daring pirate leader would march into the interior the population would join him and, as the king is occupied with the conquest of Navarre, all would go to ruin.[1] While the

[1] Pet. Mart. Angler. Epist. 499.

Granada rebellion was in progress, the Venetian envoy, Sigismondo Cavalli, in 1570, pointed out that assistance from Barbary would throw the whole kingdom in the greatest peril for there were about 600,000 Moriscos in Spain ready to assist the invader, and, in 1575, Lorenzo Priuli described them, whom he estimates at 400,000, as the source of perpetual danger.[1] If those of Granada alone, assisted by a few hundred adventurers, had only been subdued after exertions which taxed the whole energies of the monarchy, what might be expected if a powerful fleet and army should encourage a rising of the united Morisco population? As their numbers were constantly increasing, while those of the Christians diminished, they cherished the hope, if Fray Bleda is to be believed, of eventually reconquering the whole land, with the aid of the Moors and the Turks.[2]

Meanwhile there was an intermittent warfare on foot, which, though not threatening to the national integrity, was infinitely galling and vexatious. It is remarkable that Spain, while sending her fleets to the Indies and the North Sea and to the Italian waters, could not protect her own coasts from the ravages of insignificant corsairs, so that it became a proverb that the Spanish shore was the Indies of these sea-rovers. The blame was thrown on the Moriscos, who undoubtedly afforded all the aid they could, maintaining intelligences with the Moors, sending information and availing themselves of the raids to escape in large numbers to Barbary, to the great discomfiture of their lords. But the primary fault lay in the foreign policy of Charles V. and Philip II.,

[1] Relazioni Venete, Serie I. T. VI. pp. 165, 241.

[2] Bledæ Defensio Fidei, pp. 272, 276, 285.

who directed their attention to distant enterprises and consumed the power of Spain in quarrels which were of no national importance. So completely were the Spanish coasts left unguarded that, in 1542, the Moors entered Gibraltar, leading the córtes of Valladolid to petition Charles to provide for the national defence, and in 1604 the córtes of Valencia begged for additional fortifications and the protection of four galleys of the Naples squadron, for which they offered to pay.[1]

Complaints of the ravages of corsairs commence with the enforced Christianization of Granada. While, in 1499 and 1500, the court was there, occupied with superintending the baptism and with suppressing the consequent revolt, we are told that when the people saw that they were made Christians by force they invited the Moors from Africa, who penetrated to many places and carried away the Christians, especially the clerics.[2] These complaints continue until the final expulsion, when Fray Bleda, in 1618, enumerating the blessings conferred by it, includes freedom from the attacks of the Moors whom the Moriscos sheltered and aided.[3] Spanish ballad and story bear ample witness to the frequency of these incidents, and the reality scarcely needed the romantic coloring of fiction, as one or two instances will show. In 1529 certain Moriscos of Valencia made arrangements with Barbarossa to transfer them to Barbary, in execution of which agreement he sent his lieutenant, Hardin Cachadiablo, with a squadron. October 17th, at the river Altea, he landed by night six hundred men and sent them off in

[1] Colmeiro, Córtes de Leon y Castilla, II. 198.—Danvila, p. 263.
[2] Bernaldez, Historia de los Reyes Católicos, II. 155, 156.
[3] Bleda, Crónica, p. 1033.

bands of a hundred. They penetrated to the towns of Parchent and Murla, gathered together seven hundred Moriscos and returned in safety to their vessels. At Parchent they besieged the lord of the place, Pedro Perandreo, in his house; for nine hours he resisted bravely with seven men, but his vassals showed the Moors how to gain the roof and he was captured. The Count of Oliva, who had lost two hundred Moriscos, pursued the Moors with sixty horse, but vainly, and offered Pedro de Portundo, commander of the Spanish galleys, ten thousand crowns to recover them. Cachadiablo meanwhile hoisted a flag of truce to treat for the ransom of Perandreo, which was fixed at eleven thousand ducats, but, while waiting for the money to come from Valencia, he heard that Portundo was seeking him, and he set sail to avoid him. Foul weather caused him to put into Despaldar, where Portundo came up with him. He landed the Moriscos on the island of Formentera and engaged the Spanish fleet, October 25th, sinking all their galleys but two, killing Portundo and capturing his son. Reimbarking the Moriscos, he sailed for Algiers, carrying Perandreo with him, and handing him over to Barbarossa. Four times his ransom was sent, but each time the agent ransomed others and left him in captivity. In 1535 his wife sent her son, Pedro de Roda, with Charles V. to Tunis in hopes that he might capture a Moor of importance with whom to effect an exchange. Failing in this, Pedro went to Flanders with letters of credit, and thence to Venice, intending to go to Constantinople, whither Barbarossa had taken his father in 1533, but on reaching Ragusa he learned that Barbarossa was coming with a large fleet to resist Charles's expedition to Algiers in 1541. Then he procured letters from Renée, Duchess of Ferrara, to the Turkish ambassador at Paris with whom he concluded a bargain for 5000 ducats. Barbarossa came to Toulon and Pedro hastened to meet him, but at Genoa he had letters from Constantinople announcing that his father was dead and from Valencia that his mother was also no more.[1] Somewhat less successful than Cachadiablo was the corsair Amuratarraez, in 1602, who came with nine well armed galiots and landed six hundred men at Lorca, on the coast of Cartagena. The people took refuge in a tower, but he burnt it and departed with sixty captives and considerable booty. Thence he went to Málaga to catch the bishop, Tomás de Borja, at his country-seat, but the latter had warning and escaped. In the summer of 1609 the whole southern coast of Spain was kept in a state of alarm by the exploits of an Englishman, Simon Dancer, who carried motley crews of Moors and Christians, had a safe conduct from France and a safe harbor of refuge in Algiers. He captured vessels without much regard to nationality and ravaged the shores of Andalusia. Among other prizes were a ship of the Mexican fleet with 300,000 ducats and a couple of vessels with 150 Biscayans, whom he took to Tetuan and sold as slaves.[2]

The Moriscos were held responsible for this, chiefly in consequence of their desire to escape to Barbary, for which their correspondence with the corsairs afforded them the best opportunity. This was frequently effected

[1] Sandoval, Lib. XVIII. §§ x. xi.—Danvila, p. 109.

[2] Cabrera, Relaciones, pp. 153, 368, 373, 375, 382. Amuratarraez is evidently Captain Amurath—*arraez* being the Moorish term for ship-master.

in large numbers. In 1559 Dragut carried off 2500; in 1570 all those of Palmera were taken; in the summer of 1584 the Algerine fleet visited the Valencian coast and carried away twenty-three hundred souls, and the next year another fleet took off the whole population of Callosa. It was said that the king of Algiers had received from the Grand Turk some deserted lands which he proposed to populate in this manner.[1] So complete was the conviction that the trouble lay with the Moriscos that all devices were tried except the natural one of efficiently guarding the shores. In 1505, Peter Martyr describes the coast as being ravaged by Moorish corsairs, to prevent which, in 1507, Ferdinand undertook to depopulate it from Gibraltar to Almería, for two leagues back, and to replace the Moriscos with Old Christians, but the experiment was a failure.[2] In 1532, the córtes of Segovia attributed the evil to the Moors brought from Africa and set free, who maintained secret intelligence with their friends at home, and they petitioned Charles that within a year after manumission they should remove to a distance of twenty leagues from the coast, under pain of death, but Charles modified the distance to ten leagues and the penalty to a hundred lashes for a first offence and the galleys for a second.[3] In Valencia these troubles

[1] Danvila, pp. 161, 182, 205, 207. Cervantes (Persiles y Sigismunda, Lib. III. cap. xi.) gives a picturesque description of such an embarkation. The castellated church, in which the few Christians took refuge and defended themselves, conveys a vivid impression of the insecurity in which lived the inhabitants of the coast.

[2] Pet. Mart. Angler. Epist. 499.—Mariana, Hist. de España, Tom. IX. p. 217 (Ed. 1796).

[3] Colmeiro, Córtes, II. 165.

were ascribed to the Moriscos. A viceregal proclamation of January 11, 1530, states that they held relations with the corsairs and were always endeavoring to go to Africa, for which reason they were forbidden to change their lords under pain of confiscation, and any one receiving them was fined five hundred florins, while death and confiscation were threatened for any Morisco found travelling without a permit in the region between the coast and the highway from Alicante to Barcelona or for any one going to a group of towns—Polop, Callosa, etc.—not on the sea-coast, or for any of those converted within eight years who shall give aid or counsel to the corsairs. In the execution of these laws it was found that the kindred of culprits impoverished themselves to redeem them, to prevent which Charles, in 1536, ordered that there should be no redemption, but that the penalties of death or the galleys should be irremissible. In 1541, there was further legislation of the same kind, and the forbidden district was extended to the region between Orihuela and the coast, all of which was virtually repeated in 1545, and in the same year a royal order forced the Inquisition of Valencia to contribute two thousand ducats for the guard of the coasts. In 1567, a law of December 10th assumes that the damage inflicted by corsairs is attributable to the aid rendered by Moriscos and is fostered by the negligence of the authorities in punishing the guilty; it threatens death and confiscation for all connivance with the enemies of the faith, while all damage inflicted on Christians by corsairs, including the ransom of captives carried off, is to be levied and assessed on the Moriscos. All this was inefficacious, and in 1585 another proclamation prohibited their approaching the shore.[1] If legislation could cure the trouble there was plenty of it, but it was directed at the wrong end. A more feasible plan was that proposed by the córtes of Valencia in 1604—that, if the rigor of the Inquisition should be relaxed and the evidence of Moriscos should not be received against each other, they agreed to redeem all Christian slaves captured by the Moriscos on the Valencian coast. This, it was argued, would stop the ravages of the corsairs, who would be deprived of the aid and information given by the Moriscos, and the latter would be interested in repressing them.[2] Of course the petition was not granted.

While all this was humiliating and exasperating and served to keep up a healthy detestation of the Moriscos, it affected but a narrow strip of territory. Far more menacing to the whole monarchy was the generally accepted fact that the oppressed population was always yearning for an invader and plotting to invite an invasion. During the latter half of the sixteenth century, and especially after the terrible warning of the rebellion of Granada, this was an anxiety ever present to the minds of Spanish statesmen. They felt themselves walking on the thin crust of a crater, watching for evidence of an eruption; they were always in search of a fresh conspiracy, and, thanks to the Inquisition, they obtained it at not distant intervals. That the Moriscos were a recognized source of weakness to the monarchy is seen in a careful report on the condition of Spain made, in 1594, by

[1] Danvila, pp. 109-12, 118, 129, 132, 210.—Nueva Recop. Lib. VIII. Tit. ii. ley 20.—Archivo de Simancas, Inquisicion, Libro 940, fol. 69, 184.

[2] Fonseca, pp. 341, 343.

the Nuncio Caetano to Clement VIII. He describes the land as internally peaceful and loyal except that the Moriscos are much to be feared. They were converted by force and they "Judaize;" they number about 300,000 and multiply rapidly, and as they are industrious and thrifty they are thought to be rich, so that altogether they are a subject of much solicitude.[1]

When Philip II. returned to Spain, in 1559, he called for a report on the condition of the Moriscos, to serve as a guide for his policy toward them, and among other information gathered was that of a plot with the Turk for an invasion when they would rise.[2] In 1567, the trial of Hieronimo Roldan by the Inquisition of Valencia developed testimony of recent envoys from the king of Algiers with a letter urging the Moriscos to rebel and of efforts to organize and arm them.[3] Then came the revolt of Granada, which, though it showed that the Moslem powers were not so ready to invade Spain as was supposed, at the same time revealed its weakness to resist an invasion supported by a rebellion. In 1583, there was a scare over an asserted combination of Henry of Navarre with the Turk for an invasion in which the Moriscos had agreed to rise, which led the Suprema, January 13, 1584, to order the tribunal of Aragon to prepare a detailed report of all the evidence, rumors and suspicions of risings, which was duly furnished at considerable length.[4] This

[1] Hinojosa, Despachos de la Diplomacia Pontificia, p. 381 (Madrid, 1896).

[2] Danvila, p. 158.

[3] Archivo Hist. Nacional, Inq^{n} de Valencia, Legajo 30.

[4] Archivo Hist. Nacional, Inq^{n} de Valencia, Cartas del Consejo, Legajo 5, fol. 192.

affords so clear an impression of the incessant anxieties and vigilance of the period that a condensed abstract will best enable us to appreciate them.

The report begins by stating that, since 1526, when the Moors of Valencia and Aragon were baptized, the Inquisition has kept a special watch over them, and from the accumulated evidence it is clear that they have always lived openly as Moors and that the efforts to Christianize them have been wasted, for they are now more obstinate than ever. There was nothing, however, to foreshadow a general rising until 1565, when the tribunal of Aragon captured Juan Acevedo, and in Madrid were arrested Francisco Hernandez and Diego Torilla, Moriscos of Valladolid and Arévalo, from whose confessions it appeared that those of Aragon and Valencia were arranging with the Turk for a rebellion. Then, in 1568, came the troubles of Granada, when those of Aragon were in great agitation and laid in stores of arms and munitions and provisions, believing that the Turk would help them. From Grisel near Tarazona it was reported that when the disarmament took place they only gave up their cross-bows and swords and concealed their firelocks. Two loads of firelocks were sent from Daroca to Villa Felice, where four powder mills were hard at work; at Torrellas many guns were imported from Biscay, and the gunmakers reported an incessant demand from Moriscos. On the Valencia border, in 1569, a familiar seized two wagon loads of lead and tin in charge of Morisco muleteers. At Celda one came with his mule loaded with two skins, apparently of oil; the people, who were in want of oil, seized one, and the muleteer suddenly disappeared, when the skins were found to be filled with powder. There is an immense mass of testimony going to show that there was a plan for concerted action at Easter, but the Granadans rose prematurely at Christmas, and the rest waited to see the result and were disconcerted by the progress of the royal arms.

The vicissitudes and final suppression of the rebellion of Granada seemed to promise exemption for awhile, but, in 1573, there was information that the rulers of Tlemecen and Algiers were planning an attack on Mazalquivir, in which they were to be aided by a rising of the Moriscos, to avert which those of Valencia were disarmed. It was found that this was complicated with an invasion from beyond the Pyrenees, for in January, 1575, a French Huguenot named François Nalias, on trial for heresy in Saragossa, confessed under torture that two years before he had conducted negotiations between the Moriscos of Aragon and Baron de Ros, son of M. de Ros, viceroy of Béarn; he implicated Lope Darcos, a Morisco, who likewise confessed under torture. The leading Moriscos agreed to rise if Ros would invade Aragon with his Huguenots, and they would give him all the money they could raise; apparently he wanted an advance of ten or twelve thousand crowns. Envoys were also sent to the King of Algiers and the Grand Turk, who favored the plan and urged its speedy execution, but the coming of Don John of Austria to Valencia and disarming the Moriscos frustrated the plan for a time. It was not abandoned however. A certain Jusuf Duarte was sent to Constantinople and returned in December, 1576, with a letter from the sultan which he exhibited to all the aljamas. There were to be three fleets, one disembarking between Barcelona and Perpignan, one at Denia and one between

Murcia and Valencia; the Moriscos were advised to keep quiet until the arrival of the fleets, which was necessarily uncertain, and not to be impatient like those of Granada. In February, 1577, a spy named Luis Moreno was sent out to gather information, and reported that everything was organized and ready in Valencia and Aragon and that they were only awaiting the arrival of the fleets which had assembled at Farinana and Goletta. He was not the only traitor, for the Inquisition had several in its pay who were of the inner councils of the Moriscos. Towards the end of April it obtained a copy of a letter written April 16th, by Juan de Benamir of Valencia, advising the Moriscos of Aragon that the King of Algiers had sent word that the fleet was delayed, but that it would come and they must keep ready, and then in May information was had that it was not expected until August. Then there was a copy of a letter from the King of Algiers giving details of the plans; the attack of the fleet is to be simultaneous with an invasion from France; when the French come the Moriscos are to take to the mountains. How much of all this was true, and how much was manufactured by the detectives to earn their pay, it would be impossible now to decide, but the concurrent confessions of a number of those arrested and punished from 1576 to 1579, during which the Inquisition was busily investigating and prosecuting, would seem to prove that there was substantial foundation for the plot and that hopes were held out to the plotters both from France and Barbary, and it may well be that the desire to give the Huguenots occupation at home was one of the motives stimulating Philip to the organization of the League and to the assistance of the French Catholics.

When a political spy has not a real conspiracy to unravel it is his business to make one. In December, 1582, the tribunal of Valencia reported to that of Saragossa certain intercepted correspondence with Algiers, showing that the Moriscos of Valencia were planning a revolt for Easter, which led to several arrests. This did not come off, but in May the informer Luis Moreno brought in an alarming report that Constantinople and Algiers were still making the old promises, the execution of which was said to depend on the result of an embassy sent by the sultan to the King of France asking him to invade by land while the Turks attacked by sea. On this another spy named Gil Perez was sent to France and returned with information, on the strength of which some eight or ten Moriscos were arrested and their papers seized, but though they were duly tortured nothing could be learned from them. The inquisitors knew Perez to be a rogue of the first water for, in 1581, on his denunciation they had arrested a number of Moriscos of Huesca, who when tried confessed to apostasy but to nothing of what he accused them, and one of them had disabled his evidence by proving him to be a thief, a ruffian and a forger.[1] Finally Perez himself was placed on trial, and while he continued to assert the truth of his revelations he admitted that he was under pay by the Moriscos to keep them informed of the proceedings of the Inquisition. It was proved, moreover, that he had suborned witnesses and forged letters; the inculpated Moriscos were dis-

[1] A number of executions in connection with this pretended plot took place in Saragossa in 1581, which the Moors of Algiers revenged by torturing to death a Carmelite who was in their hands.—Guadalajara y Xavierr, in Historia Pontifical, V. 128 (Madrid, 1630).

charged and he and his witnesses were punished. The pretended plot was clearly a fraud, but it served to keep up the strain of anxiety and shows how perpetual were the apprehensions excited by the unnatural position of the Moriscos. A letter of the Suprema, June 22, 1585, to the inquisitors of Valencia, reflects this in reminding them of one from the king, of February 12, 1582, as to the diligence expected of them in discovering Morisco plots, and urging them afresh to penetrate into these evil designs and to keep the tribunal of Saragossa advised of whatever they find.[1]

This anxious watchfulness and these instructions to be vigilant were incessant. A letter of the Suprema, September 3, 1589, to the Inquisition of Valencia relates that the king has recently learned the wicked intentions of the Moriscos and some of the means proposed to attain their ends. Three loads of powder have been discovered which they were carrying as merchandise from Baeza to Avila. The inquisitors are, therefore, ordered with the utmost caution and secrecy to discover the plots on foot, and with whom the Moricos are communicating, whether they are dealing in sulphur and saltpetre and making powder and whether they have arms and warlike implements, concealed or openly. All that can be learned is to be transmitted under seal with their opinions and advice.[2]

[1] The report of the Inquisition of Saragossa is in Archivo de Simancas, Inq[n] de Valencia, Legajo 205, fol. 4. The correspondence of the Suprema is in Archivo Hist. Nacional, Inq[n] de Valencia, Cartas del Consejo, Legajo 5, No. 1, fol. 5, 32, 33, 37, 50, 72, 134, 192. See also Janer, pp. 269–71, and Guadalajara y Xavierr in the *Historia Pontifical*, Tom. V. p. 127.

[2] Archivo Hist. Nacional, *loc. cit.* fol. 217.

With the cessation of the religious wars in France and the consolidation of the power of the monarchy in the able hands of Henry IV., who had ample cause to seek revenge on Spain, the danger on that side grew visibly more imminent. In May, 1600, the Count of Benavente, then viceroy of Valencia, was ordered to report whether the Moriscos of that kingdom had any intelligence with France. He replied in the negative, but that they had relations with the Turk, now closer than usual, in consequence of the pressure brought upon them by the recently published edict of grace. Those of Aragon would be more likely to plot with France; there were vast numbers of Frenchmen there, and even in Valencia there were fourteen or fifteen thousand—a matter worthy of serious consideration. The Council of State, in a consulta of August 10th to Philip III. on this report, speaks of the subject as the one of all others the most important and requiring speedy action. Six months later the council repeated this opinion, in reporting on a letter from Tetuan, written by Bartolomé de Llanos y Alarcon, who had been captured when on his way to Sicily; he said that the Moriscos had been corresponding with the King of Morocco and that lately an envoy to the Turk came from Córdova to urge an expedition to Spain; he had at first been well received, but the enterprise seemed difficult and he was dismissed.[1]

The hopes of the Moriscos based on these constant appeals to Turk and Moor were illusory, but in 1602 there appeared substantial reasons for expecting an effective intervention on the side of France. The aljamas of

[1] Janer, pp. 277, 279.

Valencia had appointed five syndics to organize a rebellion. Martin de Irionde, a Frenchman, resident in Alacuas, brought into communication with them a French spy, Pasqual de S. Étienne, who was informed of what was on foot and that they desired to make over the country to France. He took Miguel Alami, one of the syndics, to Henry IV. with a memorial in which the Moriscos stated that in Valencia they numbered 76,000 families, divided into five tribes, each with three syndics who alone need to be cognizant of the matter. They could furnish 60,000 men who would cost nothing save arms, for they would furnish everything else and even pay a subsidy in addition.. Valencia lay at their mercy, and with aid from France they would make him its king. The castle of Bernia was the only one garrisoned; in the Morisco towns and villages there were no Christians save one or two officials. If a fleet were sent to Denia the Spaniards would fly; the city of Valencia would fall into their hands, where there was ample store of arms. They could no longer exist as they were, for the Inquisition was stripping them of their property; not content with making them pay to it two reales per annum for each family, amounting to 152,000 reales a year, it had subtle means for grasping more, and told them it was merciful in not taking all. The fueros granted to them and to those of Aragon by the ancient kings had been demanded by Charles V. who had burnt them. In Aragon there were more than 40,000 families who would furnish 40,000 men, for they were similarly oppressed and had to pay the same to the Inquisition. If the king would march through Navarre he would find more friends than enemies, for many Christians would join him. In Catalonia there were 3000 families and in Castile 5000 ready to die in the cause, and there were Protestants and Jews, numerous though concealed—all knew and consoled each other, praying God for an opportunity to attack the Spaniards.

Henry was sufficiently impressed with the proposal to send Alami, September 2, 1602, to the Marshal Duke of la Force, Governor of Navarre and Béarn, with instructions to send back with him to Spain a man of experience to survey the situation accurately. La Force suggested that if Pampeluna could be seized and if Queen Elizabeth would simultaneously attack Coruña, the King of France could help the Valencians. Therefore, while he sent an emissary to Valencia with Alami, S. Étienne was despatched to England, where he discussed the matter with a secretary of the queen who encouraged him, but when at a further stage of the plot he returned there in 1604 with an Englishman named Thomas Oliver Brachan Elizabeth was dead, and Lord Burghley told them that the treaty just concluded with Spain rendered it impossible for England to take part in the enterprise, but he gave them money and advised them to apply to Holland.[1]

Meanwhile la Force's emissary remained in Valencia fifteen months, acquainting himself with the situation, and on his return a Gascon gentleman named Panissault was sent there disguised as a merchant. He was present at an assembly of sixty-six syndics, held at Toga about Christmas, 1604, where Luis Asquer, of Alacuas, was

[1] Hume (Spain, its Greatness and Decay, p. 211) says that, on the conclusion of the treaty, James I. sent to Philip III. some documents found among Elizabeth's papers showing that the Valencians had been endeavoring to induce her and the Swiss Protestants to aid them in a rebellion. The Burghley of the text is doubtless Robert Cecil, then Viscount Cranbourne and subsequently Earl of Salisbury.

elected king and arrangements were made for a rising on Holy Thursday (April 7) 1605. Ten thousand Moriscos were to gather in the vicinity of the city of Valencia, rush in during the night, set fire to the "Holy Sepulchres" erected in the churches, which would draw all the Christians to extinguish them, and by the cry of "Francia! Francia!" secure the support of the innumerable Frenchmen residing there, so that the city could be pillaged and a large store of arms be secured. Panissault returned to France perfectly satisfied; the Moriscos promised to raise 80,000 fighting men, to deliver three cities, one of them a seaport, and as an earnest they paid over at Pau 120,000 ducats to la Force, who took Panissault to the king and showed him the map which he had made, the places necessary to be fortified, and every requisite for the execution of this great design, which would overturn the Spanish monarchy. Henry was much pleased, but la Force tells us simply that circumstances at the time were not favorable, and the plan was postponed. The truth probably is that one of the original five deputies, Pedro Cortes, of Alacuas, turned traitor; the plot in some way was revealed, and when, June 23, 1605, he and S. Étienne, Alami and Irionde were sentenced by the viceregal court of Valencia, his life was spared. It was also said at the time that information came from James I.; that the Inquisition of Aragon discovered the matter when trying some Moriscos for apostasy, and that details of the plot were received from several other sources.[1]

[1] Mémoires du Duc de la Force, I. 217-20, 339-45.—Bleda, Crónica, pp. 925-29.—Guadalajara y Xavierr, fol 94-96; Guadalajara in Historia Pontifical, V. 129-30.

This failure resulted in quiet for two or three years, but, in 1608, there was a fresh alarm, which was not easily allayed. In Morisco a civil war was raging between King Muley Xeque and his brother Muley Cidan. The Moriscos of Valencia sent fifty envoys to the latter, representing to him that it would be much better for him to reconquer Spain, which was destitute of soldiers and of arms, for nearly all the latter were in their possession. They would furnish 200,000 men, and if he would bring 20,000 and seize a port he would find no resistance inland, for Spain was exhausted and in no condition to resist. Negotiations were also entered into with some Hollanders to furnish ships, who replied that they would bring enough to build a bridge from Africa to Spain. The full significance of this is apparent when, early in 1509, Muley Cidan overcame Xeque, and the latter sought shelter in Spain and offered the port of Alarache in exchange for assistance. Philip III., considering the danger imminent, in 1608 communicated these reports to the Royal Council and ordered it to consider the situation to the exclusion of every other subject, as it was the one of the most extreme importance. He admitted the defenceless condition of Spain; Muley Cidan was their declared enemy; Sultan Ahmed I. was released from the war with Persia and with his own rebels; Spain's Italian possessions were exhausted and discontented and ready for rebellion, while at home the multitude of Moriscos was eager to throw off the yoke, and God must be offended with the long toleration shown to these heretics and apostates, who had obstinately resisted every effort at conversion. He therefore commanded the council to consider the means of preserving the peace of the kingdom, short of slaughtering them all, and also plans for organizing a military force sufficient for defence.[1]

This immediate danger passed away; when the Moriscos sent another mission to the victorious Muley Cidan he laughed at them and told them he was not seeking adventures outside his own dominions; though he came in sight of Tangier he did no damage, for he desired to avoid irritating Spain, and he assured the merchants that they could trade without interruption. Besides, the tables were turned when Muley Xeque's son defeated Cidan, and, moreover, Ahmed I. sent his fleet against the Italian coasts.[2] But however unfounded these fears may have been, there was genuine peril from another quarter. In the comprehensive plans of Henry IV. for the permanent humbling of the power of Spain, the Moriscos were not forgotten. Although those of Valencia were expelled in the autumn of 1609, and those of Aragon in the spring of 1610, it was thought that enough were left to cause grave embarrassment to Spain. While Lesdiguières, with the assistance of Savoy, was to invade Italy, and Henry himself was to lead into Flanders an army assembling at Châlons, la Force, with ten thousand men, was to attack Spain with the co-operation of the Moriscos, with whom relations had been resumed. He and the king were consulting over it on the fatal fourteenth of May, 1610, and he was in the royal carriage that afternoon when in the Rue de la Ferronerie the knife of Ravaillac released Spain from a most serious danger, for although

[1] Janer, p. 274.—Cabrera, Relaciones, pp. 364, 366, 367, 374.
[2] Cabrera, Relaciones, pp. 367, 372, 380-1.

the expulsion had by this time been virtually accomplished, the Spanish forces by land and water were in no condition to make head against the comprehensive plans organized by Henry.[1] As the Baron de Salignac, the ambassador at Constantinople, wrote to Henry, May 2, 1610, no matter how many Moriscos are banished, there will be enough left to give the Spaniards trouble; war, which elsewhere would cost a crown, will not cost a farthing there, and when it breaks out there, Spain will find it harder to raise a maravedí than it would be to raise a doubloon anywhere else.[2] Fruitless as were all these plots and plans they at least show that the most experienced men of affairs in Europe clearly recognized that the relations which Spain had created with her Morisco population weakened her essentially both for attack and defence. In the existing political situation this was a position from which extrication was necessary at almost any cost.

[1] Mémoires du Duc de la Force, I. 217, 221–22.

[2] Ambassade en Turquie de Jean de Gontaut-Biron, Baron de Salignac, II. 353 (Paris, 1889).

CHAPTER X.

EXPULSION.

THE problem of what to do with the Moriscos had long occupied the minds of Spanish statesmen. The situation was one of ever-present danger, for which permanent relief was essential, while the halting efforts to bring about unity of faith by a combination of persuasion and persecution had been a conspicuous failure. It was difficult to revert to the ancestral policy of toleration and fairly equitable treatment, which for centuries had proved successful with the Mudéjares; for the irrevocable law of the Church forbade the release of those who had received the saving waters of baptism, and the greed of noble and prelate demanded their oppression. There is one document, however, though unfortunately dateless and without signature, which shows that there were persons who could take a sagacious view of the situation. It was natural, the writer says, that those who are enslaved and oppressed in the land of which once they were the lords, should hate the oppressor and his faith. They must be won over by kindness. Prelates and priests, engrossed in worldly aims, should devote their time and their wealth to this. Direct effort at conversion should be dropped, the Inquisition should be suspended, those who desire to emigrate should be allowed to go. Every effort should be made to alleviate their position and to punish those who wrong them by word or act. There has been great expenditure of words and very little of ducats. There are prelates who have spent thousands in pious works, who if they had done it in seeking the conversion of the Moriscos of their dioceses would have rendered in this manner much greater service to God and the king. Seeking to convert the infidel in China and Japan is like a man who goes hunting lions and ostriches in Africa, leaving his house full of vipers and scorpions. If a hunter can tame and train a wild falcon, why cannot a wise and learned prelate, by the right methods, gain the heart of a Morisco?[1]

Such views were too foreign to the dominant tendencies in Church and State to obtain a hearing. Because the violent methods of the Inquisition, supplemented by the perfunctory and niggardly system of the rectories, had failed to secure more than an outward show of conformity on the part of those who had been coerced to baptism, it was held that the only remedy lay in the further use of force and injustice. The milder forms of this are exhibited in some of the suggestions made with more or less authority. Garcia de Loaysa, Archbishop of Toledo, in 1598, proposed that the Moriscos be prohibited from

[1] Janer, p. 266. An allusion to the Escorial would indicate that this paper probably belongs to the last quarter of the century.

In the junta held in Valencia, in 1604, in presence of Philip III., a learned doctor of theology argued for kindly treatment. He pointed out that the Moriscos had been baptized by force—dragged to the Church by the hair—and then treated as apostates, as though they had voluntarily accepted the faith, whence it arose that they abhorred the Christians and their religion. The only remedy for this, he said, was to treat them with loving kindness. In this sense Padre Ignacio de los Casas, S. J., wrote to the Pope, pointing out that in England forty years of persecution had made no perverts.—Fonseca, pp. 536-7.

marriage except with Old Christians; but Fonseca points out that such marriages are illegal, and, moreover, that Old Christians would not agree to such unions under the existing rules of limpieza, which are the cause of so many perjuries, scandals, and quarrels. Besides, the Moriscos are so obstinate in their faith that more perverts than converts would result. Then there were some who urged that the Moriscos be allowed to live in their faith and that baptisms should cease, for it was a profanation of the sacraments to impose them on those who hated them, but that they should be so crushed with taxes and imposts that they would voluntarily seek conversion; but again Fonseca proves this to be impossible, for the pope would not permit it; it would be recognizing freedom of conscience, forbidden by all the canons; baptism is an indissoluble marriage of the soul with God; the Church as a kindly mother embraces all and does not willingly part with any; the Council of Trent insists on baptism at birth, and all children of baptized parents must be baptized and be coerced with penalties to lead a Christian life; it is a Protestant heresy to claim that faith must be free and voluntary; besides, if the Moriscos were allowed to perform their rites publicly there would not only be the scandal, but many Christians would be seduced to join them.[1] Then there was another suggestion, to take all the children and distribute them among Old Christians to be brought up, but Archbishop Ribera showed that there were forty thousand births among them yearly; to take the children by force would produce a rebellion, and, even without this, the burden on Christians

[1] Fonseca, pp. 360–70.

to provide for them up to the age of ten or twelve would be unbearable and it would be impossible to collect the expenses from the parents.[1] There were not wanting impracticable humanitarians who argued that if good schools under faithful teachers were established in every Morisco community, and if the parents were compelled to send their children to them, and if the rectors and confessors and preachers were men sincere, exemplary, chaste, and zealous the trouble would disappear in twenty years; but to this Utopian suggestion it was deemed sufficient to point to the failure of the royal colleges founded in Granada, Valencia, and Tortosa—the one in Granada, named San Miguel, was reserved for the converts only for fifteen years after the baptism, when it was turned over to the Old Christians.[2] Plans and projects, indeed, there were in plenty. In 1584 the Licentiate Antonio de Córdova de Lara addressed a memorial to the king, proposing that all the Moriscos should be herded together in Sayago, which was a flat country, far from the sea, where they would lose the pride conceived from their victories in the rebellion of Granada.[3] In 1609 there was talk of prohibiting to them the callings of muleteers or traders or shopkeepers, and of confining them strictly

[1] Ximenez, Vida de Ribera, p. 387. About 1575 Dr. Miguel Tomás Taxaquet (subsequently Bishop of Lerida) in his book "De Collegiis instituendis" advocated seizing on a given day all Morisco children, placing them in colleges to be taught and then giving them to Old Christian masters. Bishop Perez of Segorbe, in 1595, quotes this with favor and says the expense could be met by taking the property of the parents.—Archivo de Simancas, Inq^{n} de Valencia, Legajo 205, fol. 3.

[2] Fonseca, p. 376.

[3] Danvila, p. 205. Sayago is a *partida* of Zamora, along the river Duero—a district absurdly insufficient.

to husbandry, to avert the evils of intercommunication between them.[1]

Although these speculations have their interest, as indications of public opinion, their importance otherwise was purely academic. Rulers and statesmen were concerned with measures far more radical and heroic. In 1598 the Venetian envoy, Agostino Nani, writes that expulsion is considered too prejudicial, as it would depopulate the land; that sometimes the idea has been entertained of a Sicilian Vespers, at others the castration of all male infants, and the former measure was advocated by Gomez Davila of Toledo in a long memorial addressed to Philip III., in which he drew a frightful picture of the impending dangers.[2] Hideous as was this project, it was resolved upon at one time and came near being attempted. In 1581, when Philip II. was in Lisbon, regulating his newly acquired kingdom of Portugal, a junta of his chief counsellors, including the Duke of Alva, the Count of Chinchon and Juan de Idiaquez, concluded to send the Moriscos to sea and scuttle the vessels, reserving only those who could be catechised and those who desired to stay, for it was not deemed wise to add to the already numerous population of Africa; it was resolved that when the fleet returned from the Azores the matter should be executed by Alonso de Leyva, but it was abandoned, because when the fleet arrived it had to be sent to Flanders. When, in 1602, Philip III. was informed of this he expressed his pleasure on account of the justification which it afforded for what was then in

[1] Cabrera, Relaciones, p. 371.

[2] Relazioni Venete, Serie I. T. V. p. 486.—Guadalajara y Xavierr, fol. 74.

contemplation.[1] A variant of this was the proposition, in 1590, that the Inquisition should proceed against all the Moriscos of the crown of Castile, without sparing the life of a single one—either inflicting natural or civil death, or perpetual exile, or the galleys for life.[2] Not much more humane was the suggestion of Archbishop Ribera to enslave all the males of proper age and send them to the galleys or to the mines of the Indies, perhaps depleting them gradually by taking every year four thousand youths for each service.[3]

Ferocious and inhuman as were all thêse projects, they evoked no scruples of conscience. Theologians there were in plenty to prove that they were in accord with the canons. By baptism the Moriscos had become Christians; as such they were subject to the laws of the Church, and as heretics and apostates they had incurred the death penalty. Anything short of that was benignity and mercy, while their guilt was too notorious to demand proof or trial. A common sentence involving them all would be a service to God. So reasoned Archbishop Ribera, who did not merely reflect the brutality of the age, for, in the proceedings for his beatification which were concluded in 1796, all his writings were closely scrutinized by the Sacred Congregation of Rites, and there was found in them nothing contrary to orthodox doctrine and practice.[4] Even more outspoken was Fray Bleda, who proved by irrefragable authorities that the Moriscos could all be massacred in a single day, or the king could condemn all the adults to death and the

[1] Danvila, pp. 250–4.

[2] Ibid. p. 221.

[3] Ximenez, Vida de Ribera, p. 384.

[4] Ibid. pp. 323, 380–84.

rest to perpetual slavery, or he could sell them all as slaves to Italy or the Indies, or could fill his galleys and liberate the Christians serving there, especially the clerics, and abolish the custom by which the superiors of the Orders send their peccant brethren to the galleys to save the expense of keeping them in prison. He urged massacre in preference to expulsion, arguing that it would be a work of great piety and edification to the faithful and a wholesome warning to heretics, and, when expulsion took place, his aggressive piety found expression in the hope that, when piled upon the African coast, they would, by dying, aggravate the pestilence which, the previous year, had carried off 100,000 Saracens. Bleda's work was not only approved by all the authorities in Spain and the expense of its printing defrayed by Philip III., but when his rival, Fonseca, sought to prevent its introduction in Rome, it was authoritatively examined and pronounced free from error, and Clement VII. read it with pleasure at the suggestion of his confessor, Cardinal Baronius.[1]

In the midst of all these conflicting projects the idea of expulsion gradually forged to the front. It had been

[1] Bledæ Defensio Fidei, pp. 20, 287, 298-301, 303, 304, 309-10, 345, 535; Crónica, pp. 948, 957.

I have met with few books more calculated to excite horror and detestation than the *Defensio Fidei*. Christianity as there presented is a religion of ruthless cruelty, eager to inflict the most pitiless wrongs on the defenceless. Moloch has usurped the place of Christ, and the bloody sacrifice of those of different faith is the most acceptable offering to their Creator. The most deplorable feature is that the learned author has incontrovertible authority for all his hideous conclusions—utterances of the Fathers, decrees of councils, decretals of popes and decisions of the most eminent theologians.

rendered familiar by the action of Ferdinand and Isabella for Castile and of Charles V. for Aragon, although the artificial barriers thrown around it showed that it was then merely a device to coerce the Moriscos to baptism. After this and the expulsion of the Jews in 1492, there could be no doubt as to the competence of the crown to decree such a measure, and the only question was as to its expediency. There were powerful parties on both sides. In the kingdoms of Aragon, which, after the rebellion of Granada, were those chiefly concerned, owing to the denseness of the Morisco population, the interests of the nobles and gentry and ecclesiastical foundations were deeply involved in retaining a class from which their revenues were chiefly derived; their influence was great, and they made it felt whenever action on the subject was proposed. It is to their fear of losing their vassals that we must doubtless attribute the curious fact that in all the prolonged discussion of the subject the simple expedient seems never to have been seriously considered of allowing the discontented ones freely to expatriate themselves, although their increasing numbers and the diminution of the Spanish population was a matter of great anxiety. Fray Bleda, who for twenty-five years devoted his energies to ridding the land of the hated race, during which he paid three visits to Rome, complains bitterly of the opposition which he experienced. The nobles, he says, for eighty years had postponed a decision of the question, involving it in a thousand clouds of disputation, and they expect to continue it for ages to come. The junta, assembled by the king to consider the matter, consisted largely of laymen whom the nobles could influence, and it was in the habit of reporting to Rome that the trouble lay in the avarice of the bishops and the evil example of the rectors; it had sole control, and no one dared to act independently. Archbishop Ribera once asked him, with regard to his visits to Rome, whether he was not afraid of the junta, to which he replied that he must obey God rather than man. In 1603 Inquisitor-General Guevara induced the vicar-general of Bleda's Dominican Order to forbid him to treat of the matter in either Rome or Madrid, but, in 1607, he obtained licence to go to Naples, and he managed in May, 1608, to obtain an interview at Frascati with Paul V., who granted him permission to go to Rome in spite of a remonstrance from his vicar-general.[1]

Still, as the only practicable remedy, expulsion grew in favor as the danger of revolt and invasion increased and the prospect of converting the Moriscos or of reconciling them to their fate appeared more hopeless. As early as 1551 Pedro de Alcocer says that the evil of the pestilent communication of the Moriscos will go on increasing if it is not stopped by driving them all out.[2] The rebellion of Granada was a warning not to be lightly overlooked, and the remedy of dispersing them throughout Castile had only spread and intensified discontent. The ferocious expedient suggested by the junta of Lisbon, in 1581, shows how real was the terror felt by experienced statesmen, and when that was abandoned there seemed to be nothing left but deportation abroad. In 1582 the Inquisitors of Valencia presented an elaborate report in which they discussed the various alternatives and

[1] Bledæ Defensio Fidei, pp. 227, 228; Crónica, pp. 882, 964, 971.

[2] Pedro de Alcocer, Hystoria ò Descripcion de la imperial cibdad de Toledo, Lib. I. cap. 117 (Toledo, 1554).

concluded in favor of a scheme of shipping the Moriscos of Valencia to the fisheries of Newfoundland, under the guard of soldiers, who should receive grants of land and allotments of vassals, as did the conquistadores in the Indies—the main difficulty in the way being the nobles, who oppose all change. Ribera at the same time submitted an alternative plan of exile or of extensive executions of justice by which in a short time none should be left. All these propositions were laid before Philip, who replied with characteristic irresolution, discussing details, as though expulsion from Valencia was settled, and referring the matter back to his advisers, as though everything had to be considered afresh, to which the junta responded by suggesting that he consult with four or five of the principal lords of Moriscos.[1] It was the eternal story of vacillation under which nothing was done and everything drifted. In 1584 he again seriously considered the project of expulsion, but laid it aside in favor of the enterprise of the Great Armada, and, in 1588, the Council of State urged him vigorously to come to some decision in view of the perilous state of the land, filled with enemies burning to avenge their wrongs, and rapidly increasing, while the Old Christians were diminishing. Soon afterwards it reported that Quiroga, the inquisitor-general and Archbishop of Toledo, was alarmed about the great numbers of Moriscos in Castile and especially in Toledo, to which Philip responded by suggesting that the Inquisition should ascertain how many families of them there were.[2]

That, in 1590, the whole subject was to be threshed out

[1] Danvila, pp. 196–200.

[2] Guadalajara y Xavierr, fol. 61.—Danvila, pp. 217–18.

anew appears from a circular letter of Inquisitor-General Quiroga to the several tribunals, asking in the name of the king for opinions as to whether the Moriscos ought to be allowed to remain or had better be expelled, with the arguments on each side, and the means they would propose for carrying out expulsion.[1] This letter was probably suggested by a consulta of the Council of State, May 5, 1590, in which, after suggesting several more or less cruel propositions, it leans in favor of perpetual banishment.[2] No action resulted, and the royal secretary, Francisco de Idiaquez, in a letter of October 3, 1594, expresses natural impatience that some speedy decision was not reached in place of eternally debating the subject and then forgetting it, as has been the case hitherto and, he fears, will continue to be. He had twice spoken to Quiroga about making the Inquisition take a census of the Moriscos, but did not know whether anything had been done. The king had recently sent him a paper from some zealous but unpractical person, who argued that the existing scarcity arose from over-population, which would be relieved if the Moriscos were expelled. So far from this being the case, Spain had less inhabitants than for the last two or three centuries. If the presence of this vile race, adds Idiaquez, were as safe as it is profitable, there is not a corner of land that should not be placed in their hands, for they alone would bring fertility and plenty by their skill and their thrift, which would reduce the price of provisions and, through these, of other products. Cheapness is not caused by scanty

[1] Archivo Hist. Nacional, Inqn de Valencia, Leg. 5, No. 1, fol. 254. (See Appendix No. XII.)

[2] Danvila, p. 221.

population, but by dense, if they will work; the high prices are the result of the vice, the idleness, the luxury and the excessive superfluity of all classes.[1] It is refreshing to hear the voice of a rational being rising in the desert of prejudice, passion and fanaticism.

Philip's feeble health by this time was forcing him to take a constantly diminishing part in the active business of government, and to his habitual irresolution was thus added the impossibility of preserving a consistent line of policy amid the conflicting views of his ministers, lay and clerical.[2] It is not surprising, therefore, that, in 1595, there was a change of policy. Philip convened another junta to organize another effort to instruct the Moriscos. It was assumed that this was the duty of the bishops, who were ordered to undertake it and to endow the rectories. The aljamas complained of the ignorance of those appointed, and asked for pardon of past offences and time for future instruction, all of which resulted in the Edict of Grace of 1599 and the final futile effort to get the Moriscos to take advantage of it.[3] At the same time the bishops of Valencia had been called upon for reports on the situation; some of these have been preserved, and among them that of Perez, Bishop of Segorbe, who reviews the whole subject in detail, and, after considering the various projects for relief, enters at much length into the question of expulsion, which is evidently regarded as the one effective measure; all the arguments in

[1] Danvila, p. 227.

[2] See the despatch, April 27, 1594, of the papal envoy, Camillo Borghese, in Hinojosa, *Despachos de la Diplomacía Pontificia*, I. 378 (Madrid, 1897).

[3] Danvila, pp. 227, 228.

its favor are given and then those against it, which are answered with a good deal of doubtful casuistry to prove that it is licit.[1] Bishop Esteban, of Orihuela, concludes in favor of giving a reasonable time for instruction, and if that failed the king could commence by taking the adults in other parts of Spain, and then the children, when, if this did not suffice, he should reduce them all to slavery and scatter them among the Old Christians.[2]

We have seen (p. 170) the conflicting opinions and interminable discussions which occupied the last year of Philip's life. His end came at last, September 13, 1598, in a fashion which the innumerable victims of his policy might well regard as retribution for their wrongs. Consumed by gout, strangled with asthma, for almost two months he lay nearly motionless and with but enough of life to render him capable of suffering. Covered with tumors and abscesses, which when opened continued to discharge till the stench in the death-chamber could not be overcome by the strongest perfumes, the long-drawn agony was greater than any of his executioners had invented for the torture chamber. Yet his bearing through all this showed the sincerity of conviction which had inspired the most ruthless of his acts. No spectre of Cazalla or Carranza, of Montigny or Egmont came to disturb the serenity of his conscience. He never lost his patient resignation to the will of God, nor his steadfast conviction that the death for which he prayed was but the gateway to a happier life. Such sins as were inseparable from

[1] Archivo de Simancas, Inq^{n} de Valencia, Leg. 205, fol. 3.

[2] Danvila, p. 229.—In 1597 Dr. Martin Gonzalez de Cellorigo, advocate of the Inquisition of Valencia, addressed a memorial to Philip urging the scattering of the Moriscos of Valencia.—Ibid. p. 232.

human frailty were washed away in the general confession, to which he devoted three days, and the resultant purgatory disappeared before the papal indulgences conferred on the relic of Sant' Albano, which he grasped in his dying hand.[1] Thus he passed away peacefully, his weary life-work conscientiously accomplished. God had entrusted him with power almost supreme; that power carried with it the responsibility of defending the kingdom of God on earth, and he had so used it according to the light vouchsafed him. If this had resulted in the impoverishment of his people and the misery of countless thousands, the fault lay not with him, but with the beliefs in which he had been trained. Yet he could scarce hide from himself that his laborious reign of forty-two years had been a failure. The three great objects of his most strenuous endeavors had been England, France and the Netherlands. England had destroyed his armada, and her corsairs plundered his shipping and his colonies with impunity. In France the League, on which he had lavished his resources, had gone to pieces, and Henry IV., his deadliest enemy, had been recognized and favored by the papacy. Holland had been irrevocably lost, and it was exhausting his strength to maintain his grip on Flanders. The only substantial success which he had to show for his tortuous policy and squandered millions was the robber-conquest of Portugal, to be wrenched from the enfeebled hands of his grandson.

With the accession of his son, the young Philip III., the position of the Moriscos became distinctly worse,

[1] Gustav Turba, Beiträge zur Geschichte der Habsburger, cap. VI. (Wien, 1899).

although, curiously enough, neither in the will and codicil, nor yet in the minute detail of the secret instructions drawn up by the dying king for the guidance of his successor is there an allusion to them.[1] Popular religiosity was rising, as seen by the foundation about this time of innumerable monasteries and other similar establishments. Still more menacing was the absolute subjection of the monarch to his favorite the Duke of Lerma, who, as Marquis of Denia, was lord of numerous vassals, whence he might be expected to favor them were it not that his estates on the Valencian coast were peculiarly exposed to the ravages of corsairs. His temper with regard to them is sufficiently indicated by his presenting a written opinion, February 2, 1599, arguing that all between 15 and 60 years of age were Moors and deserved death; they could well be enslaved and sent to the galleys and their property be confiscated, while the women and men over 60 could be shipped to Barbary and the children be educated in seminaries—a project which was recommended by the Council of State, although it also discussed a plan of scattering them among Old Christians, one to every fifty inhabitants in places of

[1] Testamento y Codicilo del Rey D. Felipe 2º (Madrid, 1882) — Gustav Turba, *op. cit.*, pp. 119-43.—Palma Cayet, Chronologie Septenaire, fol. 29-31 (Paris, 1611).—Sully, Œconomies d'Estat, I. 409-12 (Amstelredam, *potius* Château de Sully, 1638).

The letter of Bongars to Sully, enclosing a copy of the Instructions, Oct. 27, 1598, describes the sufferings of Philip with evident relish—"ce grand Monarque qui avoit tant vexé et trauaillé les autres, a luy mesme esté crucié et miserablement affligé plus de huict ou neuf mois durant, de tres-espouuentables et langoureux accidens, son corps estant extenué et descharné comme une Schelette, couuert de sordides et boüeux ulceres, puans comme une sentine et rongé de poux et de vermine comme un Herodes."—Ibid. p. 408.

not less than 500 population. That speedy action was deemed inevitable was shown by the decision of the council during 1599 to gather secretly the necessary forces, to ascertain the numbers of the Moriscos, to commence with Castile and then determine what to do with Valencia and Aragon.[1]

Still, the papal briefs for the Edict of Grace had been received, and it remained to be seen what would be the result. Archbishop Ribera sought to render it more effective by issuing a printed pastoral in which he warned the Moriscos that if gentle means proved fruitless the king had resolved on expulsion, and he told the nobles that the only way to keep their vassals was to induce them to turn Christian. This frankness alarmed the Council of State, which ordered the withdrawal of the letter; if the priests and preachers had said anything of the kind they must take it back. In no way must the Moriscos be informed in advance of their approaching destruction. Orders were also sent to the Count of Benavente, Viceroy of Valencia, to the effect that, during the progress of instruction, steps be taken to guard the kingdom, and he was asked whether it would be possible to disarm the Moriscos.[2]

The Edict of Grace, as we have seen, of course proved nugatory, and towards the close of 1601 Archbishop Ribera addressed a memorial to the king, reciting his personal experience of its futility. Religion was the foundation of the kingdoms of Spain, and on the failure of the Armada he had told Philip II. that it was a warning from God to purify his own dominions before endeavoring to sup-

[1] Danvila, pp. 233, 239, 240. [2] Ibid. pp. 243, 244.

press the heretics of other lands, while the same lesson was taught by the defeat of the recent expedition to Algiers. He dilated with much force on the dangers to which Spain was exposed, abhorred as it was by all other nations and exposed to attack by England through Portugal, by France through Navarre and Aragon, and by the infidel on the coast, with 90,000 fiercely hostile fighting men in its midst to aid them. Roderic lost Spain when there was not a single Moor in it, and the rebellion of Granada required troops to be brought from Germany and Italy; it cost 60,000 Spanish lives, and finally terms had to be made with the rebels, including free passage to their five or six hundred Turkish auxiliaries. For his memorial Ribera was warmly thanked by the Duke of Lerma and by Fray Gaspar de Córdova, the royal confessor, and, December 31, 1601, the king also thanked him and asked him to set forth the gentle and profitable remedies which he stated that he could suggest. To this he replied in a long paper, which was practically an exposition of the opening sentences, in which he quoted the Old Testament texts ordering the enemies of God to be slain without mercy and setting forth the duties of kings to extirpate them. The Moriscos are obstinate, dogmatizing heretics, and the only remedy is to drive them out of Spain: evils to be cured must be torn up by the roots, leaving no fragments to send up fresh shoots. This is the benignant and gentle method to which he had alluded—that the king shall, by secret inquisition through bishops and priests, obtain proof of the apostasy and treason of the Moriscos, and then by public sentence condemn them to exile and confiscation. That it is benignant and gentle he proves because they have merited death, and benignity is a virtue proper to kings, and besides, to massacre such a multitude would cause general horror. The only scruple lies in the invasion on the jurisdiction of the ecclesiastical judges, who would be deprived of inflicting the punishments provided by the canons, but this could be remedied by the pope. Otherwise the king need have no scruple of conscience; he will liberate his faithful vassals from oppression and enrich the royal treasury.[1]

Ribera claimed and received the credit of producing the final catastrophe, but this was undeserved. He may have had some influence in quieting the royal conscience, if Philip had any scruples, which is doubtful; but there were much more learned theologians in plenty to do this, and probably the most that he accomplished was to call attention to the fact that the secular power, in a matter of heresy, could act only under ecclesiastical mandate. To obtain a papal decree or an inquisitorial sentence against a whole race, as had been suggested by churchmen, would be incompatible with the secrecy which the preparations for expulsion demanded. It was probably on this account, and to avoid trenching upon the spiritual jurisdiction, that the measure when resolved upon finally, seven years later, was treated exclusively as an affair of state and, except a vague allusion to the service of God, only secular reasons were advanced in its justification.[2]

[1] Ximenez, Vida de Ribera, pp. 367 sqq., 374–5, 376 sqq.

[2] So far as credit is concerned, Fray Bleda had been a much more efficient agitator than the Blessed Juan de Ribera. His account of his own career shows how completely the rectories were used as mere preferment. In 1585, when he was yet only an acolyte, Ribera gave him the rectory of Corvera and admitted him to deacon's orders. He served his rectory with a vicar and, on his second visit to it, he chanced to enter the church as the vicar was elevating the host on a feast-day. He was

The fact is that, on January 2, 1602, the junta, consisting of Lerma, the Count of Miranda, Juan de Idiaquez, and Gaspar de Córdova, the royal confessor, had already presented an important consulta which virtually outlined the eventual action. It stated that the matter was the most important one that the king had to consider. The French intrigues in Aragon were known or suspected, for they were alluded to as something that might at any moment become serious. In place of commencing with Castile, as formerly proposed, the work should begin in Valencia and also, if possible, in Aragon, sufficient forces

shocked at the irreverence of the Moriscos, who made a jest of it; he returned to Valencia and offered to resign his rectorship, but Ribera refused to permit this, and he concentrated his thoughts on the best way to rescue the sacrament from these insults. When he was ordained to the priesthood he entered the Dominican Order to escape from the rectory, and, after the usual residence of new members for some years in a convent, he went to Rome in 1591 to represent the irreverence of the Moriscos to the sacrament. Gregory XIV. gave him a letter to Philip II. and Cardinal Alexandrino one to Ribera, who rewarded him with the commendation to the rectory of Sollana for a year, which he employed in writing his book on the miracles of the sacrament. To acquaint himself thoroughly with the misdeeds of the Moriscos he devoted eight years to teaching them in Ayelo, Alcocer, Gavarda and other places, and thus was fully equipped for the agitation which he carried on unceasingly to the end. Ribera's activity, he says, was aroused somewhat tardily. When, in 1597, he showed the archbishop his treatise on the apostasy of the Moriscos, and told him that he proposed to print it, the latter discouraged him, saying that their errors were not cause of infection of the faithful, but when subsequently he learned of some cases of perversion he ordered Bleda to print it. Although, as a theologian, Ribera held the theoretical opinion that the Moriscos were apostates, in practice he followed the common view that they were excused through ignorance, admitting them to mass and to burial in consecrated ground, thus adopting the allowable plan, when there are two probable opinions, of following either, according to circumstances.—Bleda, Crónica, pp. 940, 942–44.

being provided. Idiaquez and Miranda were in favor of sending them to Africa, reserving the children and those who desired to stay; they were not in favor of massacre or scuttling ships, because there may be innocent ones among them and the pope would not permit it. On the other hand, Lerma and Fray Gaspar thought it terrible to send the baptized to Barbary, where they would become Moors, and dangerous besides, there being 80,000 Spaniards, crazed by being torn from their wives and children and stripped of their property; they would at once return to regain them. The pope should be consulted. All four recommended that the work be done when the spring was well advanced, and that meanwhile troops be raised in Italy and the galleys be well manned to keep the French in check. In reply to this the king charged the junta not to drop the subject until it should be fully decided; if the Moriscos can be expelled with a good conscience he prefers that; it should commence with Valencia, and if Aragon can be added, so much the better; the largest possible land and naval forces should be assembled at once and the militia of the kingdom should be organized, and all haste be made with the preparations. In compliance with this a pragmática was drafted, which in its comparative mildness reflects the fears which prevailed of exciting to rebellion. The Moriscos were given a month in which to sell their property and depart from Spain, going whither they might choose; to those who wished to pass to Barbary safe passage was offered; if to other lands of Christendom measures would be taken to ensure their good treatment, but death and confiscation were threatened for all who should overstay the term.[1]

[1] Danvila, pp. 250–4.

All this, as usual, came to nothing. Probably, after the fashion of the government of the period, interminable discussion over details postponed action until the immediate danger of the French invasion passed away and peace was concluded with England in 1604. Then, as we have seen (p. 175), a fresh attempt was made to reform the rectories and provide efficient instruction, which, of course, was as illusory as ever, although, as late as 1607, we find the Council of State resolving to await its results before attempting severer measures. An efficient reason, indeed, is found for these delays and shifting policies in the absolute exhaustion of the royal treasury—as Juan de Idiaquez remarked, the execution of the project of Lisbon, in 1581, had to be suspended for lack of means, and the same difficulties existed still.[1] Yet, if Philip had been actuated by the zeal for the faith attributed to him in the expulsion of the Moriscos, he might have employed on this pious work a part of the 1,860,000 ducats paid to him by the Jewish New Christians of Portugal, in 1604, for procuring, in spite of the protests of the bishops, a papal bull to absolve them for all past offences of Judaism—a bargain which led to the report that the Moriscos proposed to offer the same for a similar pardon.[2]

Then, in 1608, came the alarm about Muley Cidan. On January 30th a full meeting of the council was held, where all the antecedent documents were reviewed and the opinion of each member was taken. Archbishop Ribera despaired of the conversion of the Moriscos, for the rectories were of no service in consequence of their meagre

[1] Ibid. pp. 265–66. [2] Cabrera, Relaciones, p. 227.

revenues; ignorant and dissolute persons were sent to fill them, who did more harm than good, but the pope had ordered the new effort at instruction and the holding of a provincial council, and it ought to be tried; nevertheless, the mildest course would be to deport them all to Barbary. Cardinal Sandoval, Archbishop of Toledo, said that a sentence could not be pronounced against a nation; the king ought to resolve as God should inspire him and act without further conferences. The other members all seemed to regard expulsion as inevitable; the Moriscos were increasing and the Old Christians diminishing, and in time the former would be in the majority; it would be a blow to the barons, but they would be consoled by giving to them the property of their vassals, and in a few years their lands would fill up. The discussion turned rather upon means and details, the precautions to be taken and the necessity for profound secrecy; but the question of what to do with the children was an embarrassing one, as there were conscientious scruples about sending the young, who had been baptized, to be brought up as infidels. It is significant, moreover, that there were ominous hints of putting all the adults to the sword or reducing them to slavery.[1] The provincial council ordered by the pope was duly held, November 22d, but expulsion may now be considered to have been fully resolved upon, and whatever outward efforts were made to instruct and convert were merely to conceal from the victims the fate in store for them.

It was impossible to keep them wholly in ignorance that some decisive measure was on foot, and the situation

[1] Danvila, pp. 267–9.

grew steadily more agitated. In October, Tomás de Borja, Archbishop of Saragossa, reported that many were passing to France, while the whole body was becoming more restless than usual; in some places they were forming bands, infesting the highways and killing all Christians. In Valencia, the Viceroy Caracena was exhausting himself in proclamations ordering the seizure of arms, the registering of all strangers, the enforcement of the curfew, the prohibition of shows and games attracting vagabonds.[1] The shocking condition of the currency, attributed to the Moriscos, was also a subject of grave solicitude. By this time the circulation, almost to the exclusion of the precious metals, consisted of a debased coinage known as *vellón;* when the State was a counterfeiter it was impossible to prevent individuals from following so profitable an example, and the Moriscos were especially active in order to provide themselves against expected eventualities. As early as 1605, there were some of them condemned for it in Aragon, when it was shown that they not only counterfeited the small vellón coinage, but issued reales of half-weight, in which the silver and the alloy were equal. In Valencia they were bolder, and as the future grew more threatening they turned out nail-heads and circular scraps of iron and tin, which were eagerly bought in quantities, for silver or gold, by Christians at one-fifth their nominal value; this stuff was deposited in the bank of Valencia, which paid it out as good money, and for fear of riots it was ordered to pass current, leading to troubles which we shall see hereafter.[2]

[1] Danvila, pp. 271, 273.

[2] Bleda, Crónica, pp. 923, 999.—Fonseca, pp. 202–4, 256.

Matters were now finally ripening for action. In answer to a call from Philip, in April, 1609, the Council of State presented a consulta which is a characteristic mixture of the spiritual and the temporal, representing the duty to prevent the offences to God which may invoke his wrath to imperil the State, which is the chief bulwark of Christianity. The opinion is unanimous that the Moriscos must be expelled; the fear of the Moors and Muley Cidan is acute, and Lerma even assumes that there is danger of their conquering Spain. If other suggestions are alluded to it is only to dismiss them, and it is evidently a comfort to the members to know that learned and pious men have proved that the Moriscos have all merited death, and could be put to the sword or enslaved, although it is agreed that the milder course of expulsion is preferable. It is substantially determined that the blow be struck in the autumn, when there will be less danger of foreign interference, and that the interval be employed in preparation by organizing the militia, bringing troops from Italy and assembling squadrons to command the coasts. The present year is assumed to be the time to act, as there is less to be apprehended from Moor and Turk. The fate of the Moriscos was thus determined, and no time was lost in starting the preliminary preparations. Early in May orders were sent to the Viceroys of Sicily, Naples and Milan to have the galleys in readiness, together with all the troops that could be spared, and at the end of June the several squadrons were required to rendezvous at Majorca by August 15th. The necessity of such action to deter or suppress resistance is manifest from a letter to the king from the Viceroy Caracena, as late as August 19th, dwelling on the unprotected condition of Valencia and the utter deficiency of its military establishment. Some months previously, he says, he had taken steps to organize and train the militia companies, which Lerma had ordered when viceroy, and save this the land was apparently defenceless.[1]

Early in August Don Augustin Mexia, a commander of high repute, was sent to Valencia, under pretext of inspecting the fortifications, with full powers to execute the plans of expulsion. He bore a letter from the king to Ribera, expatiating on the influence which the latter had had in assuring him that he could do what he chose with the Moriscos. It dwelt on the dangers to which the defenceless land was exposed by their appeals to the Turk and to Muley Cidan and the promises of the latter, and on the little fruit to be expected from further efforts to convert them. For which reasons and chiefly for the service of God, and confiding in the divine favor, he had resolved on the expulsion of this evil race. In this there was not an hour to be lost in suggesting other methods or in weighing difficulties, the chief of which lay in the lords of Moorish vassals, and to remove this he relied greatly on Ribera's efforts.[2] Even at the last moment, however, the councillors were not unanimous. August 29th Juan de Idiaquez and Manuel Ponce de Leon presented consultas calling in question the wisdom of the action. The former evidently feared the opposition of the whole kingdom, and pointed out the difficulty of repopulation; the latter argued that the coast could be amply protected and fortified at the expense of the Moriscos and that they could be held in subjection by

[1] Danvila, pp. 274-86. [2] Ximenez, Vida de Ribera, p. 397.

vigorous repressive measures.[1] It was too late; the decisive steps had been taken, and there could be no withdrawal.

Ribera thus had gained the object for which he had so earnestly been laboring. Yet when Mexia reached Valencia, August 20th, and, after conferring over details with Caracena and Francisco de Miranda, who was in charge of the local militia, Ribera was sent for and read the royal letter, his opinion suddenly changed. He selfishly argued that the Moriscos of Castile and Andalusia should be expelled, when those of the crown of Aragon, finding themselves isolated, would be converted. He urged the loss of the censos which they owed, the damage to their lords, and the diminution of the tithes and ecclesiastical revenues. He proposed that all three should join in a letter to the king, urging him to commence with Andalusia, and when the conference ended at 4 P.M. he was still firm. He was told that a courier for Madrid would start at midnight, when he could write what he pleased; but on consideration he concluded that the king did not want advice but obedience, and he sent to the palace his letter in time for the courier, informing the viceroy and Mexia that the royal resolution came from heaven and he would further it with all his power. Still, he could not reconcile himself to the prospect of poverty, and on September 3d he said to Bleda and to the Dominican prior Alcocer, "Padres, we may well in future have to eat bread and herbs and mend our shoes," and he wrote to the king pointing out the difficulties and dangers impending.[2]

[1] Janer, pp. 282–91.

[2] Bleda, Crónica, p. 988. Where his own interests were not concerned Ribera gave full play to his impracticable fanaticism. On June

The secret had been well kept. The assembly of the bishops, ordered by the pope, had sat until March 9, 1609, and had resolved to undertake anew the task of instruction. No one anticipated the sudden resolution, although suspicion was aroused when Mexia came ostensibly on a duty so much beneath his military rank, and it was strengthened by his frequent secret conferences with Caracena and Ribera. The Moriscos grew anxious and sent one of their number to Francisco de Miranda, with a request for a loan of considerable amount in the customary form of a censo, arguing that he would refuse to take what would prove valueless in case of expulsion, when Miranda, penetrating his object, with prompt self-sacrifice accepted it and gave an order on his wife for the money.[1] In spite of this they commenced to fortify their houses, to cease laboring and bringing provisions to the city, which suffered in consequence; the nobles conveyed their families to the city in preparation for the worst, and Ribera's action in increasing the number of his retainers and laying in stores of victuals increased the excitement. The members of the *Estamento Militar*, or House of Nobles of the córtes, who were in Valencia, assembled in the Diputacion, or Parliament house, and sent a deputation of inquiry to the viceroy, but got nothing but fair words, which increased their anxieties; a proposition to appoint en-

24th of this year he had written to Lerma protesting against the twelve years' truce with Holland, because in the articles he did not see a word providing for the inviolable maintenance of the Catholic faith (Ximenez, p. 400). He would probably have been still more aggrieved had he known that a secret article prohibited persecution for religious belief in both Holland and the provinces retained by Spain (Hubert, Voyage de l'Empereur Joseph II. dans les Pays Bas, p. 205.—Bruxelles, 1900).

[1] Fonseca, p. 150.

voys to the king led to a violent debate, which was continued in a second meeting, when hot words passed and swords were drawn. A third meeting was held, which resolved on the appeal to the king to represent to him the evils of expulsion, the poverty it would entail on the nobles, the churches, the monasteries, the gentry and citizens, whose wealth was invested in the rents charged upon the Morisco settlements, amounting to eleven millions of ducats, the diminution of the royal revenues for guarding the coasts, the desperation of the Moriscos leading to rebellion, and the enmity of the people to the nobles, inherited from the times of the Germanía. The envoys performed their duty, but were told by the king that they were too late, for the edict had already been published in Valencia.[1]

Early in September the fleet had left Majorca and by the 5th it reached Iviza, where it was joined by the home squadrons and the galleons from the Indies. In all there were sixty-two galleys and fourteen galleons, carrying about eight thousand disciplined troops, which, with the land forces, formed an aggregate indicating the magnitude of the undertaking and the dangers anticipated in the execution. By the 17th they arrived at their several destinations at Alicante, Denia and the Alfaques of Tortosa, and commenced landing the men. Possession was taken of the Sierra de Espadan, and the frontiers were guarded to prevent the entrance of Aragonese Moriscos.[2] On the 21st royal letters of the 11th, addressed to the Jurados, Diputados, and Estamento Militar were read,

[1] Guadalajara, fol. 109.—Fonseca, pp. 148–58.

[2] Bleda, Crónica, pp. 984, 989.—Danvila, p. 296.

reciting the renewed appeals of the Moriscos to the Turk, to Muley Cidan, to the Protestants and to other enemies of Spain, who all had promised to aid them; pointing out the evident danger of this and the service to God of ending the heresy and apostasy of that evil race, and announcing that he had resolved to expel them all. In this enterprise he summoned every one to aid Mexia; the viceroy would tell them what they would gain from the property of their vassals, and in addition they might be assured that he would in every way seek to repair the damage that would result.[1]

On the 22d was published the edict of expulsion, which had been sent to the viceroy August 4th. This commenced with the customary recital of the treasonable correspondence of the Moriscos with the enemies of Spain and of the necessity of placating God for their heresies, wherefore, in view of the failure of all efforts to convert them, the king had determined to send them all to Barbary. That, in comparison with the measures of Ferdinand and Isabella and of Charles V., the conditions of the expulsion were less inhuman, reflects the consciousness of weakened power to overcome resistance. These conditions were that, under irremissible pain of death, within three days after the publication of the edict in the several towns and villages, all Moriscos of both sexes, with their children, should depart for embarkation at the ports designated to them by a commissioner. They could take with them of portable property what they could carry on their backs; they would find vessels ready to convey them to Barbary, and would be fed on the voyage, but they must

[1] Janer, p. 297.

take what provisions they could. During the three days all must remain in their places of residence, awaiting the orders of the commissioner, and after the three days any one found wandering from his habitation could be robbed by the first comer and carried to the magistrates, or be killed in case of resistance. As the king gave to the lords all real estate and all personal property not carried off, if any one should hide the latter or bury it, or set fire to houses or harvests, all the inhabitants of the place were to be put to death. In order to preserve the houses, the sugar mills, the rice crop, and the irrigating canals, and to instruct the new settlers, six per cent. of the Moriscos were allowed to remain, the selection to be made by the lords, and in places belonging to the crown by the viceroy, but these were to be only husbandmen, the oldest and those who had manifested the best tendency to become Christians. Children under four years of age desiring to remain could do so with consent of their parents or guardians. Children under six, whose fathers were Old Christians, were to stay, as well as their Morisca mothers; if the father was a Morisco and the mother an Old Christian, he was to go, and children under six were to stay with the mother. Also, those could stay who for two years had lived among Christians without attending the meetings of the aljamas, and also those admitted to communion by their priests. Hiding or sheltering fugitives was forbidden under pain of six years of galleys, and all soldiers and Old Christians were strictly forbidden to insult or injure the Moriscos by word or deed, while to prove to them that the transfer to Barbary was to be executed in good faith, after every instalment had been carried over ten Moriscos were allowed to return to report to their fellows what their treatment had been.[1]

[1] Janer, p. 299. The provisions in the edict concerning children were a compromise after long discussion, and were not the final policy adopted. The question, which to us seems an exceedingly simple one —that they should not be separated from their parents—was in reality exceedingly embarrassing, owing to the conscientious scruple about allowing those who had been baptized to be taken to a land of infidels where they would grow up as Moors. To Fray Bleda this had been an insuperable obstacle to expulsion—they could not be allowed to go, and would be too expensive to retain, so he prefers the alternative of massacre. After the expulsion he expresses his deep regret that they could not all have been kept (Bledæ Defensio Fidei, pp. 345, 352, 557). Ribera, in his memorial of 1602, urged that all children under seven should be kept and distributed among Old Christians, to whom the king could grant them as slaves (Ximenez, p. 379). When at this time a project of expulsion was formulated by the junta, it was proposed to retain all children, to be brought up in Christian families and taught trades and serve until they were 26, but a discussion respecting wet-nurses shows the inherent difficulty of the subject, and it proved an embarrassing one in the discussion of the Morisco question by the Royal Council, Jan. 30, 1608 (Danvila, pp. 255–7, 269). After the expulsion edict had been sent to Valencia the matter was still undecided. A junta presided over by the king, September 1, 1609, unanimously agreed that the children below the age of 10 or 11 should be kept (Danvila, p. 294). This was in accordance with a letter from Ribera, in answer to a demand from Philip for his opinion, and it greatly pleased the king, but the impulsive archbishop speedily changed his views, after consulting three learned and prudent theologians, and wrote to the king that there was no hope of making Christians of those so old—in six years they would be marrying, and the whole trouble in time would come over again, so that he reduced the limit of age to 5. Then, on subsequent consideration, he changed his mind again, and, on Sept. 4th, he wrote another letter pointing out that according to the best estimates there must be in Valencia not less than 60,000 Morisco children under 5—how could they be cared for, and where could at least 6000 wetnurses be obtained? Add to this the difficulty of keeping them in the faith, the fact that the Moriscos would let themselves be torn in pieces rather than part with their offspring or, if they did so, they would infest the coasts in the hope of recovering them, and the plan of retaining the children becomes im-

No time was lost in making the necessary arrangements. On the 24th five chief commissioners were appointed to

practicable. He had submitted these views to his previous advisers, adding three more to the number, and he encloses their conclusions as his own—which are those which appear in the edict (Ximenez, p. 406). Yet as late as September 15th at a full meeting of the Council of State it was resolved to see about providing wetnurses, and that the fruits and movables of the Moriscos should be applied to the children, as well as the revenues of the two seminaries, while juntas of theologians were ordered to be held in Valencia and Madrid to consider the subject. The one at Madrid met under the presidency of Inquisitor-general Sandoval, and it probably adopted Ribera's suggestions (Danvila, p. 292). Simultaneously with the publication of the edict, Sept. 22d, Ribera issued a letter to all the priests, ordering them to lend all assistance to the officials, explaining the details as to the children, and charging them to use all tenderness and charity with them (Ximenez, p. 428).

Considerable efforts were made to neutralize the permission finally given for children to accompany parents. Balaguer, Bishop of Orihuela, exerted himself throughout his bishopric to have them left, pledging himself to have them brought up as carefully as if they were his own, but the parents declared that they would rather dash out their brains than have them brought up as Christians (Bleda, Crónica, p. 1023). Even guardians, although poor, paid nurses to suckle their wards, and women were seen who had undertaken three or four. We are told that, amid all the ruin caused by the expulsion, nothing so afflicted the people as seeing that hell had to swallow so many innocent lambs, and arrangements were made to steal as many as possible. Doña Isabel de Velasco, wife of the viceroy, set the example, and by the advice of theologians employed her servants, who brought her several, whom she rejoiced to see snatched from Satan ; she also sought out women about to be delivered and hid them so that the infants should be baptized (Fonseca, p. 177). When, in the expulsion from Aragon, some 12,000 were quartered in a meadow on the banks of the Tagus, they saw an Old Christian couple steal a child, when they raised such a tumult that it was necessary for the commander, Don Alexos Mar y Mon, to come and quiet it ; he ordered the most riotous to be hanged in front of his quarters, which subdued them, after which he commuted the sentence to the galleys (Bleda, Crónica, p. 1049). Still, despair occasionally overcame the claims of nature. When provisions ran out while in confinement awaiting embarkation they sometimes sold their children

superintend the embarkation at the designated ports of the Alfaques of Tortosa, Vinaroz, Denia, Valencia and

to escape starvation for all (Cabrera, Relaciones, p. 393). The same thing occurred among those who rebelled in the sierra del Aguar, after they surrendered and were on their way to embark at Denia, when children were sold for a handful of figs or a little bread (Guadalajara, fol. 119).

In this disastrous attempt at resistance and that at Muela de Cortes the soldiers captured large numbers of children and sold them, both at home and abroad, for 8, 10, 12 and 15 ducats apiece. The legality of this was questioned, and the king decided that he did not grant them as slaves, and that those who held them must register them as well as those distributed by the royal officials; they were to be instructed up to the age of 12 and then serve for as many years as they had been taken care of. Ribera protested against this: they should all be enslaved, so that there would be a chance of saving their souls; people were sending them adrift, and there would be 2000 helplessly abandoned. By no means all were registered, and many were sent to Italy and elsewhere to be sold, leading Philip to ask the pope to make the same regulations as he had done. Very large numbers were found, both on this occasion and subsequently, among whom were some 12 or 15 years old, giving rise to fresh anxiety, for they were infidels and, being very fruitful, they would eventually infect the whole world. There was much discussion over them. Ribera wanted them sent away, and most of the theologians sided with him. Philip decided that those over 7 should be expelled and the rest be kept, but it seemed cruel to send such young children to Barbary without protectors, and the matter was allowed to drift (Fonseca, p. 252; Ximenez, p. 445).

As we shall see, a somewhat different policy was adopted in the other kingdoms. The whole question is an interesting illustration of the pious eagerness to save souls at any cost to bodies (Guadalajara, fol. 151) and of the fanatical determination to free the land from heresy.

There was another class of cases which gave rise to doubts—those which were under trial or sentence by the Inquisition. The tribunal of Valencia submitted a number of queries as to its duties in view of the altered relations caused by the edict, which were answered October 7, 1609, to the effect that those who were undergoing penance in prison were to be sent off as well as those who had been arrested and were under trial. Those who had been sentenced to appear in the next auto de fe were to be kept for it, except such cases as were at large under bail,

Alicante, and thirty-two subordinate ones to gather and conduct the exiles, with 1500 of the local militia to serve as guards and escorts. On the 27th Ribera preached a sermon, which was greatly lauded at the time as having largely facilitated the acceptance of the royal policy. With considerable skill he justified the expulsion by scripture texts forbidding friendship and intercourse with the infidel and the heretic. He told his hearers that the Moriscos had offered to aid the Turk with 150,000 men, that the next spring would have seen the Turkish fleet upon their shores, and he drew an awful picture of the time when their brethren and children would have been slain and throughout Spain the name of Mahomet would have been venerated and that of Christ blasphemed. It was to prevent this that the king had employed a remedy which, besides being the only one, was so admirable, so divine, that it could not have been devised by human prudence without illumination from above, as an example for the whole world and the admiration of all who live and shall hereafter live. Who could exaggerate the Christianity, the prudence, the magnanimity and the greatness of this work? The churches, which had been filled with dragons and wild beasts, will be filled with angels and seraphim. All should humbly make confession, and he first of all, that he had lived for forty years in peace with the Moriscos, seeing with his own eyes the blasphemies which they committed. Nor did he neglect to offer material conso-

who were to have a special auto. Those who subsequently to the proclamation declared themselves to be Moors were not to be arrested unless they committed some overt offence or blasphemed the faith, in which case they were to be tried and punished as usual.—Janer, p. 306.

lation to the nobles and gentry for the temporary diminution of their revenues until matters should settle themselves, assuring them that this would be fully made up by the greater certainty of their collections.[1]

The die was cast, and was followed by some days of anxious suspense. The people, we are told, rejoiced, for they hated both the Moriscos and the nobles, and there were symptoms of an uprising against the latter. The nobles and gentry grieved over the ruin of their lands, and the religious establishments over the loss of their enormous investments in censos on the Morisco communities. The Moriscos at first were inclined to resist; they sent envoys to the viceroy, making large offers of a servicio to the king and to pay for the defence of the coasts, and when these were rejected they busied themselves in endeavoring to procure arms, forging their ploughshares and reaping-hooks into pikes, on which, together with slings, they mainly depended.[2] Then, to the general surprise and inexpressible relief of all, obstacles seemed to vanish with a completeness in which the pious plainly discerned the finger of God.[3] The nobles, for the most part, obediently accepted the situation and loyally lent their aid to facilitate the execution of the decree. The Duke of Gandía, who, next to the Duke of Segorbe, held the largest number of vassals, wrote to the king, October 9th, saying that, on September 28th, the Marquis of Santa Cruz had embarked for him five thousand of them, whom he desired to be the first in order to quiet

[1] Fonseca, p. 212.—Bleda, Crónica, p. 997.—Ximenez, pp. 411–27.

[2] Fonseca, pp. 165, 198.

[3] Guadalajara, fol. 151.—Juan Ripol, Dialogo de Consuelo por la Expulsion de los Moriscos de España, fol. 20 (Pamplona, 1613).

the apprehensions of the rest as to the safety of the voyage. It was the ruin of his house, for just then the sugar crop should be gathering, but he was content in carrying out the holy intentions of the king, to facilitate which he had allowed them to sell what they wished of their property. This had aided greatly, and had enabled him, with only eight men, to go among them and get them off, returning home he knew not whether more edified at their willingness or grieved at the ruin of the land or anxious to hurry off the rest from the baronies and the county of Oliva.[1]

The Moriscos, in fact, had suddenly changed their purpose. They were awed at the sight of the well-armed and disciplined troops which had been landed and marched to Játiva and by what they heard of the Castilian cavalry which was guarding the border. A meeting of their alfaquíes and leaders was held in which it was agreed that resistance was hopeless and submission inevitable, the most potent argument being that after defeat their children would be taken and brought up as Christians, while prophecies were talked of which promised an unexpected blessing. It was consequently resolved that all should go, including the six per cent. allowed to remain, and any one staying was held to be an apostate. This had such an effect that those who had been striving to be chosen in the six per cent. and offering large sums to their lords now refused to stay, although promised whatever terms they chose to ask. The Duke of Gandía suffered especially from this; the cane-crop was the largest ever known; all the operatives in his sugar-mills were Moriscos, and no one else knew the processes; he could

[1] Danvila, p. 301. See also his letter of Sept. 24th in Janer, p. 293.

not import skilled workmen from Madeira or Calabria or Granada, and he vainly proposed to grant whatever they wanted to induce them to remain. The only inducement that would tempt them he could not meet, for they offered to stay if guaranteed the free exercise of their religion; he applied to the viceroy, but Ribera declared that this was a concession beyond the power of either king or pope, for they were baptized.[1]

When once this resolution was reached the Moriscos lost no time in converting into coin whatever movables they possessed. The land became a universal fair. Horses, cattle, sheep, fowls, grain, sugar, honey, cloths, household effects were sold at a fraction of their value, and finally were given away. Farm animals were turned loose, and strangers went around bargaining and purchasing for almost nothing. While some of the nobles followed Gandía's example in allowing this, others complained of it, for under the edict most of these things enured to them. The viceroy, therefore, October 1st, issued a proclamation forbidding, under pain of nullity, the sale of all real property, animals, grains, oil, censos or debts, but this led to imminent danger of rebellion and was not enforced.[2]

When once the shock was over of abandoning their possessions and leaving the homes of their ancestors, the prospect of reaching a land where they could openly enjoy the practice of their faith and be free from grinding oppression inspired many of them with intense eagerness to be off. They competed for places in the first embarka-

[1] Fonseca, pp. 199 sq.—Archivo de Simancas, Inq^{n} de Valencia, Leg. 205, fol. 2.—Bleda, Crónica, p. 1000.

[2] Fonseca, pp. 202 sq.—Janer, p. 303.—Bleda, Crónica, p. 1004.

tion, and the commissioners had no trouble in marshalling them and conveying them to the designated ports in large companies. The troops marched out to meet them and escort them to the galleys, which was necessary to protect them from the robbers who flocked thither. Food was furnished to those who needed it, the sick were tended, and strict orders were issued that no one should injure them by word or act, so that good reports might encourage those who were to follow. While thus all proper effort was made to smooth the path of the exiles it was impossible to restrain the savage greed of the Old Christians, who had been accustomed to regard the Morisco as a being entitled to no rights. They sallied forth in squads, robbing and often murdering all whom they encountered. Fonseca tells us that in going from Valencia to San Mateo he saw the roads full of dead Moriscos. To check this a royal edict was issued, September 26th, ordering that guards should be provided to keep the roads safe, at the cost of the towns and villages. This proved ineffectual and, on October 3d and again on October 6th, the viceroy reported to the king that the robberies and murders were increasing, giving rise to more anxiety than the deportation of the Moriscos, although gallows were erected along the roads and swift justice was executed. Philip, after due delay, replied that the measures taken had been insufficient, the delinquents must be rigorously punished, some of the commissioners had been cowardly and should be made examples of, for to this was attributable the risings of the Val del Aguar and of the Muela de Cortes. To protect and reassure their vassals some of the nobles, like the Duke of Gandía, the Marquis of Albaida and others, accompanied them and saw them safely embarked; the Duke of Maqueda even sailed with his to Oran.[1]

The first shipment of the exiles was made from Denia, October 2d, when the seventeen Neapolitan galleys took two hundred each. Besides these, many other vessels were brought there, so that the whole number amounted to nearly six thousand. These were speedily followed by similar departures from the other ports, bringing the total of the first embarkation to about twenty-eight thousand. On arrival at Oran they were received by the Captain-General, the Count of Aguilar, and lost no time in asking to be received as vassals by the ruler of Tlemcen, about 90 miles from Oran. Understanding that they brought money with them, he gladly assented and sent Cid Almanzor, a captain, with 500 horse to escort them. He was accompanied by a rich Jew named Camillo, with a thousand camels, to carry the women and baggage, to whom they paid 1500 crowns, but they would not start till Almanzor left his son as a hostage. Those who were sent back to Spain to report carried many letters assuring their friends of the good faith with which they had been treated, which vastly increased the eagerness to go. Yet such was the inbred distrust of the royal word that vast numbers preferred to charter ships rather than sail gratuitously in the king's vessels, where they were supplied with provisions free, although it cost them 75 reales a head for all over 12, and 35 for those younger. To protect those who adopted this plan the passage-money was deposited in Valencia and was not paid until the ship-

[1] Fonseca, pp. 215 sq., 228.—Bleda, Crónica, p. 999.—Janer, pp. 76, 307–9.—Danvila, p. 304.

master brought certificates of the safe landing of his passengers, and to facilitate it all the Spanish ports were ordered to send their ships to the Valencia coast, even discharging those which were loaded, and all arrivals at Valencia ports were pressed into service. Some 14,500 thus embarked at the Grao, or port of Valencia, affording a spectacle which attracted the ladies and gentlemen of the city, and while the ships were waiting for fair winds it became a fair in which exquisite Moorish garments, rare embroideries, rich gold and silver laces and similar articles were bought for a song. At Alicante they came with music and song, as though going to a festival, and thanking Allah for the happiness of returning to the land of their fathers. One of the chief alfaquíes being asked why they obeyed a simple letter of the king, replied: "Do you not know that many of us bought or stole boats in which to cross to Barbary with much danger? Then why, when we are offered safe and free passage, should we not avail ourselves of it to go to the land of our ancestors, under our king the Turk, who will let us live as Moors and not as slaves, as we have been treated by our masters?"—which suggests how simple a relief from the long-drawn agony it would have been half a century earlier to have permitted the expatriation of those who desired it. Doubtless it was this eagerness to go and readiness to pay that led the king to break his word, for after the first embarkation the royal ships charged passage-money like the private ones.[1]

In all there were three regular embarkations, the process lasting for about three months, including, according to the

[1] Fonseca, pp. 212–22.—Bleda, Crónica, pp. 1001–3, 1005–7.

lists kept at the ports, over 150,000 souls.[1] Yet it had not all been peaceful. There were some whose distrust of the royal promises indisposed them to accept the decision of the assembly of alfaquíes, and, as early as September 27th, news was brought that those of the Marquisate of Lombay were making slings and pikes and grinding meal—the sure signs of a rising. There were others who were badly treated by the officials sent to gather them together—at Dos Aguas for this reason they slew the governor and ten or twelve men who abused them, and were held to have been justified in doing so, and for the same cause some six thousand of the younger men took to the mountains. Others refused to go because their lords endeavored to deprive them of what they were allowed by the edict to take with them. Then there came sinister rumors, unfortunately well grounded, of the outrages committed by the Moors on those of the first embarkation; these were confirmed by letters from Oran, and were exaggerated by the Old Christians, who desired to provoke resistance in order to have opportunities of plunder. It began to be noticed at the ports that there was an absence of the younger men and an undue proportion of the older ones and of women and children. The Sierra de Espadan had been providently occupied in advance by Pedro of Toledo, with 550 men of the Italian regiments, who built and garrisoned two forts, and thus

[1] Bleda, Crónica, p. 1020.—The Inquisition of Valencia, which was likely to be well informed, put the number at the more moderate figure of 100,656, viz.: at Valencia, 17,766 (of whom 3269 were less than 12 years of age and 1339 were infants at the breast); at Alicante, 32,000; at Denia, 30,000; at Vinaros, 15,200; and at Mancofa, 5690.—Archivo de Simancas, Valencia, Legajo 205, fol. 2. (See Appendix No. XIII.)

anticipated the Moriscos who had designed to seize it; but there were plenty of other mountain refuges for the disaffected. One of these was an almost inaccessible peak in the Val del Aguar, to which, as October drew to a close, those who refused to go streamed in bands, travelling by night, and when they had established themselves others came flocking to them from all parts, till their numbers were estimated at from 15,000 to 25,000. They hoped to maintain themselves till spring, when they looked for the ever-promised ignis fatuus of assistance from abroad, and they elected as king Melleni Saquien, a Morisco, who had been travelling around and exhorting them to rise. Another similar gathering took place in the Muela de Cortes, an almost inexpugnable spot, being a deep valley surrounded by precipitous heights, of which the passes were easily defensible. The Moriscos of that region had been disposed to resist the commissioners; they were in a state of excitement and were readily persuaded to rise by an outlaw named Pablillo Ubcar. They elected as king Vicente Turixi, who sent a proclamation through the sierra for all to join him under pain of treason. From their strongholds they made raids on the surrounding country, gathering cattle and provisions, burning villages, and desecrating churches. Mexia, absorbed in the work of embarkation and fearing to interrupt it, for awhile paid no attention to these movements, and, when reproached by Fray Fonseca, replied that his troops would do more damage to the country than the rebels, who could readily be reduced when the time came.[1]

[1] Bleda, Crónica, pp. 999, 1000, 1006, 1009, 1016.—Cabrera, Relaciones, pp. 385, 389.—Fonseca, pp. 227–34.

His previsions were justified. Against the rebels of Aguar he sent, toward the end of the first week of November, a couple of thousand men, who occupied strategical positions. On the 15th there was a smart action in carrying the castillo del Pop, which the Moriscos had fortified, in which many of them were slain, including their king. Then Mexia came himself, increasing his forces to about 6000. As the royal orders had been to avoid bloodshed, he offered the rebels most liberal terms—that they should return to their villages, where they should have fifteen days to collect their property and then thirty days more in which to sell it, after which they must embark, taking with them the proceeds. They were irresolute, and, as his troops were short of provisions, to hasten their deliberations he cut off their water-supply. They reopened negotiations, but demanded months in which to embark, which Mexia refused, and on the 21st he attacked them. It was a massacre rather than a battle; slings and pikes, with an occasional arquebus or cross-bow, were no match for the well-armed Spaniards, who mowed them down, and, when they broke and fled, slaughtered them without sparing women and children. Three thousand Moriscos lay dead, and only one Spaniard, Battista Crespo, who was killed by his own firelock. The booty taken, chiefly by rifling the bodies of the dead, was reckoned at 30,000 crowns. The great mass of the insurgents found refuge on the top of the mountain, where they could get neither food nor water. As the end was inevitable Mexia did not assault them, and when news came that those of the Muela de Cortes had surrendered, they came down, November 28th, and gave themselves up at discretion, in numbers of which the estimates vary from 11,000 to 22,000, so starved with hunger, thirst, and cold that even the soldiery were moved to compassion, although this did not prevent their stealing numbers of women and children and selling them as slaves. Mexia granted them their lives and property and escorted them to the port of embarkation, but the valley of Aguar was given up to pillage for twelve or thirteen days.[1]

When news was received of the gathering at Muela de Cortes, Francisco de Miranda was sent thither. He found the insurgents in large numbers, computed at about 9000, and he called for troops, when the tercio of Lombardy was despatched to him and the militia of the region were called out. There was some negotiation in which the insurgents demanded a year in which to prepare for expatriation, but they lost heart when they heard of the defeat of those of Aguar, and were disappointed as to the appearance of the Moor Alfatami on his green horse, whom tradition reported to be concealed under the mountain since the days of King Jayme. When, at daybreak on November 21st, the Spaniards advanced no Moriscos were seen until some were met at 9 o'clock, who in the name of the rest asked for passage to Africa. It was agreed that they should be safe in person and property, provided they would go to embark within three days. The rapacious soldiery, who had promised themselves abundant plunder, in their disappointment threw off all discipline; they sacked the village of Royaya, outraged the women and seized numbers of children as slaves. Only three thousand Moriscos were brought to the port of embarkation, the rest having scattered and taken to

[1] Fonseca, pp. 234–46.—Bleda, Crónica, pp. 1009–15.—Danvila, pp. 305–7.

the mountains to escape the fury of the soldiers. These, estimated at two thousand in number, for several years gave infinite trouble, killing all the Christians they met and committing constant depredations. At one time the Governor of Játiva induced many of them to come down, but finding that they were to be enslaved they fled back to the mountains. A reward was offered for King Turixi, dead or alive; he was tracked to a cave, captured, and brought to the city, when he was sentenced to have hands and ears cut off, to be drawn, torn with pincers, hanged and quartered; but at the execution, December 18th, the cutting of hands and ears was omitted. He had been confessed twice and reconciled twice, and died as a good Christian, making a most edifying end, for we are told that he had been a liberal almsgiver and devoted to the Virgin and the religious Orders. The miserable remnants were hunted down gradually, the viceroy paying twenty ducats a head for them as galley-slaves. To escape this they offered to come in if they should not be sent to the galleys but become slaves of individuals, and this was conceded to them, so that at length, February 20, 1612, Philip formally thanked Viceroy Caracena for having cleared the mountains. It is characteristic of the monarch that while this tragedy was being enacted in his dominions during the autumn and winter of 1609–10, Philip was occupying himself with hunting and feasting, dances and maskings, bull-fights, *juegos de cañas* and jousting at the ring.[1]

[1] Bleda, Crónica, pp. 1016–20.—Fonseca, pp. 246–9.—Cabrera, Relaciones, pp. 385, 388, 390, 393, 404.—Danvila, pp. 307–8.—Janer, pp. 326, 354.—Archivo de Simancas, Inqn de Valencia, Legajo 205, fol. 2.

Valencia had been the most dangerous district to deal with. The slight resistance there, so readily overcome, showed that there need be no apprehension as to the remaining kingdoms, and measures were promptly taken to complete the expulsion by successive steps. Aragon and Catalonia, although not strictly next in order, were so intimately connected with Valencia that they may properly be considered here. It is true that the whole affair was a violation of their fueros, but we are told that it was resolved to pay no attention to this in so holy a work, so agreeable to God and so advantageous to the whole land.[1] The promulgation of the Valencia edict of expulsion had naturally alarmed both the Moriscos and their lords in the neighboring kingdoms. To calm them, Philip, October 20, 1609, ordered the new viceroy, the Marquis of Aytona, to learn secretly of the archbishop the condition of the Moriscos, and if necessary to assure them, without involving the royal name, that the matter did not concern them. Besides the warning from Valencia, those of Catalonia were disturbed by a disarmament ordered in Lerida, while in Aragon the arrest of the leading members of the aljamas by the Inquisition was a source of great disquietude. Aytona was sworn in as viceroy, November 15th, and made every effort to quiet them, telling them that the Valencians had rendered expulsion necessary by their audacities and that the king had paid no attention to Aragon, and he reissued the royal proclamation, published at the time of disarmament, guaranteeing them protection. Their bitter experience of royal faithless-

[1] Bleda, Crónica, p. 1048.

ness, however, rendered them incredulous, especially as the Old Christians began to threaten and maltreat them. They abandoned their agricultural labors and commenced to sell their movables for what they could get, while their creditors and the holders of censos became alarmed and proceeded to collect their debts with rigor. The disturbance of industry and the impending losses led the kingdom to send two Diputados to the king with a prolix memorial, pointing out the enormous damage involved in expulsion, the impolicy of driving population out of Spain, which needed men in view of the emigration to the Indies and the armies maintained in Flanders, Italy, and the African presidios, and the difference between the population of Valencia and that of Aragon, in the latter of which conversion might confidently be expected. The king vainly made efforts to prevent this mission, as well as others that came from other parts of Spain, and when they arrived put them off with reassuring generalities.[1]

The question of the children would not stay settled. There were rigid churchmen who protested against allowing those who had been baptized to be damned by permitting them to be taken to infidel lands, and who refused to listen to questions of policy or to the argument that this was no worse than allowing them to be brought up as infidels in Spain. As late as April 19, 1610, the matter was still under debate among theologians called into consultation, although, on the 17th, Mexia had received his orders and had started from Valladolid for

[1] Lanuza, II. 429.—Bleda, Crónica, p. 1045.—Danvila, p. 311.—Guadalajara, fol. 124–8.

Saragossa with the edicts and all necessary papers and letters. The terms of the edicts were the same as in that of Valencia, with two exceptions. In the one for Catalonia there was a concession to the theologians in a clause retaining all children, under seven years of age, of parents going to infidel lands, the result of which was to lead large numbers to make their way to France, whence they sailed to Barbary. The facility with which the expulsion from Valencia had been executed and its costliness, which was reckoned at over 800,000 ducats, led, moreover, to an economical provision by which the exiles were required to pay all expenses—not only of their journey and voyage, but of the wages of the officials deputed to conduct and superintend them, and also half a real a head as export duty on what they carried with them. The rich were obliged to pay for the poor, so that the whole matter was managed without cost to the crown. Taking their cue by this, the commissioners fleeced them unmercifully, making them pay for the water in the brooks and the shade of the trees on their toilsome journey, besides extorting from them vastly more money for their wages than they were entitled to.[1]

The edicts were published simultaneously on May 29th in Saragossa and Barcelona. The fleets and shipping had been assembled at the Alfaques of Tortosa, the port of embarkation designated for those who went by sea; troops had been landed, the borders guarded, the passes to the mountains garrisoned; resistance was hopeless, and none was attempted, though there went up a cry of de-

[1] Janer, p. 280.—Bledæ, Defensio Fidei, pp. 602–6, 612-18.—Watson's Philip III., Appendix B.—Guadalajara, fol. 135–41.

spair which moved even their persecutors to compassion. They protested that they were Christians and would die as such, even though torn to pieces. Protestations were useless, and they were submissively led in bands of from one to four thousand, without troops to keep them in order, although they suffered greatly from the brigandage of the Old Christians. The number expelled from Aragon was computed at 74,000 souls and from Catalonia at 50,000. As there was no disturbance none were left behind, and the last embarkation was made on September 18th. The submissiveness of the Moriscos was most fortunate for Spain, for it would have been difficult to overcome resistance. The troops had not been paid since they left Italy; after vainly clamoring for their money, when landed they disbanded, leaving none but the officers, who hastened to replace them with raw levies.[1]

Large numbers—estimated at between 20,000 and 25,000—passed from Aragon through Navarre or over the mountains into France. The Spanish writers give a deplorable account of their sufferings on the road and state that they were at first refused admittance, but were subsequently allowed to enter on payment of a ducat a head; that they eagerly purchased licences to carry arms, and then, after spending money on the weapons, they were deprived of them.[2] In fact, this was a very different

[1] Bleda, Crónica, pp. 1046–50.—Guadalajara, fol. 142.—Janer, p. 90.—Lanuza, II. 429.

[2] Lanuza, II. 429.—Bleda, Crónica, p. 1049.—Cabrera, Relaciones, p. 404.—Guadalajara, fol. 143. Guadalajara says (Historia Pontifical, V. 160) that they were charged 6 reales for a sword and 4 for licence to carry it, and then were deprived of what they had bought.

outcome than the French had expected from their intrigues with the Moriscos, and this dumping upon them, without notice or agreement, of what was regarded as an undesirable population, was not likely to be looked upon favorably. In anticipation of it Henry IV., in February, issued an ordonnance permitting those who would profess the Catholic faith to settle in the lands beyond the Garonne and Dordogne, while vessels should be provided to convey those who desired to go to Barbary.[1] Under this, as we shall see hereafter, nearly 17,000 from Castile had entered France up to May 1st, soon after which the assassination of Henry threw everything into confusion. La Force tells us that, on his return to Béarn after the assassination, he found that the Viceroy Aytona had sent a band of four or five thousand old men, women, and children to the summit of the mountains on the Béarnese frontier, where they were stopped by the garrisons; the Spaniards refused to let them return, leaving them with scanty provisions, and only

[1] Mémoires de Richelieu, I. 88 (Paris, 1823).

There had been considerable correspondence between the French court and the Porte respecting the voluntary emigration through France which preceded the expulsion (see p. 190). France had thrown difficulties in the way and had even returned to Spain some of the refugees as prisoners. In May, 1609, the Sultan sent a Morisco named Agi Ibraham, as a special envoy to Henry IV., to arrange for keeping a permanent agent at Marseilles to facilitate the passage of the emigrants, and Ambassador Salignac gave him a letter to the Duke of Sully recommending the project. Subsequent letters of September 19th and November 27th show the importance attached to the subject by Salignac and that Venice was endeavoring to ingratiate itself by offering free passage by way of its territories (Ambassade de Salignac, II. 310, 324, 327, 434). The emulation and jealousies of the Christian powers at Constantinople ought to have ensured better treatment of the exiles.

furnishing more at extortionate prices. Then Don Pedro Colonna led to Jacca a troop of five or six thousand, mostly his own vassals, for whom he asked safe passage. A large number, moreover, were endeavoring to pass at another place, four or five leagues distant. La Force ordered passage refused everywhere, when Colonna sought an interview, informing him that Aytona had ordered him to request passage for them, and begging him to write to the queen-regent. He did so, June 25th, expressing apprehension that the despairing wretches would endeavor to force a passage, when he would be obliged to massacre the unarmed masses, which would be an unexampled barbarity. He therefore proposed that they be admitted in bands of a thousand, so as not to oppress the population in the sterile and scantily inhabited district through which they would pass, paying for what they got and protected from pillage. July 7th the queen replied, approving his suggestion and expressing sympathy with the Moriscos, and then again on July 9th she ordered him to admit as few as possible, as it would oppress her subjects, who were to be considered rather than the miserable exiles. On these terms they were admitted, and then, on August 6th, la Force writes to M. de Gourgues, the commissioner whom he had appointed to conduct the matter, that there were six or seven thousand more on the frontier who cannot be prevented from passing, as they throw themselves like despairing persons across the mountains. It seems that when the Moriscos asked Aytona to obtain passage for them through France they offered to pay a crown per head to defray the expenses, and la Force wrote to Aytona and Colonna that each troop must raise a common purse, sufficient to carry them through. All this was promised, but he found that the Spaniards had so maltreated and despoiled them that they were in great poverty, and when they reached Nay and Orthez he returned to them, in the presence of the consuls, the money they had paid, after deducting a little for guards and other expenses.[1] Thus they struggled on in diminishing numbers towards Marseilles and other ports where they hoped to find shipping.

Even thus they were probably more fortunate than a body of some fourteen thousand who were refused admittance after they had reached Canfranc, the last Spanish town on the mountain road over the Pyrenees. They had paid 40,000 ducats for the permission to go to France, besides export duties on what they carried and the expenses of the commissioners in charge of them. They were forced to turn back on the long road to the Alfaques, and so many of them sickened and died in the summer heat that it was feared they would bring pestilence to the ships. At the Alfaques those who embarked in the royal vessels were required to sail direct to Barbary, but those who, for the sake of keeping their chil dren, preferred to go by way of France, were free to do so in vessels that they might charter.[2]

Prior to the expulsion from Aragon and Catalonia, action had been taken covering the kingdoms of the crown of Castile. Towards the end of October, 1609, Juan de Mendoza, Marquis of San German, was sent to Seville to prepare for removing the Moriscos of Murcia,

[1] Mémoires de la Force, II. 8–12, 288–311.
[2] Cabrera, Relaciones, pp. 410, 413, 415, 418.

Granada and Andalusia, to which was added the town of Hornachos, in the kingdom of Toledo, the evil reputation of which we have seen—although the work was not to be commenced until the completion of the deportation from Valencia should permit the fleet and troops to be sent to him. Murcia, however, succeeded in escaping for a time. Like most of the other kingdoms of Spain, it had taken alarm at the events in Valencia and had presented a remonstrance in advance, which had the good fortune to be listened to. The authorities of the city of Murcia in a memorial of October 17th represented that the Valencia expulsion caused apprehension that it would be extended to other places. They had under their jurisdiction 978 Morisco households, who were merely what were needed for the wants of the Old Christian population and gave no cause for anxiety. They were mostly natives; they had made such progress in the faith that for a long time none had been punished by the Inquisition, and they were affronted when regarded as descendants of New Christians. It was, therefore, hoped that the king would do nothing to cause disquiet or to give occasion to the populace, their ordinary ill-wishers, to injure them. This memorial was followed, October 20th, by one from a Carmelite fraile, asking the king not to believe the magistrates. Of the 10,500 inhabitants of the city, he said, 5500 were Moriscos who were all traitors and should be removed to some place far from the sea.[1] The Carmelite failed for the time; the Moriscos of Murcia were Mudéjares whose ancestors had been living there peacefully since

[1] Cabrera, Relaciones, pp. 386, 390.—Janer, pp. 317-19.

the conquest in the thirteenth century; intermarriage with Christians had become frequent; many were wealthy and occupied positions of honor; they were left to the last, and the sentence of expulsion was not executed until 1614.

Granada and Andalusia were not so fortunate. December 9, 1609, the edict was sent to San German in Seville; the galleys and troops were brought from Valencia as soon as they could be spared, and on January 12, 1610, the edict was published. Its form was somewhat different from that of Valencia. It required the Moriscos to depart, under pain of death and confiscation, without trial or sentence; it gave them thirty days in which to make their preparations; it allowed them to sell all their movable property and carry with them the proceeds, invested in merchandise purchased of Spanish subjects, on payment of the regular export duties; it forbade the taking of money, bullion, jewels or bills of exchange, except what was barely sufficient to defray the expenses of the journey by land and sea, and it confiscated their lands to the king for the service of God and the public.[1] The simplicity of this left many points undetermined which were settled by subsequent orders. The thirty days were reduced to twenty. Cases of mixed marriages were treated as in Valencia, except that a Morisco could not take a Christian wife to an infidel land without her consent. Children were treated as in Catalonia, which led many to charter vessels ostensibly for France but in reality for Africa, while orphans of tender age who had no one to care for them were retained and lists were made of them. It will be seen

[1] Nueva Recop. Lib. VIII. Tit. ii. ley 25.

that in some respects the terms were harder than in Valencia, but no resistance was offered; the Moriscos, we are told, came cheerfully and contentedly, though the reports of the cruelty of the Arabs led most of them to seek other regions, and many of them settled in Morocco. Among these was probably a colony from Seville, which Bleda tells us that he found in Agde, to whom the indifference felt with regard to their religion in France was more than neutralized by the abomination of hogs allowed to run at large and the constant sight and odor of pork and lard. They built an oven for themselves in order to bake and cook free from contamination, and some returned to Seville, in the hope that the king might change his mind. San German's methods were so expeditious that by April Andalusia was reported clear of Moriscos, save the excepted ones, and that a few remained in Granada, waiting on the coast for vessels to convey them, and suffering greatly from want. The number in all was variously estimated at from 80,000 to 100,000, including 20,000 who had voluntarily departed in advance. They were said to carry much wealth with them, which was not unlikely, as many of them, especially those of Seville, were rich and prosperous and had held offices of honor and dignity.[1]

[1] Bleda, Crónica, pp. 1038–42.—Cabrera, Relaciones, pp. 396, 402.

The city of Córdova, January 22, 1610, proposed to petition the king to allow six per cent. of the Moriscos to remain, but the corregidor forbade it, saying that it would be useless. Then, on the 29th, it was resolved to supplicate for the retention of two Morisco saddlers who were necessary for the encouragement of equitation, especially as they were old and childless (Janer, pp. 295, 296). Apparently, in Córdova, so renowned of old for its leather fabrics, there were no Christians who could make harness.

It was represented to Philip that there were many descendants of Mudéjares who had been voluntarily converted prior to the enforced baptism; these were Spaniards in dress and language, regular and devout in their religious duties, and among them were many *beatas* or others under vows of chastity. To meet such cases the king issued, February 9, 1610, an order to the bishops of Murcia, Granada, and Andalusia, reciting that after mature consultation with theologians he had decided that such Moriscos should not be expelled; wherefore the bishops were to examine all such cases, without fraud or deceit, and report to San German those whom they found worthy. Many in Aragon, as we are told, sought to avail themselves of this, but few succeeded, and even these in time disappeared, some for fear of punishment for their enormous sins and others by the hands of the Inquisition.[1]

Hornachos, it is almost needless to say, was depopulated—that is, what had been left of it by the rigorous execution of justice by Madera. He was subsequently charged with its repopulation, and his execution of this duty was such as to lead to serious accusations against him. A *visitador* was sent to investigate, whose report was expected to deprive him of his office of alcalde, in spite of his being a favorite at court. Although he escaped this he was sentenced, in January, 1614, to a fine of 150,000 maravedís (400 ducats) and was kept from his regular functions by being detached on various commissions. In July his son went to San Lorenzo to represent to the king the injury thus inflicted on his

[1] Guadalajara, fol. 144.

father's reputation; he had an audience, on leaving which he sank upon a bench and died, to the horror of all the court.[1]

The Moriscos of Castile were treated on a somewhat different basis. Their expulsion had been resolved upon by the Council of State, September 15, 1609, but it was not to be attempted until the result in Valencia should be known. So serious were the apprehensions entertained that, in October, attempts were made to organize the local militia by enrolling one in five of all able-bodied men. Philip II. had twice attempted this measure, but had been forced to abandon it on account of the opposition which it excited, and now his son had the same experience—there was no military ardor in Spain, even for home service. Orders were also issued to enumerate the Moriscos in each locality in order that the government might know with what it had to deal. All this, in conjunction with events in Valencia, aroused much agitation among the Moriscos, and envoys were sent from many quarters petitioning against expulsion and promising to be faithful vassals, but they received no answers. Still, to keep them quiet, a decree of October 11th was sent to all corregidores and alcaldes, reciting that the king had learned that, in consequence of the Valencia expulsion, the Old Christians were maltreating the Moriscos, wherefore it was ordered that all abuse by word or act should be severely punished. Experience of Christian faith caused this merely to increase the alarm, and so strong became the conviction of their impending doom that

[1] Guadalajara, in Historia Pontifical, V. 137–8, 160.—Cabrera, Relaciones, pp. 396, 461, 560.

numbers commenced to sell their lands in order to be prepared for whatever might happen. This interfered with the object of the court, which was reckoning upon the prospective confiscations, and towards the end of October they were forbidden to make sales, and purchasers were warned that they could not acquire title. This proving insufficient, on November 14th a proclamation was issued prohibiting such transactions under penalty of confiscation to be incurred by both parties. At the same time the local officials were instructed to assure the Moriscos that there was no intention to disturb them; but this did not calm their fears, and the sales continued, with the precaution of antedating the contracts.[1]

No time was lost when the results in Valencia removed apprehensions. November 3d Philip appointed the Count of Salazar to superintend the expulsion from Old and New Castile, La Mancha and Extremadura. He was averse to using force, and, judging from their efforts to dispose of their lands, that the Moriscos would mostly depart voluntarily, he suggested that permission should be granted for expatriation, designating the route of departure and the provisions respecting their property. His suggestion was adopted, and a royal cédula of December 28th permitted them to leave Spain within thirty days, selling their movables and buying merchandise to carry with them, but they were only allowed to take money sufficient for the journey and were not to pass through the southern provinces or through Aragon. Assuming from

[1] Danvila, p. 292.—Cabrera, Relaciones, pp. 386, 389, 390.—Bleda, Crónica, pp. 1036-7.

this that expulsion was at hand, such numbers arranged to go by way of Biscay to France that the term was extended by twenty days more and, on January 19, 1610, Salazar was sent to Búrgos, through which they were to pass, where he was to register them and issue certificates. Under this arrangement 16,713 persons of 3972 families were registered up to May 1st, when intimations that they would be refused admittance to France caused the stream to be diverted to Cartagena, where 10,642 embarked, nominally for Christian lands, in order to keep their children, though it was found that the shipmasters were largely bribed to convey them to Africa.[1] The order prohibiting them to take money and jewels was naturally evaded as far as possible, and for attempted infractions of it more than thirty unfortunates were hanged at Búrgos, but there were convenient Portuguese brokers at hand who for a consideration engaged to transmit the forbidden articles, and when this was discovered they naturally became the objects of prosecution. A safer agency was found in the French ambassador at Madrid, who received very large sums to be repaid at Marseilles and other places. He despatched his steward with the documents, but the Spanish authorities were on the scent; they arrested the messenger at Buitrago and brought him back to Madrid, whereupon the ambassador threatened that if the letters were opened no Spanish courier should pass through France without having his papers seized. An angry correspondence ensued, in which the ambassador was victorious; the captured mail was sur-

[1] Danvila, p. 310.—Bleda, Crónica, p. 1051.—Cabrera, Relaciones, pp. 393, 396.

rendered and the steward was allowed to depart with it unmolested.[1]

Then, July 10th, came an edict banishing all Moriscos of Granada, Valencia and Aragon who were settled in the Castilian kingdoms, followed, August 2d, by a similar provision for the kingdoms of Aragon. They were to embark from the southern sea-ports, and, at their own request, they were allowed to carry with them money and jewels on condition of registering the amount and surrendering one-half to officials appointed for the purpose at the ports; but those availing themselves of this privilege were debarred from taking merchandise. From this order were excepted those who had lived as good Christians, but this was a point difficult to determine aright, both here and in the case of those similarly exempted in Granada and Andalusia. The number claiming the exemption was large, and the evidence presented to the prelates and judges to secure certificates was mostly of somewhat dubious character. We can readily conceive that the patience of all concerned was speedily exhausted by the multiplicity and intricacy of the questions which arose; it was easier to decide them all adversely in advance, and an end of the business was made by banishing all who had thus far been exempted, including even the *Moriscos antiguos*, the descendants of the old Castilian Mudéjares. Accordingly, March 22, 1611, an order was sent to all the corregidores, supplemented by another of May 3d, stating that it was for the service of God and the kingdom that the matter be per-

[1] Tapia, Historia de la Civilizacion Española, III. 272.—Cabrera, Relaciones, p. 402.—Bofarull y Broca, Historia de Cataluña, VII. 292 (Barcelona, 1878).—Watson's Philip III., Appendix B.

fected, wherefore all who had previously been exempted and all who, after being expelled had returned, were given two months in which to depart, under irrevocable pain of death and confiscation. This included all *antiguos* who had lived in separate quarters or had paid the farda or other Morisco tax and had been listed as such, except wives of Old Christians, with their children, and those who were priests and monks or nuns. Those who had obtained from competent judges decisions pronouncing them to be good Christians were allowed the poor privilege of selling their lands and taking the proceeds to some Christian country, subject to the previous edicts. Under this last provision the local authorities promptly undertook to seize one-half of the proceeds of sales in the name of the king, but were sharply rebuked in a letter of May 27, 1611, telling them not to interfere, for this division only applied to money and jewels.[1]

With the exception of Murcia, this was intended to make an end of all the remaining Moriscos, of whom many had succeeded in hiding themselves. There was often nothing to distinguish them from Old Christians in dress or language or mode of life, and there was no lack of persons to harbor them, whether from compassion or from the profit to be derived from their services. To ferret them out commissioners were sent to the different provinces with instructions that no privileges or antiquity should avail them, while the courts were expressly prohibited from interference, although, as some restraint on the opportunity for arbitrary injustice and extortion thus afforded, it was added that those who had the reputation

[1] Janer, pp. 344, 345, 350.—Bleda, Crónica, pp. 1051–2; Defensio Fidei, pp. 524–5, 607–12.—Cabrera, Relaciones, p. 415.

of being Old Christians could appeal to the king. Under this the cases were multitudinous and prolonged; the commissioners were finally discarded and the business was restored to the local courts with appeal to the Council of Justice, where these questions took long to decide, involving much undeserved hardship. The expulsions occasioned by these measures were reckoned at about six thousand, exclusive of the young children, who were retained and given to Old Christians to bring up. An incident was the complaint of the local authorities that they were burdened with maintaining in prison many who had nothing wherewith to pay their way to the seaports, and a royal letter of September 19, 1612, directed that they should be passed from one district to another, which should lodge and feed them, to the point of embarkation—the king, who was deriving large sums from the confiscations and exactions imposed on those whom he was driving from their homes, refused even to defray the cost of removing those unable to pay for themselves.[1]

The difficulty of hunting up those who were hidden was complicated by the numbers of exiles who persisted in returning in spite of an edict of September 29, 1612, which consigned them all to the galleys. Between both classes the work seemed endless. January 16, 1613, orders were sent to the local magistrates to be active in cleansing the land of infidels, and this was followed, April 20th, by a cédula reciting that there were still many concealed Moriscos and many returned exiles; licences exempting from expulsion had been fraudulently issued, and the Council of Justice could not permit its

[1] Cabrera, Relaciones, pp. 434, 437, 440.—Bleda, Crónica, pp. 1044, 1057-8.—Janer, pp. 351, 355, 356.—Danvila, pp. 212, 213.

regular business to be set aside by the multitude of suits and appeals brought before it. The whole affair was, therefore, placed exclusively in the hands of the Count of Salazar, with full authority, in conjunction with his assessor, the Licentiate Avellaneda Manrique, to hear and decide all cases summarily; the ordinary courts were divested of jurisdiction and were directed to refer everything to him. In this arduous work he labored long and strenuously, aided by Manrique, who devoted himself to it at his own expense and without pay. At Almagro Salazar found more than eight hundred returned exiles, of whom he despatched some to the galleys, others to the quicksilver mines of Almaden, and the rest he sent abroad at the expense of the magistrates who had been remiss in detecting and punishing them; but his greatest trouble, we are told, lay in determining the suits of those who claimed that they were not comprised in the edicts. Some light is thrown on the situation by an edict which he issued in the name of the king, October 26, 1613, ordering all Moriscos to leave the kingdom within fifteen days; the local officials were warned that any neglect in looking after returned exiles would be reported to the king; all persons receiving or harboring Moriscos were threatened with confiscation, and as this included fiefs, castles, vassals and royal grants, it shows that nobles were sheltering them; and finally a reward of ten ducats, payable from the property of those detected, was offered for information leading to the capture of a Morisco.[1]

In all these measures Christian property rights had

[1] Janer, pp. 357, 360.—Cabrera, Relaciones, p. 522.—Bleda, Crónica, pp. 1058, 1060.

been respected by excepting slaves, of whom many had been made in the risings of Valencia. The Inquisition looked after these, and that it was active in the work may be inferred from the records of the little tribunal of Mallorca. For many years it had only had an occasional Morisco case; but suddenly, in 1613, we find, in an auto de fe of August 18th, twenty-six Moriscos reconciled, of whom all but one were slaves.[1] A further echo of this appears, in 1615, in a complaint of the Inquisition that Moors, captured as corsairs or shipwrecked on the coast, lived and dressed as such, although they were really Moriscos duly baptized and subsequently expelled, and that when the tribunals arrested and proceeded to try them their masters interfered. Thereupon Philip addressed, February 12, 1615, a cédula to the viceroys and governors of all the maritime provinces, ordering them to see that no impediment was placed on the inquisitorial jurisdiction, and that when such Morisco slaves were released by the Inquisition they should be subjected to the penalties provided for returned exiles (the galleys) unless, indeed, the Inquisition had sentenced them to something severer.[2]

At last the time came for the Moriscos of Murcia and the Val de Ricote to share the fate of their brethren.

[1] Archivo de Simancas, Inquisicion, Libro 595. After this there are none until 1626, when there is one described as "de los expulsos de Valencia." This record is only of those relaxed or reconciled, and there may have been many minor cases.

[2] Archivo de Simancas, Inquisicion, Libro 927, fol. 187.—A subsequent instruction of the Suprema, Oct. 31, 1629, forbids the tribunals to prosecute exiles captured at sea and brought back as slaves—also those in the royal galleys, unless they gave occasion for scandal.—MSS. of Royal Library of Copenhagen, 318b. p. 224.

They had made interest enough to procure for themselves the suspension of the edict of December 9, 1609, and the proclamation of San German, January 12, 1610, but the success of the measure elsewhere and doubts as to the sincerity of their faith led to another edict of October 8, 1611, ordering all the Mudéjares who lived in separate quarters to be deported from Cartagena, which was duly published in Murcia, November 10th, by Don Luis Fajardo, captain-general of the Atlantic fleet. Again they had influence enough to secure a reprieve, but after the work was completed elsewhere, the Duke of Lerma and the royal confessor, Fray Aliaga, sent investigators to Ricote and other places who, of course, reported that the Moriscos held relations with the infidels abroad and were Christians only in name. Armed with this, Lerma insisted, the king yielded, and Salazar was ordered, by a cédula of October 19, 1613, to enforce the expulsion under the preceding edicts. The Murcians must already have enjoyed the reputation for violence which they still retain, as shown in the *refran* "el cielo y suelo es bueno, el entresuelo malo"—the heaven and the earth are good and all between is bad—for somewhat elaborate preparations were made to crush resistance or to protect the Moriscos. Philibert of Savoy, the general of the sea, was ordered to take his galleys, with the tercio of Lombardy on board, to Cartagena and place them at Salazar's disposition. Land forces from various quarters were also held in readiness, the frontiers were guarded, and Philibert was instructed to collect all the vessels necessary to carry away the exiles, who were to defray all expenses. Salazar was hurried from Madrid, November 20th, in a heavy snowstorm, with directions to lose no time; he reached Hellin, on the border, on the 29th, and from there despatched commissioners to publish the proclamation everywhere and to execute it. It embodied the general provisions of the previous edicts and allowed ten days for departure. The Moriscos hoped that with demonstrations of Christianity they could again procure its suspension; they organized processions with disciplines, in which the maidens walked barefooted with hair unbound and heads covered with ashes, like the Ninevites, and they made no preparations for departure. To undeceive them Salazar established himself at Cieza, at the entrance of the Val de Ricote, ordered a disarmament, and on December 18th issued a proclamation stating that, as they asked for time on the plea of not having disposed of their lands, they might empower agents to make sales in their absence. This convinced them that there was no alternative, and they made no resistance, but allowed themselves to be led to the port of embarkation, although many succeeded in escaping. Then, on January 4, 1614, there was another proclamation remitting the penalties on those who had been absent for just cause, and permitting them to appoint agents to sell their property, although the ten days had expired. About fifteen thousand were thus deported, but many old people and invalids, who could not undertake the journey without risk of life, were allowed to remain. Many women married Old Christians in order to obtain the exemption, and many husbands and wives who were of honorable birth entered religion to the great enrichment of the monasteries, for which the bishops and the superiors of the Orders cheerfully granted licence. The children were retained, but the parents were allowed, when they could, to place them with Old Christians, who obligated themselves to bring them up, to pay them for their services, to keep them in evidence, and not to sell them. Early in February Salazar returned to Madrid with his work accomplished, though there were still some remnants to be gathered. In 1615 he reported that he had sent Manrique to Murcia to complete the expulsion, and that he had consulted with the vice-chancellor of Aragon as to what was necessary to drive out the Moriscos of Tarragona; there was still question as to those of Mallorca, where there were seventy households, and he knew that there were Moriscos in Mallorca, Menorca, the Canaries and Sardinia.[1]

Although, as late as 1623, there were still investigations on foot as to Moriscos scattered and hidden in Spain, the pious work of purifying the land of infidelity was considered to be accomplished by the expulsion from Murcia. It had been undertaken as a matter of state policy and necessity, but the untiring zeal shown in eradicating the last vestiges indicates how large a part of the impelling motive was the duty recognized as owing to God, and the consummation was fitly celebrated. In 1614 the Archbishop of Granada suggested that such a triumph of the faith should be commemorated by a solemn feast, to which Philip promptly assented and wrote, March 24th, to all the prelates of the realm to determine whether it should be held on the day when the final resolution was adopted or on that on which its execution was commenced.[2]

[1] Bleda, Crónica, pp. 1058–60.—Janer, pp. 361–66.—Cabrera, Relaciones, pp. 531, 546.—Danvila, pp. 314, 317.

[2] Janer, p. 366.

The estimates of the number of exiles vary greatly, and the details given by contemporary writers are too fragmentary to allow of an accurate summing up. Guadalajara alludes in passing to a total of 600,000, but he subsequently reduces this to 400,000 exiles, besides voluntary emigrants. Navarrete speaks of 2,000,000 Jews and 3,000,000 Moriscos having been at various times expelled from Spain, and he is copied by Gil Gonzalez Davila, the official historiographer of Philip III. and IV. Von der Hammer reduces the number to 310,000, exclusive of those sent to the galleys, while Alfonso Sanchez raises it to 900,000. In modern times Llorente assumes a total of a million, while Janer estimates the whole Morisco population at the same figure, of whom 100,000 perished or were enslaved, leaving 900,000 exiles. Vicente de la Fuente, on the other hand, reduces the number to 120,000 souls, while Danvila y Collado, after a careful comparison of all official statistics, reaches an estimate of something less than 500,000 souls, which is probably not far from correct.[1] No computation, that I am aware of, has been attempted of the number of children taken from their parents and

[1] Guadalajara, fol. 163; Historia Pontifical, V. 161.—Navarrete, Conservacion de Monarquias, p. 50 (Madrid, 1626).—Davila, Vida y Hechos del Rey Felipe III. p. 151 (Madrid, 1771).—Von der Hammer y Leon, Felipe el Prudente, fol. 33 (Madrid, 1632).—Alfonsi Sanctii de Rebus Hispan. Anacephaleosis, p. 390 (Compluti, 1634).—Llorente, Hist. Critique de l'Inquisition, I. 455 (Paris, 1818).—Janer, p. 143.—V. de la Fuente, Hist. eclesiastica de España, III. 229 (Barcelona, 1855).—Danvila, pp. 337–40.

The computation of 3,000,000 Moriscos and 2,000,000 Jews originated with Vicente Gonzalez Alvarez, in a little book on the expulsion from Avila. In this he computes six successive expulsions of both races.—Guadalajara in Historia Pontifical, V. 161.

retained, nor is there material to make one, but it must have been considerable. In the then existing population of Spain, reckoned at over 8,000,000, the prolonged alarm inspired by the comparatively insignificant number of Moriscos, disarmed and unorganized, indicates the profound conviction entertained by Spanish statesmen of the internal weakness of the monarchy.

When we compare the inconsiderable number of the exiles with the original large Moorish population of the lands recovered during the reconquest we can realize how great a proportion of the Mudéjares must have become Christians and have been merged indistinguishably with their conquerors. Medieval toleration had won them over, and its continuance would in time have completed the process. Not only would an infinite sum of human misery have been averted, but Spain would, to some extent, have escaped the impoverishment and debility which served as so cruel an expiation.

The fate of the exiles was deplorable. Torn from their homes without time to prepare for the new and strange life before them, and stripped of most of their property, at the best the suffering was terrible, but man's inhumanity multiplied it tenfold. In whatever direction they turned they were exposed to spoliation or worse. While the voyage to Africa, in the royal ships, was doubtless safe enough, the masters of the private vessels which they chartered had no scruples in robbing and murdering them. Many who sailed were never accounted for as arriving; others were merely deprived of their valuables and forced to sign the letters which enabled the masters to claim the passage-money deposited. It was not that the Spanish authorities were indifferent. Fonseca relates that he witnessed in Barcelona, December 12, 1609, the execution of the captain and crew of a barque which had started from Valencia for Oran with seventy Moriscos. Falling in with a Neapolitan felucca, the united crews conspired to kill the passengers and divided the spoils, amounting to 3000 ducats. Under promise of pardon a dissatisfied sailor revealed the crime in Barcelona, when not only were the Spaniards duly punished, but the Viceroy of Catalonia wrote to the Viceroy of Naples with details which enabled him to seize and execute the crew of the felucca.[1]

Those who escaped or postponed these dangers by passing overland to France were objects of pillage rather than of murder. We have seen la Force's account of how he treated the unexpected and unwelcome multitudes suddenly thrust across the border; he no doubt did what he could to alleviate the embarrassing situation, but the exiles were hardly used. Some of them reached Constantinople and spread reports of their treatment, doubtless exaggerated, which Ambassador Salignac felt were well calculated to reverse the favorable impressions which he had so sedulously cultivated. August 24, 1610, he wrote to the queen-regent, in terms more forcible than courtly, that the outrages and pillage to which these poor creatures had been exposed were so cruel and horrible a brigandage that there could be no excuse for leaving them unpunished, and this was followed, October 5th, by a letter from Ahmed I. himself, in which he alluded to having sent Agi Ibrahim in 1609; he now

[1] Fonseca, pp. 222–6.

sends him again to ask the royal protection for the exiles, because the governors and officials had stripped them of their property and had put some of them to death, while others were scandalously ill-treated by the shipmasters, who robbed them and landed them on desert islands, carrying off to slavery their wives and children. That this, however, was not universal is shown by a letter, October 30th, from M. du Carla (the brother of Salignac, who had meanwhile died), announcing the arrival of a vessel from Marseilles with a number of Moriscos who speak in the highest terms of their treatment.[1] Cardinal Richelieu tells us that some of the officials, commissioned to superintend the passage of the exiles, were guilty of much thievery, and even permitted murders, but they were punished so severely that the outrages ceased.[2] Perhaps the most accurate statement is to be found in a letter of July 25, 1511, from one of the refugees to a friend in Spain, relating how about a thousand of them, mostly from Extremadura, reached Marseilles, where they were welcomed with promises of good treatment, but this suddenly changed when the news came of the assassination of Henry IV., which was attributed to the King of Spain. Victims were wanted, and the Moriscos were accused of being Spanish spies; they were in much personal danger for awhile and were stripped of most of their money by a judicial sentence. To remedy this the queen sent a judge, but he was so greedy that when one of the Moriscos bribed him with a hundred ducats he returned one of light weight and demanded to have it

[1] Ambassade de Salignac, pp. 389, 434.
[2] Richelieu, Mémoires, I. 89 (Paris, 1823).

replaced. In hopes of better fortune elsewhere they went to Leghorn, but met the same treatment. There was nothing for them to do in Italy but to work in the fields, for which they were unfit, being all merchants or officials, so they finally sailed for Algiers. Apparently the writer and his friends were Christians, for he emphasizes the fact that there they are not obliged to renounce their faith.[1] The Moslem of Tetuan were not so tolerant, and it adds a new horror to the whole unhappy business to learn that there the Christian Moriscos who were firm in their religion were lapidated or put to death in other ways for refusing to enter the mosques.[2] The Church which had impelled them to martyrdom, however, took no steps to canonize these obscure victims.

In Barbary, as a rule, the sufferings of the exiles were terrible. They were landed at Oran, whence they had to make their way to the Moorish states; they had the reputation of bringing money with them, and were plundered and slain and their women were taken from them without mercy, after the first embarkation had been safely convoyed. Before the year 1609 was out the Count of Aguilar, Captain-general of Oran, wrote that through fear of the Arabs many remained there and were starving. Twenty of their principal men had come to him and declared themselves to be Christians; that they had not known what to believe until they had seen the abominations of the Moors, and now they desired to remain and die as Christians. Not knowing what to do,

[1] Janer, p. 350.

[2] Cabrera, Relaciones, p. 404. Fray Bleda (Crónica, p. 1042) naturally discredits the statement of these martyrdoms, as it militates against his theory that all the Moriscos were apostates.

the count threw them in prison and applied for instructions. We may doubt the story, contained in a report of the Inquisition of Valencia, that the crew of a transport, wrecked on the African coast, in making their way to Oran, counted nine thousand corpses of those who had been slain, but there is little reason to suspect the statement of the Comendador de N. Señora de las Mercedes of Oran, that what between disease and the atrocities of the Arabs two-thirds of those deported had perished. In fact, the general estimate was that the proportion was at least three-quarters.[1]

This explains the number who returned to Spain in spite of the savage edicts which consigned them to the galleys. Many came, professing a wish to be Christians and to serve as slaves, and they found persons to accept them as such. The question was raised whether this was permissible under the edicts, and a number of theologians signed an argument, addressed to the Viceroy of Valencia, to prove that, as the Church receives and baptizes Moors desiring to become Christians, it could not reject those already baptized who returned to its bosom, even although moved by servile attrition, which is defined as sufficing by the Council of Trent. Fray Bleda took the alarm, and, May 7, 1610, addressed the king on the subject, warning him of the fate of Saul for sparing the Amalekites. To this Philip replied, May 23d, thanking him and telling him that orders had been issued to the viceroy that not a single Morisco should be left in the kingdom. The officials made efforts to accomplish

[1] Cabrera, Relaciones, pp. 391, 396.—Archivo de Simancas, Inq^{n} de Valencia, Legajo 205, fol. 2.—Juan Ripol, Diálogo de Consuelo, fol. 20.—Bleda, Crónica, p. 1021.

this, but kindness and covetousness combined to render it impossible. Six months later Archbishop Ribera found that in his see there were at least two thousand, and twice that number in all Valencia. Thinking that there were probably as many more concealed he issued, November 13th, a *mandement* commanding, under pain of major excommunication *latæ sententiæ,* that all should be reported, but his efforts were fruitless. The royal orders were frequently repeated, but finding them useless the Royal Council at length grew tired of issuing them, and Fray Bleda, writing in 1618, deplores the fact that he will die without seeing his land purified of this evil seed. Apparently it never was wholly purified. We are told that in Valencia, la Mancha and Granada there are still communities which in dress, customs and tendencies may be regarded as Moriscos, having scarce any notions of Christianity.[1]

Thus, nine centuries after the fatal day of Jerez de la Frontera, the descendants of the conquerors were driven from the land which the labors of their ancestors had enriched and adorned. History records many vicissitudes, but few so complete as this. When Cardinal Richelieu characterized the act as the boldest and most barbarous recorded in human annals,[2] he did not foresee that in his own land, before the century was out, the Most Christian King would, in a somewhat different fashion, emulate the barbarity without the excuse of state necessity.

[1] Bleda, Crónica, pp. 1021-3.—Vicente de la Fuente, Historia eclesiastica, III. 228.

[2] Mémoires de Richelieu, I. 86.

CHAPTER XI.

RESULTS.

THE ecclesiastics, who had labored so strenuously to bring about the catastrophe, were loud in their pæans of joy at the accomplishment of their purpose. Fray Bleda breaks forth in a rhapsody in which he assures the king that his treasury will be filled and his debts be paid, the land will be thoroughly tilled and its waste places will flourish and it will grow rich; there will be a golden age for Spain; unified in religion and freed from its domestic enemies, it will prosper as never before and become a terror to all enemies of the Christian name; it is the most glorious event for Spain since the resurrection of Christ and its conversion from paganism. Guadalajara is equally enthusiastic; the great conjunction of the stars in December, 1603, the Sibylline and other prophecies, Spanish and Arabic, which he recounts, prove that Spain, after this great achievement, will recover Jerusalem and break utterly the Moslem power. The Moriscos, he tells us, were accustomed to say that the prosperity of Spain ceased when they were forced to baptism; but this only shows that the land was cursed with sterility for tolerating their apostasy, and since the expulsion there has been abundance, the price of wheat has fallen, trade is more freely conducted, the coasts are free from corsairs, men travel without fear and voyage without danger, the currency is free from false coinage, the land is delivered from the fear of treason and rebellion, murders are less frequent, there is no lack of soldiers, all live in the one Catholic, Apostolic and Roman faith, there is peace throughout the land and the sleeper is not afraid.[1]

If such was the temper of the fanatic enthusiasts who had urged the measure, there were others who approved of it, but who felt that its advantages were dearly bought, and that the consolations of philosophy were required to reconcile the people to their losses. These are represented in a little tract which makes no endeavor to disprove the material damage endured, but teaches the Christian stoicism that earthly possessions are vain, that poverty is a blessing, that the only true riches are virtue and the disdain of mundane things. It is well that there shall be less rumbling of carriages and that the nobles who used to ride shall be forced to walk. It is well that when we are too prosperous we should be humiliated. Our position was such that but for this there is no saying to what point our pride and haughtiness would have reached; we would have been ruined by our own abundance. We had employed our wealth for uses other than those for which it was given to us, and it is just that we should lose it. The poor, moreover, rejoice at seeing that their labor has become necessary to the rich. Against this comes the argument that Spain has hitherto been reputed sterile on account of its deficient population, to which the answer is that if we are few we shall be united, and union is the source of strength.[2]

[1] Bledæ Defensio Fidei, pp. 490, 513, 516, 561.—Guadalajara, fol. 157, 160-3.

[2] Juan Ripol, Diálogo de Consuelo por la Expulsion de los Moriscos, fol. 9, 13, 17 (Pamplona, 1613).

Fray Bleda sought to administer more material consolation when, writing in 1618, he said that the villages which these infernal demons inhabited were deserted but for a very short time, especially where the lords attended to repopulating them, as might be seen in the marquisate of Elche, the county of Elda, the baronies of the Duke of Infantado, the marquisate of Lombay, and most other places, so that as regards population and the harvests of wheat and other important crops the absence of the Moriscos is imperceptible. It will be seen, he asserts, that the first-fruits and tithes of the Church will be little less, and in a short time will be much more, than with the Moors. Thus for only eight or nine years will their absence have been felt in the incomes and in the general prosperity of the kingdom, although some lords of sterile lands where there is no irrigation will have to wait longer to bring them up to the point in which the Moriscos kept them, but then they will need fewer Christians, for the Moriscos were miserable laborers. It is very certain that as regards important products, such as wheat, the Moriscos will not be missed, and if the Christians who have replaced them had their implements and cattle there would be a third more wheat gathered than in their time, and in proof of this may be cited the baronies of the Duke of Infantado, in which this year an infinite crop of wheat has been gathered.[1]

As regards the economical effects of the measure, vague generalities such as these are readily offset. A modern writer, who seeks to minimize its injurious influence, admits that it reduced greatly the revenues of the churches

[1] Bleda, Crónica, pp. 1030–1.

and the nobles ; that in the dioceses of Valencia, Saragossa and Tarazona there was scarce a benefice of which the income was not cut down one-half, and they never returned to their former value.[1] A concrete example of the effect on the nobles is furnished by the statistics of the dukedom of Gandía, which embraced over 60,000 Morisco vassals in the lordships of Gandía, Oliva, Fuentedeu and Murla, yielding a revenue of 53,153 libras, 8 sueldos. In 1610 this fell to 15,349 libras, 5 sueldos, rising in 1611 to 17,179 libras, 10 sueldos, 3 dineros, and in 1611 to 24,353 libras, 12 sueldos, 2 dineros. In ten villages alone, in the vicinity of Gandía, 417 houses were vacant, five hamlets were demolished and four were uninhabited.[2] It is highly significant of the embarrassments brought upon the duke that, in 1518, we find the Suprema ordering the Inquisition of Valencia to send authentic copies of the censos due by him to it and to report whether the agreement reached in the suit with him had been carried out, and in what condition were his estates and vassals since the Moriscos departed.[3] Thus, in spite of the grant to the nobles of the lands of their vassals, they were impoverished. They were required to repopulate the abandoned districts, which was not easy in a land already suffering from inadequate population. When they sought to at-

[1] Vicente de la Fuente, Historia eclesiastica de España, III. 230.

In a memorial presented to Urban VIII. by Philip IV. in 1634, it is stated that in some provinces of Spain, owing to depopulation and diminution of production, the revenues of many prebends and benefices are less than a third of what they formerly were.—Bodleian Library, Arch. Seld. A. Subt. 17.

[2] Danvila, p. 302.

[3] Archivo Hist. Nacional, Inqn de Valencia, Legajo 6, No. 2, fol. 144.

tract immigrants from Majorca the authorities there interfered, to prevent the loss of inhabitants; they endeavored to get a larger share of the fruits in virtue of the incorporation of the *dominium utile* with the *directum* of the lands held by the Moriscos, but in view of the heavy burdens on the lands they were obliged to be content with a portion ranging from a sixth to a ninth of the product in place of the third or the half which the Moriscos had been accustomed to pay. On these terms three places were repopulated before the year 1609 was out, fifteen more in 1610, thirty in 1611, and so the process went on. We hear of 8000 immigrants from the Pyrenees and 7000 from Catalonia, but these were a very partial substitute for the 100,000 or 150,000 exiles from Valencia, and if the house of Osuna, as is alleged, in comparatively a few years brought its rentals up to the old standard there must have been exceptionally capable management.[1]

The process of repopulation was greatly retarded by the censos or ground-rents with which most of the Morisco holdings were charged. The lords took the lands subject to these liens, and were unable to pay the interest or rent, and newcomers were unwilling to assume them. The rate ranged from six and a half to ten per cent., although the customary charge in Spain was only five; these censos were the chief support of all who had capital to invest—nobles, widows, convents, parish churches, cathedral and collegiate chapters, etc.—so that the confusion was inextricable and the suffering universal, especially in Valencia.

[1] Cabrera, Relaciones, p. 392.—Ximenez, Vida de Ribera, p. 435.—Danvila, pp. 334-6.—Boix, Historia de la Ciudad y Reino de Valencia, II. 50-1 (Valencia, 1845).

Francisco Geronimo Ramo, a gentleman of Murviedro, thus lost 20,000 ducats of censos in Almunia, a property of his ancestors since the time of the conquest, and Bernardino Zanoquera, Maestre Racional of Valencia, lost 6000 ducats in Alzira. To straighten matters out Salvador Fontanet, regent of the royal court of Valencia, was commissioned to investigate the whole subject, and, on the basis of his report, a pragmática of April 2d, and a cédula of June 9, 1614, laid down general principles and gave full instructions what to do in each case. From this it would appear that a horizontal reduction of interest on the censos was made to five per cent., while allusions to the pro-rating of creditors and allowing of executions indicate how complete was the financial disturbance and how wide-spread were the losses. It was not only the Morisco villages which were depopulated, but many Christian communities were ruined in consequence of the intimate relations existing between them. The *tabla de los depositos* of Valencia—presumably a bank of deposit—was bankrupted and had to be assisted by the imposition of an impost to repair its losses. The tabla of Barcelona, which was regarded as exceptionally strong, was likewise bankrupted, and only the one of Saragossa managed to retain its credit. The nobles who, in Fontanet's report, were shown to have suffered exceptionally were assisted by annual payments from the king, "para alimentos," as though they were in danger of starving. Thus, to the Count of Castellar was awarded the sum of 2000 ducats a year, to Don Juan Rotla 400, to Doña Beatriz de Borja 600, to the Marquis of Quira 600, to the Count del Real 2000, to the Duke of Gandía 8000, and so forth. The barony of Córtes, belonging to

Don Juan Pallas, had suffered especially, troops having been quartered there who razed the houses, cut down the trees and destroyed everything, in compensation for which he was granted 4000 ducats worth of royal lands and a pension for life of three hundred libras.[1]

These were liberal grants, in view of the fact that the royal treasury was an especial sufferer and that it was habitually in a state of penury. In 1611 Philip, in appealing to the córtes for relief to the necessities of the state and enumerating the reasons for his poverty, included the expulsion of the Moriscos, in which he had postponed the interest of the treasury to the service of God and the state.[2] This was not entirely candid, for the king enjoyed a compensating source of profit denied to the nobles and churches. In Aragon and Valencia he suffered with them, and in the latter kingdom he was the largest landholder, for at the conquest all lands not granted to vassals were reserved to the crown. In the kingdoms of the crown of Castile, however, as we have seen, he escheated the lands of the exiles or made them surrender one-half of the wealth they carried with them. What sums were derived from this we have no means of knowing, but they were undoubtedly large, and, in fact, among the arguments urged in advance for expulsion a prominent place was given to the permanent relief to the state that the confiscations would bring, enabling it to clear off its enormous and increasing indebtedness. As early as October, 1610, the Council of Finance reported that the property of the Moriscos of Ocaña and Madrid

[1] Boix, *op. cit.* II. 344.—Bleda, Crónica, pp. 1032, 1033.—Danvila. pp. 333-9.—Cabrera, Relaciones, p. 546.

[2] Cabrera, Relaciones, p. 458.

had mostly been sold and that seventy-five millions of maravedís (200,000 ducats) had been already paid in.[1] This indicates total receipts of considerable magnitude, but they afforded no relief to the treasury, for greedy favorites were always at hand to profit by the reckless improvidence of Philip, as the Flemings had done in the early years of Charles V. In letters of Sir Francis Cottington, the British ambassador, to Lord Salisbury, March 4th and May 16, 1610, he states that commissioners had been sent to the provinces to sell the houses and farms of the exiles, but that the king did not propose to utilize the proceeds for the service of the state, for he was dividing them in advance among his favorites with scandalous prodigality—250,000 ducats to Lerma, 100,000 to the Duke of Uceda, Lerma's son, 100,000 to the count of Lemos, and 50,000 to the Countess of Lemos, Lerma's daughter.[2]

Better use was made of at least a portion of the escheats in Aragon and Valencia. A statement of January 7, 1613, shows that those of Aragon amounted to 471,533 libras, 5 sueldos, out of which 49,188 were bestowed on the Inquisition, 84,949 to new inhabitants in the form of ground-rents on which they were to pay interest, and a considerable sum was devoted to repopulating the barrio de San Juan in the town of Borja, and the village of Torroles, which were deserted.[3] In 1614 Adrian Bayarte was sent to Valencia with full powers to settle all matters connected with the large amount of property left by the Moriscos in the royal cities and towns, to sell it, to verify and pay all claims on it of every kind, to collect

[1] Janer, p. 343.
[2] Watson's Philip III., Appendix B.
[3] Danvila, p. 332.

all debts due by Christians to Moriscos which enured to the fisc, to restore the population of Segorbe, Navajas, Corvera and the suburbs of Játiva, together with many other matters arising from the expulsion. In all this he had plenary authority, and the courts were deprived of jurisdiction in the premises. The task occupied him for two years and a half, during which he settled an infinity of suits and sold the royal properties at prices considerably larger than their valuation, so that the king was able to pay all debts and claims and had a surplus for distribution to the barons, monasteries and other sufferers —it was doubtless from this source that were met the awards made under the report of Fontanet. It is said that Bayarte satisfied every one and that no appeals were made from his decisions, and, in September, 1616, the king ordered that his settlements should be final, that no court should take cognizance of any suit brought to disturb them, under penalty of forfeiture for the pleader and exemplary punishment of the judge entertaining such action.[1] It is easy to imagine the multitude and complexity of the cases arising from this sudden dislocation of business when the active trading element of the community was ordered out of the kingdom on a three days' notice.

How long, indeed, it took to settle all the questions arising from this arbitrary act, and the still more arbitrary methods used in its enforcement, may be seen from the fragment of a suit, brought about 1640, by the Licentiate Herrador, a priest, to recover some property which had been sold at the time of the expulsion by Francisco

[1] Bleda, Crónica, pp. 1033-6.

de Santander, the *juez de comission*, as an escheat to the king. The argument for the plaintiff sets forth that he is descended from the noble Moors of the five cities of the Campo de Calatrava, who voluntarily embraced Christianity and who were granted by the king all the rights and privileges of Old Christians. His father, Juan Herrador, had been alcalde and regidor; the family had appealed against being included in the edict of expulsion, but the case had been delayed in consequence of their documents being in the hands of a certain Doña Leonora Manrique, who profited by their misfortune and received the price of the property sold. They made good their claims of exemption finally, but it was not until 1627 that they obtained a reversal of judgment in the Royal Council, which reinstated them in their rights, and since then Padre Herrador had been seeking to obtain restitution of the property of his father which had been wrongfully sold.[1] Here was a family which for hundreds of years had been undoubted Christians, holding positions in the Church and magistracy, yet obliged to struggle as though for life against peremptory exile and confiscation, nor is it likely that among the hundreds or thousands of similar cases, embraced in the orders to disregard all attempts to prove Christianity, there were many so fortunate as it was to escape the proscription.

The Inquisition also was a sufferer from the expulsion which it had done so much to necessitate. In Valencia it lost the 2500 annual ducats which replaced the confiscations, and also the fines and penances which it levied so liberally. In Aragon and Catalonia it lost the confis-

[1] MSS. of Bodleian Library, Arch. S. 130.

cations, and in all three kingdoms the censos in which its capital had been invested. In Valencia alone these losses amounted to 17,679 libras of revenue. The Inquisition habitually pleaded poverty, and, whatever its revenues were, it was always grasping for more, and now it had substantial reasons for seeking a share in the general plunder. As early as November, 1610, it was reported that the king had granted to the Inquisition all the lands that had fallen in to the crown in Valencia and Aragon, subject to the liens and censos on them.[1] If this was proposed the Inquisition probably hesitated to make so dubious a bargain, for, as we have seen, the royal lands were sold. It had presented consultas to the king, June 22d and July 27, 1610, representing the poverty to which the tribunal of Saragossa was reduced by the expulsion, and this was partly met, in 1614, by the donation alluded to above, from the sales of the escheated lands, of 49,188 libras, which, invested in censos at five per cent., brought in a revenue of 24,524 reales. The tribunal of Valencia continued to suffer, and, in 1612, those of Granada and Seville were ordered to lend it a thousand ducats each to pay its salaries, while in 1614 Philip procured from Paul V. a brief, authorizing the diversion to it of 650 crowns of revenue from the foundations of the Morisco colleges, 2500 crowns having already been given to it from them. Then, in 1615, on the occasion of a royal visit to Valencia, an effort was made to get from the king for it a portion of the lands which had reverted to the crown, but with what success does not appear. Whether successful or not, its poverty was not relieved, for in 1617 it had not

[1] Cabrera, Relaciones, p. 423.

money for the salaries, and its receiver of confiscations was ordered to distribute ratably among the officials his collections as fast as they were made; there was probably some attempt on foot to relieve its chronic distress, for in 1618 we find the Suprema ordering it to submit a detailed statement of all its property and sources of income and also of its expenses. January 30, 1617, the Suprema again appealed to the king in favor of the Inquisition of Saragossa, and in 1619 it represented to him that the tribunals had been reduced to such extreme poverty by the expulsion that he must either suppress some of them or make good the deficit out of his own purse. This appears to have failed of its object, for on May 30, 1620, there is another appeal for Saragossa; it had suffered a reduction of 19,000 reales of revenue and was unable to pay the salaries of its officials.[1]

A burdensome legacy left by the Moriscos, which created great excitement at the time, was the large amount of counterfeit coinage which they succeeded in issuing, and which, as we have seen, found eager purchasers at four or five to one in silver or gold. These deposited it in the bank of Valencia, which paid it out as good money. Then there came a proclamation forbidding its circulation, and the confusion was inextricable, as there was no other currency, leading to frequent quarrels and murders in the daily petty transactions for bread and meat. There were

[1] Danvila, p. 331.—Archivo de Simancas, Inquisicion, Libro 19, fol. 100; Libro 30, fol. 31; Libro 940, fol. 44.—Archivo Hist. Nacional, Inq^{n} de Valencia, leg. 6, No. 2, fol. 28, 58, 81, 140.—Bulario de la Orden de Santiago, Libro —, fol. 434.—Biblioteca Nacional, Seccion de MSS. X 157, fol. 244.

threats of a popular rising, and another proclamation appeared permitting the circulation of all coins bearing a stamp and discriminating only against those which were merely nail-heads or pieces of tin or lead. Other proclamations followed, for the country was full of coiners, taught by the Moriscos, who sold them stamps and instructed them in the art. In the frightful condition of the Spanish currency, consisting almost wholly, for daily transactions, in the debased and worn vellón coinage, the business was easy and profitable, and the Christians followed it eagerly, choking up the channels of trade, until the city felt obliged to redeem all the spurious money. The guards at the gates searched all who entered and registered all the counterfeits found on them, which were redeemed at a specified place, and in a few days there was accumulated in the sacristy of the cathedral, where it was stored, more than 300,000 ducats of it. In all, the redemption cost the city 401,500 gold crowns. This was but a temporary relief, for fresh issues kept pouring forth, and though the coiners were prosecuted they laughed at the punishment, which was only a fine of 300 ducats, so that all they could make over this was pure gain. This was represented to the king, who promptly made it a capital offence, and there were so many convictions that scarce a week passed without two or three executions. In the single district of Murviedro over a hundred and fifty persons, some of them high in station, were arrested or fled, and in the little town of Torrente twenty persons were implicated, and so it was everywhere, and above all in the city. May 8, 1610, a gentleman from Murviedro was beheaded, and on the 10th the fiscal, or prosecuting officer, denounced a company of forty-six persons who carried on the manufacture as an established business, employing workmen at regular wages. Quite a number of familiars of the Inquisition were detected by the civil authorities in the work. They were, as usual, claimed by it as subject to its exclusive jurisdiction, and consequently escaped the death penalty. In fact Salvador Mir, one of them, tried in 1614, had already, ten years earlier, been punished by the Inquisition for the same offence, but it had not removed him from office; on the contrary, it had appointed his son, Joseph Mir, also a familiar, and both of them were sentenced as accomplices in 1614. Barcelona suffered as much as, if not more than, Valencia, though we have not the details, and the trouble long continued, for as the State was the chief counterfeiter, the temptation to imitate its example was irresistible. In 1614 some attention was excited by the arrest for this crime of Don García de Alarcon, of Granada, the son of a rich and prominent father; he confessed and his tools were found, and as his indiscretion was coupled with sorcery it was expected that he would be burnt.[1]

The diminished incomes of churches and landed proprietors were only a symptom of the permanent injury to the agriculture and productive industry of Spain, resulting from the exile of so large a body of its most efficient workers. It was a notorious fact that the Christian population had a settled aversion to labor, which was contemptuously regarded as dishonoring. This is repeatedly dwelt upon by the Venitian envoys in the sixteenth cen-

[1] Fonseca, pp. 256–60.—Bledæ Defensio Fidei, p. 505; Crónica, p. 923.—Archivo de Simancas, Inquisicion, Libro 688, fol. 601–607.—Cabrera, Relaciones, p. 549.

tury as a marked national characteristic, applicable alike to husbandry and the mechanic arts; the Spanish are described as most indolent cultivators and so lazy in hand-work that what in other lands would be done in a month would in Spain not be completed in four. Agriculture was admittedly distasteful, and the great resources of the land were most imperfectly developed, yet of what was produced but little was consumed at home; it was exported in the raw state to be worked up abroad and brought back after the skilled labor of other lands had been profitably employed on it. As Federico Badoero says, in 1557, the fine Spanish wools were woven in only four places in Castile, while 60,000 bales were annually sent to France, Flanders, and Italy, whither Spaniards resorted for their cloths and tapestries.[1] It was universally recognized that no Spaniard brought up his children to honest industry. Those who could not find a career in the army or service of the State were thrust into the Church; a single daughter would be furnished with a marriage portion, and the rest would be placed in convents. Navarrete deplores the existence of four thousand Latin schools, crowded with the sons of peasants, while the fields were deserted, and those of the pupils who, with a smattering of learning, could not gain a living in the Church, became beggars or tramps or robbers.[2]

[1] Relazioni Venete, Serie I. T. III. p. 256; T. V. pp. 82, 139, 163, 286. Dom Clemencin (Elogio de la Reyna Isabel, p. 301), in his enumeration of the causes of the decadence of Spain, includes "el desonor del trabajo, la calificacion de viles prodigada á los oficios y profesiones utiles." See also the representation of the córtes of 1594 to Philip II. as to the universal poverty, the diminution of the population and falling off in production.—Ibid. p. 302.

[2] Navarrete, Conservacion de Monarquias, pp. 67, 299.

This inordinate growth of the clergy, and especially of the regulars, while the productive population was diminishing, was a subject of earnest solicitude to Spanish publicists, especially as the lands acquired by them were relieved from taxation, and it goes far to explain the exceedingly slow recuperation from the loss of the Moriscos. Throughout the middle ages there had scarce been an assembly of the córtes that had not called attention to it, and now the abnormal growth was proceeding with increased rapidity, stimulated by the universal misery, for, as Francisco Solano Salazar said, in 1627, in a memorial to Philip IV., it is only in the convents that people are not dying of hunger.[1] In 1603 Philip III. held a secret consultation with learned theologians, including the heads of some of the religious Orders, who all advised that a check be placed on this excessive growth. In 1618 the córtes petitioned him in the same sense, and in 1619 a celebrated consulta of the Council of Castile enumerated this as one of the causes of the increasing public distress.[2] In 1624 Fray Angel Manrique deplores the fact that there is not a town in which the number of convents had not trebled within fifty years, while Búrgos, which used to have 7000 hearths now has only 900, Leon which

[1] Picatoste, La Grandeza y Decadencia de España, III. 36 (Madrid, 1887).

[2] Gil Gonzalez Davila, Vida de Felipe III., pp. 214, 215, 225 (Madrid, 1771). Davila adds that, though he is a priest himself, he must confess that there are too many ecclesiastics. In the year he writes (1635) there were 32,000 Dominicans and Franciscans in Spain, and in the sees of Calahorra and Pampeluna 24,000 secular clergy, and he asks how many are there in the other orders and other bishoprics (p. 215).

Some fifty years earlier there were in Seville alone 15,000 priests, including both seculars and regulars.—Miscelanea de Zapata (Memorial Hist. español, XI. 59).

formerly had 5000 now has but 500, while the smaller places are depopulated, the middle-sized ones are rapidly becoming so, and the wealth of the Church was similarly overgrown to the great detriment of the republic.[1] In 1625 Doctor Pedro de Salazar, Penitentiary of the church of Toledo, says that in spite of a privilege from Alfonso the Wise, prohibiting the erection of additional convents within the confined limits of the city, the six older ones had been enlarged and numerous new ones founded, so that they had occupied more than fifty royal and noble palaces and over 600 smaller houses, and he attributes to the growth of the ecclesiastical bodies the fact that Spain had but a fourth of its former population.[2] The process went on with increasing momentum to escape the burden of the heavier State taxation, which thus fell with added weight on the diminishing lay population. In 1670 the attention of the government was called to it by an appeal for relief from the town of Camarma de Esteruelas, representing that by the purchase of lands by convents its population had been reduced from 300 families to 70, of which 30 were *labradores*, on whom thus fell the whole burden formerly borne by the 300. The Finance Council, to which the petition was referred, replied that this was the case with many other towns, but that the cure lay with the Council of Castile.[3] Seven years later, in 1677, there was a futile attempt to check these evils by a royal edict complaining of the disorders arising from the over-

[1] Campomanes, Tratado de la Regalía de Amortización, p. 255 (Madrid, 1765).

[2] Pedro de Salazar y de Mendoza, Crónica del Gran Cardenal de España, Lib. I. cap. 68 (Toledo, 1625).

[3] Campomanes, p. 209.

grown numbers of the secular clergy and from the devices and frauds employed to evade the salutary regulations of the Council of Trent, which the bishops were ordered to enforce strictly ; as for the excessive number of convents, application had been made to the pope for power to regulate them.[1]

While indolence and religious ardor thus combined to reduce the numbers and productive energy of the population, its most energetic members were drawn off for service in the endless foreign wars and in developing the colonies of the New World. It was under such circumstances that Spanish statesmanship yielded to its fears and to the pressure of bigotry to eject the only class on which it could rely for the development of the resources and the prosperity of the land—a class which could so readily have been retained, perhaps even at the last moment, by wise measures of conciliation and by permitting the expatriation of those who were irreconcilable.

The economical results of Spanish intolerance are epitomized in Ciudad-Real, the capital of la Mancha. Founded in the thirteenth century by Alfonso the Wise, the liberal privileges which he granted attracted to it many Jews and Moors. An assessment of 1290 shows that its Jewish aljama already contained 8828 tax-payers (heads of families and adult males) paying, at three gold maravedís a head, 26,484 mrs. At the expulsion of the Jews, in 1492, it of course lost these—or what was left of them after previous massacres, persecutions, and forced conversions. To some extent their place was supplied by the Moriscos sent there, in 1570, from Granada. These,

[1] Autos Acordados, Libro IV. Tit. i., Auto 4, §§ 20, 21, 27.

again, with all the ancient Mudéjares were expelled in 1610, leaving the once flourishing city desolate and almost depopulated. In 1621 it numbered only 5060 souls in all; the hidalgos who remained disdained to cultivate its lands, and the cloth industry which the Moriscos hàd built up was destroyed. To resuscitate it, Philip IV., in 1623, granted it a free market in a charter in which he said that formerly it contained twelve thousand households, but now it had little more than a thousand, most of them steeped in poverty; that in the expulsion of the Moriscos it had lost five thousand persons of those who chiefly contributed to its prosperity and provided for its support. More than a century elapsed before it recovered from the blow.[1] In the face of such facts it is not difficult to identify one of the chief factors in the rapid decline of Spanish population and prosperity.

In the terrible atrophy which fell upon Spain as the seventeenth century advanced there were earnest inquiries made as to its causes and suggestions for its relief. By royal order the Duke of Lerma, June 6, 1618, called upon the Council of Castile to consider the rapid depopulation of the land and to devise a remedy. The answer was delayed until February 1, 1619, when it presented a consulta describing the condition as most deplorable, the population diminishing and towns and villages becoming deserted. It makes no allusion to the expulsion of the Moriscos, to the overgrown numbers of the clergy, to the shocking condition of the currency, or to the popular aversion to honest labor, but ascribes the evil chiefly to the ex-

[1] Padre Merchan, La Judería y la Inquisición de Ciudad-Real, pp. 148, 151, 245 (Ciudad-Real, 1893).

cessive burden of the most injudicious system of taxation which perhaps any civilized nation ever devised, which led many to abandon their properties in despair. Other subsidiary causes were enumerated, among which were the drain caused by the importation of silks, embroideries, and other luxuries, and the prodigality with which the king had enriched his favorites with excessive grants, the resumption of which it recommended in imitation of former monarchs, such as Henry III., Juan II., and Ferdinand and Isabella.[1] In 1625 the córtes concerned themselves with the matter, and, at the request of some of the members, Miguel Caxa de Leruela drew up a long memorial which found so much favor that it was printed at the royal expense. In it he attributes the evil to the diminution of the cattle and sheep industry through injudicious legislation and the absorption of common pasturages by the nobles. His arguments are not of value, but some of his facts show the rapid decadence in progress at the time. In 1600, he says, at Cuenca there were 6,250,000 pounds of wool washed for export and 3,750,000 dyed for working up at home; now there are only 200,000 exported and 250,000 worked. To this falling off in production he attributes the fact that there are no manufactures, and that for lack of employment so many are driven into the Church. Within thirty-six years the number of cattle had fallen off by 12,000,000 head, and when, in 1627 and 1628, the scarcity of meat in Madrid caused commissioners to be sent out to seize cattle and bring them to the city they were obliged to take half-grown steers and to carry off oxen from the plough, to the

[1] Gil Gonzalez Davila, Vida de Felipe III. p. 216.

despair of the husbandmen.[1] Of course, no country could flourish in which the government permitted itself such arbitrary abuses.

While these publicists seem by tacit agreement to avoid complaining of the expulsion as one of the causes of Spanish decadence, there was no hesitation on the part of the sufferers to attribute to it their evil case, as we have seen in the grant to Ciudad-Real in 1623. Similarly in 1622 Philip IV., in conceding to the cities of Valencia a reduction of their burdens, points out how they have been affected both by the withdrawal of inhabitants to people the deserted lands and by their loss of revenue from the excise on the articles which the Moriscos in their districts formerly consumed, the traffic in which moreover was a source of profit to their merchants.[2] In every way the community suffered, both in production and in consumption. It was long before the wounds thus inflicted could even be partially healed and industry recover from the confusion entailed by the blow. In 1645 the Brazo Real of the córtes of Valencia represented that the royal revenues suffered greatly by reason of rich and fertile lands capable of raising many thousand bushels of wheat lying idle, for they could be neither sold nor rented on account of the liens and debts hanging over them, which no one dared to encounter. It was therefore suggested that the magistrates of each town should fix a term within which the owners or creditors should cultivate the lands, failing

[1] Caxa de Leruela, Restauracion de la Abundancia de España, pp. 50, 53, 75, 87 (Madrid, 1713). The first edition of this work appeared in 1631, and it was printed a third time in 1732, showing in what high estimation it was held.

[2] Coleccion de Doc. inéd. T. XVIII. p. 148.

which they should be rented for money or kind, payable to an official who should, after making proper deductions, hand the balance to the creditors. To this the king assented in so far as concerned lands belonging to the members of the Brazo Real which had lain untilled for six years.[1] This represents one of the innumerable questions which arose and took long to settle, and another is suggested by the córtes of Saragossa, in 1646, when, in ordering a new assessment of the *fogaje* or hearth-tax, it gives as a reason the diminution of the fogajes in some places by the expulsion of the Moriscos and other troubles and their increase in others.[2] A population, on which for centuries had rested so large a part of the productive industry and financial arrangements of the land, could not be suddenly torn up and cast out without scattering ruin broadcast and raising a cloud of complications the settlement of which dragged on for weary decades. It is characteristic of the Spanish statesmanship of the period that no thought was given to these matters and no provision made for them in the long-drawn consultations over the Morisco question. There were endless debates as to the comparative expediency of the various projects proposed, and, when expulsion was determined upon, as to the methods of effecting it, what the exiles should be allowed to take with them, and what should be done with the children, but the collateral consequences were left to chance, with a contempt for practical details and for the welfare of the subject which goes far to explain the failure of Spanish administration.

[1] Danvila, p. 341.

[2] Fueros y Actos de Corte en Zaragoza, 1646 y 1647, p. 4 (Zaragoza, 1647).

Whatever else was gained or lost, at least the end was virtually attained of eradicating the hated faith of Islam, in so far as is revealed by the accessible records of the Inquisition, the exceptions being scarce more than sufficient to show that its vigilance was not relaxed. It is true that for awhile there were Morisco slaves to be looked after—those captured and sold in the risings at del Aguar and the Muela de Córtes, and those who voluntarily returned from Africa to become slaves. A letter of March 14, 1616, from the commissioner of the Inquisition at Denia to the tribunal of Valencia, asks for instructions concerning some baptized Morisco slaves who had plotted to escape to Barbary, thus showing how carefully they were watched.[1] In the incessant maritime warfare of the Mediterranean, Moorish prisoners were perpetually being brought in and sold as slaves, and there grew to be an objection even to these unless they were baptized. Repeated prohibitions of keeping such in Madrid were issued, and as these were not observed an edict, in 1626, orders all unbaptized slaves to be removed within fifteen days under pain of confiscation. In view of their owners' rights it was impossible to expel them from the kingdom, but they were not infrequently manumitted or purchased their freedom, and their presence then was regarded as obnoxious. An edict of 1712 orders their expulsion within the term that may be allowed by the local magistrates to collect their families and property and transfer them to Africa.[2] The unreasoning fanaticism, which had been so sedulously culti-

[1] Archivo Hist. Nacional, Inq^{n} de Valencia, Legajo 372.

[2] Autos Acordados, Libro VIII. Tit. ii. Autos 4, 6.

vated in these matters, was exemplified by an occurrence in Málaga, June 9, 1637, when a fugitive Moorish slave girl applied to the almoner of the bishop for baptism. He sent for a priest, but before he came she changed her mind, and he went away, carrying the sacrament as usual. Some foolish women, seeing him departing hurriedly, began to cry out that some Moorish friends of the girl had trampled on the sacrament. Immediately the city rose in a tumult; women rushed forth like furies, assailing with sticks and stones all the Moors they encountered, and slaying them without mercy, although they declared themselves to be Christians. A cry arose that the Moors were trying to burn the city; the bells were rung, and bands sallied forth throughout the vicinity, killing all the slaves they could find. A Portuguese vessel was leaving the port; some one said they were Moors, and immediately a brigantine started in chase, overtook her, and massacred the whole crew. The number of slaves of both sexes butchered in the affair was reckoned at sixty.[1]

In a population animated by such ferocious religious zeal it was not easy for any Morisco or descendant of Moriscos guilty of adhering to the religion of his fathers to escape denunciation to the Holy Office, so that the rarity of the cases in the records proves how thoroughly the land had been purified by the heroic treatment administered. The Inquisition, on its side, kept itself in readiness to deal with such culprits. In a manual of instructions drawn up in Saragossa, about 1625 or 1630, there is a fairly complete list and description of Moorish ceremonies with which it says inquisitors must be familiar

[1] Cartas de Jesuitas (Memorial Histórico español, XIV. 143).

in order to examine properly those accused of Mahometanism.[1] A few scattering cases occur which may probably be referred to baptized slaves or to the children retained at the time of expulsion—as, for instance, Geronimo Buenaventura, described as a Morisco of Alcaneta in Valencia, condemned to relaxation for pertinacity by the tribunal there and transferred for execution, in December, 1635, to Valladolid, where he was still lying at the end of 1637, awaiting an auto de fe—for these costly solemnities were growing infrequent with the increasing poverty of all departments of the government—and in May, 1638, he was finally sent to Saragossa where he doubtless was duly despatched.[2] In 1649 the Valencia tribunal prosecuted some baptized slaves detected in an attempt to escape to Barbary, which was presumptive evidence of unsoundness in the faith.[3]

An occasional Christian renegade, captured at sea and handed over for trial to the Inquisition, serves to account for the casual appearance of Mahometanism in the autos de fe. In that of Córdova, December 2, 1625, there were sixty-eight Judaizers but only one Mahometan, Francisco de Luque, a renegade who had sailed as a corsair and had made the pilgrimage to Mecca, of which he gave an account more picturesque than veridical; he was reconciled with two hundred lashes, four years of galleys, and perpetual imprisonment with the sanbenito. In the Barcelona auto de fe of June 21, 1627, there were three renegades who had been brought in by the galleys; of these one was an old man, pertinacious in his faith,

[1] Archivo Hist. Nacional, Inqn de Valencia.
[2] Archivo de Simancas, Inquisicion, Legajo 552, fol. 22, 23.
[3] Archivo Hist. Nacional, Inqn de Valencia, Legajo 387.

who was duly relaxed, but as he was garrotted before burning it shows that he recanted at the last.[1] In the Córdova auto de fe of December 21, 1627, there were eighty-one culprits, but not a single Mahometan, while in that of May 3, 1655, out of eighty-seven cases there was but one, Talfa, a Moorish woman slave, who had been baptized and who was reconciled with a hundred lashes for endeavoring to escape to Barbary.[2] So, in the great Madrid auto de fe of June 30, 1680, to which victims were brought from all parts of Spain, there was but one Mahometan, Lazaro Fernandez, alias Mustafa, a native of Cadiz, who had apostatized and sailed as a corsair; he was pertinacious in his adopted faith and was burnt alive.[3] In the Toledo auto de fe of April 7, 1669, there appeared a Moorish slave from the mines of Almaden, named Soliman or Francisco de la Candelaria, for ridiculing the sacraments when taking communion, for which he was punished with a hundred lashes.[4] Scattering

[1] Parets, Sucesos de Cataluña (Memorial Hist. español, XX. 17–18).

[2] Matute y Luquin, Coleccion de los Autos de Fe de Córdoba, pp. 37, 65, 189 (Córdoba, 1839).

[3] Olmo, Relacion del Auto de la Fee celebrada en Madrid 30 de Junio de 1680, p. 262 (Madrid, 1680). Padre Jeronimo Gracian, the spiritual director of Santa Teresa, who lay a captive in Tunis for two or three years, about 1595, says that he met there many renegades who would gladly have escaped to Spain but for fear of the Inquisition, saying that they would be punished if they did not bring testimony from some well-known person that they came home voluntarily with a desire to return to Christianity. Gracian was supposed to be an inquisitor or an archbishop, and was frequently applied to for such certificates, which he gave, although if detected he would have been burnt alive. He subsequently knew of four of these who had been mercifully treated by the Inquisition in absolving them with secret penance. —Escritos de Santa Teresa, II. 464 (Madrid, 1877).

[4] Archivo Hist. Nacional, Inq^{n} de Toledo, Legajo 1.

cases such as these show that vigilance was unrelaxed, yet in the reports of the tribunal of Valladolid for twenty-nine of the years between 1622 and 1662, there is only a single case of Mahometanism, and a record of all the cases decided by that of Toledo from 1648 to 1794 shows only five.[1] In a similar record of cases tried by the Inquisition of Madrid from 1703 to 1820 there is but a single Mahometan, and he was a renegade.[2]

There were still, however, descendants of the Moriscos whose pedigree seems to have been jealously preserved by their neighbors, causing them to be known as such. In the trial at Toledo of Angela Nuñez Marquez for Judaism, she confessed that before her arrest, October 24, 1678, she hid a quantity of silk in the house of Isabel de Bernardo, *Morisca*, of Pastrana.[3] In some places, moreover, these remnants managed to preserve a secret organization for the maintenance of their ancestral faith. Such a one was discovered in Granada, in 1727, leading to profitable confiscations for which the Inquisition rewarded the chief informer, Diego Diaz, with a pension of a hundred ducats a year, continued to his family, and when, in 1769, his daughters, Maria, Francisca, and Luciana, begged for a Christmas gift the Suprema granted them 200 reales *vellón*.[4] It was possibly one of these Granadans, Ana del Castillo, who had removed to Jaen, who was condemned in the Córdova auto de fe of March 4, 1731, as a *hereje Mahometana*, to reconciliation, with confiscation and irre-

[1] Archivo de Simancas, Inquisicion, Legajo 552.—Archivo Hist. Nacional, *ubi sup.*

[2] Archivo de Simancas, Inquisicion, Libro 879.

[3] Proceso de Angela Nuñez Marquez, fol. 169 (MS. *penes me*).

[4] Archivo de Simancas, Inquisicion, Legajo 1479, fol. 2.

missible perpetual prison.[1] Somewhat similar was the report, in 1769, of the Inquisition to Carlos III., that it had verified the existence of a mosque in Cartagena, maintained by the New Christians.[2] What was the result of this does not appear, but if there were prosecutions and convictions they may safely be assumed to be the last suffered by Moriscos. There exists a complete record of all cases decided by all the tribunals of Spain, from 1780 to the suppression of the Inquisition in 1820, and in this voluminous catalogue there is not a single Morisco. Renegades still occasionally made their appearance; when forced labor in the African *presidios* took the place of the galleys as a punishment, there were opportunities afforded for escape to the Moors which inferred apostasy, and there was still the capture and enslavement by corsairs. Sometimes these were recaptured and handed over to the Inquisition; sometimes they presented themselves voluntarily for reconciliation; of the former class there were five cases in the decade 1780–89; four between 1790 and 1799, and none subsequently; of the latter there were four in 1788, seven between 1790 and 1799, and two after 1800.[3]

[1] Matute y Luquin, p. 268. [2] Danvila, p. 318.

[3] Archivo Hist. Nacional, Inq^{n} de Valencia, Legajo 100.

In 1727 the gloomy piety of Philip V. awoke to the scandal of tolerating Mahometanism among the *Moros de paz* of his territory of Oran. November 7, 1727, the inquisitor-general wrote to the tribunal of Valencia that the king has been reflecting upon this; these Moors reside on the frontier, some of them maintain as many women as they can and redeem female slaves, others even ride on horseback, and bear arms, and conversions among them are rare, while their numbers may be very injurious to religion and the State. The inquisitors were, therefore, asked to suggest remedies for these evils, and they in their turn handed over the inquiry to the commissioners at the sea-ports.—Archivo Hist. Nacional, Inq^{n} de Valencia, Legajo 14, No. 1, fol. 121.

The judgments rendered by modern Spanish authorities on the tragedy of the expulsion and its effects naturally vary with the conservatism or liberalism of the writer. The *a priori* view of the independent reasoner necessarily must be that the sudden ejectment of half a million of industrious workers from a population rapidly diminishing, and in a land that was ever sinking deeper into poverty and inertia, could not but inflict a virtually immedicable wound, which though in time it might heal over superficially, yet would leave the sufferer weakened and lowered in vitality. Whether this was so in reality is a plain question of fact about which there ought not to be a dispute among those who have studied the abundant sources of information and can exercise their powers of observation on the existing situation, but the answer to the question involves such deep-rooted convictions in religion and politics that the diversity of opinion expressed affords an instructive illustration of the subjectivity from which so few historians can emancipate themselves. One with ecclesiastical sympathies, like Vicente de la Fuente, ridicules the notion that the expulsion was a cause of the decadence of Spain; a nation, he says, will lose 150,000 men in an epidemic or a civil war, and he scornfully asks why there should be such clamor against Philip III.[1] A conservative such as Menendez y Pelayo contents himself with declaring it to have been the inevitable result of an historical law, in which the only source of regret is that it was so long delayed; Valencia was rapidly repopulated, the new settlers soon learned the arts of agriculture, and the admirable system of irrigation has been pre-

[1] V. de la Fuente, Historia eclesiastica de España, III. 230.

served to the present day; it is a mistake to ascribe to it the decadence of manufactures which had never been largely in the hands of the Moriscos; that decadence had set in half a century earlier, caused by the discovery of America, which converted Spain first into a land of adventurers and then into one of beggared hidalgos.[1] Danvila y Collado, from whose researches I have quoted so largely, sums up the philosophy of the event in saying that humanity and religion had a struggle in which the latter was victorious; there was no mercy for the Moriscos, but religious unity shone with radiant splendor in the Spanish heavens, and that country is happy which is as one in its great sentiments; it is only an historical ophthalmia which regards the Moriscos as industrially useful to Spain; had they been so they would have carried prosperity to Barbary, whither they went.[2] Janer, who rates highly the industry and skill of the Moriscos in the arts and crafts as well as in agriculture, agrees with Campomanes in assigning to the expulsion the point of decadence of Spanish manufactures. Arabia Felix, he says, was converted into Arabia Deserta; famine speedily made itself felt everywhere; to the active movement of the people succeeded the mournful silence of the *despoblados;* to the travel on the roads succeeded the highwaymen who infested them, and who found refuge in the deserted villages. Yet he adds that the expulsion was only one of the causes of depopulation and decadence; these had already made alarming progress when the expulsion made them more manifest and precipitated the

[1] Menendez y Pelayo, Heterodoxos españoles, III. 632, 634.

[2] Danvila, pp. 320–3.

ruin, for the proscribed race was the most agricultural, industrious, and productive in the land, but, notwithstanding this, expulsion was a religious and political necessity, and to-day religious unity is the most precious jewel of the Spanish people.[1] Modesto Lafuente, the liberal historian of Spain, has no hesitation in characterizing the expulsion as the most calamitous measure that can be conceived from an economical point of view, inflicting a blow on the public wealth from which it is not too much to say that it has not yet recovered.[2] Picatoste, whose researches into the history of the period are minute, presents what, in some respects, is the most reasonable view of the situation. The expulsion he holds to have been the greatest of calamities, and the responsibility of Philip III. and his predecessors lies, on the one hand, in not guarding the material interests which would have satisfied the industrious Moriscos, and, on the other, in not having strength to repress their rebellious tendencies. The reduplication of imposts, the contempt for labor, religious persecution, the oppression of the Inquisition, inflamed them against a weak and short-sighted government till this extreme remedy became a necessity. The historians and publicists who have defended it commit the gravest of errors in looking only to the necessity of the moment, for, in admitting its political necessity, we cannot forget that this deplorable relation was created by the faults of the government. As for its results, the loss of their labors in agriculture and many arts and crafts, the contempt with which not only the race but its

[1] Janer, pp. 95-109, 113.

[2] Lafuente, Historia general de España, XV. 393-4.

industry was regarded, the improvidence of the government, which made no effort to replace that industry, the increase of taxation to make good the deficit arising from their absence, were the most efficient causes of the misery which overtook Spain—a misery which reached a point incomparably beyond that of the most downtrodden races of the earth, while the court was rioting in the most extravagant festivities. The procurador, Lobon, declared that one-half of the Spanish people were feeding on the herbs of the field which they disputed with the herds of cattle.[1]

If, as Menendez y Pelayo asserts, the expulsion was but the inevitable outcome of an historical law, that law can only be that retribution follows wrong. If it was a necessity under Philip III., that necessity was a purely artificial one, created by the fanaticism and infatuation of the sixteenth century. If, from the times of the Kings of Leon and Counts of Castile and Barcelona, it was safe to keep Mudéjares in the land, while the Christian chiefs were involved in almost constant strife with each other and making head against the powerful Arabs and Almoravides and Almohades—if during these tumultuous ages they could rely upon their Moorish subjects during war and profit by their industry during peace, the political necessity of uniformity of faith when Spain had become a united and powerful State and the Moors were scattered subjects, was self-evidently the merest illusion, born of intolerance. That intolerance was the result of the assiduous teachings of the Church, listened to and respected

[1] Picatoste, La Grandeza y Decadencia de España, III. 101–2 (Madrid, 1887).

only when Spain emerged from her isolation and began to take part as a world-power in the general movement of European politics, when Aragon wrested Sicily from Charles of Anjou, when the quarrel between Pedro the Cruel and Henry of Trastamara made Castile the battle-ground between England and France, and when the Great Schism, which so weakened the papacy elsewhere, first brought Spain directly under its influence. Once set in the direction of intolerance, the intensity of the Spanish temperament carried it to its ultimate conclusions with a completeness that finds no parallel elsewhere, and when the impetuous arrogance of Ximenes destroyed Moorish faith in Spanish justice and honor, the fatal step was taken in a path that had but one ending. The Mudéjares had been faithful subjects in times of stress and peril from their fellow-religionists over the borders, and there was no reason why they should not have remained so when isolated in a united Spain, gradually becoming Christianized under the influence of equitable treatment. The Moriscos were inevitably domestic enemies trained in every way to abhor a religion imposed on them by force and symbolized by injustice, oppression, and the horrors of the Inquisition. Under the theocratic influences which were becoming dominant in Spanish policy, it was impossible to apply to them the kindliness and tolerance which alone could render them contented and prosperous and the Christian religion attractive; every effort to amend the situation only rendered it worse. They became a perpetual invitation to foreign enemies, a perpetual object of dread to Spanish statesmanship, and, as the power of Spain declined and her rulers lost the superb self-confidence of Ferdinand and of Charles V., the only course that they could devise was to crown a century of faithlessness and wrong by expatriation. To them the limb seemed incurably gangrenous, and amputation the only remedy to save life, even though it left a crippled and mutilated body. History offers few examples of retribution so complete and so disastrous as that which followed on the fanatic labors of Ximenes.

Yet, severe as was the shock, it could speedily have been overcome had Spain possessed the vigorous vitality which has enabled other nations to recover from even more serious misfortunes. It has been rather the fashion with Spanish writers to explain its long-drawn agony and paralysis by the exhaustion of its foreign wars and the drain of colonization, but the argument is fallacious. The Thirty Years' War in Germany wrought greater ruin than all the conflicts in which Spain was involved, and though its traces long remained they were in time obliterated. The wars of Louis XIV. and of Napoleon exhausted France to a greater degree than those of Charles V. and Philip II. exhausted Spain, yet in each case France showed an elasticity which soon restored her to her place among the nations. England, with a narrow territory and starting with a population about one-third that of Spain, peopled North America and Australia while constantly gaining in numbers at home and maintaining heavy armaments abroad. Where there is intellectual life and intelligent industry, where agriculture, the arts and manufactures bring employment and wealth, the recuperative power of a nation is incalculable, and it rebounds with marvellous rapidity from the depression of war, while the swarming colonies which it sends forth are merely the overplus of its natural increase.

The decadence of Spain was not caused merely by its loss of population in banishing Jews and Moriscos, for that loss could readily have been made up. It was that the Jews and Moriscos were economically the most valuable of its inhabitants, whose industry in great part supported the rest. The pride that was taught to regard work as unworthy an Old Christian and led the beggared hidalgo to starve rather than to earn an honest living; the indolence that preferred beggary or robbery to labor; the fanaticism that regarded religious unity as the summum bonum to be maintained at the cost of any and all sacrifice; the impulses that consigned so many thousands to a life of celibacy; a financial system so elaborately bad that in the effort to favor the consumer it wellnigh strangled production; a theocratic spirit which stifled intellectual progress—all these united in preventing Spain from filling the gap in population and productiveness left by the expatriation of Jews and Moors.

It is true that efforts were made to replace them by inviting foreigners to come as tradesmen and craftsmen, and in the larger cities many of them ministered to the follies and luxuries of the rich, but they were birds of passage who carried away with them such gains as they could accumulate, and no permanent settlement of desirable immigrants could be expected in a land where they were regarded as degraded by labor and were subject to the sleepless supervision of the Inquisition for any careless word or any neglect of the observances of religion. The fanaticism which expelled the Jew and the Morisco hung like a pall over the land, benumbing its energies and rendering recuperation impossible. Spain was the one land in which the Church had full opportunity to fashion at her will the lives and aspirations of the people, and the result is seen in the misery and decrepitude which blasted the illimitable promises of the opening sixteenth century. While the rest of Europe, in spite of wars and revolutions, was bounding forward in the eager competition of progress, Spain, sacrificing everything to religious unity, sank ever deeper in poverty and misery—a paradise for priests and friars and familiars of the Inquisition, where every intellectual impulse was repressed, every channel of intercourse with the outer world was guarded, every effort for material improvement was crippled. In vain the riches of the New World were poured into the hands of a race whose natural aptitudes were inferior to none, in a land of which the resources were as great as when Moorish ingenuity and industry rendered it the most flourishing in Europe. Great as were the undoubted services of Isabella the Catholic and Cardinal Ximenes, the latent evil in their work overbalanced the good, for they taught the nation that religious unity was the paramount object to be attained, and in the pursuit of this it sacrificed material prosperity and intellectual development.

APPENDIX.

I.

Permission for the Moors of Portugal to Pass Through or Settle in Castile (p. 23).

(Archivo de Simancas, Patronato Real, Inquisicion, Legajo único, fol. 4).

En la ciudad de Merida veinte y tres dias del mes de Marzo año del nascimiento de nuestro salvador Jesucristo de mill e quatrocientos e noventa e ocho años un tal honrado e discreto señor el bachiller Alonso de la Torre, teniente de corregidor en este ciudad de Merida e su tierra por el muy magnifico señor Luys Portocarrero señor de la villa de Palma gobernador de la provincia de Leon e corregidor de la dicha ciudad de merida e villa de Xerez cerca Badajoz por el Rey e la Reina nuestros señores e en presencia de mi diego de caravajal escribano del Rey e de la Reina nuestros señores e escribano de la . . . e juzgado del dicho señor teniente de corregidor e de los testigos de yuso escriptos e sus nombres parescio Ali valiente moro vecino de la ciudad de Merida e presento ante el dicho señor teniente de corregidor una carta de sus altezas firmada de sus reales nombres e sellada con su sello e refrendada de Juan de la Parra su secretario e señalada en las espaldas de los del su muy alto consejo segun e por la dicha carta parescia, su tenor de la qual es este que se sigue. Don Fernando e doña Isabel por la gracia de Dyos Rei e Reina de leon de aragon de cicilia de granada de toledo de valencia de galicia de mallorcas de sevilla de cerdeña de cordova de corcega de murcia de jaen de los algarbes de algecira e de gibraltar e de las islas de canaria condes de barcelona señores de viscaya e de molina duques de atenas y de neopatria condes de Ruysellon e de cerdania marqueses de orestan e de gociano, por quanto por parte de vos los aljamas e moros del Reyno de Portugal nos fue fecha relacion diciendo que por el serenisimo rey de portugal nuestro muy caro e muy amado primo vos esta mandado que dentro de cierto termino todos saliesedes fuera de sus reinos e señorios e que no podiades salir dellos a parte ninguna sin yr y pasar por nuestros reinos e señorios ni menos venyr a bivir a los dichos nuestros reynos syn nuestra licencia e por vuestra parte nos fue suplicado e pedido por merced que husando con vosotros de piedad e clemencia vos mandasemos dar licencia para que vosotros e vuestras mujeres hijos e omes criados e vuestros byenes pudiesedes venir a estos nuestros reinos e señorios e estar en ellos el tiempo que vosotros quisieredes e yr de ellos cada e quando quisiesedes e asi mesmo para que pudiesedes pasar por los dichos nuestros reinos e por sus terminos asi por la mar como por la tierra e yr vos con vuestras cosas e hasiendas a otros reynos e parar donde quisiesedes e por bien toviesedes e que sobre ello proveyesemos como la nuestra merced fuese e nos por facer merced e limosna a vosotros los dichos moros por la presente vos damos licencia e facultad para que vosotros e vuestras mujeres e fijos e omes criados e con vuestras haziendas podais entrar, estar y venir en estos dichos nuestros Reynos y señorios todo el tiempo que quisieredes e por bien tovieredes e se quisieredes salir dellos lo podades fazer e sacar todos los bienes que en ellos tovieredes a los reynos e partes e logares e donde vosotros quisieredes e por bien tovieredes cada e quando que quisieredes sin que en ello vos sea puesto ni mandado poner embargo ni empedimento alguno contando que no podais sacar ni llevar fuera destos nuestros Reynos oro ni plata ni las otras cosas para nos vedadas e por esta nuestra carta tomamos a vosotros e a vuestros bienes so nuestra guarda e hanpara e defendimiento real e mandamos e defendemos que persona ni personas algunas vos no fieran ni maten ni ligen ni prendan ni prenden ni mande ferir ni lijar ni matar ni prendar ni prendan ni tomar ni ocupar cosa alguna de lo vuestro contra razon e derecho e mandamos al principe don juan nuestro muy caro e muy amado fijo e a los infantes duques perlados condes marqueses ricos ombres maestres de los ordenes e a los del nuestro consejo e oydores alcaydes de los castellos e casas fuertes e llanas e a los alcaldes e alguaciles merinos prebostes e a otros jueces e justicias qualesquier asi de la nuestra casa e corte e chancilleria como de qualesquier ciudades villas e logares de los nuestros reynos e señorios e qualesquier maestros capitanes de naos que andan o andovieren de armada o en otra qualesquier manera por los mares e puertos e a vuestros (?) de nuestros reynos e qualesquier personas de qualesquier lei estada condicion dignidad e priminencia que sea que esta nuestra carta o todo lo en ello contenido guarden e cumplan e fagan guardar e cumplir todo e por todo segun que en ella se contiene e contra el tenor e forma della no vayan ni pasen ni consientan yr ni pasar por alguna manera e los unos ni los otros no fagades ni fagan andeal por alguna manera so pena de la nuestra merced y de dyez mill maravedises para la nuestra camara y demas mandamos al ome que vos esta nuestra carta mostrare que vos emplaze que parescades ante nos en la nuestra corte donde quier que nos seamos el dya que vos emplazare fasta quince dias primeros syguientes so la dicha pena so la qual mandamos a qualquier escribano publico que para esto fuere llamado que de ende al que vos la mostrare testimonio sygnado con su sygno porque nos sepamos como se cumple nuestro mandado. Dada en la ciudad de Burgos veynte dias del mes de abril año del señor de mill e quinientos e noventa e syete años. Yo el Rey e yo la Reina. Yo Juan de aparra su secretario del Rey e de la Reina nuestros señores la fize escrebir por su mandado.

E asi presentada la dicha carta de sus altezas en la manera que dicha es luego el dicho Ali valiente moro e dicho que por quanto el siguiente dia aprovechar de un traslado de la dicha carta que pedia e pidio al dicho señor teniente de corregidor le mande dar un traslado de la dicha carta original sygnado e autorizado en la manera que fagase qualquier traslado ponga su autoridad e decreto para que valga e fagase como la dicha carta de sus Altezas.

E luego el dicho señor teniente de corregidor dixo que vista la dicha carta de sus Altezas como no estaba rota ni chancellada ni en parte alguna sospechosa que mandaba e mando a mi el dicho diego de Carvajal escribano que saque un traslado de la dicha carta e lo de al dicho Ali valiente moro qualquier traslado dixo que ponia e puso su autoridad e decreto para que valiese e eciese fe bien asi e a tan complidamente como la dicha carta original de sus altezas e testigos que fueron presentes a lo que dicho es e vieron ler e corregir este dicho traslado con la dicha carta original de sus altezas Anton desquivel alguazil mayor e Martin gonzalez su lugar teniente de alguazil en la dicha ciudad de merida—e yo el dicho diego de Carvajal escrivano susodicho a todo lo qual dicho es en uno con los dichos testigos presentes fuy e este traslado fize sacar e saque de la dicha carta original de sus altezas el qual va cierto e corregido en fe de lo qual fize aqui este mio signo a tal en testimonio de verdad.—Diego de Carvajal (Signo e rubrica).

II.

General Pardon of the New Converts (p. 37).

(Archivo de Simancas, Patronato Real, Inquisicion, Legajo único, fol. 26).

Don Fernando por la gracia de Dios Rey de Castilla, de Leon, de Aragon, de Sicilia, de Granada, de Toledo, de Valencia, de Galicia, de Mallorca, de Sevilla, de Cordoba, de Murcia, de Jaen, de los Algarbes, de Algecira, de Gibraltar, e de las islas de Canaria, Conde de Barcelona, Señor de Viscaya e de Molina, Duque de Atenas e de Neopatria, Conde de Rosellon e de Cerdania, Marques de Oristan e de Gociano, por facer bien e merced a los vecinos e moradores mis vasallos nuevamente convertidos de la moreria de esta grande e nombrada cibdad de Granada e de todas sus alquerias e acatando los buenos e leales servicios que vos habeis fecho es mi merced e voluntad de vos remitir e perdonar todas las culpas e casos pasados fasta que vos convertistes a nuestra santa fe catolica e todo qualquier derecho que yo como vuestro Rey e señor natural habia e podia haber de justicia a vosotros e a vuestras mugeres e fijos e a todos vuestros bienes por razon de las dichas culpas e casos fago merced por la presente e por su traslado signado de escribano publico sacado con autoridad de juez o alcalde por vos facer bien e merced e entendiendo ser ansi complidero a servicio de Dios e mio vos remito e perdono todas las dichas culpas e excesos que cometistes fasta el dicho dia que vos convertistes a nuestra santa fe catolica como dicho es e todo el derecho e accion que por razon de las dichas culpas e excesos tengo a vuestras personas e bienes e vos doy por libres e quitos de todo ello e mando a los del mio consejo e oidores de la mi audiencia e chancilleria e al mi corregidor e a otras qualesquier mis justicias que son o fueren desta nombrada e grand cibdad de Granada e a qualesquier dellos que por razon de las dichas culpas e excesos que cometistes fasta el dicho dia que vos convertistes a nuestra santa fe catolica non procedan contra vuestras personas e bienes antes vos guarden este mi perdon e remision que yo vos doy a todo e per todo segun que en este mi carta se contiene so aquellas penas e casos en que cahen e incurren los que pasan e quebrantan perdon e remision, dado e concedido por su Rey e señor natural.

Dada en la dicha cibdad de Granada a veinte y seis dias del mes de Febrero, año del nacimiento de nuestro salvador Jesucristo de mil e quinientos años.

Yo El Rey.

Yo Fernando de Çafra secretario del Rey nuestro señor la fice escribir por su mandado.

En las espaldas: Juan Fernandez de Fontecha, chanciller.

III.

Ferdinand's Reproof to Inquisitors (p. 59).

(Archivo de Simancas, Inquisicion, Libro 926, fol. 76).

El Rey.

Inquisidores: a nos a sido recorrido por parte del duque y duquesa de Cardona y del conde de Ribargoça castellano damposta y de otros que tienen vasallos moros en ese principado de Cataluña con grande quexa diciendo que algunos de los dichos moros sus vasallos son compelidos por vosotros y otras personas por via indirecta que se tornen cristianos y se bapticen no teniendolo ellos in devocion y que a causa que algunos de los otros moros dicen y amonestan a algunos que no se tornen cristianos y se les impiden an sido presos por ese sancto oficio y se procede rigurosamente contra ellos excediendo en algo el termino del derecho con mucho escandalo de los dichos moros y daño de cuios son, por lo cual avemos sido suplicado fuese de nostra merced proveer y mandar que la dicha fuerza y capcion en los dichos moros no se faga aqui adelante y los moros que por la causa susodicha han sido presos sean sueltos y puestos en su libertad, y porque nos parece que a ninguno se debe hacer fuerça para que se convierta a nuestra sancta fe catholica y sea baptizado pues dello no es Dios servido sino cuando la conversion viene de puro corazon y voluntad, haviendo raçones persuasivas para ello y no violentas, ansi mesmo que no es raçon porque algunos moros ayan dicho o digan a otros simplemente que no se tornen cristianos que sean tomados presos si ya no lo an dicho o fecho de tal manera que por derecho deven ser presos y punidos por ese sancto oficio—Por ende encargamos vos y mandamos que de aqui adelante no fagais ni consintais que ningun moro de ese principado sea convertido ni baptizado por fuerça sino que el quiera ser cristiano de su mera voluntad y que si algunos moros teneis de presente presos por solo an dicho simplemente a otros que no se convirtiesen los solteys y pongais luego en su libertad, imbiando la pesquisa e ynformacion que contra ellos teneis al reverendo obispo de Vich nuestro confesor general inquisidor para que visto por el se os escriba lo que fuere justicia y que agora adelante no mandeis proceder ni procedais a capsion de moro alguno por la causa susodicha sino que primero recevida por vosotros informacion de lo que cada un moro abra dicho o fecho sobre la conversion de los dichos moros la ayais embiado al dicho obispo y general inquisidor y recevida su repuesta sobre ello y porque algunos de los dichos moros diz que se an ausentado de sus casas por temor que no se fagan cristianos por fuerça o que los tomen presos por lo que dicho es proveereis que luego vuelvan libremente asegurandolos de tal manera que sin recelo y temor de violencia alguna puedan volver y estar en sus casas, y no se faga lo contrario en alguna manera por quanto nos deseais servir. Dada en la ciudad de Cordova a cinco dias del mes de Octubre, año de mill y quinientos y ocho. Yo el Rey.—Calcena Secretario.—Dirigitur Inquisitoribus Cathalonie.

IV.

Letter of Cardinal Manrique to Charles V. Concerning the Coerced Converts of Valencia (p. 74).

(Archivo de Simancas, Inquisicion, Libro 4, fol. 97).

Sacra Catolica magestad : Los inquisidores de Valencia me han escripto lo que creo vuestra alteza sabe como en tiempo de la Germania los moros de aquel Reino ó casi todos se tornaron cristianos y que las mesquitas fueron consagradas, y como despues de algund tiempo estos se volvieron á su secta y las iglesias que eran nuevamente reducidas a nuestra religion Cristiana se volvieron á facer sus templos e mezquitas e dicen que sobre esto tienen presos algunas personas ansi mesmo mi informan como vuestra magestad hobo proveido en esta materia mandando al gobernador de Valencia que se juntase con dichos inquisidores de alli e congregasen personas doctas, teologos y juristas para que platicasen en ello, e que conforme á lo que hallasen que se debia de facer se proveyese. Visto todo esto yo lo he comunicado con el Consejo y á nos parescido que por ser este caso general que no solamente toca á aquellos infieles de nuestra santa fe catolica mas á todos los de estos Reinos y tambien podria acaescer en casos que sucederan y por ser ansi mesmo materia de tanta sustancia y que tanto toca á nuestra relixion que seria bien que aquella congregacion que vuestra magestad manda que se haga en Valencia que yo la haga, juntando algunos de sus Consejos Reales y otros teologos y juristas, porque por esta via ternia mas sustancia e autoridad e no solamente se platicaria en el articulo dicho mas tambien porque asi viene dependente de ello se hablaria e platicaria en los de Granada y en todos los otros que eran moros y se convertieron y darse ia en todo lo dicho tal orden, mediante Dios, qual conviniese al bien e salvacion de sus animas e aumento de nuestra Religion cristiana. Suplico á vuestra magestad tenga por bien que se tenga este modo porque se vuestra magestad no ha de venir aqui tan aina yo me iria á su corte e irian conmigo los de este Consejo de la sancta Inquisicion e alli se haria la congregacion, ó si no mandandolo vuestra magestad á que los podria congregar vea vuestra magestad lo que es servido que se haga, ó agora sea aqui ó en su corte paresceme que sera bien que vuestra magestad escriba á su gobernador de Valencia haciendole saber que la congregacion que mandaba se hiciese por el y por los inquisidores tenia determinado que yo la hiciese aca y que para esto que nombrasen algunos letrados teologos y juristas de aquella ciudad e reino, porque se hallasen en la platica de estas materias. Esto digo porque enviando de aquella tierra semejantes personas que hallandose en la dicha congregacion quedarian mejor satisfechos con lo que se determinase que segun se dice como los caballeros resciben daño e detrimento en sus bienes e haciendas temporales favorescen á estos que se volvieron á su secta e para que no sean compelidos á que sean reducidos á nuestra religion cristiana alegan que se convertieron con miedo, asi que conviene que personas de aquella tierra se hallen presentes en esta platica e yo invio á los inquisidores para que largamente me informen de como fue la dicha conversion, porque si intervino miedo sepamos de que calidad fue y modo, e porque vuestra magestad sepa lo que los inquisidores me escribieron por su mesma relacion ahi lo invio al fiscal para que sobre todo lo mande ver y proveer, y suplico a vuestra magestad que sea con brevedad que el caso lo requiere porque en verdad es casa de gran dolor ver que los que fueron reducidos y traidos á nuestro baptismo y á nuestra Iglesia se hayan ansi vuelto á su secta vana y los templos nuevamente fechos iglesias nuestras se hayan tornado templos á do se blasfema el nombre de Cristo y su honor y pesame en gran manera en que en tanto tiempo haya habido este daño, y ansi es necesario pues la cosa esta en tales terminos que mediante Dios vuestra magestad lo mande proveer y remediar y con todo la instancia que puedo se lo torno á suplicar. . . .

De Burgos á veinte y tres de Enero de mil quinientos veinte y quatro años.

Humil siervo de vuestra magestad que sus muy reales manos y pies besa.

El Arzobispo de Sevilla.

V.

Informacio super Conversione Sarracenorum (p. 75).

(From the Original in my possession).

Commission from the Inquisitor-General.

Nos Don Alonso Manrrique por la divina miseracio Arzobispo de Sevilla del Consejo de sus Magestades Inquisidor apostolico general contra la heretica pravedad y apostasia en todos los sus Reynos e Señorios hazemos saber a vos el Reverendo licenciado Joan de churruca chantre de Almeria Inquisidor contra la heretica pravedad en la Inquisicion del reyno de Valencia y el magistro doctor Andres palacio assessor en la dicha Inquisicion que nos havemos sido informado como al tiempo de la comocion desse reyno muchos moros se convertieron y recibieron agua de bautismo y las mezquitas se hicieron yglesias y despues todos o los mas dellos tornaron a vivir como moros y las yglesias a ser mezquitas como eran antes de su conversion, cosa por cierto de grandissimo dolor y menosprecio de nuestra santa religion cristiana, y venido esto a noticia del Emperador y Rey nuestro Señor su catholica magestad ha scrito a la serenissima reyna de Aragon lugartiniente general en esse dicho reyno que nombre personas ydoneas para que vengan a la Corte de su Magestad y se junten con otros letrados ante nos, e sabido lo que ha passado acerca de la dicha conversion se provea conforme a derecho lo que pareciere que mas cumpla al servicio de dios y al bien y augmento de nuestra santa fe catholica. Por ende mandamos vos que lo mas presto que pudieredes recibays entera Informacion de todo lo que passo en la dicha conversion y de lo que despues han hecho los dichos moros bautizados y de las causas y razones pordonde ellos pretienden que no son obligados a vivir como cristianos ni dexar las mezquitas que antes de su conversion tenian y de todo lo demas que convenga a la buen y sancta expedicion del negocio, y aquella recebida la traygays a nos vos el dicho assessor Palacio para que se vea en la dicha congregacion y se provea como dicho es, que si necesario es por la presente vos damos y cometemos cumplido poder para todo ello con todas sus incidencias y dependencias, annexidades y connexidades. Datus en la ciudad de Burgos a xx dias del mes de hebrero del año del nacimiento de nuestro Señor de mil y quinientos y veynte y quatro.

A. HISPALENS.

De mandato reverendissimi Archiepiscopi Hispalens, Inq[ris] generalis.

Jo. GARCIA Sectius

INTERROGATORY.

Las cosas de que se ha de tomar informacion sobre la conversion de los nuevamente convertidos de moros a nuestra sancta fe catholica en el reyno de Valencia son las siguientes.

I. Primeramente quanto tiempo ha que se convertieron y que fue la causa de su conversion.

II. Item si les fue hecha alguna fuerza y que fuerza fue, y quien la hizo, lo qual se inquira con mucha diligencia para que enteramente se sepa la verdad si hovo fuerza y que tal fue.

III. Item si fueron amenazados por personas poderosas que les causasse justo temor para que se convertiessen a nuestra sancta fe Catholica.

IV. Item si despues de convertidos permanecieron por algun tiempo en nuestra sancta fe Catholica y que tanto tiempo fue.

V. Item si bautizaron sus hijos despues de su conversion y quanto tiempo estuvieron sin que la contradixessen.

VI. Item si han sido induzidos por algunas personas para volver a sus herrores y declaren que personas eran.

VII. Item si todos de cada lugar donde se bautizaron se convertieron a nuestra sancta fe catholica o quanto dellos fueron.

VIII. Item quien fueron los principales movedores de la dicha conversion y que manera se tuvo en ella.

IX. Item si las mezquitas que tenian los dichos nuevamente convertidos antes de su conversion se hizieron yglesias y si fueron benditas y si se celebraron en ellas los divinos officios y si se enterraron en ellas como yglesias y si se confessaron los dichos convertidos y comulgaron y recibieron otros sacramentos y si se dixeron missas y los otros divinos officios en ellas.

X. Item si despues denterrados algunos convertidos en las dichas yglesias se han desenterrado algunos dellos y enterrado en otra parte y adonde se han enterrado.

Despachose en Valladolid a xiii de Setiembre de Mil D xxiiij años.

Jo. Garcia Sectius.

Specimen of Testimony (p. 64).

Precontentis loco die et anno.

[In villa de Albayda, die decima septima novembris anno MD xxiiij.] Eadam die coram R^do^ domino Joanne de Churruca Inq^dor^ et magnifico Andrea de palacio assessore, assistentibus dominis Martino Sanchez et Marco Joanne de bas, vocatus per nuncium comparuit magnificus Galcerandus destanyo domizellus ville de Albayda habitans qui per dictos dominos, juramento mediante fuit interrogatus super primo articulo E dixo que se acuerda que estando el Campo de Oriuela en la presente villa de Albayda, que entonces el visorey era en beniasar que a su parecer devia ser en el anyo D. xxj, estando este testigo retrahido en su possada en la presente villa que no osava sallir palesamente porque no lo matassen vehia passar los moros del Condado de veinte en veinte y de cinquenta en cinquenta que los trahian a babtizar a la yglesia los de la yglesia los quales mostravan que no yuan de buen grado sino forçados y por lo que tiene dicho no los vio baptizar ni este testigo fue a la yglesia y que la causa de la conversion destos crehe este testigo que fue por que hoyo dezir publicamente que fueron ciertos sindicos de la Jermania de Albayda con siete o ocho moros desta moreria e condado a Urgeles que entonces se dezia Capitan de la Jermania a pedirle si se podria scusar el babtismo destos moros e que les respondio que no podia bolver la bandera a Valencia hasta que todos los moros del Reyno de Valencia fuessen cristianos y que con esta respuesta eran bueltos y lo havian dicho a los moros y que por esto crehe este testigo que esto fue la causa por salvar la vida, y acuerdasse que en el dicho tiempo hun moro de bufali por que dixo que no se queria hazer cristiano le quisieron matar los de la villa de Albayda y este testigo tuvo harto que hazer que no le matasse y al fin por salvar su vida se hizo cristiano.

Int[us] si estos que dize este testigo que los levavan forçados a hazerse cristianos si pudieran hir a bernia o a otra parte por salvar sus vidas.

E dixo que lo tiene por muy impossible que se pudieran salvar.

Super secundo articulo. E dixo que ya lo tiene dicho.

Super tercio articulo. E dixo idem.

Super iiij[o] a[o]. E dixo que tanto tiempo quanto duro el temor que fueron dos meses desde Julio al Agosto perserveraron en vivir como cristianos y no mas.

Super v[o] a[o]. E dixo que ha hoydo dezir publicamente por la villa que los hijos que les nascian entonces que los hazian babtizar.

Super vi[o] a[o]. E dixo que no lo sabe.

Super vij[o] a[o]. E dixo idem.

Super viij[o] a[o]. E dixo que ya lo tiene dicho que los sindicos fueron los principales promovedores.

Super viiij[o] a[o]. E dixo que hoydo ha dezir que bendixieron las mesquitas pero no lo ha visto.

Super x[o] a[o]. E dixo que no lo sabe salvo que ha hoydo dezir que en la yglesia o cimenterio de la villa de Albayda enterraron dos o tres de los nuevament convertidos que murieron.

Int[us] si alguna persona ha hablado antes o despues para que fuesse testigo en esta causa. E dixo que no.

Generaliter fuit int[us] de odio, amore, timore, etc. Et ad omnia dixit non.

VI.

Complaints of the Cortes of the Kingdoms of Aragon, in 1537, Concerning the Treatment of the Moriscos, with Replies of the Inquisitor-General (pp. 98, 122).

(Archivo de Simancas, Patronato Real, Inquisicion, Legajo único, fol. 38, 39).

Reverendisimo y muy ilustre Senor.

Su magestad nos dexo mandado diesemos a v. s. reverendisima noticia de todas los cosas tocantes a la sancta Inquisicion de que sintiesemos que los congregados en estas cortes se quexan, poniendoles nombres de eceso o abuso que se hare contra el sancto officio por los inquisidores particulares que han exercido y exercen el dicho sancto officio en estos reynos de aragon y cataluña y valencia los quales cumpliendo el mandamiento de su magestad nos ha parescido de dar por escrito a v. s. reverendisima porque mejor pueda deliberar sobre ellos que son los siguientes—

* * * * * *

Undezimo se dize que a v. s. reverendisima es muy sabida la manera que se tubo en la conversion de los moros a la santa fe catolica y assi mesmo la poca o ninguna doctrina y ensenança que despues aca de nuestra santa fe catolica se les ha dado ni yglesia que les hayan fecho en los lugares donde biven y que sin embargo de no haver sido doctrinados ni enseñados como dicho es se procede contra ellos como contra hereges y que en esto ay gran exceso y que queriendolos castigar sin dotrinarlos primero hay poca necesidad de proceder contra ellos por Inquisicion pues a todos es notorio que estan y biven en la ynfidelidad que primero tenian.

Duodecimo se dice que los dichos Inquisidores proceden a ocupacion de las tierras que tienen estos moriscos condenados por los señores de los lugares donde biven en tributo o censo o infiteosin y que ya por sus delitos devan ser presos y sus personas castigadas por la Inquisicion y tomadoles los bienes propios que tubiesen assi muebles como rayzes por que los que poseyeren por los titulos sobredichos se deven volver a los primeros señores de quien los hobieron y fue la tierra por diverzas raçones que para ello hay.

Trezeno se dize que han tentado de ocupar por la dicha causa bienes feudales que los tales presos y condenados por los dichos delitos tenian deviendose de bolver a los señores del feudo.

Catorzeno se dice que algunos poseedores de los bienes de los tales condenados que los hovieron y compraron dellos mayormente por titulo honeroso y con buena fe estando los tales condenados en possesion de catolicos cristianos e haviendo con la dicha buena fe hecho en los tales bienes muchas mejoras y reparos, los dichos Inquisidores se los piden y demandan ante el juez del santo oficio.

Lo que el Cardinal Inquisidor general responde a lo que su cesarea magestad le ha mandado comunicar de lo que sintiesen los señores de su real consejo que los congregados en estas cortes se quejan tocante al santo oficio de la inquisicion es lo que se sigue. . . .

Al 11. Que en esto de los nuevos convertidos se ha procedido y se procede con toda benignidad y templança y que en lo demas con acuerdo y consulta de su cesarea magestad se proveera como convenga al servicio de dios y salvacion de las almas de los dichos convertidos.

Al 12. Que hasta agora no se han ocupado tales bienes y quando se ofreciere tal caso se hara justicia.

Al 13. Que si esto se entiende con los nuevamente convertidos tal cosa no se ha fecho y si se entiende generalmente con todos que se ha guardado y se guardara lo que de derecho esta proveydo.

Al 14. Que si se dize con los nuevamente convertidos que tal cosa no se ha fecho y si generalmente que siempre se ha fecho y se hara justicia, y si se agraviare alguno ya tiene el remedio de apellacion y recurso al superior.

VII.

Delegation by Inquisitor-General Valdés of Power to Hear Confessions (p. 102).

(Archivo de Simancas, Inquisicion, Libro 4, fol. 262).

Nos Don Fernando de Valdés, por divina miseracion arzobispo de Sevilla Inquisidor apostolico general contra la heretica pravedad y apostasia en los reinos y señorios de S. M., usando de la gracia y facultad que la felix recordacion del papa Paulo quarto nos concedio por virtud de su breve cuyo tenor es el que se sigue—Paulus Papa IV. etc.

Confiando de la integridad, prudencia y recta conciencia del Sr. Don Francisco de Navarra, arzobispo de Valencia, damos poder y facultad á su señoria ó á su oficial que presente es ó por tiempo fuere en la dicha ciudad, siendo clerigo presbitero, para que pueda oir las confesiones de los nuevos convertidos del reino de Valencia que ovieren cometido ó hecho algunas zeremonias ó ritos de moros ó cosas contra nuestra santa fe catolica que sean tales que se puedan provar en juicio, aunque hayan sido apostados ó relapsos y admitillos á reconciliacion secreta, imponiendoles las penitencias que les pareciere, con que la dicha confesion y abjuracion se haya ante un notario del secreto de la Inquisicion ó ante otro notario que tenga las qualidades necesarias, y la entregue á los reverendos inquisidores de aquella ciudad y reino el qual dicho poder y facultad y subdelegacion le dava y hacia por vertud del dicho breve de su Santidad supra scripto por el tiempo que fuere su voluntad. Dada en Madrid á 12 de Julio 1561. F. Hispalensis. Por mandado de su señoria ilustrisima, Pedro de Tapia, con señales de los Señores del Consejo, Andres Perez, Don Rodrigo de Castro y Guzman.

Don Fernando de Valdés por la divina miseracion arzobispo de Sevilla, inquisidor apostolico general contra la heretica pravedad en los reinos y señorios de su Magestad etc. Por quanto oy dia de la data de esta dimos poder y facultad al Señor arzobispo de

Valencia ó a su oficial para que puedan oir las confesiones de los nuevos convertidos de moros de la ciudad y reino de Valencia que ovieren cometido ó hecho algunas ceremonias ó ritos de moros que sean tales que se puedan provar en juicio y admitilles á reconciliacion secreta imponiendoles las penitencias que les pareciere con que la dicha confesion se haga ante un notario del secreto de la Inquisicion y hecha se entregue á los reverendos inquisidores de la dicha ciudad por virtud del breve de su Santidad que en el dicho poder y facultad va inserto, damos poder al dicho señor arzobispo y á su oficial que es ó por tiempo fuere para que á los que ovieren cometido los dichos delictos secretemente los puedan oir y absolver sacramentalmente y reconciliallos à nuestra sancta fe catolica impusiendoles las penitencias spirituales que les pareciere con que ayan cometido los dichos delictos de manera que no se puedan probar en juicio y para ello les damos nuestro poder cumplido y cometemos nuestras veces. Dada en Madrid a 12 de Julio, 1561.—F. Hispalensis, Por mandado de su señoria ilustrisima, Pedro de Tapia.

VIII.

Cardinal Manrique's Instructions to Calcena and Haro (pp. 142, 185).

(Archivo de Simancas, Inquisicion, Libro 77, fol. 228).

Que si los rectores tienen emolumentos bastantes con que ellos se puedan mantener y sobre esto dar emolumentos a capellanes que residan en los lugares y a sacristanes que se les mande que asi se lo efectuen y si no los tuvieren que suplan lo que faltare con prelados y las otras personas eclesiasticas que llevan los diezmos y primicias á cada uno segun la parte que lleva y lo que toca á los rectores se entiende por la vida de los que agora poseen las rectorias y despues de sus vidas se guarde la instruccion que sobre esto se dara á los subdelegados.

Item que si los señores dotaren los beneficios que sean patrones de ellos y presenten las personas que ovieren de servir las Iglesias á los prelados para que les hagan colacion de ellos y en los lugares donde los señores no dotaren se provean los beneficios con los naturales del mismo lugar si los huviere y no habiendolos que sean de los lugares de la diocesis mas cercana y que se tenga en esto el modo que se tiene en nuestras Iglesias de Palencia y Burgos y para ello se haga bula apostolica.

Item que con diligencia se provea que los clerigos que agora se proveen sean tales quales conviene por tan grande necesidad como al presente hay.

Item que los subdelegados con los ordinarios tasen y moderen la cantidad de los reditos que ha de tener cada beneficiado.

Asi mismo que se procure que se pongan muy buenos sacristanes porque demas de lo que es necesario para la buena administracion de la justicia y limpieza de las Iglesias convendra que fueren tales que pudiesen enseñar la doctrina cristiana á los niños de los pueblos y todo lo que es menester para su instruccion y con los subdelegados con los ordinarios tambien taxaran lo que se debe dar á los dichos sacristanes.

Item que de las rentas de las [mezquitas?] se dé una parte que parezca suficiente para la fabrica de las Iglesias y la otra se dé para la sustentacion y la otra se dé para los rectores pues en el lugar donde el rector tiene suficiente para la sustentacion que todas las dichas rentas de las [mesquitas?] sean para la fabrica de la Iglesia del dicho lugar y para ornamentos y otras cosas necesarias del culto divino y que esto se entienda sin perjuicio de los que fueron alfaquies sino que se les guarde en ello lo que se asento y otorgo en Toledo el año de quinientos veinte y cinco.

Item parece que es cosa muy necesaria que se provea de predicatores para que prediquen y dotrinen á los dichos nuevamente convertidos y que se platique de que seran proveidos para su sustentacion.

Item ha parecido que para que todo lo susodicho se pueda conservar y aumentar se deve hacer un colegio para que sean enseñados los niños en las cosas de la dotrina y en religion y buena crianza porque de alli redundaria el fruto que se ha alcanzado en otras partes donde se ha hecho y despues estos niños podrian enseñar y dotrinar á sus padres y deudos y hase de platicar en el modo como se efectuaria esto.

Item que Su Magestad mande guardar lo que se asento en Toledo con los dichos cristianos nuevos que serian tratados en todo como cristianos viejos.

Asi mesmo procurareis con los ordinarios que administren y hagan administrar los santos sacramentos gratis ó se moderen los derechos de manera que por no pagarlos no se escusen los nuevamente convertidos de recibirlos.

Item procurareis que no los apremien confiesen sino los primeros dias de pasqua y de la incarnacion y asuncion de nuestra señora y de todos Sanctos.

Item procurareis con los ordinarios que en los matrimonios se moderen los derechos de manera que los convertidos no se quexen y si en esto no vinieren á lo razonable nos lo consultareis con vuestro parecer sobre ello.

Despachada en la ciudad de Çaragoça á catorze dias del mes de Enero año del nacimiento de nuestro Señor de mil quinientos treinta y quatro.

A. Cardinalis.
J. Garcia, secretarius.

Otra instruccion. Demas de lo contenido en la instruccion general quando fueredes á los lugares de los señores donde hay nuevamente convertidos harreis informacion secretamente de los derechos que los dichos nuevamente convertidos solian pagar quando heran moros por respetos de ser vasallos moros y agora despues que son cristianos se los llevan y han llevado sus Señores y de los agravios y tratamientos que se les hacen agora por sus señores como si fueren moros y hechas las dichas informaciones con vuestra parecer y todo lo que sintieredes nos las embieis para que se provea lo que convenga y esto se ha de hacer solamente con parecer y consulta del Excelentisimo Señor Duque.

Despachada en la ciudad de Çaragoça á catorze dias del mes de henero año del nacimiento de nuestro Señor de mil quinientos treinta y quatro.

A. Cardinalis.
Joan Garcia, secretarius.

IX.

BRIEF OF CLEMENT VII., FEBRUARY 28, 1597, AUTHORIZING ABSOLUTION FOR RELAPSE (P. 170).

(Archivo de Simancas, Inquisicion, Libro 926, fol. 71.—Bulario de la Orden de Santiago, Libro IV., fol. 128).

Venerabili fratri Petro episcopo Cordubensi in Regno Hispaniarum generali Inquisitori

CLEMENS PAPA OCTAVUS.

Venerabilis frater salutem et apostolicam benedictionem. Nihil est quod magis deceat catholicos Reges et Principes quam se profiteri veræ fidei quam sancta Romana Ecclesia omnium fidelium mater et magistra perpetuo docuit et docet atque hac una in re potissimum hujus sanctæ Apostolicæ sedis in qua Deo auctore præsidemus sollicitudinem adiuvare ut eadem fides catholica in eorum regnis et provinciis inviolata conservetur et quantum fieri potest divina adiutrice gratia propagetur. Quo nomine merito imprimis commendandus est charissimus in Christo filius noster Philippus Hispaniarum rex catholicus, cujus fidei zelus et insignis pietas cum multis aliis in rebus eminet tum valde etiam elucet in novorum conversorum qui ex Maurorum gente sunt animarum salute procuranda. Nam cum ex veteri calamitate multi adhuc in Hispania sint ex ea natione homines et præsertim in regno Valentiæ qui sacro baptismatis lavacro regenerati et Christianum nomen palam professi, animo tamen et secretioris vitæ genere a pravis maiorum suorum institutis atque imitatione non discedunt et impios ac detestabiles Mahumetis errores et superstitiones observant, non cessat idem pius Rex omnem diligentiam adhibere omnique studio conari ut ijdem noviter conversi Christianam et catholicam fidem, omni impietate reiecta, vere atque ex animo complectantur. Ceterum cum ea quæ hactenus adhibita sunt remedia, etiam auctoritate dictæ sanctæ Sedis Apostolicæ et præsertim fe. re. Clementis VII., Pauli IIII., Pij IIII., Pij V., Gregorij XIII. et Sixti V. Romanorum Pontificum prædecessorum nostrorum, vigore etiam sacrorum canonum et Apostolicarum constitutionum contra ejusmodi apostatas et fidei desertores mitigato, minus profecisse videantur, rursus quoque id nostræ

Apostolicæ auctoritatis adiumento expereri desiderat si forte cum eadem benignitate et lenitate eorum durities emolleri possit. Itaque desiderij tam pij causas nobis accurate exponi curavit nobisque humiliter supplicavit ut Fraternitati tuæ eam facultatem benigne tribueremus quam opportunam esse et magis in Domino expedire censeremus. Nos autem, qui nihil ardentius optamus quam animas Christo Domino lucrari et errantes ad viam salutis atque ad salutarem pœnitentiam reducere, eiusdem charissimi filij nostri Philippi Regis supplicationibus inclinati et novellas et teneras in fide plantas donec altiores in agro Domini radices agant et firmius coalescant benigne confovere atque excolere nec semper peccantes graviori pœna aut acerbiori supplicio coercere, sed ubi et quando pro animarum salute tempus et locus ac personarum ratio ita postulant mitiori etiam cultura lethales hujusmodi radices ac fibras extirpare atque evellere cupientes, deque tua singulari prudentia ac in religionem et fidem Christianam zelo plurimum in Domino confisi, Tibi ut per te vel per alium seu alios inquisitorem seu inquisitores hæreticæ pravitatis quem vel quos ad id specialiter duxeris deputari, adiunctis etiam dicti regni Archiepiscopo vel Episcopis diœcesanis sive eorum vicarijs seu officialibus in spiritualibus generalibus, vel ipsis recusantibus etiam absque illis, omnes et quoscunque utriusque sexus filios, nepotes et alios descendentes ex Mauris seu e prædicta secta Mahumetana ad fidem conversis in Regno Valentiæ prædicto et quibuscunque ipsius Regni partibus et jurisdictione inquisitorum civitatum eiusque Regni ac in eis eorumque subjectis locis existentes seu inhabitantes et commorantes cuiuscunque sint status ordinis et conditionis qui in apostasiam a Christi fide aut in alias hæreses vel errores contra fidem catholicam quomodolibet lapsi aut etiam sæpius relapsi fuerint illasque et illos semel vel iterum aut etiam forsan pluries in iudicio generaliter vel specialiter abjuraverint et detestati fuerint, qui intra tempus seu tempora gratiæ ut vocant, vel terminum seu terminos abs te vel ab inquisitore sive inquisitoribus locorum per te deputandis, prædictis publicis propositis edictis, eorum arbitrio præfixum seu præfigendum coram Fraternitate tua vel inquisitore seu inquisitoribus deputatis ac ordinarijs seu diœcesanis locorum prædictis aut eorum aliquo sponte seu personaliter comparuerint vel se constituerint atque a fide apostasiam, hæreses et errores prædictos aliaque contra eandem fidem per eos eorumve aliquem verbo, scripto vel facto aut alias quomodolibet perpetrata crimina et excessus integre tam de se quam de alijs confessi fuerint atque habentes firmissimum propositum ab illis et alijs similibus in posterum abstinendi, de illis humiliter veniam petierint, si et postquam apostasiam, hæreses et errores huiusmodi coram notario et testibus publice vel privatim prout Tibi vel inquisitori aut inquisitoribus deputatis et diœcesanis seu ordinarijs prædictis videbitur, detestati fuerint anathematizaverint et abiuraverint, ac præstito juramento promiserint se talia deinceps non commissuros nec committentibus consensuros neque opem, auxilium consilium vel favorem præstituros tam ab his quam ab aliis similibus, etsi maiores et graviores sint, excessibus, etiam si pluries in abiuratam apostasiam sive hæreses et errores relapsi tentijs censuris et pœnis iniunctis inde eorum cuilibet juxta qualitatem excessuum prædictorum ac pro modo culpæ, tuo vel deputatorum inquisitoris seu inquisitorum et ordinariorum præfuerint, necnon ab excommunicatione alijsque ecclesiasticis sendictorum arbitrio, pœnitentijs salutaribus non tamen pecuniarijs et alijs iniungendis, in forma ecclesiæ consueta, ut sponte comparentes etiam si in indicijs in iudicio præventi fuerint aut quomodolibet inquisiti, non tamen qui condemnati aut detenti in carceribus reperiuntur, in utroque foro absolvere et liberare eosque ad unitatem et gremium sanctæ matris ecclesiæ recipere et reconciliare, et quascunque etiam temporales et corporales perpetui carceris et immurationis ac traditionis seu relaxationis brachio sæculari faciendæ et ultimi supplicii et confiscationis omnium bonorum perpetuæque infamiæ et inhabilitatis tam ipsorum quam filiorum nepotum et descendentium tam a jure quam a quibuscunque provincialibus aut synodalibus aut etiam Apostolicis constitutionibus et ordinationibus in quas quomodolibet incurrerint inflictas et irrogatas seu infligendas et irrogandas pœnas gratiose remittere et condonare, omnemque notam et maculam contra eos eorumque filios et descendentes ex præmissis insurgentem tollere et abolere ipsosque in pristinum statum et quoad bona temporalia restituere reponere et reintegrare cæteraque omnia et singula in præmissis et circa ea necessaria et quomodolibet opportuna et quæ notam et expressionem exigerent magis specialem et sub generali commissione non veniunt, facere, gerere, mandare et exequi libere et licite possis et valeas seu inquisitores deputandi, et diœcesani prædict possint et valeant plenam, liberam et omnimodam facultatem et potestatem ad quadrennium dumtaxat a data præsentium numerandum et non ulterius duraturam auctoritate Apostolica tenore præsentium concedimus et impertimur præsentibus literis et facultatibus Tibi ac inquisitori seu inquisitoribus per te ut præfertur deputandis locorumque ordinarijs per ea attributis, post dictum quadrennium minime valituris. Nonobstantibus constitutionibus et ordinationibus Apostolicis et legibus etiam imperialibus sive prædictorum regnorum et quarumcunque civitatum et locorum etiam municipalibus ac in generalibus, provincialibus aut synodalibus consilijs editis aut prædicti officii sanctæ inquisitionis in quolibet ex prædictis locis instituti etiam iuramento, confirmatione Apostolica vel quavis firmitate alia roboratis, statutis et consuedinibus privilegijs quoque indultis et literis Apostolicis quomodolibet concessis, approbatis et innovatis. Quibus omnibus illorum tenores pro expressis habentes hoc vice duntaxat specialiter et expresse derogamus cæterisque contrarijs quibuscumque. Datum Romæ apud Sanctum Petrum sub annulo Piscatoris, die ultimo Februarij MDLXXXXVII. Pontificatus Nostri anno sexto.—Marcus Vestrius Barbianus.

X.

Report of Inquisition of Valencia on Result of the Edict of Grace of 1599 (p. 173).

(Archivo Historico Nacional, Inquisicion de Valencia, Legajo 5, fol. 298).

Señor:—A los 21 del presente el Virrey desta ciudad embio a este santo officio dos cartas de Vuestra magestad, sus fechas de 24 y 27 de Julio proxime pasado, por las quales Vuestra magestad nos manda demos aviso á Vuestra magestad con mucha particularidad y brevedad del fruto que ha hecho el Edicto de gracia que se concedio á los nuevamente convertidos deste Reyno y del que se puede sperar y se ha seguido de las diligencias que se han ydo haziendo para que mejor fuesen instruydos en nuestra santa fe y la profesasen perfectamente y de lo que mas pareciese se podria pedir á su santidad y mas nos occuriese digno de consideracion para este fin.

En año y medio que duro el edicto de gracia y prorrogacion della la gosaron solo treze haziendo confessiones tan fictas y simuladas y encubriendo tanto los conplices que antes merescian ser condenados que absueltos por ello, y destos treze algunos estavan ya testificados en este santo officio de suerte que se entendio que mas por temor de la testificacion que por convertirse gosaron de la gracia, y todos en general en lugar de enmienda la tomaron por occasion para delinquir con mas libertad y escandalo y ayunaran su ayuna del Ramadan toda la luna que cayo por quaresma en tanta publicidad que todos los christianos viejos chicos y grandes lo vieron y notaron, porque en todo el dia en sus casas no salia humo de los ximeneas ni havia rastro de encenderse lumbre ni guisarse de comer hasta el caher del sol y todos andavan derramados de dia por los campos, calles y plaças, y al salir de la estrella se recogian á cenar sin que pareciese ninguno: y muy de atras se tiene experiencia en este santo officio y al presente mayor que nunca por los muchos exemplares que en el ay de que muy pocos ó ninguno de quantos se ha Reconciliado dizen enteramente la verdad ni se convierten de coraçon; y los señores cuyos vasallos son y otras personas graves y fidedignas y los curas de sus lugares y todos los que los tratan dizen y certifican que todos son y seran moros se dios nuestro señor no usa con ellos de particular misericordia y les alumbra el entendimiento para que dexen de serlo y que ni professan cosa de nuestra santa fe ni quieren ser instruydos en ello, ni van a missa sino es por fuerça y por temor de la pena que les llevan sino van y quando estan en la yglesia oyendola es con mucho desacato y menosprecio y volviendo los ojos y cabeça á otras partes al tiempo de la elevacion del santissimo sacramento por no verle y asi por estos efectos sacamos que de la gracia y misericordia que Vuestra magestad como tan christianissimo a sido servido de usar con ellos procurando su conversion y no ha Resultado ni se spera Resultara de su parte buen fruto sino el dicho de quererla y pedirla para tener occasion de delinquir con mas libertad y sin temor al castigo y al fin el que haze ellos el santo officio de la Inquisicion ya que no les aprovecha para Reduzirlos aprovechales para que se abstengan de vivir en su secta con tanta publicidad y scandalo y para que no dañen como podrian dañar á otros christianos si assi la professasen y usasen. Guarde y prospere nuestro señor á Vuestra magestad por muy largos años como para bien de la christiandad y exaltacion de su santa fe es necessario. De Valencia y de agosto 22, 1601.

El Doctor Pedro cifontes de loaste.
El Licenciado Pedro serraro de mieres.
El Licenciado Antonio canseco de quiñoñes.

XI.

Report of Inquisition on the Moriscos of Granada, 1526–1561 (p. 215).

(Archivo de Simancas, Inquisicion, Libro 926, fol. 80).

Memorial de lo que resulta de las escrituras y papeles que estan en el Consejo de la General Inquisicion tocantes á la Inquisicion del Reino de Granada y á los nuevamente convertidos del—es lo siguiente.

Año de 1526.

En el año de 1526 su Mag^{d} con parecer de una congregacion de prelados y otras personas del Consejo real y del Consejo de Inquisicion que se hizo en la ciudad de Granada, mando poner la Inquisicion en aquel Reino, y al tiempo que se puzo hizo S. M. merced a todos los moriscos de los bienes que por delito de heregia y apostasia que fasta entonces avian cometido tenian perdidos y conforme a derecho les estavan confiscados y se les hizo perdon general de todas las otras penas de carcel y cadahalso y sanbenito y la dicha congregacion ordeno ciertos capitulos tocantes a la buena gobernacion de los moriscos del dicho reino quanto al hablar y vestir y otras cosas y ciertas instrucciones y capitulos de cosas que el arzobispo de Granada avia de mandar y proveer.

Despues de lo qual, pasado el termino de gracia, a los moriscos que fueron presos y declarados por hereges en algunos años no se les tomaron sus bienes sino que se les mandaba que pagasen alguna cantidad y a la pagar se les daba algun tiempo porque sin dificultad y trabajo la pagasen.

En el año de 1532 el marques de mondejar escrivio a S. M. una carta por la qual dice que la inquisicion se avia puesto en aquel Reyno contra los confessos y contra ellos no se hazia nada porque no se hallava cosa ninguna contra ellos y que S. M. mandase que por estonces no se procediese contra ellos.

El consejo de Inquisicion informo a S. M. cerca de lo que el marques decia en su carta que especial que hablaba como muy prevenido e ymportunado y por entonces no se hablo mas en ello.

El año de 1537 se dieron ciertos capitulos por parte de los moriscos del dicho reyno por los quales entre otras cosas pedian perdon de todos los delitos que fasta estonces oviesen cometido, y que de alli adelante no se les confiscasen los bienes ni se les impussiesen penas pecuniarias y que se podria dar orden como el oficio de la sancta ynquisicion se sustentase.

El Consejo de inquisicion respondio a los dichos capitulos en efecto que no era justo que se quitase la confiscacion de los bienes ni los penitencias pecuniarias por ser penas estatuidas por los sacros canones y por las leyes imperiales y por las leyes destos reynos y que si el perdon de los delitos por ellos fasta estonces cometidos pareciese que lo pedian con deseo de reducirse a nuestra santa fe catholica y de salvar sus anymas y no fingida ni simuladamente que se les podria conceder un termino de gracia dentro del qual diesen sus confesiones de los delitos pasados enteramente y por escrito ante los ynquisidores y que todos los que dentro del dicho termino veniesen a confesar en la manera dicha fuesen absueltos de sus delitos, y con esta respuesta del Consejo por entonces no se hablo mas en ello.

Despues en el año de 1539 en Toledo por parte de los moriscos del dicho reino se dieron otros capitulos y el marques de mondejar escrivio en su favor a S. M. y en ellos entre otras cosas pidieron las dos susodichas que antes en el año de mil y quinientos y treinta y siete avian pedido, la una perdon general de todo lo pasado sin ninguna condicion de confesion ni otra cosa, la otra que los que dellos fuessen condenados a muerte y habito de penitencia por el delicto y crimen de heregia no perdiesen sus bienes ni les pudiesen ser tomados por via de confiscacion ni por via de composicion ni por via de alimentos excesivos, y su Mag[d] mando juntar los prelados del reino de Granada y al obispo de mondoñedo y a otras personas del Consejo Real y consejo de inquisicion y despues de haver visto los dichos capitulos y platicado sobre ellos toda la dicha congregacion en conformidad acordaron y fueron de parecer que el perdon general en la manera que lo pedian no se les podia ni devia conceder, mas que siendo S. M. servido que se usase con ellos de misericordia, puesto que se les avian concedido dos terminos de gracia, por algunos justos respectos y consideraciones se les podria conceder de nuevo otro termino de gracia dentro del qual los que veniessen a confesar sus delitos y errores enteramente y diesen sus confesiones por escrito ante los ynquisidores fuesen recebidos al gremio e union de la santa madre iglesia y fuesen absueltos en forma sin confiscacion de bienes ni carcel ni habito sino en penitencias espirituales, y que no se les devia quitar la confiscacion de los bienes y que cerca della se devia guardar la disposicion del derecho, y visto lo que acordo la dicha congregacion por entonces no se hablo mas en lo contenido en los dichos capitulos y peticiones de los dichos moriscos.

Despues, en el año de 1543, queriendo los moriscos del dicho reyno de Granada tornar a pedir lo que diversas veces se les avia denegado se concertaron y obligaron que darian a christoval mexia vecino de Ciudad Real, hermano de fray Pedro de soto que entonces era confesor del emperador, seis o siete mil ducados en caso que se les concediese lo que antes el año mill quinientos y treinta y siete y el año de mill y quinientos y treinta y nueve avian pedido y ofrecieron al marques de mondejar veinte mill ducados porque los favoreciese e intercediese con S. M. para que consiguiesen lo que pedian, y con esto tornaron a pedir lo que antes avian pedido el año de mill y quinientos y treinta y siete y el año de mill y quinientos y treinta y nueve, en especial que a los moriscos de aquel reino se les concediese perdon general de todos los delitos e crimenes de heregia que fasta estonces oviesen cometido sin que precediese confesion ni reconciliacion y que no se les confiscase los bienes de alli adelante ni se les echasen penas pecuniarias, y el cardenal tavera inquisidor general y el consejo de inquisicion respondieron que aquello mesmo se avia pedido el año de mill y quinientos y treinta y nueve y la congregacion que sobre ello se avia tenido en toledo de prelados e otras personas del consejo real y el consejo de inquisicion avian acordado y determinado que no era cosa justa que se les quitase la confiscacion ne se les podia ni devia conceder perdon de los delictos que oviesen cometido fasta aquel tiempo sin confesion mas que se les podria conceder edicto sin gracia para los que dentro de cierto termino viniese a se confesar los delictos de heregia y apostasia que oviesen cometido y lo que supiesen de otros no se les confiscasen sus bienes y fuesen absueltos de sus culpas sin salir a cadahalso ni carcel ni sanbenito sino solamente con penitencias espirituales, y esta respuesta que dieron el cardenal tavera inquisidor general y el consejo de inquisicion parece que fue mostrada al marques de mondejar el qual replico y dixo que los moriscos de aquel reino no se satisfarian con lo que se les podia conceder conforme al parecer del inquisidor general y del consejo de inquisicion, porque dando las confesiones ante los inquisidores por escrito quedarian a peligro de ser relapsos y querian mas estar en lo aventura de lo que les podia suceder y que si para lo que pedian fuese necesario se podria traer facultad o aprobacion de nuestro muy sancto Padre y que la confiscacion de los bienes se les podia quitar pues S. M. podia hacer merced dellos y la hazia a quien era servido, y despues a 27 de Octubre del año de mill y quinientos y quarenta y tres S. M. imperial escribio de davenes a su magestad rreal y al inquisidor general y al consejo de inquisicion que lo havia mandado ver todo y que comunicado con personas de letras y consciencia avia parecido que se les podia conceder a los moriscos del dicho reino de Granada perdon general en lo pasado sin que precediere confesion ni reconciliacion y que los bienes no se les confiscasen en lo de adelante por tiempo de veynte y cinco o treinta años, y tambien escrivio al marques de mondejar otra carta de davenes a veynte y siete de Octubre de quinientos y quarenta y tres por la qual le decia que le agradecia y se tenia por servido de lo que en este negocio de los moriscos avia fecho. el cardenal tavera inquisidor general y el consejo de inquisicion tornaron a responder a su Mag[d] despues de aver visto su determinacion quanto al perdon general de lo pasado en efecto lo mismo que antes avian dicho y dado por su parecer y que les parecia que seria harto pequeño servicio que los dichos nuevamente convertidos sirviesen a su magestad con los ciento y veinte mil ducados por su parte ofrecidos con que se les hiciese remision general de todos los delitos por ellos cometidos fasta estonces confesandolos por escrito ante los inquisidores o ante las personas por ellos deputadas como se requeria para la salvacion de sus animas y que fuesen por ellos absueltos sin imponerles pena alguna temporal y remitiendoles todas las otras del derecho y la confiscacion de los bienes por los delitos hasta estonces cometidos.

Y quanto a darles termino de veyinte y cinco o treinta años para que en el dicho tiempo no pudiesen ser confiscados sus bienes aunque tornasen a cometer delictos de heregia o apostasia les parecia que no le podrian aconsejar a S. M. con seguridad de conciencia porque las disposiciones canonicas repugnaban mucho a la tal impunidad porque della se seguiria ocasion y atrevimiento para que ellos y todos sus hijos sin temor fuesen moros teniendo segura la vida y no aviendo confiscacion de bienes, mas porque deseaba que S. M. fuese servido en todo lo que se pudiese hazer con conciencia les parecia que seria harta piedad que S. M. les hiciese merced que por el dicho tiempo no se les confiscasen sino la mitad de los bienes, aplicando la otra mitad de que se les hiciese remision a los hijos y descendientes catholicos porque ellos tuviesen algun temor y los hijos se animasen a ser buenos cristianos y que tenian por cierto que dando a entender las personas que interviniesen en esto a los dichos moriscos la gran merced y piedad de que S. M. en esto usase con ellos y que en efecto se les concedia quasi todo lo que habian pedido que ellos se satisfarian, lo qual parece que se mostro al marques de mondejar y torno a replicar a esto diciendo que no se satisfarian los moriscos de aquel Reino. Despues de aver visto S. M. lo susodicho escrivio otra vez S. M. al inquisidor general y al consejo de inquisicion de metz a seis de julio de mil y quinientos y quarenta y cuatro diciendo que ya se avia resolvido en que se ficiese conforme a lo que antes avia escrito de davanes y que a don Juan de vega embajador que entonces era en Roma se avia escrito que entendiese en despachar la bula que fuese necesaria para que se concluyese y pusiese en ejecucion, y Juan de vega despacho una bula cuyo traslado esta fol. 179 y la original tiene el señor arzobispo de Sevilla inquisidor general, la qual con un memorial de la dificultad que sobre ello se puso en Roma cuyo traslado esta fol. 178, fue dado al señor arzobispo de sevilla por mandado del comendador mayor de leon covos y la bulla viene cometida al inquisidor general que es o fuere y a los inquisidores, que es muy diferente de lo que se pretendia por parte de los moriscos.

En aquel año de mil y quinientos y quarenta y quatro un morisco mudejar que se decia Antonio Serrano dyo aviso al señor Inquisidor general que los moriscos de aquel reino de Granada holgarian de poner en razon los capitulos que avian dado y se contentarian con que se les concediesse lo que fuesse justo y harian un largo servicio a S. M. e insistio que se cometiese a alguna persona para que tratasen dello, y el inquisidor general escrivio a Diego de Deza obispo de canaria, oydor que entonces era de la real audiencia de Granada, para que se informase si era verdad lo que decia el dicho Antonio Serrano y comunicado y tratado con los principales moriscos de aquella ciudad algunos dellos dixeron que querian pedir licencia al conde de tendilla para tratar y hablar en ello y se la pidieron y despues hablaron y comunicaron los dichos moriscos con el dicho diego de deza y le dixeron que holgarian que por mano del inquisidor general y del consejo de la inquisicion se les hiciese la merced y pondrian en razon lo que antes tenian pedido y se contentarian con lo que fuere justo y servirian a S. M. con doscientos mil ducados y como el conde de tendilla vio que tratava dello un francisco martinez muley ciego y otros amigos y servidores del marques de mondejar y conde de tendilla y de su opinion procuraron de estorbar a los moriscos de aquella ciudad que no tratasen dello sino que querian lo que el marques de mondejar fiziese y el conde de tendilla envio a llamar a muchos de aquella nacion y les dixo palabras muy asperas y a manera de amenazas poniendoles delante la necesidad que del tenian y que el se quedava alli y el oidor diego de deça que de ello trataba se iria otro dia y que ya el tenia el despacho que S. M. avia fecho la merced al marques su padre de concederle los capitulos que avia dado muy cumplidamente por lo qual no se tomo la resolucion en lo que pedian y pretendian el dicho serrano y los otros moriscos.

Despues en el año pasado de mil y quinientos y cincuenta y cinco el dicho conde de tendilla trato con los convertidos de moros de aquel reino de granada de procurarles que su santidad permitiese que confesando los delitos de heregia y apostasia que oviesen cometido a los confesores que ellos eligiesen fuesen absueltos sin otra solenidad ni pena y que S. M. les hiciese gracia de los bienes que en qualquiera manera oviesen perdido por los dichos delitos de heregia y apostasia y que despues de la dicha remision y gracia por espacio de quarenta años, aunque cometiesen delitos de heregia y apostasia e hiciesen ceremonias de moros no les fuesen confiscados los bienes ni el sancto oficio de la inquisicion se entrometiese en sus causas, y aviendo tratado esto envio personas por todas las ciudades villas y lugares de aquel reino de granada a hacer saber a todos los convertidos lo que cerca desto se avia tratado y platicado y a darles a entender quanto les importaba y a persuadirles que ofreciese cada uno la cantidad de dineros segun su posibilidad asi para que se hiciese un buen servicio a su magestad como para gratificar a las personas que en ellos entendiesen y a los que intercediesen con su santidad y con su mag[d] y el dicho conde les dio instruccion para ello firmada de su nombre y las personas que envio fueron por el reino a todos los pueblos con la dicha negociacion con escandalo y mal exemplo y hicieron algunas estorsiones y malos tratamientos a los que no les parecia bien, de lo qual algunos prelados de aquel reino escandalizados de lo que se hacia dieron noticia al inquisidor general y los inquisidores de granada recibieron informacion dello y procedieron contra los culpados, y el inquisidor general y el consejo de inquisicion escribieron a sus magestades sobre ello y su magestad real les respondio y el conde de tendilla tambien escribio a su magestad y le envio una relacion de lo que dice avia pasado en este negocio tocante a los moriscos de granada y torno a insistir y pedir que se les conceda perdon general de lo pasado y que no se les confisquen los bienes ni se les echen penas pecuniarias en lo porvenir y alega causas e razones para lo justificar y el señor arzobispo ordeno una respuesta a lo que decia el conde de tendilla respondiendo a cada capitulo cuyo traslado esta fol. 181 lo qual su magesta real lo remitio al inquisidor general y al consejo de inquisicion y les escribio de bruselas a once de mayo de mil y quinientos . . . . tanto lo uno y lo otro le informasen particularmente lo que sobre todo les pareciese y a esto se respondio a su magestad por el reverendo señor inquisidor general y el consejo entre otras cosas que se les escribieron a cinco de diciembre de mil y quinientos y cincuenta y seis que se entenderia en ello como S. M. lo mandaba y por la consulta que se le haria veria S. M. que lo que en ello avian ynformado era muy al reves de lo que avia pasado.

Despues en el año de mill y quinientos y cinquenta y ocho los moriscos del dicho reino de Granada enviaron sus solicitadores a flandes adonde estaba su Mag[d] real los quales le dieron memoriales en que en effecto supplicavan y pedian lo que las otras veces antes tenian pedido que se les hiciese perdon general de los delictos passados con que se confiesen a los confessores y que de alli adelante no se les confisquen los bienes y en estos memoriales piden otras cosas muy exorbitantes como son que aya carceles publicas y que se les de los nombres de los testigos y que cuando pecaren en sus errores no se proceda contra ellos por rigor sino por via de doctrina y quexanse que el marques de mondejar y el conde de tendilla los an traido en palabras y que el dicho conde les dixo y certifico que el tenia el despacho della en su arca y ofrecieron haziendoseles merced de lo que en sus memoriales pedian que servirian a S. M. con cien mill ducados por una vez y que darian tres mill ducados de renta en cada un año para siempre jamas para la sustentacion del santo officio. Su Mag[d] en consulta proveyo que por ser negocio de tanta importancia y que conviene mirarse mucho en ello se escriviese a los del consejo de la inquisicion que tornase a ver y tratar lo que antes de agora se pidio cerca desto y lo que al presente de nuevo pedian los moriscos que avian ydo a flandes y con comunicacion de las personas que S. M. mando que entendiesen en ello y vistos los pareceres que sobre ello han dado lo toviesen apuntado tratato y platicado para que venido S. M. a estos reynos lo pudiese con brevedad oyr y ver y proveer como mas conviniese al servicio de Dios y salvacion de las animas de los dichos nuevamente convertidos, y conforme a lo susodicho que se decreto, su Magestad escrivio al consejo de inquisicion y le embio el Memorial que por parte de los dichos moriscos se le avia dado en flandes y despues de lo aver recibido por parte de los dichos moriscos se pidio al reverendo Señor Inquisidor general y al consejo de inquisicion que se les diese licencia para que se pudiesen juntar los moriscos de aquel reino de Granada para tratar lo que tocava al dicho negocio y otorgar poderes para que por ellos los pudiesen obligar y pidieron una minuta de lo que se avia de contener en el poder y dioseles licencia para que en presencia del arzobispo de granada y del presidente y los oydores licenciados salas y arana y de uno de los inquisidores se juntasen a tratar del negocio, e dioseles una minuta del poder y sobre ello se les escrivio a los dichos arzobispo y presidente e oydores e inquisidor, e los dichos moriscos se juntaron e se otorgaron los poderes aunque no estan en estos papeles y el arcobispo de granada escrivio que no convenia que se les quitase la confiscacion de los bienes y despues cuando estuvo en esta corte dio sobre ello capitulos a S. M. los cuales se remitieron al consejo de inquisicion. Despues de aver pasado todo lo susodicho por parte de los dichos moriscos de granada se han presentado muchas peticiones con que suplican a su magestad les haga la merced que tienen pedida pues se concedio a los moriscos de valladolid y de otras partes y dizen que en ellos ay mayor razon, y al presente estan en esta corte ciertos moriscos de granada procurandolo y solicitandolo para que su magestad les haga la merced que tantas veces han supplicado y pedido y agora suplican y piden y por la ultima peticion dan a entender que se contentaran con que se les haga la merced que se hizo a los moriscos de aragon y de valladolid la qual presentaron a 12 de março 1560, tambien presentaron otra peticion a 20 de febrero 1560 en que pidieron no se vendiesen los bienes que fuesen confiscados en el auto que ya estava publicado ni los que estavan por vender de los otros autos de antes por la paga de la farda y por la situacion de lo que se ha de dar para la paga del salario de los inquisidores y officiales que se ha de cargar tambien sobre aquellos bienes.

En 29 de Octubre de 1561 dieron otra peticion por la qual dizen que piden lo que por otras antes desta tienen pedido y suplicado attento lo mucho que han gastado en prosecucion deste negocio, asi en dar los poderes como en las ydas y venidas que han hecho en flandes y en esta corte.

XII.

Moorish Ballad of 1568, Prior to the Rebellion of Granada[1] (p. 234).

Let the God of love and mercy's name begin and end our theme;
Sovereign He o'er all the nations, of all things the Judge Supreme.
He who gave the book of wisdom, He who made His image, man,
He chastiseth, He forgiveth, He who framed creation's plan.

---

[1] By Mohammad ben Mohammad aben Daud, the chief agitator in the movements which led to the rising.—Cartulario de Alonzo del Castillo (Memorial Histórico español, 1852, Tom. III. p. 41).

He the One sole God of Heaven, He the One sole God of earth,
He who guards us and supports us, He from whom all things had
birth;
He who never had beginning, Lord of heaven's loftiest throne,
He whose providence guides all things, subject to His will alone.

He who gave us Holy Scripture, who made Adam, and who planned
Man's salvation, He who gives their strength to nations from His
hand;
He who raised the Saints and Prophets, ending with Mahoun the
greatest—
Praise the One sole God of Heaven, with all His Saints, from first
to latest!

Listen, while I tell the story of sad Andalusia's fate—
Peerless once and world-renowned in all that makes a nation great;
Prostrate now and compassed round by heretics with cruel force—
We, her sons, like driven sheep, or horseman on unbridled horse.

Torture is our daily portion, subtle craft our sole resource,
Till we welcome death to free us from a fate that's ever worse.
They have set the Jews to watch us, Jews that know nor truth nor
faith,
Every day some new device they frame to work us further scaith.

We are forced to worship with them in their Christian rites unclean,
To adore their painted idols, mockery of the Great Unseen.
No one dares to make remonstrance, no one dares to speak a word;
Who can tell the anguish wrought on us, the faithful of the Lord?

When the bell tolls, we must gather to adore the image foul;
In the church the preacher rises, harsh-voiced as a screaming owl.
He the wine and pork invoketh, and the Mass is wrought with
wine;
Falsely humble, he proclaimeth that this is the Law divine.

Yet the holiest of their shavelings nothing knows of right or wrong,
And they bow before their idols, shameless in the shameless throng,
Then the priest ascends the altar, holding up a cake of bread,
And the people strike their bosoms as the worthless Mass is said.

All our names are set in writing, young and old are summoned all;
Every four months the official makes on all suspect his call.
Each of us must show his permit, or must pay his silver o'er,
As with inkhorn, pen, and paper, on he goes from door to door.
Dead or living, each must pay it; young or old, or rich or poor;
God help him who cannot do it, pains untold he must endure!

They have framed a false religion; idols sitting they adore;
Seven weeks fast they, like the oxen who at noon-tide eat the more.
In the priest and the confession they their baseless law fulfil,
And we, too, must feign conversion, lest they work us cruel ill.

Albotado and Horozco[1] shear us like a flock of sheep,
Cruel judges and unsparing, who their tireless vigils keep,
And whoever praises God into destruction's net they sweep.
Vain were hiding, vain were flight, when once the spies are on his track,
Should he gain a thousand leagues, they follow him and bring him back.

In their hideous gaols they throw him, every hour fresh terrors weave,
From his ancient faith to tear him, as they cry to him "Believe!"
And the poor wretch, weeping, wanders on from hopeless thought to thought,
Like a swimmer in mid ocean, by the blinding tempest caught.

Long they keep him wasting, rotting, in the dungeon foul and black,
Then they torture him until his limbs are broken on the rack,
Then within the Plaza Hatabin[2] the crowds assemble fast,
Like unto the Day of Judgment they erect a scaffold vast.
If one is to be released, they clothe him in a yellow vest,
While with hideous painted devils to the flames they give the rest.

---

[1] Albotado was a converso and a priest of the New Christians to whom Francisco Abenedem, a bricklayer at work on the Alhambra, revealed in confession the conspiracy on foot in the Albaycin. Antonio de Horozco was a canon of Sacromonte. The houses of both were attacked on the night when Abenfarax entered Granada.—Marmol, Lib. IV. c. 2, 4.

[2] The Soq el-hattabin or the wood-market.

Thus are we encompassed round as with a fiercely burning fire,
Wrongs past bearing are heaped on us, higher yet and ever higher.
Vainly bend we to their mandates; Sundays, feast-days though we keep,
Fasting Saturdays and Fridays, never safety can we reap.

Each one of their petty despots thinks that he can make the law,
Each invents some new oppression. Now a sharper sword they draw!
New Year's day in Bib el Bonut[1] they proclaimed some edicts new,
Startling sleepers from their slumbers, as each door they open threw.

Baths and garments, all our old ancestral customs are forbidden,
To the Jews we are delivered, who can spoil us still unchidden.
Little reck the priest and friar so they trample on us yet;
Like a dove in vulture talons, we are more and more beset.

Hopeless, then, of man's assistance, we have searched the prophets o'er,
Seeking promise in the judgments which our fathers writ of yore;
And our wise men counsel us to look to God with prayer and fast,
For through woes that make youth aged, He will pity us at last!

I have done; but life were short our sorrows fully to recall.
Kind Señores, do not blame me, if I am too weak for all.
Whoso chants these rugged verses, let his prayers to God arise,
That His mercy may vouchsafe me the repose of Paradise!

---

[1] The Gate of the Banner—the principal plaza in the Albaycin.

XIII.

LETTER OF INQUISITOR-GENERAL QUIROGA SUGGESTING THE EXPULSION OF THE MORISCOS (P. 302).

(Archivo Hist. Nacional, Inquisicion de Valencia, Cartas del Consejo, Legajo 5, No. 1, fol. 254).

Muy R^dos^ Inquisidores. Considerando la multitud de nuebos combertidos de Moros que ai en estos Reinos de Castilla y en todos los lugares dellos y en los de la Corona de Aragon ansi en ese como en el de Aragon y que de cada dia va creziendo y quan mezclados estan entre los catolicos cristianos y quan ladinos y entendidos en las cosas dellos y que en su manera de bivir y profesion de cristiandad se vé y espera tampoco fructo y que son tan enemigos nuestros como se ha visto y vee y la esperiencia lo muestra de cada dia pone en cuidado de mirar en ello y obligarnos a saver y aun su Magestad lo desea si convenia questos estubiesen entre nosotros como de presente estan, ó si seria bien dar orden y medio como apartarlos y alejarlos, quitandoles la ocasion que se puede muy bien tener dellos si la viesen en alguno tiempo, que nuestro Señor no permita, para inquietar estos Reynos y desasosegarlos, y en caso que esto pareciese que orden se podria tener para ello y que se habia de hazer dellos y adonde y en que parte se podrian poner para estar con la seguridad que conviniese, pasando este negocio como lo requiere la qualidad y gravedad del, mirando las razones que para la una parte y otra podrian conbencer y avisandonos dellos muy puntual y particularmente y con la mas brevedad que ser pueda. Guarde nuestro Señor vuestros muy R^das^ personas. Madrid, 7 de Mayo, 1590.—G. Carlis. Toletan.

XIV.

Brief Relation of the Expulsion from Valencia (p. 320).

(Archivo de Simancas, Inquisicion, Sala 51, Legajo 205, fol. 2).

En 22 de Setiembre 1609, se publico un real bando de S. M. en la presente ciudad de Valencia, mandando por las causas en el contenidas que todos los moriscos del reyno de Valencia dentro de tres dias despues que en cada lugar de ellos se hiciere pregon para que se fuesen á embarcar so las penas en el contenidas, saliessen de sus casas y lugares con lo que pudiesen llevar á cuestas y solo quedasen los niños de quatro años abaxo con voluntad de sus padres ó curadores.

Fueron señalados para la embarcacion de dichos moriscos tres puertos, Alicante, Denia y Vinaros, ofreciendo S. M. pasaje franco y bastimentos, el qual bando se hizo con apercibimiento que pasados los tres dias pudiesen ser desbalijados y traidos al primer lugar para entregallos á la justicia y haziendo resistencia les pudiesen matar y que los bienes muebles y raices de los moriscos fuesen de los señores de los lugares.

En la playa de Alicante estaban aprestados los galeones de la Armada con Don Luis Fajardo general de ella y otras naves, y entendia en la embarcacion por tierra Don Baltasar mercader.

En Denia estuvo de principio don Agustin Mexia maese de campo general y las galeras del Marques de Santa Cruz y otros vaixeles que acudian; tambien asisteron a dicha embarcacion don Cristobal Sereno y el dotor Noto Rodriguez, Juez de corte.

A Vinaros acudio Don Pedro de Toledo con las galeras de España y antes de publicarse el dicho bando estaban desembarcadas las compañias del tercio de lombardia y parte de ellas subieron á la sierra de espada donde en otra ocasion los moriscos del reyno se subieron, y en el marquesado de Denia estuvo el tercio de Napoles.

Despacharonse luego comisarios por el reyno y a un tiempo en la gobernacion de Alicante, en el ducado de Gandia y marquesado de Denia y a las partes mas vecinas de Vinaros para sacar los moriscos á embarcar, aunque de noche y á horas cautas entre las aljamas principales del reino corrian muchos avisos tratando si se rebelarian, sus mayores alfaquies resolvieron que no, por dos causas principales, la una que tenian pronostico que les havia de venir un bien impensado á tiempo que perderian una coxida negra y que era este el cumplimiento del pronostico, la otra porque no tenian fuerzas para vencer ni aun para defenderse y si se alçavan serian presto vencidos y sus mugeres cautivas y sus hijos christianos y serian causa de este grande pecado. Con este consejo de los alfaquies, aunque por falços pareceres, determinaron de obedecer y fueron saliendo de sus casas y embarcandose y para mas facilitar su embarcacion se les dio libertad que hasta sallirse de sus casas pudiesen administrar sus bienes, y por este camino vendieron y gastaron quanto tenian, dando el trigo á dos y á tres reales la hanega que es grande estremo de barato en este reino, aunque despues se les quito libertad de vender ganados, trigo y azeite.

Don Pablo Sanoguera persuadio á los moriscos de Alcacer, vasallos de don Christobal sanoguera su hermano, que fuesen á embarcarse al Grao de Valencia y pagasen el flete e hiziesen su bizcocho para el viaje que de esta suerte serian de los mas bien librados del Reino y se ahorrarian el largo camino y gastos hasta Denia ó Vinaros, y assi los que primero dexaron sus casas para embarcarse en el Reino fueron los de Alcacer que, dia del Señor St. Miguel á 29 de Setiembre, por la mañana salieron y llegaron al Grao á medio dia á cavallo con sus carros y vagajes con mucha ropa que trahian. A estos siguieron los de picacente sus deudos, vecinos y amigos, y otros muchos señores de lugares con sus vasallos hizieron despues lo propio de suerte que en este Grao de Valencia con asistencia del dotor Francisco Pablo bazieron, juez de corte, se an embarcado hasta veynte y uno de Deziembre que fue continua la embarcacion, decisiete mil setecientos sesenta y seys moriscos, esta es nueve mil ochocientos noventa y siete hombres y mugeres de doce años arriba, tres mil doscientos sesenta nueve de doce años abajo, mil trescientos treinta y nueve de teta. En Alicante treinta y dos mil entre hombres y mugeres. En Denia treynta mil entre hombres y mugeres. En Vinaros quinze mil y doscientos entre hombres y mugeres. En Mancofa cinco mil seyscientos y noventa, que todos son 100,656.

Pocos dias despues de començada la embarcacion los moriscos fueron subiendo á los montes en dos partes distintas y apartadas del Reyno, esto es en los montes de Alaguar y en la muela de

Cortes y de cada dia fueron creciendo el numero de suerte que en el de Alaguar llegaron á doce mil hombres y mugeres grandes y pequeños de la vall de guadeleste, confirdes, sella, xalon, gata, orba, Alcalali, mosquera y Alaguar y de algunos otros lugares. A muchos hicieron salir por fuerça de sus casas y rebelarse. Estos escogieron y levaron por rey á Geronimo Mellin, valiente moro.

En la muela de oro que es la misma de cortes se juntaron mas de nueve mil entre hombres, mugeres, grandes y pequeños. Estos nombraron por su Rey á Vicente turiri, hombre de buen entendimiento y valeroso. En ambas partes se proveyeron bien de bastimentos de trigo, arroz, pasas, higos, miel y mucha arina. Aunque estaban muy mal armados hicieron grandes insolencias de robar y quemar yglesias, acuchillar las imagines y en particular el Santisimo Crucifixo y de la gloriosisima reyna de los Angeles, y el dotor baziero prendio á tres de estos sacrilegos [que] quemaron y robaron a yglesia de bicorbe.

Despues de muchas embajadas y tratos que huvo entre los moros de Alaguar y don Agustin mexia maese de campo general con que procuraban entretenerse los moriscos, pidiendo plazas largas para embarcarse, determino de apretallos poco á poco con la gente que tenia de los tercios de napoles y secilia y con las compañias de la milisia efectiva del Reyno que acudieron y lo mismo fue á esta otra parte de la muela de cortes que don Joan de Cordoba, maese de campo del tercio de lombardia estaba con su tercio y don Alvaro vique sorogado de gobernador con las compañias del tercio de la Rivera de la milicia efectiva donde asistian tambien don Joan pacheco carrillo y don Esteban su hermano y fue Dios servido que en ambas partes los campos á un mesmo tiempo fueron apretando los moros de suerte que de dia de la presentacion de nuestra Señora [21 Nov.] al amanecer envistieron á los enemigos y el campo de don Agustin mexia cerro con ellos y luego volvieron las espaldas como á gente bisoña y desarmada y en el encuentro y seguida de la Vitoria les mato mas de dos mil y les gano los lugares do estaban y el pendon que hera lo mas fuerte y los demas subieron á lo mas alto donde ni tenian que comer ni gota de agua para bever y ansi les tuvo apretados el campo unos quantos dias hasta que se rindieron para embarcarse y baxaron con tanta furia y tan sedientos que de pechos se arrojaban en el agua y algunos rebentaron beviendo, y de alli los llevaron á embarcar á Denia.

Don Juan de Cordova llegandose con el campo al lugar de cortes el dicho dia de la presentacion de nuestra Señora y adelantandose la cavalleria donde iban dichos don Joan pacheco y don Esteban haviendo caminado como media legua hallaron catorze morillos con banderillos blancos, señal de paz, los quales postrados por tierra pidieron misericordia en nombre de todos, y haviendolos remitido á Don Joan de Cordoba que dixo que se rindiesen en buena ora que el habia lo que le parcciesse y les admitio prometiendoles que no serian robados ni maltratados, y no lo pudo cumplir porque los soldados les desvalixaron todos sin dexarles cosa alguna y al ultimo estos moriscos baxaron en veces y dias diferentes y los unos fueron á embarcarse á Denia y mas de tres mil al grao de Valencia.

Geronimo Mellin murio pelando valerosamente el dia de nuestra señora que fue vencido y luego despues levantaron por cabeza á su hermano Christobal mellin cuyo cuerpo difunto dias despus fue traido á la ciudad de Valencia.

En la muela de cortes quedaron mas de dos mil moros despues de haver baixado la mayor parte de ellos con seguridad para embarcarse y por ser los montes muchos y muy espelos llenos de barrancas y que nos han dado mucho trabajo en reduzillos ó prendellos haciendo extraordinarias diligencias y poco á poco los han sacado del monte, unos reducidos con seguridad de sus vidas para embarcarse, otros presos y cautivos, y entre otras diligencias que se han hecho fue publicar con bandos que los que estaban en la muela rebelados dentro de tres dias baijassen pasados los quales pudiese qualquier particular prendellos y cautivallos y si hiciesen resistencia les pudiesen matar, reservandose libertad el Virrey de tomallos para las galeras pagando veinte ducados por cada uno, con lo qual salia mucha gente de diferentes lugares y fueron por los montes cautivando muchos y han quedado solo hombres . . . . y los mas dellos mozos al pie de ciento y cinquento con diez ó onze mugeres.

Estan dichos moriscos tan aborrecidos por no embarcarse que por medio de don bautista pallas hermano del señor de Cortes an pedido de merced al Virey que les asegure de no embarcallos ni ser exclavos de las galeras y se rendiran voluntariamente para ser exclavos de particulares para lo qual han baxado cinco moros de los principales y se les ha concedido esta seguridad hoy que estamos 6 de março 1620 [1610?] con lo qual se tiene por cierto baxaran los que quedan.

Buscando los moros por los montes unos soldados del conde de Carlet allaron en una cueva á Vicente Turiri, mujer, hijos y otros hombres y mugeres los quales truxeron á este ciudad de Valencia y á dicho Turiri le dieron sentencia que fuese atenaceado y cortadas las orijas y hecho quartos y su cabeça puesta al portal de esta ciudad dicho de St. Vicente, executose asi y murio como buen cristiano confesando y pidiendo perdon á nuestro Señor y encomendandose al Señor y a su madre bendita de quien havia sido devoto y viviendo hizo muchas limosnas.

Hanse hallado por los montes muchos moriscos muertos, unos de hambre, despues que fueron rendidos, otros despeñados voluntariamente solo por no embarcarse ó quedar en manos de christianos, otros muchos luego de principio quando se hecho el bando general se salieron del reyno para Aragon, Cataluña y á Francia muchos de ellos.

En el discurso de la embarcacion del Grao han sucedido varios casos porque de algunos de los moros era tanto el deseo y gana que tenian de embarcarse que estando en las taraçanas muriendose y boqeando se hicieron llevar al navio por no quedar en tierra y luego tuvieron desengaño de su dañada secta, muriendo y hechando su cuerpo á los peces, otros hivan como si fuesen á bodas vestidas los mugeres de fiesta con lo mejor que tenian y una que vio embarcar sus deudos no hizo mas que parir y con la criatura en los brazos se fue á embarcar en dia aspero, ventoso y muy frio, no embargante que se le ofrecio muy buen recoximiento si se queria quedar. La gente pobre y tullida traian de los lugares algunos de ellos á brazos, pareciendoles que hacian una grande obra de caridad, otros no embargante que se quedaban en tierra maridos, hermanos ó hijos se an embarcado con el mayor contento del mundo.

Por el contrario se han visto grandes extremos de muchas personas que querian quedarse, ofreciendo primero al cuchillo al garganta que embarcandose, algunos han deixado ir sus padres y mugeres y se an quedado no embargante se quedaban sin hacienda, otros se han escondido y huydo del Grao por no embarcarse, haciendo grandes demonstraciones de christianos y escogiendo el estado de exclavitud antes de salir de España, y en particular una moça de quince años hizo particulares diligencias para quedarse estando ya en la taraçana y fue Dios servido darle una grande enfermedad para su salvacion porque viendose apretada de la enfermedad llamo un christiano que pasaba por delante su Rancho y le dixo que le truxese un confesor que queria morir como buena cristiana, hizolo asi y dicha moça se confeso y dio la alma á Dios á lo que se puede creer piamente, y su cuerpo fue enterrado en la yglesia del Grao.

En los viajes hubo diferentes sucesos, porque aunque el mar navegando no se a perdido ningun baixel de los que han embarcado moriscos en el Grao, pero estando muchos de ellos con otros de Denia y Mancofa en el cabo de Palos aguardando buen tiempo les sobrevino fuerte cierzo con el qual se perdieron y ahogaron como cien moriscos de piles y de otras partes y se perdieron tres saetias, dos de Denia y la otra de Marzella, y el dia siguiente se hallo en una destas saetias una niña de quatro años viva, estando el baixel lleno de agua y de cuerpos muertos. Una nave del capitan pedro nicolas llegada á Arzen y haviendo desembarcado la mayor parte de los moros dio al traves en tierra y se perdio.

Una saetia del patron Pedro fita catalan assi mismo haviendo llegado á Arzen el viejo se perdio y todos los moros salieron á salvamento á tierra mas no se pudieron librar de los alarves que á todos los desbalijaron dexando aun las mugeres en cueros y este patron y sus marineros quentan que escapandose de los alarbes y caminando á Oran vieron degollados y muertos mas de nueve mil hombres y mugeres y entre ellos un niño asido á los pechos y tetas de su madre muerta.

El comendador de nuestra Señora de las mercedes de Oran ha escrito que es tan grande la Rissa que los alarves han hecho en los moriscos por los campos y despues han muerto tantos de enfermidades que entiende que de todos los que han desembarcado por aquel paraje no queda la tercera parte.

Agora se van recogiendo algunos moriscos que hay por el Reino entre personas particulares para embarcallos y sienten lo tanto que los pocos moros que estan en esta ciudad para embarcarse de buena gana se quedarian exclavos si les permitiese estar en el Reino.

INDEX.